Views from the Margins

Views from the
Margins

Creating Identities in Modern France

Edited and with an introduction by
Kevin J. Callahan and Sarah A. Curtis

UNIVERSITY OF NEBRASKA PRESS

LINCOLN AND LONDON

© 2008 by the Board of Regents
of the University of Nebraska
All rights reserved. Manufactured
in the United States of America
♾
Set in Quadraat.
Designed by Ashley Muehlbauer.

Library of Congress
Cataloging-in-Publication Data
Views from the margins: creating identities in
modern France / edited and with an introduction
by Kevin J. Callahan and Sarah A. Curtis.
p. cm.
Includes bibliographical references.
ISBN 978-0-8032-1559-7 (pbk.: alk. paper)
1. National characteristics, French. 2. France—
Colonies—History. 3. France—Civilization.
4. Immigrants—France—History. 5. France—
Social conditions. I. Callahan, Kevin J. II.
Curtis, Sarah Ann.
DC33.V535 2008
944—dc22   2008032895

In memory of William B. Cohen
Scholar, teacher, friend

Contents

᭗ ᭗ Views from the Margins

KEVIN J. CALLAHAN & SARAH A. CURTIS

Introduction

What constitutes "Frenchness"? Until recently we thought we knew. After all, France is regarded as "the oldest nation of Europe," a recognizable geographic and political entity dating from the early Middle Ages. Fernand Braudel, arguably France's most influential historian of the twentieth century, has located the essence of French identity in the deeper patterns of French geography, demography, and the environment that emerged over centuries.[1] France has been historically at the center of Europe in terms of power and the influence of its culture and civilization. As early as the thirteenth century, students from across Europe attended the University of Paris. In the seventeenth century Louis XIV's splendid court culture became the rage of the day, so much so that imitations of Versailles popped up everywhere, most notably Schönbrunn Palace in Vienna and Sans Souci in Potsdam outside of Berlin. Already, the French language had replaced Latin as the de facto lingua franca of diplomacy and culture. And until the Revolution, France, as the "eldest daughter of the Church," rivaled Rome as the center of European Catholicism.[2]

The striking feature of French history, especially from 1648 until the nineteenth century, has in many ways been its posture as the geopolitical core of Europe, from which the periphery has been delineated. Related to this geographical centrality is the historical development of the French state from Louis XIV until its completion under Napoléon. First in abstraction and later in reality, the French state has served as the tangible glue that has unified the French territory in modern times. And the center of that state has been Paris, the unquestioned center of France in terms of population, language, culture, economy, and political significance. In no other European country save England is the dynamic between the capital city as core and the provinces as periphery as pronounced as in France. French identity, therefore, has been most easily understood as the product of a centralized state and culture emanating from Paris that were themselves central to European history and civilization.[3]

Yet the elements of that understanding have come under question and with it the definition of Frenchness. A fine collection of essays edited by Michael Wolfe points to the fluid nature of French identity in the early modern period.[4] Likewise, the origins of French nationalism, long assumed to be the product of the French Revolution, are now sought in the eighteenth century. David Bell's work on nationalism in this period suggests that French national identity was shaped in part by a conflict far away from France's shores, the Seven Years' War in North America.[5] The relationship between Paris and the provinces has been debated and revised for the past quarter-century, ever since Eugen Weber published *Peasants into Frenchmen* (1976), arguing that the early Third Republic in the 1870s and 1880s imposed a set of urban and Republican values on a rural peasantry not yet entirely assimilated into the French center.[6] Historians now believe that French identity has been shaped not merely by centralizing forces from Paris but also by a complex process of negotiation between competing loyalties to village, region, and nation.[7]

Recent events in France, as the country assimilates unprecedented numbers of non-European immigrants, suggest that French identity continues to be shaped by peripheral forces, within and without Europe. France has long been a country that has welcomed refugees and migrants, a historical phenomenon first explicitly recognized with the publication of Gérard Noiriel's *Le Creuset français* in 1988.[8] Ongoing historical work on immigration seeks to examine the ways in which outsiders have created French identity as they have become French themselves.[9] The French government's decision to open a museum dedicated to immigration, Cité National de l'Histoire de l'Immigration, located at the Palais de la Porte Dorée, is a belated recognition of this reality. Since the 1980s debates about French immigration and naturalization policies in national politics have been an unveiled discourse on national identity and what it means to be a French citizen.[10] In the 2007 presidential elections the question of Frenchness emerged as a campaign issue when candidate Nicolas Sarkozy proposed creating a ministry of national identity and immigration.[11] Sarkozy, subsequently elected, is himself the son and grandson of immigrants who nonetheless defines himself as entirely French. Only the far Right denies that the French national soccer team, les Bleus, made up in great majority of individuals whose families migrated from elsewhere, are not French.

Linked to the new awareness of immigration history is the significance of France as one of the preeminent European and world colonial powers. The study of the history of France, like so many other aspects of early twenty-first-century life, has gone global. Over the last decade scholarship on the French Empire has exploded,[12] calling into question some long-standing truths regarding the creation of French identity as well as the relationship between metropole and colony. Like Paris's relationship with the provinces, historians long assumed that the relationship between France and its colonies was unidirectional, examining the impact of policies and decisions made in Paris (or in Lyon, Marseille, and Bordeaux) on the lives of individuals in Dakar, Saigon, and Algiers. This literature was often both nuanced and critical, acknowledging the messy reality on the ground as well as the destructive quality of much of this colonization. We now know a great deal more about the workings of France's empire and the discourses that sustained it, the impact of colonization on non-French peoples, the way the empire was represented in France, and the paradoxical claims of citizenship and republicanism. But in order to write a history of greater France that truly integrates center and periphery, much more work remains to be done. Few studies, for example, take seriously the French claim after 1850 that Algeria was part of metropolitan France, nor do they take up the thought-provoking possibility that remote French regions were treated like colonies.[13] Nor has this scholarship explored the impact of colonization on French identity at home or the ways in which peripheral identities and events shaped and created French policies at the center that were then transmitted back to the periphery.

This collection brings together nine essays that use the ordering principle of core and periphery as an analytical tool to explore the creation of French identity from the Revolution to the aftermath of World War II. In using the core/periphery analytical framework, the volume sets forth the following main points. First, seven of the nine essays explore the creation of French identity by making a contribution to an imperial history of France, treating the history of both metropole and colony in a single interpretive frame. Calls to write this type of history are more often evoked than actually put into practice, and these essays provide models of metropolitan/colonial interaction. Second is our belief that empire is only one of multiple categories and themes for which the process of identity creation in a core/periphery framework is useful. This perspective also adds much to understanding other fields of history that upon first glance would not necessarily come into association with each other. In short the core/periphery framework opens up a wide range of possibilities that allows us to investigate modern French identity in relation to race, class, religion, and politics. Three essays, therefore, address the nexus of gender and forms of legal and civic engagement in the context of French identity not related to the history of imperial France while overlapping with the essays on French Empire in their consideration of issues such as religion, consumer culture, and national and regional politics. Third, all of the essays point to the fact that identity creation occurs invariably within a framework of authority, whether it be the state, the church, political parties, a legal system, an international corporation or organization, or prevailing social and cultural norms. Likewise, it seems that changes in authority patterns—gradual or dramatic—permit the reshaping and reshuffling of identity markers. Finally, these essays as a whole challenge the notion of a hegemonic core, which impinges upon and determines peripheral identities. Whether the hegemonic core is understood in the traditional sense of the power of the state, the neo-Marxist/Gramscian concept of the hegemony of culture, or Michel Foucault's notion of the hegemony of power, these explanatory models do not adequately account for the power of the periphery and the agency of peripheral actors and identities.[14] In some cases it is the periphery itself that permits more fluid and dynamic notions of identity, while in others peripheral developments can drastically upset or change identity patterns emanating from Paris or the center.

The core/periphery framework allows us to investigate the salient features of modern French identity in multiple ways. Variables that encompass the core/periphery approach include most notably metropole/colony but also others such as Paris/province, urban/rural, national/local, French/non-French, normal/abnormal, Left/Right, self/other, and male/female. (This list is, of course, by no means exhaustive.) The essays in this book explicitly address these kinds of oppositions as building blocks of identity formation in the history of modern France. We do not presume to privilege the core at the expense of the periphery, nor do we regard the periphery as merely a mirror that reflects the interests and intellectual constructs of the core.[15] Nor do we assume a single core versus a single periphery automatically structured in terms of binary oppositions, a history limited to the study of the representations of difference. Instead, we regard the nexus between the core(s) and periphery(ies) as contested terrain and/or negotiated space, the crucible of identity creation. The actual processes and strategies of identity creation might be inclusive or exclusive, contested or conciliatory, democratic or hegemonic, negotiated or imposed, or a combination of these characteristics. In short, we have deliberately chosen the word *create*, as opposed to *contest* (which assumes that society is conflictual) or *construct* (which assumes that society is structural rather than processual and implies a division between subjective and objective, society and culture), in order not to prejudge or predetermine as much as possible the way in which a particular identity is fashioned.

To borrow from Ronald Grigor Suny's insightful explanation of identities, we conceive identity to be "fluid, multiple, fragmented, and constantly in need of hard work to sustain."[16] Identity is not created in a vacuum but, rather, is shaped by the strictures of culture, which itself is mutable but provides a "thin coherence," as William Sewell has argued.[17] Therefore, one of the key questions with respect to identity creation "is that of the different ways in which groups or individuals make use of, interpret and appropriate the intellectual motifs and cultural forms they share with others."[18] It is our belief that identity—rooted in culture—is anchored in social, economic, political, and other realities, although in a nondeterministic manner. Similar to our hesitancy to privilege the core over the periphery, or vice versa, we are suspicious of assuming ipso facto the primacy of any specific force or social category such as class, power, or religion devoid of context.

The first six essays presented in this volume take up the theme of imperial France, illustrating how the creation of Frenchness was at stake in the interconnections between the core and periphery. By the early nineteenth century France had lost most of its North American holdings and its land empire in Europe, but the Restoration and July Monarchy saw a resurgence of interest in leveraging France's existing colonies around the Atlantic basin as well as its new imperial conquest in Algeria. By the time of the "new imperialism" in the decades before World War I, France was again one of Europe's most significant imperial players, with important colonies in West Africa and Southeast Asia, which it held until the wave of decolonization efforts after World War II. Among them the loss of Algeria was the most contested, in France as well as Algeria. Temporally, the first six essays cover aspects of this history from the 1820s until the 1980s; geographically, they span the continents of Europe, Africa, Asia, and South America; and topically, they tackle issues such as religious, consumer, political, and regional identities in the broader context of empire and French identity. Three trends come to the fore: the multidirectional nexus between the core and periphery, the relative autonomy of peripheral forces, and the instability of authority relations.

Sarah A. Curtis's essay explores identity creation on the very margins of empire, the colony in Mana, French Guiana, established by Catholic missionary Anne-Marie Javouhey and populated by former African slaves. Here, far from French "civilization," Javouhey—literally and figuratively—carved out a space to forge her own utopian experiment based on a Catholic rural identity, seeking to transform "uncivilized" African slaves into paragons of pious French peasant farmers. But it was Javouhey herself who was most changed by the experiment, as she rejected the church's teachings on slavery and became an abolitionist, earning her the disdain of local colonists, who resisted innovation that threatened the traditional plantation model, sustained by African slavery, as well as the interference of Paris in colonial affairs. The gradual unraveling of the French slave trade allowed a charismatic nun such as Javouhey to establish a missionary utopia. In the opinion of both her admirers and her detractors, Javouhey's assumption of authority in Mana brought her very gender identity into question, as King Louis-Philippe called her (admiringly) a "great man."

Jeremy Rich argues that the colonial origins of the ultraconservative Catholic identity of Marcel Lefebvre have been forgotten. In interwar Gabon a religious revival caused a generation of French male missionaries to internalize lessons about heroism and authority that were unavailable to them in France. Some, like Lefebvre, transferred what they learned—or what they thought they learned—in Africa back to France after World War II in order to confront the liberalizing efforts of Vatican II. Lefebvre thus paradoxically reclaimed for metropolitan France an authoritarian Catholic identity he had fashioned in France's colonial periphery. Here the effects of the colonial experience were directly opposed to those of Anne-Marie Javouhey in French Guiana a century earlier. By leaving France for Africa and South America, Javouhey was radicalized, using her new experience and knowledge to challenge the very basis of the pre-1848 French Empire, slavery, as well as the position of women like herself in the church. Lefebvre in Gabon, on the other hand, reaffirmed the most traditional and authoritarian of Catholic teachings, to the point where he, too, stood outside the mainstream of the established French Catholic Church. In both cases, however, it was their real-life experiences in the colonies that marginalized them within the established structures of church and state.

Stephen L. Harp's essay on the complex relationship between colonial production and metropolitan consumption shows how French consumer and tourist identities at home deliberately obscured the realities of production. In the interwar period a consumer society in France, in the form of automobilism, was built on the labor of indigenous Vietnamese who harvested the rubber that made the Michelin empire, from tires to tourist guides, run. But the French in the metropole who bought tires and used Michelin guides to tour France were encouraged to forget about empire, creating their consumer identities on the basis of Michelin ads rather than imperial realities. Although Harp demonstrates that the periphery, Indochina, and the center, France, were in fact intimately interlinked through the production of rubber, this relationship was made invisible in France, forgotten and ignored in favor of a constructed, self-contained French consumer identity.

Lee Whitfield's essay on French public opinion during the 1954–62 Algerian War examines the regional identity of the Rhône-Alpes in light of the imperial conflict in Algeria. Whitfield traces significant divergence among this population from the Algerian policies designed by politicians in Paris. After World War II up through the Algerian conflict, entrepreneurs, civic leaders, and farmers in the Rhône-Alpes were far more interested in bolstering and selling their own regional identity (or perhaps identities) than supporting the state-sponsored imperial nationalism of the Fourth Republic on full display in a losing cause in North Africa. The crisis spurred by the Algerian conflict led the citizens of the Rhône-Alpes to reorient their sense of Frenchness away from imperial prerogatives and toward regional pride and revival.

The next two essays by Samuel Huston Goodfellow on right-wing politics in interwar Alsace and Kevin J. Callahan on left-wing politics in the international socialist movement also shed light on the processes of contested national identity creation and core/periphery relationships in politics. Equally important, they challenge us to reconceptualize our understanding of an imperial history of France beyond the traditional French metropole and its colonies. After all, the history of France was itself largely a pattern of internal colonialism using methods of inclusion and domination from the core territory of the French medieval kings, the Île de France, outward in all directions to France's "natural" frontiers of the Rhine River and the Alps and Pyrenees Mountains. At the same time, French identity has been influenced by its peripheral relationship—both in reality and in perception—to other imperial and expansionist powers, most notably Britain in the eighteenth century and Germany from the 1870–71 Franco-Prussian War until World War II.[19]

In this context Goodfellow argues that the perceived identity of Alsace as either French or German fails to acknowledge the strong attachment Alsatians felt for their region. Alsace was the peripheral region of France par excellence, geographically marginal to both France and Germany yet always defined in terms of one nationality or the other due to cultural imperialist policies of the French and German governments. Goodfellow inverts this paradigm to suggest that Alsatians attempted to create their own distinctive ethnic identity, in which they constituted the center and the national states of France and Germany the periphery. Yet unlike the citizens of the Rhône-Alpes, who were able to resist the pressure of the central government and consequently help precipitate a crisis of France's core imperial identity, Alsatian regional identities were swept away by the dominant alternatives of French or German nationalism.

The impact of imperialism on the left-wing identity politics among French socialists was as profound as on the right-wing politics in interwar Alsace.[20] In this instance, however, the perception of foreign domination did not correspond to reality. Callahan's essay, which navigates the many fluctuations in the sectarian politics of the French Left in the movement of international socialism from 1889 to 1900, shows that the squabbles within the French Left are not adequately explained by mere doctrinal differences. Rather, they emerged from a contest over national identity, in which French socialist factions asserted their own notion of national identity and internationalism in contradistinction to an international socialist movement perceived to be dominated by a Germanic socialist imperialism. Thus, identity markers revolved around the axis of French/other in multiple forms such as French/non-French, French/Germanic, and French/international. Elements of the

French Left insisted that they alone represented the "true French worker party" while castigating their contenders as foreign/German worker parties. Paradoxically, Callahan demonstrates that it was the French disorder at the margins of the international socialist movement that prodded the Second International to develop a strong core political culture based on promoting fraternity and containing sectarianism.

The implications of these essays, taken together, in terms of writing an imperial history of France and the relationship between the core and periphery are striking. First, it is quite clear that what occurred in the periphery often directly impacted events in the center. Anne-Marie Javouhey's utopian experiment in the wilds of South America provided a model—used by both supporters and opponents—of how the emancipation of slaves might actually take place. Likewise, the essays by Rich on Marcel Lefebvre and Whitfield on the Algerian War demonstrate how events in the empire and the regions effected changes that were significant for French society in the metropole. Lefebvre spearheaded an ultraconservative French version of Catholicism that he exported back to France after his colonial experience, while the Algerian debacle resulted in Rhône-Alpes citizens refashioning their national identity, in part bringing down the French Fourth Republic and laying the groundwork for the ascension to power of Charles de Gaulle and the French Fifth Republic. Callahan argues that, ironically, the perception of a German socialist imperialism in part prompted factions within the French Left to overcome their division and unite, while their sectarian battles redefined the core identity of international socialism.

Upon first glance the essays of Goodfellow and Harp seem to testify to the power of the center. French consumer identities were indeed being forged in a self-referential vacuum, while Alsatian identity eventually gave way to the external alternatives of French and German nationalism. In both cases, however, it is undeniable that events in the periphery profoundly impacted France's center. Without economic imperialism Michelin's call for well-to-do Frenchmen to experience their Frenchness as tourists by savoring the country's regional diversity is unthinkable. In Alsace fervent resistance to French cultural imperial policies in the 1920s ended up forcing the central government to relax its approach, and Alsatian politics provided a boon for the emergence of French fascist parties, which played a key role on the French national political stage in the 1930s. Thus, a cursory assessment of the strength of the center fails to appreciate the economic realities and political consequences emerging from the periphery.

Another insight gleaned from these essays relates to the fact that actors on the periphery all enjoyed a certain degree of autonomy, albeit to varying degrees. Thus, peripheral identities were not just reactions to or constructions of a hegemonic core but, rather, were agents of their own making. It was the very margins of empire that provided Javouhey the space in which to carry out a radical experiment, Lefebvre the opportunity to internalize masculine virtues of heroism not readily available in the metropole, and Michelin to run exploitative rubber plantations in Indochina. Within French politics factions within the French Left forged their own national identities (some with an anti-foreign/German strain), even though they perceived themselves under siege from a form of German socialist imperialism. Both citizens in Alsace and the Rhône-Alpes repudiated the national government's imposition of a French imperial identity and opted instead to forge identities anchored in regional pride and revival. In one case it succeeded, while in the other it did not. Yet like the sectarian politics within French socialism, both involved contested processes of identity creation, unlike for Javouhey, Lefebvre, and Michelin, all of whom, although facing real challenges in their immediate environment, did not face the heavy-handed intervention of the French government.

Finally, these six essays suggest strongly that French identity is tested, more fluid, or significantly altered when authority patterns are weakened or severely disrupted. The unraveling of the French slave trade gave Javouhey's proposal a favorable audience within the French Colonial Ministry. No less astonishing was the fact that a Catholic nun was wielding patriarchal authority over her colony and bucking the dominant trends of the French Catholic Church in her pro-African and abolitionist views. Consequently, she was not fulfilling the expectations of a proper Frenchwoman and was even mistaken for a "man." In Gabon, as Rich explains, it was the breakdown of traditional African institutions and structures that established fertile ground for a Catholic religious revival, while Lefebvre's distance from the authority of the French Catholic Church in his homeland gave him freedom to interpret the religious revival surrounding him. Facing the French economic crisis of the post–World War I economy, Michelin responded to this challenge by trying to create the market that would consume its products through its promotion of well-heeled consumer tourist identities. The reshuffling of regional identities in Alsace and the Rhône-Alpes came in the wake of the crises of reintegrating Alsace into France after the devastation of World War I and the Algerian conflict, while French socialism underwent changes in the transitional years of reestablishing the international socialist movement in the 1890s. In sum, although the French saw their "civilizing mission" as flowing outward from the metropole to the colonies in Guiana, Gabon, Algeria, and Indochina and from Paris to the regions such as Alsace and Rhône-Alpes, these essays show that, especially in times of national or international crisis, French identity and culture could instead be shaped by the periphery.

The final three essays of this collection provide examples of the operation of the core/periphery framework on other facets of French identity to illustrate its broader application and importance for all fields of French history. They examine the processes of identity creation at the intersection of gender, civic engagement, family structure, and national identity. They also focus on the salient core/periphery binary oppositions of French male/female and French/other in contributing to our understanding of a modern (republican) French national identity and support strongly the hypothesis of weakening authority relations permitting the creation of new identities.

In *The Second Sex* Simone de Beauvoir demonstrated that societies have constructed men as the norm and women as the "other."[21] In the terms adopted by the authors in this volume men are the center and women the periphery. This gender polarity traces its roots to French Enlightenment thinkers such as Jean-Jacques Rousseau, medical researchers and practitioners in the late eighteenth and early nineteenth centuries, and the bourgeois legal order emanating from the French Revolution as ensconced in the 1804 Napoleonic, or Civil, Code. Yet the three essays written by Sean M. Quinlan, Anne R. Epstein, and Rachel G. Fuchs illustrate that this gender system was often challenged in moments of acute societal and political transformations, such as those of the French Revolution and the Dreyfus Affair, or gradually eroded due to shifting social and cultural conventions, as was the case with French family formation in the first half of the twentieth century.

In examining the sex manuals of the Napoleonic era from 1799 to 1804, Quinlan argues that instability during the early Napoleonic years opened up a public space for the publication of ideas on sex and the French citizen prior to the consolidation of the French bipolar gender system. The male doctors who authored these texts were once influential figures in France's Old Regime, but the vicissitudes of the Revolution inverted their social standing. Now as outsiders to the Paris political and medical establishment, these male medical authors used a publishing forum in order to make money and connections that would enhance their professional careers. Interestingly, the power of a female consumer market for their manuals meant that the doctors challenged the dominant model of gendered separate spheres that was beginning to emerge during the Revolution. Quinlan illustrates vividly that new sexual identities tinged with political ideologies were up for grabs in Napoleonic France. Sex and procreation took on a new national meaning because French citizens could demonstrate their patriotism in the privacy of their bedrooms for the purposes of populating the new French nation. As a result, the marginal status of these doctors servicing the market demand for such identities calls into question Michel Foucault's hegemonic model of power, which places all authority in the hands of the Parisian medical establishment, not the marketplace of identities and private interests of peripheral actors.

Epstein's essay on the *Revue de Morale Sociale* asks why the "Intellectual" in France (as stereotyped, for example, by Jean-Paul Sartre) is always imagined as male, even though intellectuals (such as Simone de Beauvoir) were (and are) often female. Like Harp's essay on Michelin, Epstein's essay deals with the processes of erasure and forgetting in the creation of Frenchness, particularly about the way in which the figure of the intellectual who emerged at the time of the Dreyfus Affair has been identified as masculine ever since, despite the active engagement of women. She argues that gender conventions in France have created and sustained a rigid male intellectual identity in spite of the historical reality. Yet women at the end of the nineteenth century challenged the dominance of men in intellectual life by using their moral authority at the margins to work their way into the center. These women attempted to redefine prevailing gender assumptions by carving out public roles for themselves beyond the formal channels of politics. In spite of this historical reality, the French archetype of the masculine Intellectual has remained.

Fuchs's examination of family law during the interwar and Vichy periods uses both gendered and imperial notions of core and periphery. In these legal cases the very identity of the French family was at stake. Fuchs explains how cases that were distant from Paris and in the colonies illustrate the gradual redefinition of the core French patriarchal family to include more complicated, peripheral relationships. Although France is renowned for its paterfamilias French family model derived from the Napoleonic Code, that model evolved in the first half of the twentieth century, as Fuchs explains, so that French society permitted more fluid and flexible family forms such as ex-nuptial children and single-mother households to the point where they could become part of the French cultural core. Surprisingly, the shifting family patterns of the interwar period continued under an overtly patriarchical Vichy regime. In using examples from Algeria and Indochina, Fuchs also brings the volume full circle back to an imperial history of France.

The final three essays reinforce the major themes of this volume in multiple ways. First, they illustrate the interconnections between gender, civic engagement, family law, and national identity in the creation of Frenchness. Quinlan points to the unstable gendered nature of French republican citizenship, an important contribution to an existing body of literature on gender and the French Revolution.[22] Although not in the form that these marginal medical authors articulated, French citizenship remained gendered long after the Revolution, some would say until the present.[23] Epstein also demonstrates the gender implications of French republican political culture in unearthing the origins of the creation of the French Intellectual. The French Intellectual remains a point of pride for the French today and, as Epstein explains, is one of France's most exportable cultural products. Fuchs's analysis of family case histories illustrates how the gradual erosion of the French patriarchical family model, long a central component of national identity, coincided with the increasing inclusion of more complex familial relationships.

In terms of authority and the interaction of the core and the periphery, the three essays exhibit convergent and divergent trends. They illustrate the emergence of (new) notions of Frenchness against the backdrop of political and societal turmoil in the form of the French Revolution and the Dreyfus Affair and the gradual cultural shift in French attitudes toward the ideal family structure. In all three cases existing authority patterns were challenged, resulting in the creation of new French gender and political identities. Revolutionary medical doctors exerted influence on French society by facilitating the process of taming the radical political impulses of the French Revolution by redirecting and reconfiguring them into the realm of the private domestic sphere. While women activists in turn-of-the-century France could relish the victory of the acquittal of Alfred Dreyfus, expanded political and legal rights were not forthcoming. The nexus of gender and French republican political culture explored in the essays of Quinlan and Epstein offer, at the very least, different historical alternatives to the dominant French political culture of distinct sex-specific public and private spheres while demonstrating that such a political culture has more often been an ideal than a historical reality.[24] Interestingly, in Fuchs's essay family formation and dissolution patterns had more to do with geography and a shift in French attitudes toward marginal figures than with the hegemonic power of the state. Notably, all three essays highlight a more fluid and complex gender model of civic engagement and family formation, which in varying degrees integrated the "weaker" sex into the social and political center and thus provides historical evidence to demythologize the so-called natural French bipolar gender order, which still holds great sway in French society today.

Together, all nine essays in this volume suggest the value of the core/periphery framework in defining Frenchness over two centuries. In the more obvious connection of metropole/colony as well as the theme of gender and civic and family identity, we hope that they open up other vistas of possible research in identity creation. Additional research might support the hypothesis that identity creation occurs within a framework of authority, while permutations in such identities often result when that authority structure is weakened. Likewise, it is our contention that future research should take into account the power of the periphery. All things French are not necessarily located in Paris or the product of a centralized state or any other perceived or constructed hegemonic core. Unidirectional center-focused explanatory models of French identity such as Antonio Gramsci's theory of cultural hegemony or Foucault's theory of power, while thought-provoking, are so concerned with the instruments of domination and manipulation that they implicitly assume that actors on the periphery lack autonomy and thus deny them any degree of historical agency. The essays in this volume, by contrast, illustrate the weakness of such theories, the relative autonomy of peripheral actors, the multidirectional flow of peripheral and core events and developments, and the primarily contested and negotiated (as opposed to hegemonic) processes of identity creation. In sum we believe that the views from the margins are well worth appreciating in understanding the dynamic nature of French identity.

Finally, this book is an outgrowth of the contributors' extraordinary appreciation for the scholarship and friendship of William B. Cohen, who inspired a generation of French and European historians. Its themes reflect both his scholarship and his life. He encouraged his students, many of whom are contributors to this volume, to look across borders or at the margins while being aware of what was happening at the center. He also taught most of us the craft (and the fun) of research, reflected in the archivally based contributions to this collection. His own work was a model of scholarship in both respects, combining meticulous research with unasked questions—many of which were neither trendy nor widespread at the time he asked them—but which in retrospect anticipated important historiographical approaches. His first two books explored the relationships between France and its African colonies, the second of which, *The French Encounter with Africans* (1980), remains the classic account of French cultural attitudes toward blacks. His third monograph, *Urban Government and the Rise of the French City* (1998), examined the growth of municipal government in the industrial age, illuminating again the interactions between the Parisian centralized core and urban regional peripheries. His uncompleted book project on the Algerian War and French memory was poised to be a landmark study, again teasing out the full implications of culture and identity between the core and periphery in a postcolonial setting. Born in Europe, raised in Africa, educated in the United States—a polyglot who spoke each of his several languages, as he joked, with an accent—Bill personified the scholar without borders, whose humanistic perspective infused both his writing and his teaching. We dedicate this book to his memory.

Notes

1. Fernand Braudel, *The Identity of France*, trans. Sian Reynolds, 2 vols. (New York: Harper and Row, 1988–90).
2. To be French in the Middle Ages connoted being a "good Christian" in the realm of the "most Christian" king, a form of Christianity deemed at times as more pure

than Roman Catholicism and the papacy itself. Liah Greenfeld, *Nationalism: Five Roads to Modernity* (Cambridge: Harvard University Press, 1992), 94.

3. This is the interpretation offered by Greenfeld, *Nationalism*; as well as Orest Ranun, ed., *National Consciousness, History, and Political Culture in Early Modern Europe* (Baltimore: Johns Hopkins University Press, 1975).

4. Michael Wolfe, ed., *Changing Identities in Early Modern France* (Durham NC: Duke University Press, 1997). Also see the helpful article by David Bell, "Recent Works on Early Modern French National Identity," *Journal of Modern History* 68 (1986): 84–113.

5. David A. Bell, *The Cult of the Nation in France: Inventing Nationalism, 1680–1800* (Cambridge: Harvard University Press, 2001), chap. 3. See also Mack P. Holt, "Burgundians into Frenchmen: Catholic Identity in Sixteenth-Century Burgundy," in Wolfe, *Changing Identities*, 345–70; and Colin Jones and Dror Wahrman, eds., *The Age of Cultural Revolutions, Britain and France, 1750–1820* (Berkeley: University of California Press, 2002).

6. Eugen Weber, *Peasants into Frenchmen: The Modernization of Rural France, 1870–1914* (Stanford: Stanford University Press, 1976).

7. See esp. Caroline Ford, *Creating the Nation in Provincial France: Religion and Political Identity in Brittany* (Princeton NJ: Princeton University Press, 1993); and Stéphane Gerson, *The Pride of Place: Local Memories and Political Culture in Nineteenth-Century France* (Ithaca NY: Cornell University Press, 2003). Note that the region as central to national identity is also the case in Germany, as explained by Celia Applegate, *A Nation of Provincials: The German Idea of Heimat* (Berkeley: University of California Press, 1990); and Alon Confino, *The Nation as a Local Metaphor: Wurttemberg, Imperial Germany, and National Memory, 1871–1918* (Chapel Hill: University of North Carolina Press, 1997).

8. Gérard Noiriel, *Le Creuset français: histoire de l'immigration XIXe–XXe siècles* (Paris: Seuil, 1988), translated by Geoffroy de Laforcade as *The French Melting Pot: Immigration, Citizenship, and National Identity* (Minneapolis: University of Minnesota Press, 1996).

9. See Ralph Schor, *Histoire de l'immigration en France de la fin du XIXe siècle à nos jours* (Paris: Armand Colin, 1996); Patrick Weil, *Qu'est-ce qu'un français? histoire de la nationalité française depuis la Révolution* (Paris: Éditions Grasset et Fasquelle, 2002); Joseph Krulic, "L'Immigration et l'identité de la France: mythes et réalités," *Pouvoirs* 47 (1988): 31–43; Yves Lequin, ed., *La Mosaïque France: histoire des étrangers et de l'immigration en France* (Paris: Larousse, 1988); Patrick Weil, *La France et ses étrangers: l'aventure d'une politique de l'immigration, 1938–1991* (Paris: Calmann-Levy, 1991); Peter Sahlins, *Unnaturally French: Foreign Citizens in the Old Regime and After* (Ithaca NY: Cornell University Press, 2004); J.-F. Dubost and Peter Sahlins, *Et si on fai-*

sait payer les étrangers? Louis XIV, les immigrés et quelques autres (Paris: Flammarion,
1999); Sophie Wahnich, *L'Impossible citoyen: l'étranger dans le discours de la Révolution
française* (Paris: Albin Michel, 1997); Michael Rapport, *Nationality and Citizenship
in Revolutionary France: The Treatment of Foreigners, 1789–1799* (Oxford: Clarendon
Press, 2000).

10. Rogers Brubaker, *Citizenship and Nationhood in France and Germany* (Cambridge: Harvard University Press, 1992), 138–64.

11. Elaine Sciolino, "Identity, Staple of Right, Moves to Center of French Campaigns,"
New York Times, March 30, 2007.

12. Even a cursory glance at the programs of annual conferences of the Society for
French Historical Studies and the Western Society for French History will confirm
this trend. Figures are cited in Alice L. Conklin and Julia Clancy-Smith, "Introduction: Writing French Colonial Histories," *French Historical Studies* 27 (Summer
2004): 497n1. This issue is entirely devoted to recent scholarship on French colonialism. Recent key texts also include Patricia Lorcin, *Imperial Identities: Stereotyping,
Prejudice, and Race in Colonial Algeria* (New York: I. B. Taurus, 1995); Alice L. Conklin,
A Mission to Civilize: The Republican Idea of Empire in France and West Africa, 1895–1930
(Stanford: Stanford University Press, 1997); Julia Clancy-Smith and Frances
Gouda, eds., *Domesticating the Empire: Race, Gender, and Family Life in French and Dutch
Colonialism* (Charlottesville: University Press of Virginia, 1998); Elizabeth Thompson, *Colonial Citizens: Republican Rights, Paternal Privilege, and Gender in French Syria and
Lebanon* (New York: Columbia University Press, 2000); Owen White, *Children of the
French Empire: Miscegenation and Colonial Society in French West Africa, 1895–1960* (New
York: Oxford University Press, 2000); Eric T. Jennings, *Vichy in the Tropics: Pétain's
National Revolution in Madagascar, Guadeloupe, and Indochina, 1940–1944* (Stanford:
Stanford University Press, 2002); Sue Peabody and Tyler Stovall, eds., *The Color
of Liberty: Histories of Race in France* (Durham NC: Duke University Press, 2003);
Laurent Dubois, *A Colony of Citizens: Revolution and Slave Emancipation in the French
Caribbean, 1787–1804* (Chapel Hill: University of North Carolina Press, 2004); J. P.
Daughton, *An Empire Divided: Religion, Republicanism, and the Making of French Colonialism, 1880–1914* (New York: Oxford University Press, 2006).

13. This idea was first introduced but not developed by Weber in *Peasants into Frenchmen*, chap. 29.

14. For Italian Marxist Antonio Gramsci's theory of cultural hegemony, refer to David
Forgacs, ed., *The Antonio Gramsci Reader: Selected Writings, 1916–1935* (New York:
New York University Press, 2000); and for Foucault's theory of power, see Michel
Foucault, "Governmentality," in *The Essential Works of Foucault, 1954–1984*, vol. 3,
Power, ed. James D. Faubion (New York: New Press, 2000), 201–22.

15. As does, for example, Edward Said in *Orientalism* (New York: Vintage Publishers,
1979).

16. Ronald Grigor Suny, "Back and Beyond: Reversing the Cultural Turn?" *American Historical Review* 107, no. 5 (2002): 1485.

17. William H. Sewell Jr., "The Concept(s) of Culture," in *Beyond the Cultural Turn*, ed. Victoria E. Bonnell and Lynn Hunt (Berkeley: University of California Press, 1999), 49–50.

18. Roger Chartier, *Cultural History: Between Practices and Representations* (Ithaca NY: Cornell University Press, 1988), 102.

19. See Bell, *Cult of the Nation in France*, chap. 3, with respect to England and the following works for the German Empire: Claude Digeon, *La Crise allemande de la pensée française (1870–1914)* (Paris: Presses Universitaires de France, 1959); Alan Mitchell, *The German Influence in France after 1870: The Formation of the Republic* (Chapel Hill: University of North Carolina Press, 1979); Raymond Poidevin and Jacques Bariéty, *Les Relations franco-allemandes, 1815–1975* (Paris: A. Colin, 1977); Hartmut Kaelbe, "Die vergessene Gesellschaft im Westen? Das Bild der Deutschen von der französischen Gesellschaft, 1871–1914," *Revue d'Allemagne* 21, no. 2 (1989): 181–96; and Michael E. Nolan, *The Inverted Mirror: Mythologizing the Enemy in France and Germany, 1898–1914* (New York: Bergahn Books, 2005).

20. On identity politics, some key works are Robert Nye, *Crime, Madness, and Politics in Modern France: The Medical Concept of National Decline* (Princeton NJ: Princeton University Press, 1984); Jerrold Seigel, *Bohemian Paris: Culture, Politics, and the Boundaries of Bourgeois Life, 1830–1930* (New York: Penguin, 1986); Jane F. Fulcher, *The Nation's Image: French Grand Opera as Politics and Politicized Art* (New York: Cambridge University Press, 1987); Marc Antliff, *Inventing Bergson: Cultural Politics and the Parisian Avant-Garde* (Princeton NJ: Princeton University Press, 1993); Herman Lebovics, *True France: The Wars over Cultural Identity* (Ithaca NY: Cornell University Press, 1994); Philip Nord, *The Republican Moment: Struggles for Democracy in Nineteenth-Century France* (Cambridge MA: Belknap Press, 1994); Kolleen M. Guy, *When Champagne Became French: Wine and the Making of a National Identity* (Baltimore: Johns Hopkins University Press, 2003); and Melissa Hyde and Jennifer Milam, eds., *Women, Art, and the Politics of Identity in Eighteenth-Century Europe* (Burlington VT: Ashgate Press, 2003).

21. Simone de Beauvoir, *The Second Sex* (New York: Knopf, 1953).

22. Joan B. Landes, *Women and the Public Sphere in the Age of the French Revolution* (Ithaca NY: Cornell University Press, 1988); Olwen Hufton, *Women and the Limits of Citizenship in the French Revolution* (Toronto: University of Toronto Press, 1992); and Joan Wallach Scott, *Only Paradoxes to Offer: French Feminists and the Rights of Man* (Cambridge MA: Harvard University Press, 1996).

23. See Joan Scott, *Parité: Sexual Equality and the Crisis of French Universalism* (Chicago: University of Chicago Press, 2005).

24. They are not, of course, the only scholars to suggest this divergence between ideal

and reality. In politics the ideal was probably more fully realized than other elements of French society. One area in which considerable research has been done on women's entry into the public sphere (albeit a gendered public sphere) is in the arena of consumerism, as explained by Leora Auslander in *Taste and Power: Furnishing Modern France* (Berkeley: University of California Press, 1996); and Lisa Tiersten, *Marianne in the Market: Envisioning Consumer Society in Fin-de-Siècle France* (Berkeley: University of California Press, 2001).

SARAH A. CURTIS

1

Missionary Utopias

Anne-Marie Javouhey and the Colony
at Mana, French Guiana, 1827–1848

In this essay Sarah A. Curtis investigates the imperial identity of missionary Anne-Marie Javouhey and her attempt to transform newly emancipated African slaves into pious peasant Catholic farmers in the remotest periphery of the French Empire, the isolated outpost of Mana in French Guiana. Precisely because of its geographical distance from metropolitan France and its marginal economic status, Guiana provided a site for radical experiments such as this one. Inspired by her own rural regional roots in Burgundy, Javouhey attempted to transpose the identity of pious French peasants onto "uncivilized" former African slaves within the French Empire. Yet it was Javouhey herself who was transformed the most by this experience. As a woman, a nun, and an abolitionist, Javouhey forged her own identity in opposition to accepted ideas about gender and race in the Catholic Church and among slave owners in Guiana. On the margins of empire Javouhey enjoyed considerable autonomy because the unraveling French slave trade from the 1820s to 1840s and her personal connections to the elite of the July Monarchy in the metropole permitted this audacious Catholic woman to launch a bold colonial experiment.

♥ ♥

When, after the Revolution of 1848, the Second French Republic emancipated and enfranchised the slaves in the French Empire, the newly liberated blacks living in an isolated settlement on the Mana River in faraway French Guiana, are reported to have insisted on casting their legislative votes for the founder of their colony, Mère Anne-Marie Javouhey, superior general of the Soeurs de St-Joseph de Cluny. "Vainly," one source writes, "did one tell them that women could not form part of political assemblies." Upon finally understanding the gender realities of French politics, they supposedly stated, "'If we cannot name our Dear Mother, name whom you like, it's all the same to us.'"[1] Another source claims that they then refused to vote altogether.[2]

What was going on here? Like first-time voters all over France and the colonies in 1848, the inhabitants of Mana apparently preferred to send a familiar candidate to the new republican National Assembly in Paris, throwing their support behind the local notable. In this case, however, the local notable was a woman and a nun, and the voters were not only former slaves but ones born in French West Africa, now living in a self-supporting, agricultural commune in the wilds of South America, 220 kilometers away from the nearest French outpost, at Cayenne. Despite the fact that King Louis Philippe had called her a "great man" and she was allegedly misidentified on the Paris barricades as "the general Javouhey,"[3] Anne-Marie Javouhey was not running for anything, nor of course, being a woman, could she even cast a vote herself. Dismayed by the disorder and radicalism of the Revolution of 1848, she was nevertheless gratified that "her dear blacks" were "wiser" than those of the West Indies, where violence broke out on the news of liberation.[4] To her peaceful liberation in Mana proved that her faith in the gradual emancipation of blacks under the moralizing influence of Catholicism had been well placed and that the experimental colony she had established there in 1828 had been a success.

This essay examines the unusual settlement at Mana, French Guiana, in which over five hundred West African slaves and their descendants—seized in the clandestine slave trade, shipped across the Atlantic, and entrusted to Javouhey's care—lived and worked under the supervision of the Soeurs de St-Joseph de Cluny beginning in the 1830s. Scarcely a household name, either to contemporaries in the nineteenth century or to historians today, Mana nevertheless presents a window onto the complex relationship between race, gender, and religion, as well as between metropole and colony, in the period between the French Revolution, which temporarily outlawed slavery, and the Revolution of 1848, which did so definitively. The Mana colony not only became a safe haven for blacks in a region where oppressive slavery was the rule; it also allowed Anne-Marie Javouhey to fulfill a long-held desire to create an independent religious utopia far away from what she considered the corruption of everyday society.

Everything about this colony defied the norm. Javouhey's insistence on working with Africans rather than only with settler populations in French colonies revived a Catholic paradigm of evangelization to non-Europeans first developed in the sixteenth century but one that few early nineteenth-century clerics embraced. Unlike most Catholics, however, she took her inspiration from contemporary utopian movements as much as from missionary precedents. She also broke with her church in championing abolitionism. But she remained an outsider to the incipient French abolition movement, which was dominated by secular Protestants. Although Javouhey shared many of the nineteenth-century stereotypes about Africans, she steadfastly defended their intrinsic equality to Europeans in the eyes of God and their potential to rise to European standards of "civilization." And her forceful direction of Mana defied the gender expectations of her day, producing conflict with male clerics, who saw her autonomy as a challenge to the accepted role of both women and Catholic nuns in the nineteenth century.

Only Mana's extreme isolation and its peripheral status in a colony that was itself peripheral made Javouhey's mission possible. For the French state Mana provided a rare opportunity to experiment with new models of slave relations and slave emancipation in anticipation of the breakdown of the slave system sometime in the near future. Such experimentation could only have taken place away from the geographical and economic centers of empire, yet Javouhey skillfully manipulated the relationship between metropole and colony in order to raise the political and financial support that she needed to make Mana feasible. Javouhey's power also derived from Mana's location on the edges of empire, where it was safe to invest political, religious, and economic sovereignty in a Catholic nun as well as the marginal status of the people she was allowed to rule, slaves and former slaves, uprooted from their homeland and implanted on new soil. For Javouhey isolation on the periphery was the very conceptual basis of her utopia, as she believed that only far away from French civilization could blacks, paradoxically, change their identity by realizing their potential as "civilized" beings, able to live in equality with whites under God.

A Colony of Her Own

Daughter of a prosperous Burgundian peasant, Javouhey founded the Soeurs de St-Joseph de Cluny with her three birth sisters in 1798, and the order was authorized by Napoléon in 1806. Like a number of other pious women in the wake of the French Revolution, she sought to bring together a centralized, uncloistered religious order of like-minded women who would consecrate themselves to God and to the religious regeneration of France through the active work of evangelization and charity.[5] After the Restoration of the French monarchy in 1814, thanks to Javouhey's good political contacts in the colonial ministry, the order rapidly expanded into missionary work, establishing houses in Bourbon (Réunion) in 1817; Senegal in 1818; Sierra Leone, Guadeloupe, and Cayenne in 1822; Gambia and Martinique in 1823; St.-Pierre-et-Miquelon in 1826; and India in 1827. By the time of Javouhey's death in 1851, the Soeurs de St-Joseph de Cluny had become one of France's largest and most important missionary orders, numbering more than 1,200 sisters in 140 communities on five continents. Like many missionary orders of this era, the Soeurs de St-Joseph primarily answered requests to provide hospital and educational services for French settlers abroad, and both church and government officials generally discouraged more active evangelization among natives. Yet not only did these limitations keep Javouhey from attaining the scope for initiative that she desired, but her own experiences in the colonies increasingly convinced her that her mission was really among Africans rather than Europeans.

Javouhey's first personal contact with Africans came in March 1822, when she arrived in the French colony of Senegal, where the order had established a school for European and mixed-race girls in 1819. Residence in West Africa was clearly an eye-opening experience that only whetted her appetite to work among native populations. Surprised by the density of inhabitants in the coastal city of Saint-Louis, Javouhey wrote, "I feel a great need to work for their happiness."[6] She quickly became attached to a young African servant named Florence, who later accompanied her back to France, and she began negotiations for seventeen promising African boys to be sent to France for training toward the priesthood. She bought and freed six slaves aged nine to twenty-five and had ample opportunity to witness the extent and brutality of the slave trade in West Africa, despite its official prohibition since 1815.[7] Evangelizing among Africans appeared to her more promising than among Europeans, whom she viewed as corrupt and irreligious: "very bad subjects who did not want to hear about religion," whereas the blacks were "good, simple . . . it would not be difficult to convince them by example."[8] Soon she was petitioning the government to open a school for "*black* children," which came to fruition in 1826, when the sisters opened a boarding school with a French Catholic curriculum for African girls in Saint-Louis, Senegal.[9]

Javouhey also hankered after a mission based on the small-scale farming familiar to her from her own peasant upbringing. As early as 1822 she imagined an agricultural settlement farmed by Africans in Dagana, 120 kilometers upstream from Saint-Louis, on lands granted to the order by the French government. "This project," she wrote, "that I have contemplated for a long time, relates naturally to the great project of civilizing Africa, of forming an agricultural, hard-working people, and above all honest men and good Christians."[10] Only in a self-sufficient religious community uncorrupted by worldly contact did she see the possibility for the true regeneration of society in harmony with God. Increasingly, she sought an opportunity, in the words of her nephew, "to found a town where she could assemble a population she raised and that would develop under her care."[11] Such an opening presented itself not in Africa but across the Atlantic in the French colony of Guiana on the coast of South America, where in 1827 the government allotted the Soeurs de St-Joseph de Cluny a tract of land next to the Mana River on which they could establish a self-supporting commune, entirely independent of religious and political authority. Although similar to her plan for an agricultural community in Senegal, Javouhey originally intended to populate her new colony at Mana with five hundred French orphans of both sexes as well as voluntary immigrants "habituated to the fatigue and deprivations of a simple and rustic life."[12] Most would be farmers, but Javouhey also sought to recruit artisans in order to make the settlement self-sufficient. Soeurs de St-Joseph de Cluny would care for the orphans and the sick, teach, make clothing, prepare food, and assist with the agricultural work when necessary. The children would learn farming and animal husbandry under the supervision of the sisters and the French settlers. Eventually, Javouhey envisioned four villages at Mana, each one housing a thousand orphans.[13]

Although Javouhey asked the government for the land grant, transportation to Guiana, building and maintenance labor, and the initial equipment and supplies, as well as continued support for eighteen months, the new colony was to be left entirely independent in matters of governance and economic livelihood. Her inspiration here appeared to be contemporary "utopian" colonies where residents eschewed private ownership and worked together for a common good. "The system of these establishments," the project proposal stated, "should be in the associational spirit of institutions created recently in England and the United States of America. All would

MAP I.I. French Guiana

be in common: work, methods of provision, food supplies, products for members, no private property of any kind in the colony."[14] In a period of poverty in France, Mana would serve a useful social purpose by providing asylum for French orphans who might otherwise be an economic burden on the French government or a blight on the "social condition."[15] At Mana these children would be raised with religious principles and work skills. Like many other Frenchmen and women in the 1820s and 1830s, Anne-Marie Javouhey saw her society in a state of moral and spiritual crisis that could best be remedied by a return to communal solidarity and common purpose in a setting far from the ills of modern life.[16] Far away from the corruption of French society, it would be easy, Javouhey argued, to raise these children "in the practice of religious virtue," and "our dear solitary society" would keep "no man who was not truly pious and God-fearing."[17] Isolation was assured by the 220 kilometers between Mana and the capital city of Cayenne, the absence of roads after Kourou (160 kilometers from Mana), and the Atlantic winds that made a return sea voyage to Cayenne take over a month (the trip from Cayenne took three days). To the west were scattered settlements of Surinam Maroons living beside the Maroni River, and behind Mana stretched the Amazon forests, inhabited only by peaceful Amerindian tribes. What better setting for a religious utopia in which Christian virtue could be nurtured among innocent children?

Javouhey's ambitions for Mana dovetailed nicely with the interests of the French government. After the loss of Canada (except St-Pierre-et-Miquelon) in 1763, the independence of Haiti in 1804, the sale of Louisiana to the United States, and the transfer of many of its colonies to Britain during the Napoleonic period, in 1817 France's recovered empire was essentially limited to its West African ports, the island of Bourbon (now Réunion) in the Indian Ocean, Guadeloupe and Martinique in the Caribbean, and French Guiana. The last, officials hoped, could be developed as a profitable territory that would, in the words of a government report, "compensate us for the colonial possessions we have lost." Based on a plantation economy, Guiana in 1819 consisted of 13,309 slaves, 1,698 free individuals of color, and a mere 987 white settlers.[18] Because the abolition of the slave trade in 1817 made importation of new African labor difficult, the colonial ministry focused on the need to attract European farmers to Guiana, to the irritation of the existing plantation owners, who saw new settlements such as Mana a waste of government resources that could be better spent in subsidizing their crops.[19] Rather than large plantations, these new colonization schemes rested on small-scale agricultural communities, and in the mid-1820s Mana had already been the site of a failed experiment to resettle a handful of families from the Jura region in France. Javouhey's project for the same site appeared to officials not only to promise more success, thanks to her obvious vision and drive, but also to reduce the costs and simplify the administration of such a settlement.[20] The religious and social regeneration she sought would work hand in hand with the colonial regeneration of Guiana itself.

The first colony under Javouhey's direction, however, was not successful. Within a short time she was disillusioned with the quality of immigrants she had attracted. "Few," she wrote, "have shown the courage and devotion necessary to such undertakings: half left halfway [through their engagement] and those who have stayed only want to live as Europeans" who "fear the least appearance of suffering."[21] Other sources suggest that the quasi-monastic life at Mana and its extreme isolation from other settlements, including prohibitions on trade and commerce, discouraged French settlers. Few of them appear to have bought into the concept of a communal utopia, especially one in which the initial establishment was so hard. After his inspection of 1829, the governor wrote that they preferred to "establish themselves individually than stay in association." He also did not see how the colony was to grow given that most of the unmarried women were nuns, leaving no European marriage partners for the single men.[22] Out of the original fifty-six colonists in 1828, by 1832 five had died, eight had left for other parts of Guiana, and twenty-nine had returned to France.[23] The orphans never materialized, in part because the government had already spent almost two hundred thousand francs on Mana and was reluctant to spend more.[24]

Evangelizing Africans

To keep her colony afloat, Javouhey returned to the concept of establishing a settlement primarily for Africans. The French government had already provided Mana with a small workforce of black slaves to help clear the land, to whom she added rescued runaway slaves from Brazil and Surinam and slaves whom she purchased from inhumane owners for forty thousand francs of her own money. The Africans proved to be harder workers than the French settlers, but Javouhey also had evangelical goals in mind, intending to "make them into good Christians."[25] By 1832 Mana was no longer a majority white settlement but one with equal numbers of Europeans and Africans.[26] To make this transformation definitive, Javouhey contracted with the government in 1835 to populate Mana with 476 Africans seized from illegal slave ships, who had been transported to Guiana to finish seven-year terms of indenture before being definitively freed. The Africans, temporarily housed in government workshops in Cayenne, were moved to Mana in seven groups between March 1836 and April 1837, with an initial shipment of fifty men who could build the cabins to house the subsequent arrivals.[27] By 1836 Mana had become a colony with a majority African population (over five hundred blacks to about twenty-five whites) of which the celibate Javouhey described herself "as a mother in the middle of her large family" and her charges as "her new children."[28]

This reinvention of Mana as a site of moralization and gradual emancipation of African slaves under the direction of the Soeurs de St-Joseph de Cluny gave Javouhey a captive population to evangelize and train. It also provided a useful service for the new July Monarchy that had come to power in 1830. Having taken a more activist role in enforcing the prohibition of the slave trade than the Restoration government, which looked the other way while slave ships sailed from Nantes and other French ports, it was nevertheless unsure what to do with the Africans it seized on the high seas.[29] Officials feared that returning them to Africa would risk their recapture yet that freeing them in the slave colonies might serve as a dangerous catalyst to slave rebellion. Instead, they distributed them between the slave colonies under seven-year terms of indenture, a system that had been developed in Senegal after 1815,[30] hoping that gradual emancipation would buy them some time.[31] Javouhey's proposal to cloister the almost five hundred individuals held in Guiana at Mana under religious rule seemed both a safe and responsible solution, especially as she promised to educate them in anticipation of their liberation. Her interest in Africans was well known and well regarded in the colonial ministry, as well as in the Tuileries palace, where Javouhey lobbied personally for her new project with King Louis Philippe and Queen Marie-Amélie.[32] In Guiana the governor praised her success in transforming the Africans she had purchased or rescued, whom he characterized as "notoriously the worst subjects of the colony, most recovered from justice or former runaways," into "honest, peaceful, and hardworking" residents of Mana.[33]

French officials even proposed that in time Mana could be used as a sort of model training settlement for slaves awaiting freedom while simultaneously increasing Guiana's prosperity.[34] "It is the Liberia of the Americans," the minister of marine and colonies was reported to have declared to the governor of Guiana, "soon slavery will be banished entirely and this new freetown will be populated not only with freed slaves of the Antilles, but undoubtedly with ransomed Africans. It is to this establishment, perhaps, that Guiana today deprived of manpower . . . will one day owe its prosperity" in a "new colonial society, born of free labor."[35] Another commentator hoped that Mana would go beyond "a place of asylum and reward," like Sierra Leone or Liberia, by becoming "a place of regeneration," where birthrates would rise and racial hostility would decline, ensuring the "future prosperity of French colonies."[36] The former governor of Senegal, Baron Roger, an abolitionist and personal friend to Javouhey, wrote, "Think of the 250,000 slaves who wait in some way for the results of your experiment. You work for them all, as well as for the blacks of Mana."[37] Although most colonial officials, unlike Roger, were not abolitionists, by the 1830s, with the slave trade outlawed and the British abolition of slavery imminent, they were eager for economically viable alternatives to slavery in the French colonies.

To most French colonists resident in Guiana, however, Mana as a home for former slaves was only useful to the extent that its distance isolated free and semi-free blacks from contact with the slaves who guaranteed their livelihood. Otherwise, they considered the Mana settlement a dangerous social and economic experiment, warning that the new Mana residents would quickly establish contact with the Maroon rebels from Surinam camped along the Maroni River and create "another enemy at our doors."[38] This particular fear appeared to have little foundation, as the great slave rebellions in Surinam between 1764 and 1776 had not touched Guiana, and French runaway slaves had made little contact with their Dutch counterparts.[39] But French settlers had long depended on slavery as the labor force that made Guiana a viable colony. Although the slave system resembled that of the Caribbean islands, Guiana was a much poorer colony, where many fewer slaves were available.[40] Even at the height of the slave trade, few ships bothered to make the journey. In the eighteenth century, due to the direction of the Atlantic winds, four out of ten ships missed the landing at Cayenne even when within sight of the port, and the trip from the Antilles could take up to two months (the outward journey took about six days). The difficulties of importation raised the price of slaves and diminished their quality. Runaway slaves could easily take refuge in the dense forests, and the colony did not have the manpower to recapture them.[41] Slaves in Guiana, therefore, were kept in somewhat better physical and material condition than their counterparts in Saint-Domingue, Guadeloupe, or Martinique because they were less easily replaced commodities. Yet as in these colonies, disease, malnourishment, and lack of medical care kept mortality rates high and birthrates low,[42] further endangering the future of the slave labor force. Under these conditions colonists were hostile to any suggestion of a change in the status quo. Furthermore, the experience of successful slave rebellion in Saint-Domingue during the French Revolution and the British abolition of slavery in 1834 made them nervous about the future security of their way of life. Javouhey's Mana experiment not only raised the specter of slave emancipation; it diverted funds and labor from their plantations without a clear economic benefit to themselves. At best Mana would become an economic competitor and pave the way for definitive slave emancipation; at worst it would gobble up scarce investment monies from Paris and incite slave rebellion.

Furthermore, the Mana settlement put administrative control in the hands of a woman, who, colonial clergy continually complained, considered herself more powerful than even the priest assigned to Mana. In fact, she was. In addition to choosing the nuns who were sent as missionaries to Mana in her role as superior general of her order, Javouhey's civilian powers there included the appointment of any administrators (whom she recruited among members of her own family) and medical personnel, the organization of a police force if necessary, a trade monopoly, the ability to authorize new construction and crops, and permission for blacks to leave the colony. She rejected the offer of anxious French authorities to place a military post at Mana, arguing that she would not need armed force to govern the individuals under her care. Likewise, she refused even a resident government agent, who might become the "real chief of the establishment." The civilizing process, she argued, required "unity of power and method."[43] Although she could call on the governor of Guiana if necessary, her authority flowed directly from the colonial ministry in Paris, which also provided the funds for personnel and materials. Here Javouhey had full support to choose the "system of education and discipline that she judges the most appropriate to the civilization of blacks."[44] Javouhey made the complete isolation of her colony "an absolute condition."[45] No one, she insisted, could come to Mana without her permission, including merchants, "which prevents intrigues from penetrating there."[46] The minister of colonies acquiesced by outlawing the use of the Mana River to Guiana ships in 1835.[47] Javouhey's ability to fulfill her vision at Mana derived directly from the confidence she enjoyed in Paris, where she received the powers and funds she needed to make her colony successful. Officials there were more willing to support progressive experiments than were local elites, whose interests were threatened more directly by both the substance and the symbolism of Javouhey's colony.[48]

The Mana Model

At Mana work, order, and devotion were the organizing principles. The main project of the colony was agriculture, but it had little in common with the plantation economy in other parts of Guiana, South America, or the Caribbean, where slaves produced large quantities of sugar, coffee, or cotton.[49] Instead, like French peasants, most inhabitants cultivated a variety of crops on a small scale. And although Javouhey implied that she and her sisters were providing instruction in farming, many of the crops grown at Mana—manioc, rice, bananas—would have been familiar to individuals native to the west coast of Africa. Along with agriculture, Javouhey added training in French artisanal trades, from shoemaking to carpentry to baking bread. Physically, the colony, Javouhey wrote, "resembles a pretty village in France; all is symmetrical, the streets are wide, the houses simple but well lined up."[50]

Mana's economic organization was something like a seigneurial domain. Javouhey, in her double role as superior of a religious community and colonial administrator, oversaw everything from prayers to crops. Unfreed residents spent approximately five hours a day on an assigned task for the community and the rest on personal plots of land. The newly freed hired themselves out two days a week to Javouhey in exchange for rations and three francs a week.[51] In exchange for their labor the African residents received food, lodging, clothing, instruction, and medical care. Nuns served as administrators, teachers, nurses, and an additional workforce. The entire community began its day at five-thirty in the morning with prayer, hymns, and catechism. Following the monastic model, the rest of the day was strictly divided into periods of work, meals, recreation, and religious instruction. According to Soeur Philémon Poulachon, who lived in Guiana from 1839 until 1890, two hundred Africans "listened with religious attention" to a sister who instructed them on "the state of mind necessary to the reception of the sacraments and the obligations that they were going to contract on becoming Christians."[52] The Soeurs de St-Joseph encouraged baptisms (the first ceremony took place in 1836 with eighty individuals) and Christian marriages, which were rewarded with small plots of land for household use. Javouhey put great stock in the formation of Christian households as a means to moralization, so much so that she proposed at one point buying and importing (and later emancipating) about thirty additional Senegalese women to serve as marriage partners for the excess population of men at Mana.[53] Until they were married, however, men and women lived in separate lodgings, and the women and children were cloistered with the sisters "night and day,"[54] only mixing with men for work, church services, and religious instruction. These precautions, Javouhey argued, as well as the isolation of the colony ensured that the Mana residents were protected from the "vicious habits to which they were so unfortunately previously inclined." Above all, they had no opportunity to pick up irreligious and immoral habits from others. "Bad examples," she wrote in the same report, "kill societies."[55]

Although her letters refer to some of the utopian experiments of the 1820s and 1830s as well as the creation of Liberia and Sierra Leone (where she had traveled in 1823), Javouhey's most important model for Mana was undoubtedly the seventeenth-century South American "reductions" established by the Jesuits to evangelize Indians. In a letter sent soon after her arrival in Mana in September 1828, Javouhey wrote, "I hope that we will make a new Paraguay where the Lord will be served, loved, and glorified."[56] Six years later, when she transformed Mana into "an asylum to place Negros who are destined for freedom, to instruct them, to direct them for five or seven years, before making them completely free," she claimed to be "following the example of Paraguay."[57] Although she does not mention them specifically, Jesuit missions for Indians also flourished in Guiana itself during the first half of the eighteenth century, disappearing after the Jesuit expulsion from France in 1762. In the reductions Jesuits protected Indians from enslavement while attempting to Christianize them.

Even though the reductions were far larger in population than Javouhey's Mana colony, the two projects had in common a desire to provide a vulnerable population sanctuary from the brutality of other Europeans in a self-sufficient settlement run according to European religious and cultural norms. The daily schedules, derived from monastic models, the enclosure of women, communal property, and the emphasis on settled agriculture were also common features.[58] But Jesuits in Guiana, while opposing the enslavement of Indians, had owned Africans, in whose culture they saw little redemptive value.[59] Javouhey, on the other hand, made only limited attempts to convert several hundred Indians who lived not far from Mana and with whom the colony had frequent contact. The Jesuit reductions operated as a source of inspiration but not as a blueprint. Instead, Javouhey followed her own sense of destiny.

The premise of the entire Mana establishment was that quasi-religious enclosure provided the best opportunity for the regeneration of society, especially that of blacks, for whom "everyone on earth seems to doom an eternal degradation." Placed in "a single establishment, under a single authority . . . and isolated from all foreign contact," Javouhey argued, the Mana inhabitants could be taught "the love of work and escape from laziness" that would allow them "to act like free men, that is to maintain themselves in peace and good order."[60] In 1841 Javouhey proposed the transfer to Mana of the three thousand slave children over the age of seven who lived in Guiana, in whom "rested all hope of the future," in order to prepare them for emancipation. Again, she argued that isolation and enclosure provided the best possibility of raising children untainted by immorality and vice: "Oh! what I would give to see raised in the middle of the Guiana forests, as in the womb of nature alone, supported on one side by religion, on the other by morality and the love of work, this population of children, led by piety and gentleness, animated with the desire to do good, strong against seduction and vice, who could show to the world that Christianity alone is capable of producing the great effects of civilization that philanthropy only dreams of in its impotence!"[61]

During her thirteen-year sojourn in Guiana, Javouhey lauded the tranquility of the Mana "forests" as preferable to "society," suggesting that they could also be a refuge for Catholics who were being persecuted in France.[62] On one administrative trip to Cayenne, she wrote, "I cannot accustom myself any longer to the problems of the world, of business; I am only fit to live in the woods . . . [where] it is sweet to serve God without distraction!"[63] And upon a return visit to Paris in 1834, she praised the newly acquired convent, where "no one could penetrate the interior," as providing solitude "as at Mana" while still being "two steps from our affairs."[64] Javouhey herself, as much as she might have expressed a longing for the forests of South America, was a charismatic and engaged leader whose 1,100-plus letters, worldwide travel, and constant communication with officials contrasted with the isolation she advocated for her colonists. In the virgin lands of Guiana, however, enclosure became the rule for all inhabitants of the Mana colony, isolation providing the possibility of reform according to religious and moral values that she saw as compromised elsewhere.

Unlike most Europeans of her time, Javouhey believed in the perfectability of blacks, provided that they were instructed in Christian beliefs and behavior. Africans, despite their race and color, she argued, were not "totally lacking in those qualities that made men in society" and could, as she saw it, be safely freed. But she was also a strong believer in gradual emancipation given the conditions in which African slaves had been held. The experience of slavery had eliminated a sense of discipline among the newly liberated, who "thought that their status as free men would give them the ability to live without any worries, without any work." Not only had slavery not provided any incentive to develop work habits, but "need, fear, dependence had made [slaves] cold and selfish." "Not having anyone to share his sorrows and his joys," she wrote of the slave, "separated early from his father and mother to be sold to another master. . . . To what end would it have served him to attach himself to places and people? He knew well that his existence did not depend on himself and that he had to sacrifice everything to the order or caprice of the person who had paid for him." Raised in such a system, the former slave had no sense of "conduct or wise habits" that he could maintain "in the middle of cities."[65] Under the tutelage of the Soeurs de St-Joseph de Cluny, however, the former slave would learn the love of work and of others as well as of "submission: not that painful obedience that is only compelled by brutal force, but that gentle and filial obedience that is obtained by benevolence and conviction."[66]

Javouhey was driven by a Christian conception of obedience to God and society in which blacks also had to be inculcated before they were ready for "civilization." After the first set of indentured slaves were freed in 1838, she hoped that they would stay at Mana. "The liberated," she wrote in a report to the colonial minister, "are too new in civilization to be able to do without the instructions that must direct them in their new life. The barely formed social and familial ties cannot have acquired the strength that hold together societies . . . the newly freed, after having caught a glimpse of the dawn of civilization, would fall again into the shadows of the savage life."

She had great hopes, however, for the second generation, which having been educated in European work habits "that are a necessity, a condition of life for civilized people," would in turn become productive members of society. Then, she proclaimed, far from the French inhabitants of Cayenne having to fear the Mana settlers, "the question would be reversed."[67] Children at Mana were enrolled in the school run by the sisters, where in addition to religion and basic literacy and numeracy skills, they were given work training: needlework and sewing for girls and farming for boys.[68] Given enough time and the right training, she implied, anyone could become virtuous; without it even whites were not immune to vice. In fact, she clearly preferred to evangelize among populations such as children and Africans, whom she saw as uncorrupted by society.[69] To her the good order of the Mana colony, which saw no outbreaks of rebellion or violence and little attrition among freed blacks, proved the rightness of both her cause and her methods.

Catholics and Abolitionists

Anne-Marie Javouhey was an unusual figure in the French antislavery movement in the early nineteenth century. Unlike the British abolition campaign, which was rooted in religious evangelicalism and gained a strong popular following in the early nineteenth century, the French movement was confined to a small, largely secular elite. The French abolition of slavery during the French Revolution and the Revolution of 1848 was based on the language of human rights developed by Enlightenment philosophers and enshrined in the Declaration of Rights of Man and Citizen of 1789. Except for the Abbé Grégoire,[70] many of the leading abolitionists in early nineteenth-century France came from the minority Protestant community, whose religious freedom was guaranteed by the very disestablishment of the Catholic Church. Yet Javouhey's attitudes toward slavery coincided with many of theirs, including cautiousness about emancipating slaves before they were deemed ready for freedom.[71] Javouhey's connection to French abolitionists came through her friendship with Baron Jacques-François Roger, who was governor of Senegal when Javouhey lived and worked there in the early 1820s. In 1834 Roger became one of the founding members of the Société pour l'Abolition de l'Esclavage and helped facilitate Javouhey's work with slaves in French colonies.[72] These groups became more active after the British abolition of slavery in 1834.[73]

The Catholic Church, for its part, unlike Protestant evangelicals in Britain and elsewhere, did little as an institution to oppose African slavery. From the first European foundations Catholic missionaries active in the Caribbean islands and in Latin America were much more interested in converting native Indians than African slaves and were often slaveholders themselves. Seventeenth-century French missionaries participated in the formation of racial discourse that justified the enslavement of Africans as a New World workforce.[74] Because the French Code Noir, first promulgated in 1724 (though poorly enforced), required baptism and the religious education of slaves, some theologians justified slavery as a means to Christian salvation.[75] Only in 1839 did Pope Gregory XVI condemn the capture and mistreatment of slaves (though not slavery itself). The Seminary of the Holy Spirit in Paris, which trained priests for the colonies, went on record as supporting slavery as consistent with church teachings as late as 1846, and most French colonial clergy, scarce as they were, only served white settler populations.[76] The French religious hierarchy at home kept their distance from the Abbé Grégoire, supporter of the Revolution, and the liberals who joined abolition societies. During the Revolution several hundred priests who refused to take the loyalty oath were deported to Guiana in 1798; freed in 1800, many of them stayed on as firm supporters of the established racial and political order, who thought religion should serve as a means for keeping slaves submissive.[77]

These priests were hostile to Javouhey and her mission, both on grounds of her independence from their authority, especially shocking in a woman, and on the impossibility, in their view, of her project. The head of the Catholic Church in French Guiana, apostolic prefect Abbé Guillier, denounced both abolitionism and Javouhey in 1838: "The project of the abolitionists, of which she is the agent, is obviously a deception and a chimera. One cannot improvise the civilization of Africans any more than the majority of children, and I do not conceive how that woman, who has a head of sense and reason, was able to let herself be fooled and throw herself headlong into the dreams of the utopians of the day." If the Jesuits had failed to emancipate African slaves systematically in South America, Guillier argued, "utopians" such as Javouhey certainly could not succeed.[78] In his fulminations against her Javouhey appeared to Guillier to have so-called masculine qualities of intelligence and rationality yet be feminine enough to be, in his view, manipulated by the partisans of abolition, whom he derided as utopians. And unlike Javouhey, he saw Africans as permanently immature, rather than temporarily so, unable to rise to "civilized" standards. By 1842 he was denouncing Mana outright and refusing Javouhey the sacraments because of her insubordination. Javouhey's experimental colony and her long residence in Mana were among the factors that led to a complete breakdown of relations with her bishop back in France, which nearly destroyed her order.[79] Although by mid-century the French Catholic Church had a few other figures who shared her vision (most notably François Libermann, founder of the Missionnaires du Sacré-Coeur de Marie) for most of her active life Javouhey stood apart from the church by insisting on ministering to Africans and slaves rather than only to white settlers.

Yet she also stood apart from many French abolitionists by grounding her belief in the perfectability of blacks in religious equality before God rather than in rights-based language. "The Blacks," she wrote, "are not deaf either to the voice of morality and religion, nor to that of civilization; sons of a common father, they are men like us."[80] For her the key to the redemption of Africans was transforming them literally into men and women "like us" by converting them to Catholicism and training them in European values and work habits in a setting designed to mimic a prosperous and pious French country village. Javouhey's strong belief in universal values, derived from her Catholic faith, was the source of her power to challenge accepted racial stereotypes. Yet while that faith allowed her, on the one hand, to support unequivocally the intrinsic equality of Africans, it also meant she universalized her own social and cultural upbringing—peasant, French, and Catholic—as the only path to "civilization." Yet even Europeans often failed to live up to her exacting standards; Mana, after all, was originally intended as a colony for the redemption of whites.

Religious Utopia or Economic Monopoly?

How successful was Javouhey's radical experiment? On one measure all commentators agreed: Mana had avoided the high death rates and low birthrates typical of slave societies, including the rest of Guiana.[81] This demographic edge was attributed to the age and gender structure of the population, the lighter workload at Mana than on other plantations, the medical care provided (including a lying-in hospital), and the somewhat healthier climate.[82] On the issue of moralization many colonial officials also gave Javouhey credit. Christian marriages, baptisms, and legitimacy rates all exceeded those among people of color elsewhere in Guiana. By 1838, when the first group of Africans were liberated, outside assessments of Mana agreed that religious instruction had achieved results. In his inspection the governor of Guiana argued that "the most constant gentleness" had improved most of the young people and even produced "respectful submission" among the older men. Those gains, most felt, resulted not only from the work of the sisters but also because the isolation of Mana kept its residents away from "the free blacks of Cayenne, who are almost all devoted to indolence and vagrancy." Even the freed blacks at Mana, by contrast, rose at half-past-five in the morning for prayer and then went to work.[83] Officials were relieved that most accepted the offer to stay on lands in or near Mana and did not desert the colony to return to Cayenne, where they might present a security risk. In 1841 the governor reported that most Mana inhabitants attended Mass, properly dressed; their cabins, built along straight and well-aligned streets, were furnished; and the number of illegitimate births was decreasing, all signs, in his view, of civilization.[84]

Marriage, in particular, had long been considered a marker of assimilation by both missionaries and officials who were frustrated by the low rate of legitimate couples among the slave population.[85] But Javouhey's enemies cast doubt on the validity of marriages when unmarried women were sequestered with the sisters. "In order to get out of prison," the colonial council suggested, "it is entirely possible that young women decide to get married without having the calling."[86] Over time, as Mana came under other kinds of scrutiny, its moralizing effects also began to be questioned, as critics charged that they were merely superficial. Contrary to earlier reports, these skeptics claimed that only women went to church, that many fewer children attended school than were officially enrolled, and that little real progress had been made at Mana. "One finds in Mana the innate habits of the African black," a 1846 report stated, "more or less modified by a poorly understood civilization."[87]

But it was the economic organization of Mana that received the harshest criticism. The order had a monopoly over the commercialization of crops, livestock, and forests as well as provisioning Mana through a single store. Beginning as early as 1839, however, these commercial arrangements received increasing scrutiny from officials. The residents themselves, officials reported, complained that, because of Mana's isolation, they could not get to Cayenne to market their products themselves, forcing them to deal only with the sisters, who bought low and sold high. The Soeurs de St-Joseph made their money on their "double monopoly" as well as the generous government subsidies that underwrote Mana.[88] Hence, they had no reason—and perhaps, officials suggested, as women, not enough knowledge—to undertake the large-scale agricultural production that would make the colony truly profitable. Instead, Mana was made up of "small producers, planters of manioc, farmers of rice, work that took no trouble, no labor."[89] In 1841 the governor contrasted the output of a state workshop (atelier d'esclaves), in which the same number of slaves produced 138,000 francs worth of sugarcane in a year, with Mana, where "revenue is absorbed by expenses."[90] The sisters harvested the valuable woods bordering the settlement to build a new church but did not think to develop them as export commodities.[91] To the colonial government Mana was redefined as a failed experiment because it enriched the Soeurs de St-Joseph de Cluny without adding to Guiana's prosperity. In 1843 the governor no longer saw the need for "the luxury of a religious order and all its expensive apparatus." "What a loss for French Guiana," he wrote, to have moved five hundred potential state workers to Mana when they could have been put to work building roads and canals instead.[92]

According to this new analysis, Mana's economic structure also prevented its residents from developing the work habits that only a free enterprise economy could sustain. Whatever moral advantages Javouhey's regime might have produced were undercut, in the view of these capitalists, by the bad example of its monopoly. Lacking incentive to produce because they could not make a profit, blacks fell back on their "natural tendency, which is laziness,"[93] preferring to hunt or fish rather than work the soil. The residents might be, as the governor wrote in 1841, "infinitely happier than those of the workshops, first because they are free . . . and second place, because they only work when they want," but they lacked the work habits that characterized a truly "civilized" society.[94]

The very isolation of the colony, which at its inception was considered the best way for training Africans in European practices of discipline and order, was reinterpreted as its fatal flaw. Without increased communication with other parts of the colony and the free trade that would follow, the Mana inhabitants would never rise above "primitive man,"[95] no matter how many church services they attended. Although a few officials worried that opening up Mana might present some risks in terms of increased desertion or a rise in criminal behavior, by the mid-1840s the general consensus had become that breaking Mana's isolation was necessary to the economic health of Guiana and the moral improvement of its residents. Capitalist imperatives and rhetoric trumped the utopian language of a mere decade earlier. In part this shift was due to the increasing likelihood of slave emancipation in the French Empire in the near future. Colonial officials saw Mana, one of the few places in Guiana with a concentrated free black population, as an experiment in free labor whose success (or failure) might guide the future. That its residents practiced only subsistence agriculture alarmed them.

The debate about production, from Javouhey's perspective, missed the point. Her goal had never been to produce in large quantities, and the combination of individual household plots and religious commons achieved her vision of a self-supporting religious commune. The economic model of the slave plantation was one she consciously rejected as inhumane and immoral, however profitable. As the head of a rapidly expanding religious order, however, she sought to balance revenues and needs throughout her organization to maximize its overall impact. Extremely well connected in the colonial ministry, she sought maximum government support for her overseas missions, which, in her view, contributed to France's colonial enterprise; Mana was no exception. She had no compunction about applying any profits the order made there elsewhere, such as transferring 5,500 francs from Guiana to subsidize its establishment in Brest in 1828.[96] Nor was she without business acumen, as when she applied to the colonial ministry in 1839 to sell goods from Mana in the Antilles or neighboring foreign colonies, where her profits would be higher than in Cayenne.[97] Daughter of a peasant, she had a shrewd eye for good land and good livestock. But ultimately the value of Mana—or any other mission run by the sisters—was not the money it made but the good it did. That good, Javouhey argued repeatedly, derived expressly from its closure to the outside world, in which economic matters were irrelevant. "We will live like the ancient hermits of [the desert]," she wrote when Mana was first established, "we will no longer be familiar with money; we will find under the soil all the needs of life."[98]

By January 1847, however, responding to multiple complaints and changing priorities, the unique regime of Mana as a closed settlement run by the Soeurs de St-Joseph de Cluny came to an end, when the government brought it under direct colonial control at considerable savings to the colonial treasury. Most significantly, it was opened to outside trade and investment. The sisters—without Javouhey, who had returned to France in 1843—remained as educators and nurses but not as administrators or commercial agents. A young Frenchman, Eugène Mélinon, was appointed as the new colonial administrator in Mana, aided by a small police squad.[99] He immediately introduced a new land system with a stronger emphasis on private property, resulting in a temporary desertion of a group of Africans to farm farther up river. He proposed bringing more European settlers to Mana—Irish immigrants perhaps—in order to provide examples of civilization and private ownership. And, perhaps fearing the residual communal lessons of the Soeurs de St-Joseph, he invited the Frères de Ploërmel, a masculine teaching order rapidly expanding into colonial missions, to establish a school for boys.[100]

In 1848 the abolition of slavery throughout the French Empire resulted in serious unrest in Guadeloupe and Martinique and widespread desertion of plantations in Guiana. In Mana, however, where the remaining slaves whose seven-year contracts had not yet expired received their freedom on August 10, almost all stayed put. Most of them already had what many newly freed Guianese slaves appeared to want: a small plot of land they could cultivate for their own families.[101] On March 4, 1849, 140 of them voted in the elections to the National Assembly. A slim majority of 73 voted for the white candidate, Vidal de Lingendes; the remaining 67 votes were for the candidate of color, Jouannet, who won overall, with 3,420 votes to 601, evoking the worst fears of French settlers. Only 201 of Vidal de Lingendes's votes came from nonwhites and a third of those from Mana.[102]

Without knowing any details about the election campaign, it appears—superficially at least—that the residents of Mana were less suspicious of whites than other Guianese of African descent. It was certainly seen as one of the few bright spots in an otherwise dismal landscape by colonial officials. Despite the "unrest that the elections sowed in Mana as everywhere," one official reported to Paris two months later, "there at least one can note in other respects a satisfactory state of affairs, a compact population attached to the soil. . . . As ownership increases, the family will put down deeper roots and in its wake ideas of morality and religion will return."[103] That same year, however, the government granted a concession at Mana to the sugar company of Frères Bare, who wanted to use black labor for sugar monoculture. Javouhey's vision of an independent black peasantry, like her religious utopia, had passed. The complete collapse of the economy after abolition led the French government to designate Guiana as a penal colony in 1851, although Mana continued as a free town proud of its distinctive heritage to this day.[104]

On the Margins of Empire

For the better part of two decades Javouhey was given an unusual opportunity, as a woman and a nun, to head a unique experiment in the annals of the French Empire that sought to solve on a small-scale the difficult and contested problem of African slavery. To the debate she added a working model of a free (or semi-free) African community that met the French criteria for stability and order. It is hard to imagine, however, its larger applicability. One of the paradoxes of the Mana settlement was that although Javouhey's ambitions for it were limitless—she saw it as a new paradigm for emancipation while also hoping it would become a literal training ground for all the slave children of Guiana—its very existence depended on isolation and enclosure that was not easily replicated elsewhere. Indeed, in the three other slave colonies (Martinique, Guadeloupe, and Réunion) where the Soeurs de St-Joseph were more dependent on the daughters of the colonial elite as pupils and their parents' fees as income, they only cautiously established institutions serving the black population. Javouhey's ability to establish such an unusual settlement depended not on her relations in the colony, which were hostile, but on the support she received from Paris, which desperately sought a way to make Guiana into a profitable colony while simultaneously reducing its dependence on slavery. Their views on how best to do this shifted like the notorious Guiana winds, while Javouhey's vision remained steady, borrowing from sources as diverse as Catholic universality, Jesuit reductions, utopian socialism, and abolitionist theory.

Javouhey represented a certain type of religious woman in nineteenth-century France—activist, independent, self-confident—that infuriated most male clerics who came into contact with her; in another paradox her strongest support came from the liberal July Monarchy rather than her own church. Her views on abolition further distanced her from fellow Catholics, few of whom embraced this cause. Yet if Javouhey was too abolitionist for the Catholics, she was too Catholic for the abolitionists, whose vision of slave emancipation did not include a commitment to Christian renewal. Despite their theological differences, Javouhey might have found herself more at home among the Baptist missionaries who created free villages for blacks in Jamaica than among secular French abolitionists.[105] Although she drew from the Catholic missionary tradition in seeking to form an ideal Christian community, she did not work among the indigenous or settler populations, as was usually the case, but instead with individuals specially imported to this remote spot, on the model of contemporary utopian communities. Like many of those utopias, the new world appeared to be a better location for experimentation than the old. Yet Mana, unlike the utopias imagined or created by socialists of various stripes, did not promise equality to all residents but, rather, bound them in a hierarchy of Christian obedience to Javouhey, through which they were offered the possibility of freedom from the literal bonds of slavery. To achieve this ideal, Javouhey saw no other solution than isolating them at the edges of empire, where they remained uncorrupted by the very French civilization they were supposed to emulate.

Marginal in multiple respects, Javouhey as an individual as well as her Mana colony demonstrate the reciprocal interactions between the center and the periphery in the French Empire under the July Monarchy. Javouhey herself forged a new identity in the wilds of South America, overstepping the boundaries of expected behavior for a woman or a nun. To fulfill this ambitious agenda, she took refuge in a location arguably as remote as one could find in the French Empire at the time, all while exploiting her relationships to the center of power in Paris, which provided her with the political and financial support that allowed her this independence. Javouhey's ability to run her own show undoubtedly derived from Mana's geographical distance from metropolitan France as well as its economic distance from the wealthy sugar plantations of France's colonies in the West Indies. Precisely because of this geographical isolation and its marginal economic status, Guiana was a fertile site for radical experiments such as this one. As such, it provided important feedback from the periphery to the metropole on solutions to France's economic and moral quandary in its slave colonies. In the end Mana's radical potential was rejected by colonial officials who preferred economic integration to religious self-sufficiency. Yet if Javouhey's experiment at Mana failed to live up to its founder's utopian vision, it did provide a humane and paternalistic—dare I say, maternalistic—alternative to the often cruel system of plantation slavery endemic to the West Indies and South America as well as an unusual opportunity for a woman to exercise autonomy and power. In the long French encounter with Africans, Mana demonstrated the creativity possible at the margins of empire.

Notes

I would like to thank the Soeurs de St-Joseph de Cluny, for access to their archives, and their late archivist, Soeur Yves LeGoff, for her welcome and assistance. This research was originally funded by the Spencer Foundation as well as a Fulbright Research Grant to France. I would also like to thank Kevin J. Callahan, Stephen L. Harp, and my colleagues in the faculty colloquium at San Francisco State University, for reading a draft of the essay and providing many insightful comments and useful suggestions for revision.

1. F. Delaplace, *La R. M. Javouhey, Fondatrice de la Congrégation de Saint-Joseph de Cluny: histoire de sa vie, des oeuvres et missions de la Congrégation* (Paris: Librairie Catholique Internationale, 1885), 2:343. The original source of this anecdote appears to have been Gen. L. Javouhey (Anne-Marie Javouhey's nephew and Mana resident), "Notes sur quelques essais de colonisation à la Guyane Française," pt. 2, 113, Archives des Soeurs de St-Joseph de Cluny (hereafter cited as ASJC).

2. Valérin Groffier, *Héros trop oubliés de notre épopée coloniale* (n.p., 1908), 362.

3. See Delaplace, *La R. M. Javouhey*, 2:225, 2:545–46, for the origins of these masculine identifications of Javouhey.

4. Anne-Marie Javouhey, *Lettres*, 4 vols. (Paris: Cerf, 1994), no. 877, to Soeur Madeleine Collonge, January 11, 1849. France liberated the slaves in its empire definitively on August 10, 1848. During the French Revolution, following the outbreak of violence in St. Domingue (Haiti), slavery had been abolished in the colonies in 1794 and reestablished by Napoléon in 1802.

5. For details on the spectacular growth of nineteenth-century female orders, see Claude Langlois, *Le Catholicisme au féminin: les congrégations françaises à supérieure générale au XIXe siècle* (Paris: Cerf, 1984). For additional biographical information on Anne-Marie Javouhey, see Geneviève Lecuir-Nemo, *Anne-Marie Javouhey: fondatrice de la congrégation des Sœurs de Saint-Joseph de Cluny (1779–1851)* (Paris: Karthala, 2001).

6. Javouhey, *Lettres*, no. 54, to father, March 1822.

7. Although outlawed during the Restoration, laws against trading in slaves were badly enforced in the French Empire. See William B. Cohen, *The French Encounter with Africans: White Response to Blacks, 1530–1880* (Bloomington: Indiana University Press, 1980), 187.

8. Javouhey, *Lettres*, no. 59, to Mère Clothilde Javouhey, end of April, beginning of May 1822.

9. This latter school failed to attract many pupils, however, and by 1832 local French administrators thought its cost not worth the effort. Denise Bouche, *L'Enseignement dans les territoires français de l'Afrique occidentale de 1817 à 1920* (Lille: Reproduction des Thèses, Université de Lille III, 1975), 402–3.

10. Javouhey, *Lettres*, no. 67, to M. de Maudit, directeur des colonies, November 25, 1822.

11. "Mana: renseignements fournis par Auguste Javouhey en 1875 pour 1821–1838," 2 A i (3), ASJC.

12. "Projet d'établissement à former à Mana par les Soeurs de St-Joseph de Cluny," August 29, 1827, 2 A i (1), ASJC.

13. "Notes de Madame la Supérieure Génerale des Sœurs de St Joseph sur l'établissement commencé à la Mana," July 1829, FM SG Guyane 60, Centre des Archives d'Outre-Mer, Aix-en-Provence (hereafter cited as CAOM).

14. "Projet d'établissement à former à Mana," August 29, 1827, 2 A i (1), ASJC.

15. "Projet d'établissement à former à Mana," August 29, 1827, 2 A i (1), ASJC.

16. This belief was, of course, most characteristic of early, or "utopian," socialists, who proposed a variety of new forms of communal life. Pamela Pilbeam reminds us that these socialists had a strong spiritual (though not necessarily Catholic) dimension. See *French Socialists before Marx: Workers, Women, and the Social Question in France* (Montreal: McGill-Queen's University Press, 2000), chap. 4. See also the introduction to Jonathan Beecher, *Victor Considérant and the Rise and Fall of French Romantic Socialism* (Berkeley: University of California Press, 2001), for a summary of the main characteristics of early socialism.

17. Javouhey, *Lettres*, no. 199, to Mère Marie-Joseph Javouhey, June 16, 1829.

18. Serge Mam-Lam-Fouck, "Apogée, déclin et disparition du système esclavagiste (première moitié du XIXe siècle)," in *Deux siècles d'esclavage en Guyane Française, 1652–1848*, ed. Anne-Marie Bruleaux et al. (Paris: L'Harmatton, 1986), 210.

19. "Précis sur la colonisation des bords de la Mana (Guyane française)," February 20, 1835, 17, FM SG Guyane 61, CAOM. The primary crops in Guiana at this time were sugarcane, cotton, and the plant dye extracted from *rocou* (annatto). See Mam-Lam-Fouck, "Apogée," 144, 219, 228–31. He asserts, however, that despite the abolition of the slave trade, about five thousand slaves were brought into Guiana between 1817 and 1831.

20. Minister of Marine and Colonies to King, Rapport, August 22, 1827, FM SG Guyane 60, CAOM.

21. Javouhey, *Lettres*, no. 241, to M. de Saint-Hilaire, directeur des colonies, and no. 243, to M. Jubelin, September 22–30, 1831.

22. Governor Jubelin to Minister of Marine and Colonies, December 31, 1829, FM SG Guyane 60, CAOM.

23. "Etat nominatif des soeurs de la congrégation de St-Joseph de Cluny et des colons composant la colonisation de Mana," August 17, 1828, to July 15, 1832, FM SG Guyane 60, CAOM.

24. "Précis sur la colonisation des bords de la Mana (Guyane française)," February 20, 1835, 104, FM SG Guyane 61, CAOM. The order attributed the failure of the project to send orphans to hostility from Guiana colonists and the change of government in France to one (the July Monarchy) more hostile to religious orders. "Colonisation de Mana," n.d., 2 A i (3), ASJC.

25. Javouhey, *Lettres*, no. 214, to Mère Clotilde Javouhey, June 25, 1830.

26. There were thirty-two of each, including the twenty-nine Soeurs de St-Joseph. Governor Jubelin, French Guiana, to Minister of Marine and Colonies, October 10, 1832, FM SG Guyane 60, CAOM.

27. The last group of 137 individuals were, "for the most part, non-producers." Governor of French Guiana to Minister of Marine and Colonies, June 2, 1837, FM SG Guyane 61, CAOM. See also "Etat des dépenses faites dans l'intérêt des noirs libérés envoyés à Mana," May 31, 1837, in the same series.

28. Javouhey, *Lettres*, no. 369, to Admiral Rosamel, minister of Marine and Colonies, August 24, 1836.

29. When slave ships were captured, it was common for the slaves to be transferred to public works projects in Senegal or Guiana or simply to "disappear" onto plantations. See S. Daget, "The Abolition of the Slave Trade," in *General History of Africa*, vol. 6, *Africa in the Nineteenth Century until the 1880s*, ed. J. F. Ade Ajayi (Paris: UNESCO, 1989), 69–71. Guiana received about five thousand slaves from 1817 to 1831 from the clandestine slave trade. Mam-Lam-Fouck, "Apogée," 219.

30. This system existed in Senegal from 1815 to 1844 to provide labor for the French military and landowners; it was then revived for the Caribbean islands and Réunion after 1852 as a substitute for slave labor. Cohen, *French Encounter*, 190.

31. The French seized a total of about 1,500 Africans, distributed as follows between the four slave colonies: Bourbon 700, Guiana 520, Martinique 250, and Guadeloupe 30. Guiana received a larger share because plantation owners in Martinique and Guadeloupe were afraid of increasing the population of free blacks. Some of those sent to Bourbon were transferred to Île Ste.-Marie off Madagascar. "Rapport: projet de remettre à Madame la supérieure générale des soeurs de St-Joseph de Cluny les noirs libérés," October 20, 1834, FM SG Guyane 61, CAOM.

32. Groffier, *Héroes trop oubliés*, 353.

33. "Notes sur les observations de Mr le Gouverneur de la Guyane au sujet de l'établissement projeté des noirs à la Mana," n.d., FM SG Guyane 61, CAOM.

34. "Rapport: Project de remettre à Madame la supérieure générale des soeurs de St-Joseph de Cluny les noirs libérés," October 20, 1834, FM SG Guyane 61, CAOM.

35. "Lettres addressées à Mère Javouhey," from St-Hilaire, Maître des Requêtes et Directeur des Colonies, August 8, 1836, 6 A 2 D, ASJC.

36. Laure Fernand, *La Guyane Française et l'ordre de Saint-Joseph de Cluny* (Paris: Imprimerie de Ducessois, 1834), 63.

37. "Lettres addressées à Mère Javohey," from Baron Roger to Marie-Joseph Javouhey, November 26, 1838, 6 A 2 D, ASJC.

38. "Extrait des délibération du conseil colonial, M. Gibelin," June 17, 1835, FM SG Guyane 61, CAOM.

39. Marie-Louise Marchand-Thébault, "L'Esclavage en Guyane sous l'ancien régime," in Bruleaux et al., *Deux siècles d'esclavage*, 43.

40. Colonists were also poorer and less able to afford slaves. In 1832 only 28 out of 469 white plantation owners owned more than 100 slaves. Twenty-three of these plantations grew sugarcane. Mam-Lam-Fouck, "Apogée," 145.

41. Marchand-Thébault, "L'Esclavage," 16–17, 30–31, 38, 41–42. Mam-Lam-Fouck points out that most slaves ran away for only short periods of time; they were only considered true runaways if they were gone over a month. Half of the runaways in 1837 returned of their own accord. "Apogée," 191.

42. Mam-Lam-Fouck, "Apogée," 256–57.

43. Untitled report from Commission, Département de la Marine, June 2, 1835, FM SG Guyane 61, CAOM.

44. "Rapport du Ministre de la Marine, M. Duperré, au Roi, sur l'état des esclaves de saisie dans les colonies," August 14, 1835, 2 A i (1), ASJC.

45. Admiral Rosamel, Minister of Marine and Colonies, to Governor of French Guiana, September 1835, 2 A i (1), ASJC.

46. Javouhey, *Lettres*, no. 380, to Mère Rosalie Javouhey, February 23, 1838.

47. Mam-Lam-Fouck, "Apogée," 259.

48. This contrast can be seen clearly in the archival documents, in which the *conseil privé* of the colony, made up of settler elites, was consistently hostile to Javouhey, while the governor of Guiana, appointed by Paris, and the minister of marine and colonies, usually supported her.

49. On the slave economy of this period, see Herbert S. Klein, *African Slavery in Latin America and the Caribbean* (New York: Oxford University Press, 1986).

50. Javouhey, *Lettres*, no. 381, to Mère Clotilde Javouhey, March 15, 1838.

51. "Rapport de Mr le Gouverneur de la Guyane Française sur l'établissement de Mana, inspection de 1838," FM SG Guyane 61, CAOM.

52. "Souvenirs de Sr. Philémon Poulachon sur la Guyane," n.d., 2 A i (3), ASJC.

53. She indeed made a stop in Senegal on her return to Mana in 1835 to effect this plan but only managed to procure a half-dozen women among the government population of "engagées." Governor of Senegal to Minister of Marine and Colonies, February 1, 1836, FM SG Guyane 61, CAOM.

54. Javouhey, Lettres, no. 383, "Exposé sur l'état de Mana" (premiers mois de 1838).

55. Javouhey, Lettres, no. 383, "Exposé."

56. Javouhey, Lettres, no. 183, to Mère Marie-Joseph Javouhey, September 17, 1828.

57. Javouhey, Lettres, no. 277, to Mère Rosalie Javouhey, January 22, 1834. The Jesuit reductions in Paraguay were well-known among early nineteenth-century Catholics.

58. On the Jesuit reductions among the Guaraní in Paraguay, see Barbara Ganson, The Guaraní under Spanish Rule in the Río de la Plata (Stanford: Stanford University Press, 2003).

59. Marchand-Thébault, "L'Esclavage," 46–47, 61–62.

60. Javouhey, Lettres, no. 463, to Admiral Duperré, Ministre de la Marine et des Colonies, June 26, 1841.

61. Javouhey, Lettres, no. 463, to Admiral Duperré, June 26, 1841.

62. Javouhey, Lettres, no. 252, to Mère Marie-Joseph Javouhey in Bailleul, May 12, 1832.

63. Javouhey, Lettres, no. 259, to Soeur Madeleine Collonge in Senegal, August 1, 1832.

64. Javouhey, Lettres, no. 311, to Mère Marie-Thérèse Javouhey in Martinique, December 9, 1834.

65. Javouhey, Lettres, no. 429, to Admiral Duperré, July 25, 1840.

66. Javouhey, Lettres, no. 463, to Admiral Duperré, June 26, 1841.

67. Javouhey, Lettres, no. 384, to Admiral Duperré, April 10, 1838.

68. "Monographie de l'école primaire des filles de Mana," n.d., 2 A i, ASJC.

69. Claude Langlois, "Anne-Marie Javouhey au miroir de sa correspondance," Mémoire Spiritaine 2 (1995): 142.

70. When the main French abolitionist society, the Société de la Morale Chrétienne, was founded in 1822, Grégoire refused to join, fearing the association with Protestants. Lawrence C. Jennings, French Anti-Slavery: The Movement for the Abolition of Slavery in France, 1802–1848 (New York: Cambridge University Press, 2000), 8. On the Abbé Grégoire, see Alyssa Goldstein Sepinwall, The Abbé Grégoire and the French Revolution: The Making of Modern Universalism (Berkeley: University of California Press, 2005).

71. On the question of gradual versus immediate emancipation, see Jennings, French Anti-Slavery, chap. 9; and Cohen, French Encounter, 150–54.

72. Lecuir-Nemo, Anne-Marie Javouhey, 224. On the Société pour l'Abolition de l'Esclavage, see also Jennings, French Anti-Slavery, chap. 3; and Cohen, French Encounter, 201–2. The membership of this group overlapped with that of the Société de la Morale Chrétienne.

73. On the British campaign to abolish the slave trade and slavery, see Adam Hochschild, *Bury the Chains: Prophets and Rebels in the Fight to Free an Empire's Slaves* (New York: Houghton Mifflin, 2005).

74. See Sue Peabody, "'A Nation Born to Slavery': Missionaries and Racial Discourse in Seventeenth-Century French Antilles," *Journal of Social History* 28 (2004): 113–26.

75. Philippe Delisle, "Clergé et esclavage aux Antilles et en Guyane françaises: de l'Ancien Régime à 1848," *Mémoire Spiritaine* 9 (1999): 161–72.

76. Jennings, *French Anti-Slavery*, 110–11, 128–29.

77. Delisle, "Clergé et esclavage," 163–64; Mam-Lam-Fouck, "Apogée," 150.

78. Abbé Guillier, Préfet Apostolique, to Bishop of Autun, August 5, 1838, 4 A c 5, ASJC.

79. Monseigneur d'Héricourt, the bishop of Autun, also objected to Javouhey's independence in ecclesiastical matters, one example of a recurring struggle between bishops and female heads of religious orders in the nineteenth century. For an account of their long-running battle, see Lecuir-Nemo, *Anne-Marie Javouhey*, chaps. 9–10.

80. Javouhey, *Lettres*, no. 384, to Admiral Duperré, Ministre de la Marine et des Colonies, April 10, 1838.

81. In the decade between 1838 and 1847 there were 290 births to 150 deaths. "Comte rendu," n.d., FM SG Guyane 61, CAOM. For a comparative view, see Richard B. Sheridan, "Slave Demography in the British West Indies and the Abolition of the Slave Trade," in *The Abolition of the Atlantic Slave Trade: Origins and Effects in Europe, Africa, and the Americas*, ed. David Eltis and James Walvin (Madison: University of Wisconsin Press, 1981), 259–85.

82. Contrôleur Colonial to Governor, French Guiana, June 26, 1846, FM SG Guyane 61, CAOM.

83. "Rapport de Mr le Gouverneur de la Guyane Française sur l'établissement de Mana, inspection de 1838," FM SG Guyane 61, CAOM.

84. Governor of French Guiana to Minister of Marine and Colonies, October 29, 1841, FM SG Guyane 61, CAOM.

85. From 1841 to 1847 this rate was never higher than 1.75 percent, despite marriage presents and other incentives given to slaves owned by the government. Mam-Lam-Fouck, "Apogée," 178.

86. "Rapport du Conseil Colonial de la Guyane Française à S.E. Mr le Ministre de la Marine et des colonies rélativement à l'établissement de la Mana," n.d., FM SG Guyane 61, CAOM.

87. Contrôleur Colonial to Governor, French Guiana, June 26, 1846, FM SG Guyane 61, CAOM. There is little evidence that would resolve how deeply Catholic Mana residents became. Elsewhere in Guiana, slaves probably amalgamated African and Catholic beliefs. Mam-Lam-Fouck, "Apogée," 183–85.

88. "Rapport de l'Ordonnateur sur la colonisation des noirs libérés établis sur les

bords de la Mana sous la direction de Madame la Supérieure générale de la Congrégation de St. Joseph de Cluny," October 5, 1839, FM SG Guyane 61, CAOM.

89. Governor, French Guiana, to Minister of Marine and Colonies "au sujet de la colonisation de Mana," October 6, 1843, FM SG Guyane 61, CAOM.

90. Governor, French Guiana, to Minister of Marine and Colonies "au sujet d'une
tournée dans divers quartiers de la colonie," October 29, 1841, FM SG Guyane 61,
CAOM.

91. Contrôleur colonial to Governor, French Guiana, June 26, 1846, FM SG Guyane 61,
CAOM.

92. Governor, French Guiana, to Minister of Marine and Colonies "au sujet de la colonisation de Mana," October 6, 1843.

93. "Rapport du Conseil Colonial de la Guyane Française à S.E. Mr le Ministre de la
Marine et des colonies rélativement à l'établissement de la Mana."

94. Governor, French Guiana, to Minister of Marine and Colonies "au sujet d'une
tournée," October 29, 1841.

95. Contrôleur colonial to Governor, French Guiana, June 12, 1846, FM SG Guyane 61,
CAOM.

96. Javouhey, *Lettres*, no. 186, to Mère Marie-Joseph Javouhey, December 31, 1828. It
was the boarding schools in Martinique and Guadeloupe, however, that were most
profitable for the congregation. See Philippe Delisle, *Histoire religieuse des Antilles
et de la Guyane françaises: des chrétientés sous les tropiques? 1815–1911* (Paris: Karthala,
2000), 52.

97. Javouhey, *Lettres*, no. 408, to Minister of Marine and Colonies, August 20, 1839.

98. Javouhey, *Lettres*, no. 164, to Mère Clothilde Javouhey, November 14, 1828.

99. Twenty-eight years old, Mélinon was attracted to Guiana because of an interest
in botanical studies; he was not part of the old colonial elite. In 1847 he mar-
ried Soeur Juliette, who left the order to marry him. Governor, French Guiana, to
Minister of Marine and Colonies, July 15, 1846, FM SG Guyane 61, CAOM; Soeur
Isabelle, Superior, Mana, to Anne-Marie Javouhey, April 7, 1847, FM SG Guyane 61,
CAOM.

100. "Compte rendu présenté à M. le Gouverneur de la Guyane Française, sur la situation de la colonie des noirs libérés," n.d., FM SG Guyane 61, CAOM. The Frères de
Ploërmel were founded in 1819 in Brittany.

101. Philippe Delisle, "Débats autour de la christianisation des Noirs aux Antilles et
en Guyane française après l'abolition de l'escalvage (de 1848 aux années 1880),"
Mémoire Spiritaine 8 (1998): 88–89.

102. "Etat Résumé des votes électoraux de la Guyane Française," March 21, 1849, FM
SG Guyane 15 (B40), CAOM.

103. Commissaire Générale de la République, French Guiana, to Minister of Marine
and Colonies, May 6, 1849, FM SG Guyane 61, CAOM.

104. Yvette Farraudière, *École et société en Guyane Française: scolarisation et colonisation* (Paris: L'Harmatton, 1989), 86.

105. On Baptists in Jamaica, see Mary Turner, *Slaves and Missionaries: The Disintegration of Jamaican Slave Society, 1787–1834* (Urbana: University of Illinois Press, 1982); and Catherine Hall, "Missionary Stories: Gender and Ethnicity in England in the 1830s and 1840s," in *White, Male and Middle-Class: Explorations in Feminism and History* (New York: Routledge, 1992), 205–54.

2

Marcel Lefebvre in Gabon

Revival, Missionaries, and the Colonial
Roots of Catholic Traditionalism

Jeremy Rich examines the emergence of the ultraconservative and authoritarian Catholic identity of cleric Marcel Lefebvre in interwar Gabon at a time when French Catholicism itself was undergoing significant changes in Lefebvre's homeland. Because of the break-down of traditional social structures and institutions in Gabon, French missionaries were presented with an extraordinary opportunity to proselytize among the indigenous population. Lefebvre and other clergy, inspired in part by French medieval Catholic crusaders, assimilated a tradition of having heroic missionary priests. Like Anne-Marie Javouhey, Lefebvre shaped his own Catholic identity on the periphery without much interference from the church hierarchy in France or French colonial officials in Gabon. Furthermore, like Javouhey, Lefebvre saw colonial Catholicism as a powerful model for the universal church. Unlike her, he used his colonial experiences to reaffirm tradition rather than subvert it. And when Lefebvre returned from the margins to the center after World War II, he was determined to bring with him the lessons of evangelization and apply them to what he believed had become an unacceptable transformed and modern French Catholic core. Only by understanding the development of Catholicism on the margins, Rich argues, can we make sense of the debate between traditionalists and reformers that took place in France after World War II.

⊹⊹ ⊹⊹

On the fiftieth anniversary of his ordination in 1979, Monsignor Marcel Lefebvre (1905–91) gave a sermon at a Parisian church crowded with supporters of his traditionalist Catholic vision, opposed to the liturgical and theological reforms of the Vatican II council of the 1960s. As a result of the Second Vatican Council, the Roman Catholic Church significantly changed its practices. These innovations included the use of vernacular languages during church services, the full endorsement of democratic institutions, and the abandonment of earlier views deemed as overtly anti-Semitic. Lefebvre was opposed to these changes and became a leading conservative critic of the council. Viewing Vatican II as a victory for liberals and modernists, he formed his own congregation, the Society of Saint Pius X, which has remained a source of controversy and dissent since its foundation in 1970.

Archbishop Lefebvre's career after 1962 has attracted a wide range of scholarly attention, but surprisingly, his early life in Gabon has rarely received much mention.[1] Yet these beginning years certainly meant a great deal to the outspoken traditionalist. Over the course of the 1979 sermon Lefebvre revisited his early career as a Holy Ghost Father missionary in the former French colony of Gabon, his home between 1932 and 1945. He chose to speak of how life in this central African colony taught him to value the Tridentine (Latin) Mass. "[In Gabon] I saw—yes, I saw—what the grace of the Holy Mass could do. I saw it in the holy souls of some of our catechists. I saw it in those pagan souls transformed by the grace of baptism, transformed by assistance at Holy Mass, and by the Holy Eucharist," he said to his audience.[2] He added that he only learned what the Latin Mass truly was through his ministry in a French colony.

On first glance Lefebvre's teachings suggest that African Christians had proven more loyal to traditional views of doctrine than Catholics in Europe. Philip Jenkins's recent overview of African and Asian Christianity denotes the conservative stance of these movements regarding sexual behavior.[3] Lefebvre himself believed that missionaries and their African congregations had been shielded from the rise of liberal ideas before the 1960s. When he speculated about why French Catholics had accepted Vatican II, he noted, "I can only see one explanation: [the bishops] were in France and they let themselves be gradually infected. In Africa, I was protected. I came back the year of the Council [1962], when the harm already had been done."[4] Recent novels about missionary life in Africa, such as American author Barbara Kingsolver's *The Poisonwood Bible*, present a similar perspective of the supposedly innate reactionary nature of Western evangelists abroad.[5]

Instead of viewing missionaries in Africa as fundamentally more conservative than their colleagues in Europe and America, as Kingsolver suggests, I contend that missionaries drew from a common experience of revival in France and Gabon from the 1920s to the mid-1940s. This sense of revitalization crossed traditional divisions between Left and Right. Historian Philip Nord, in a recent article examining the flourishing of Catholic intellectual life in France between World Wars I and II, has argued that the French Catholic community "no longer stood on the defensive but carved out for itself a vast, new civic domain."[6] Nord notes how different Catholic intellectuals and groups, despite being attracted to a range of opposing authoritarian and democratic ideas, shared the same goals of asserting themselves in public life and reclaiming France for Catholicism. In a telling phrase Nord notes, "The new Catholic culture did not reject out of hand the forms and means of communication modernity placed at its disposal. A readiness to engage with modernity, however, did not mean a capitulation to its ways."[7] Nord's views about revival confirm recent revisionary work by French historians that views French Catholicism in the 1920s and 1930s as not simply a conservative monolith that abhorred democracy and embraced the fascist Vichy regime in 1940.[8] Instead, historians are uncovering a wide range of views among Catholics who disagreed on a host of issues in metropolitan France.

Nord does not consider how missionary work in Africa might have influenced this Catholic revival in France and its aftermath after World War II. He is not alone. Studies of European Catholicism in the 1920s and 1930s rarely mention missionaries at all. In turn, historians examining African Catholicism have hardly considered how missionaries looked at French society and politics. Although J. P. Daughton has noted how Catholic missionaries were as divided on the nature of colonialism and the Third Republic as their colleagues in France, few others have tried to understand how French priests in colonies looked at republican values and conflicts between church and state.[9] Rather than ignoring the connections between the metropole and the periphery, I will trace how French missionaries in an African colony interacted with the Catholic resurgence in their homeland. To recognize how someone like Lefebvre could call upon colonial Gabon as an inspiration to reform France and the Vatican, one must recognize the varied impacts that imperial expansion had upon European cultural and social mores.[10]

This essay explores how the growth of Catholicism in Gabon between 1918 and 1945 helped to generate discourses of authoritarian politics and heroism among missionaries that greatly influenced Lefebvre. First, it will evaluate the rise of African participation in the Catholic Church in Gabon. Between roughly 1925 and the end of World War II, Catholicism in Gabon expanded dramatically, as many Africans converted to the faith. After a review of the blossoming of Gabonese Catholicism, I scrutinize how French missionaries viewed their own efforts. Priests gained confidence in the transformative power of Catholicism, thanks to their successes in central Africa. Much of Lefebvre's traditionalist agenda can be traced in part to his early life in Gabon. Although some missionaries did not endorse conservative ideas about empire and the church, priests such as the young Marcel Lefebvre generally believed in hierarchical government, the need for reform of social institutions at home and abroad based on Catholic tradition, and the superiority of Catholic teachings over indigenous beliefs and French secularism. Gabon thus served as a crucible for missionaries who, after the trauma of World War II, drew widely divergent lessons from their religious experiences and their ministry in Africa.

The last section of this essay will discuss how missionaries, especially Lefebvre, stationed in Gabon before 1945 looked at decolonization and Vatican II. Some would align with democracy after the war. Most French priests in Gabon in the 1960s openly backed Vatican II. Lefebvre, who became archbishop of Dakar and later head of the Holy Ghost Fathers mission, did not follow the same path. Lefebvre had doubts about the timing of decolonization and thought of Vatican II as an unqualified disaster. His writings present his Gabonese mission work in the 1930s and 1940s as proof of the value of pre–Vatican II liturgy and conservative values. The rise of Catholicism in interwar Gabon was a model to Lefebvre for how modern France and Vatican II–era Catholicism could be redeemed by his own traditionalist movement.

Understanding the Expansion of Catholicism in Interwar Gabon

Soon after his ordination in 1929, Marcel Lefebvre attended a seminar held by visiting missionary bishop of Libreville Louis Tardy. Lefebvre no doubt knew something of the guest prelate from his brother René, who already served as a priest in Gabon. Marcel, still working as a curate in France, was impressed by Tardy's discussion. Tardy showed his audience a range of photographs depicting animals in the Gabonese rainforest, victims of sleeping sickness, and images of model African converts. Photography, a technological hallmark of modernity, had been put to work for the faith. The moral of the tale was clear: the Holy Ghost Fathers wanted to reveal the transformative power of baptism and their efforts on the Gabonese people.[11] Tardy sought out young priests who shared his theological and political views and told Marcel that he would be selected to join him and René in central Africa.[12]

Bishop Tardy's presentation of heroic missionary life and the success of Catholic ministry in Gabon might seem to be merely a generic way of finding new recruits and soliciting funds. There was no denying, however, the increase in catechists, clerics, and lay Catholics in Gabon under his watch. One might question the narrative of progress he constructed with his photographs, but there could be no argument about the church's growth. Between 1925 and 1938 the population of baptized Catholics went from 18,660 to 69,684, and the number of catechists went up nearly tenfold, from 152 to nearly 1,500.[13] Even the interior Haut-Ogooué Province, a place where missions established in the 1890s had made little headway with local people, could boast a rapid series of conversions sponsored by local chiefs.[14] Gabon was far from alone; the ranks of Catholics expanded dramatically in much of Africa between 1918 and 1950.[15]

Lefebvre's 1979 sermon presented the supernatural efficacy of the sacraments as the root cause of the Catholic revival of Gabon, but an assortment of other factors could help explain how missionary efforts reached bigger audiences. First, the 1920s was a decade when French colonial authorities could truly boast for the first time that they controlled the length and breadth of Gabon. French naval officers first unfurled the *tricolore* in Libreville, the coastal capital of the colony, in 1849 but battled for scores of years before dissident Africans accepted French authority in the remote and rugged rainforests and grasslands of the colony.[16] The violent exploitation of Africans by concessionary companies between 1900 and 1920 caused hardship and unrest for the Gabonese people. World War I broke the autonomy of rural Gabon. International trade collapsed, much of northern Gabon became a battleground between France and German Cameroon to the north, and the global influenza pandemic killed thousands.[17] Gabonese people often fled forced labor details, obligatory military service, and high taxes by fleeing into remote forests, which put them at greater risk of contracting sleeping sickness from tsetse flies as well as death from malnutrition.

With the end of the war French timber entrepreneurs streamed into the colony to cut and process lightweight *okoumé* wood for plywood and to rebuild France's shattered railway system. French officials coerced and cajoled rural men throughout Gabon to toil in timber camps along the coast and the Ogooué River in Central Africa and used forced labor to construct roads throughout the country to survey and control local people more effectively. One unexpected result of these industrial operations was a series of famines, as the scattered populations of coastal regions battered by years of adversity could not feed thousands of male workers who did not produce food for themselves. In the annals of African colonial horrors this time of starvation has barely received a footnote, but it radically altered the lives of the Gabonese people. Better transportation, the widespread movement of people, the end of armed resistance by Gabonese communities against French rule, and the destabilizing effects of the timber business transformed Gabon.

Holy Ghost Father missionaries felt uneasy with the bewildering changes that had swept through Gabon, but indirectly the chaos of the period favored their evangelization efforts. Before the 1920s Holy Ghost Father missionaries had considered Gabon a frustrating post from the time they first arrived in Gabon in 1844.[18] Outside of coastal centers such as Libreville on the Atlantic coast, Catholic priests had little luck establishing missions until French occupation of the interior began in the 1880s. The chaos of early French rule, punctuated by warfare between various groups of Africans and between Africans and the colonial government, as well as the devastation wrought on Gabon by World War I, dampened their evangelization efforts. Besides these obstacles, World War I also made funding from French Catholics harder to obtain and created a dearth of personnel for the missions. These difficult conditions made any hope of revival difficult to imagine, yet it did occur, beginning in the mid-1920s.

Hardships ultimately drew some Gabonese to Catholicism. Time and again, elderly Gabonese people, recalling stories their parents and elders told them of the famine years, described the era of horrors as the "punishment of God" for the sins of their people.[19] An eighty-four-year-old man interviewed in 2004 noted how his community, the Fang people living in northern and central Gabon, had been ignorant of Christianity before missionaries came and so had incurred the wrath of the Lord.[20] Catastrophes often engender visions of divine retribution and expiation, as French missionaries undoubtedly knew well. French Catholics employed discourses of sacrifice and renewal in discussing the French Revolution, the Franco-Prussian War, the Commune, and World War I in counterrevolutionary traditions of the nineteenth and twentieth centuries.[21] Just as France's conflicts inspired new conversions and were understood as a means of renewing the faith, the famine years also led many Gabonese to question older beliefs and incorporate foreign religious ideas.[22] Catholics were not the only beneficiaries of the situation; by the 1930s rural Gabonese joined churches formed by French and American missionaries in droves, and Fang people also formed *bwiti* syncretic movements that stitched together beliefs and practices of southern Gabonese religious associations, Catholic regalia, Christian doctrine, and older Fang traditions of supernatural power.[23]

The leveling effects of the war and famine years also created other incentives for Gabonese people to engage with missionaries. Missionaries provided job skills, educational opportunities, and patronage in times of hardship. Gabonese men who had relied on trading ivory, timber, and rubber for European goods such as bottled spirits and cloth in the late nineteenth century faced a serious challenge, as World War I and the timber boom altered and eliminated older forms of accumulating wealth. The timber economy, dominated by European capital that could pay for heavy machinery, transport costs, and the upkeep of hundreds and even thousands of workers, did not allow much room for most African entrepreneurs to succeed in the business. Literacy rather than trading acumen was vital for younger men wishing to obtain lucrative jobs working for the colonial state and private businesses.[24]

Mission schools also became sources of patronage in other ways. During the 1920s missionaries fed thousands of hungry victims of the famine and sometimes challenged state authorities' draconian policies of requisitioning food from rural villages.[25] Children and older people accused by others of using supernatural forces to harm others could flee to missions; rather than relying on kin networks for aid, they now could form a new set of fictive family ties at the mission. Young mission-educated men in their twenties such as Léon Mba, the future president of Gabon after independence, used their education to become state-appointed chiefs and thus could dominate elderly men who previously had made up the leadership of Gabonese rural communities.[26]

For men seeking to climb up the ranks of colonial society, the best education available in the colony was at the Saint Jean seminary in Libreville. Very few of the young Gabonese who passed through its doors entered the priesthood, but the male elite of early postcolonial Gabon went through the seminary. Senator Jean Ondo, doctors such as Felicien Ndong, and other notable bureaucrats studied with Lefebvre and Jean-Baptiste Fauret.[27] Besides these luminaries, three future Gabonese bishops also received their training from Lefebvre: François Ndong of Oyem, Félicien Makouka of Franceville, and Cyrique Obamba of Mouila.[28] With only a rudimentary public school system available in the capital of Libreville, families seeking to improve the fortunes of their male children had little choice but to place their offspring and relatives at the seminary or other Catholic schools.

African gender conflicts also incited Gabonese men and women to accept membership in Catholic mission communities. Catholic priests in mission stations such as Donguila, a church in Gabon's Estuary Province where Marcel Lefebvre served from 1940 to 1943, became the patrons of women seeking to escape polygamous and arranged marriages. Maurice Briault, the self-styled chronicler of missionary life in Gabon who penned books and articles after he left active ministry in Gabon in 1918, wrote at length of women fleeing polygamous husbands by turning to the sanctuary of the church.[29] Colonial officials detested this missionary policy, as did many Fang men, who went as far as raiding Donguila to recapture their wives forcibly.[30] For Fang women missionaries proved useful in their efforts to improve their circumstances by escaping marriages, because divorce meant that their own families would have to repay their husbands.[31] Fang men currying favor with missionaries often agreed to send their daughters and younger wives to missions to learn the catechism as well. Some priests, including Lefebvre himself, tried to reform marriage practices among the Gabonese people. Lefebvre met with state-appointed Fang chiefs under the auspices of the colonial administration in 1942 to create more stable marriages by limiting divorce and bride-price costs.[32] Although few Fang people seem to have gone along with these policies, they illustrate how missionaries inserted themselves as active participants in negotiations between men and women.

Missionaries also could use forceful measures and operate in villages outside of their mission grounds with much less risk of retribution from indigenous people than before the 1920s. Until World War I armed villagers menaced some priests and catechists with violence.[33] The 1920s brought a halt to this behavior, as French officials could send in guards to destroy villages and arrest Africans quickly. Missionaries could travel throughout Gabon with little risk of harm, and if incidents did occur with recalcitrant Africans, the French government acted to protect mission interests. Priests regularly toured Fang villages from their missions on boats and by foot and tore down talismans and buildings dedicated to bwiti practices they deemed to be a satanic parody of the faith. Lefebvre himself participated in anti-bwiti campaigns while stationed in Lambaréné and Ndjolé in central Gabon during World War II.[34] Africans who assaulted the white-robed intruders risked beatings and jail from guards working for the colonial government. They also, in the name of saving children from pagan beliefs, sometimes took children away from rural parents against the will of their families; parents could protest, but the colonial administration rarely intervened.[35] Some priests chastised Catholic women who had abandoned their husbands by making them undergo penance; they had their hair shaved, wore burlap sacks, and had to beg pardon to the entire mission.[36]

Another source of missionary successes came from the key role played by African clergy and laypeople. Missionaries often could only inspect scattered settlements far from their missions several times a year, and their main goal on these visits was to hear confessions, hold Mass, and review candidates for confirmation and baptism rather than rally villagers to the faith. The bulk of the work of evangelization went to African catechists trained by Catholic missionaries, who by the late 1930s could be found in nearly every village in Gabon. African priests and nuns also became more common, and like the catechists, did much of the practical work of translating Christian doctrine in ways local people could understand. Gabonese priests and nuns such as André Raponda Walker and Cécilia Fatou-Berre wrote sermons, learned African languages other than their own tongues, and trained laypeople in Catholic dogma.[37]

Catechists literally handled much of the day-to-day affairs of ministry. In his 1979 sermon Lefebvre lauded the "noble souls of some of our catechists," but other missionaries had more pithy observations to give about their assistants.[38] The Donguila mission, for example, sent out male school graduates to settle in the many small villages that dotted the Estuary Province. Catechists often enjoyed the patronage and the mobility their occupation afforded them but often proved more willing to follow the dictates of local social demands than follow Catholic teachings. Missionary inspections of catechists in the 1920s and 1930s from Donguila were rarely positive; catechists regularly married multiple women, quit mission work to find jobs with European timber camps, or set up arranged marriages, and some even became initiated into bwiti temples.[39] Lefebvre himself proved less condescending toward his catechists than some other French missionaries, but he too believed the vast majority could only be trusted if they were kept under the watchful eye of a priest.[40] Despite the willingness of many male mission staff to profit from their positions, the numbers of the newly baptized continued to multiply.

This thumbnail sketch of Gabonese mission life does not pretend to provide a thorough explanation of the reasons behind the willingness of Gabonese people to accept missionaries and adopt Catholic teachings, but it does serve to show how the interwar period created new opportunities for the Gabon missionary work to blossom. French Catholic intellectuals and clergy sought to rally the working class as well as the bourgeoisie to the call of Christian renewal between the wars, and Lefebvre and his colleagues participated in the equally impressive feat of spreading Catholicism in the rainforests of Gabon. Their relative power in colonial society furnished them with opportunities to disseminate their idea of the French nation to Africans and European-born residents of the colony alike. They may have been dismayed by the excesses of colonial administrators and the social disruption engendered by the boom-and-bust nature of the timber trade, but lumber exports and the colonial state had created attractions and the tangible means of spreading the faith. Instead of considering social and cultural factors in the success of Catholicism in Gabon, however, missionaries viewed the renaissance of faith according to ideas emerging from the Catholic renewal in France itself.

Missionary Ideals and Conservative Views in Gabon, 1918–45

French Catholic writers and secular observers of mission work in Gabon tried to make sense of the great revival. Generally, priests who had access to a public audience presented the blossoming of Catholic Gabon as a triumph of Catholic tradition and the labor of knightly and self-sacrificing missionaries. Their idealization of medieval, rural, and Catholic France served as their paradigm for how they wanted to reshape Gabon. Priests proudly showed off their schools and churches to visitors to the colony in the 1930s as proof that their efforts were part of the civilizing mission. "The great Saint Paul had to do manual labor; so do we, and it is our work of ministry and civilization," Father Aloïse Hee, a priest stationed in the expanding mission of Franceville, succinctly noted.[41] They openly celebrated the heroism, bravery, and hard work of priests. These presentations generally lauded French missionaries and neglected the role of Africans in spreading the faith. Public discussions of Catholicism in Gabon before 1945 presented most Africans as simple children in need of constant supervision. Briault and other French Catholics also used the revival as a means of patching up older differences on religion that had once placed the French government at odds with the Catholic Church. It should come as no surprise that Bishop Tardy and many clergy, including Marcel Lefebvre, rallied to Philippe Pétain in 1940. At least in public discourse, conservative values explained the success of missionaries in Gabon. These attitudes reinforced many of Lefebvre's own ideas about Catholic tradition and politics.

The public version of the revival for French metropolitan and missionary consumption was authored largely by one man: Maurice Briault. He had been a priest stationed in the colony before World War I, and for three decades after his return to Europe, he published a series of vignettes aimed at French readers.[42] Briault's chronicles were standard reading for missionaries in Gabon, and African and European priests who wrote about the colony regularly referenced him.[43] Even Pope Pius XI turned to his expertise. In 1925 Briault helped put together an exposition of African missions for the Vatican.[44] These stories spoke of the value and challenges of Catholicism in Gabon. Briault presented himself as the public face of the Gabonese missionary community and remained in close communication with Monsignor Louis Tardy, bishop of Libreville and head of the Catholic mission in Gabon from 1926 to 1947.[45] Lefebvre's later writings and conversations between visitors and mission clergy in the 1930s suggest Briault's opinions represented those commonly voiced among French priests and monks in the colony.

Briault's ideal of a good missionary was Father Jean-Baptiste Barreau, whom Briault praised in the last chapter of his 1945 book, Sur les pistes de l'AEF (On the Paths of French Equatorial Africa).[46] Barreau consciously drew from revivalist imagery popular in metropolitan interwar French Catholicism. Like a host of other Catholics in France, Barreau's Christianity derived from a medieval foundation. Barreau was famed among the settler community in central Gabon for his unabashed royalism and idealization of the "purity" of the French language of the Middle Ages, to the point that some *colons* dubbed him the "royal monk." When Pope Pius XI's encyclical against the royalist Action Française group of Charles Maurras was announced in 1926, Barreau clearly was hurt.[47] The royalist priest found other ways, however, to serve the king.

In the early 1930s one French monarch found a home in Gabon: the medieval crusader Saint Louis. Barreau erected a church dedicated to Saint Louis in the timber town of Port Gentil.[48] Louis had a special place in the interwar French Catholic imagination. His crusading exploits against Muslims, his chaste virtue, and his dedication to the church made him a favorite among early twentieth-century French Catholics, along with Joan of Arc. Philip Nord has rightfully noted how interwar Catholics looked to such icons as Saint Louis from the French past to push for a remaking of the French present: "The heroes of these bygone ages had critical lessons to teach the modern-day believer, lessons of valor, risk, and adventure."[49] The Gabonese could serve Christendom in the same way as the medieval hero. In 1933 Barreau wrote to Briault about one of his African servants, whom he described as a "docile sheepdog" who now would become "the royal knight of the great St. Louis."[50] Just as young French Catholic group members sang songs extolling knightly virtues and the Uriage movement would put French chivalry to work for Marshal Pétain in World War II, Barreau idolized medieval male virility.[51]

Briault thought Barreau fit into the chivalrous tradition of Catholic laborers as well, even though this priest jousted with colonial challenges to the faith in the Gabonese rainforest. Briault's account lovingly treated the adversity that Barreau encountered in the remote southern Gabonese mission of Trois-Epis.[52] As a young man, Barreau had his own heroic struggles: learning local languages, building schools and churches, fighting off panthers that raided mission grounds to snatch away livestock, competing with French Calvinist missionaries, and of course, combating African resistance to missionary teachings. His daily prayers and asceticism reminded Briault of Saint Francis of Assisi, even if Barreau's mastery of weapons made the comparison with the peaceful lover of animals a bit incongruous. Knighthood still was in flower even in the twentieth century, thanks to colonial missionaries.

Briault thought of missionaries such as Barreau as representing the conscience of empire; he had no doubts, however, about the need for France to rule Gabon and the superiority of European culture over Gabonese beliefs. The missionary expert advised officials to treat the Gabonese as backward and primitive people in desperate need of tutelage. He spoke, for example, of the decline of superstitions and human sacrifice as an inevitable result of "our civilization" that, though often mocked, was in his eyes undoubtedly better than what Gabonese people could accomplish on their own.[53] Even granting basic liberties was out of the question. As he noted, "It is human to accord some excuses to these big children [Gabonese people], but from the moment one takes charge of them and that this command has to necessarily touch on their customs, it is still a form of humanity to not allow them to think their excuses and explanations will always be accepted."[54] Briault despised coastal Mpongwe people who dressed in European clothes and spoke French fluently but ignored mission teachings. European suits on black men left Briault seething. "From the moment the blacks of our villages know how to write a bit, they are hypnotized by the office and the paper that they will scribble on, the white outfit they will wear, and the glasses that they judge de rigueur," reads one of his screeds against coastal people.[55] This uneasiness was hardly unique to Gabon; fears of educated colonial subjects turning against "traditional" leaders and their European rulers were a feature of colonialism in Africa and Asia.

Missionaries such as Briault might patronize the Gabonese as a whole, but they certainly valued the revival as a genuine expression of the potential of Christianity in Gabon. Briault reassured his French readers that Christ was prevailing even in savage Africa and recounted how he and Bishop Tardy visited the Adouma mass converts of the mid-1930s. After seeing scores of new Catholics visit Franceville, Tardy proclaimed, "The presence of these Christian crowds, no matter how frustrating they may be, are for missionaries the best way to judge their own advancement."[56] In his own journal Tardy himself was awed at the progress in the Franceville mission and concluded, "Nearly 17,000 Christians and 15,000 catechumens. Zealous and courageous missionaries who have no fear of pain and suffering."[57] Briault's books also highlighted interactions between Catholic teachings and ordinary, and often deeply troubled, Gabonese. One tale focused on catechism lessons with a Fang man slowly dying from sleeping sickness;

the man battled fatigue every morning to speak with the priest so he could be ready for baptism.[58] Another discussed Anghilé, an alcoholic who still ably served the Donguila mission for twenty-five years as a clerk, interpreter, and laborer.[59] If African men could fight so nobly through their own flaws and adversities, then Catholicism would take root in Gabon.

Briault was not the only missionary who employed heroic images to persuade a secular French audience of the value of the Catholic presence in Gabon. Marcel Sauvage, a French poet, took a tour of French Equatorial Africa in 1933 and 1934, probably modeled after novelist André Gide's visit to the same colonies several years earlier. Sauvage decided to meet Father Xavier Dahin, who had spent four decades in the colony, in southern Gabon.[60] When his boat came to the Fernan Vaz missions, the tourist discovered that Dahin was on his deathbed and too ill to speak, so he met with Dahin's assistant, Brother Mathias Schmitt, instead. Even before speaking with Schmitt, Sauvage was moved by the same respect for tradition that appeared in the Catholic revival of France and Gabon. "[The mission] bell, like in a French village, sweet and clear, is something shocking on the Equator. Twenty centuries of tradition hits you in the throat and stomach. . . . Such music, in these parts of the globe where we are sad intruders, is a miracle," he wrote.[61] As the passage indicates, Sauvage understood Catholicism as a coherent heritage linked to the French past.

This past now had a future in Africa and a promising one at that. Schmitt gave Sauvage a tour that highlighted the achievements of the Catholic mission.[62] The poet marveled at seeing how Dahin had "remade [Fernan Vaz] from a corner of Hell to nearly a corner of Heaven." Well-tilled fields fed schools that taught over three hundred children. After a walk around the grounds, Schmitt then regaled Sauvage with heroic tales of Dahin's life. The dying man had marched with explorers through the rainforest, single-handedly put down a rebellion in central Gabon by negotiating with local leaders, and acted as a doctor to sick Europeans and Africans without taking note of their religious beliefs. "He worked like a buffalo . . . one hundred times he risked his life," the monk said. Missionaries not only acted heroically; they even sacrificed themselves for French unity. Dahin dragged his feeble body from his chamber to a chapel to hold Mass daily on behalf of all Frenchmen in Gabon, even though no settlers actually attended, and few were practicing Christians of any sort. Schmitt's vivid description of the brave missionary and the results of his work moved Sauvage, much as Barreau had inspired praise from Briault.

Valiant missionaries received a mixed response from administrators until World War II. During the revival missionaries and officials viewed one another uneasily, even though the fierce opposition between anticlerical and clerical forces had declined by the 1920s.[63] In Gabon the rise of timber and marriage were the two biggest sources of strife between church and state. Bishop Louis Martrou lambasted officials as utterly incompetent and blamed them for the dreadful famines of the early 1920s before his own death in 1925.[64] Tardy wrote to Briault in 1926 that the timber industry supported by the colonial government was to blame for starvation.[65] Other missionaries noted with frustration how timber profits allowed African men to marry multiple wives. Father Mesange from the Donguila mission wrote to his superior, "This timber fever won't last, but it will have done a great evil from the Christian point of view. With wealth comes polygamy!"[66] Briault wrote of an African priest upbraiding a nominally Catholic administrator for trying to have the mission release a Christian woman who had fled her polygamous husband.[67] Some officials rejected these criticisms by arguing that missionaries were disrupting the status quo. "No missionary from any church can come to this country and create with his own authority religious practices that destroy local customs," the governor-general of French Equatorial Africa, Raphaël Antonetti, warned the governor of Gabon in 1928.[68]

Despite these general differences, individual priests and officials could find common ground, especially on the social value of Catholic work and the need to command Africans forcefully. Jean-Baptiste Barreau himself used the presence of a secular French government in Gabon as a foil to show off missionary heroism and sacrifice: "Because it would be impractical, the mission does not disdain the representatives of the state, despite their prejudices and the lamentable indifference of a secular government."[69] Individual administrators received accolades, especially if they took a firm hand with the Gabonese. Donguila missionaries praised the "smiling severity" of one officer in 1929: "The Fang know that there's no joking around with Soalhat. He is just but harsh."[70] Other officials would stay at Donguila and eat with the priests.[71] Some administrators expressed their respect for missionaries. The protagonist of an autobiographical novel penned by an administrator in Gabon praised mission efforts, despite his own atheism and adherence to the Freemasons.[72]

World War II changed these relationships, and Tardy did not hide his enthusiasm for the fascist Vichy government. The bishop's distrust of democracy became evident once Marshal Pétain took power in 1940. After the fall of France, French Equatorial Africa was torn between partisans of Charles de Gaulle and Pétain.[73] Governor Félix Éboué, a Guyanese-born black administrator, rallied Chad to the cause of Free France.[74] Tardy took a key role in ensuring that Georges Masson, governor of Gabon since 1939, stayed faithful to the marshal instead of vacillating toward de Gaulle. In August 1940 Tardy and some leading timber camp owners met with Masson and convinced him to remain loyal to Vichy.[75] Henceforth, Tardy went out of his way to show off his undying loyalty to Pétain, and heroism again became a central theme.

Discourses of heroism associated with the Gabonese and French revivals featured prominently in his homily when Tardy addressed the Libreville faithful after the bombing of Dakar by Allied forces in 1940. A common bond of sacrifice for the nation promised redemption for the French Empire, according to Tardy's homily. The dead of Dakar—whether black or white, infantryman or officer, civilian or soldier—now "slept side by side in that sublime fraternity that brings together in the same sadness and glory the children of the same motherland."[76] The blood of these victims cemented a new alliance that would lead to the redemption of France, just as Christ had given Himself for all humanity. France would become a Christian nation if it returned to God and followed the wise marshal and finally would return to its rightful place "at the head of civilized peoples." He approvingly cited nationalists such as Maurice Barrès and Ernest Psichari who underlined the link between the *révolution nationale* and Christian renewal. Skeptics and selfish individualists might belittle this new greater France, but the transformation would come in the colonies as well as the homeland. Such sentiments were hardly novel in 1940, as missionaries in other parts of the Vichy empire echoed Tardy's sentiments.[77] Tardy himself kept diligent notes on articles by Action Française founder, Charles Maurras, and other writers who claimed that defeat was the prelude to a Christian rebirth of France.[78]

When Gaullist forces invaded Gabon from Cameroon and Moyen Congo, Tardy upheld the fight against Free France, and Catholic missionaries under his watch became part of the civil war. Knighthood no longer was just a metaphor; some Catholic missionaries literally became combatants. A mortar fired by Free French troops took the life of a French priest in Lambaréné in October 1940. "Soldier of God, soldier of France, Father Talabardon will not have given his life in vain," a Vichy officer declared to Tardy in a telegram.[79] The captain of the *Bougainville*, a Pétainist ship, thanked Tardy for his kind support days before Free French forces sank the boat and captured Libreville.[80] Vichy governor-general of French West Africa, Pierre Boisson, thanked Tardy for "thinking French before all."[81] The bishop stitched to his cassock his Legion of Honor medal, which General Weygand had awarded Tardy for his loyalty to Pétain when Gaullist troops detained him, and refused to chant *Te Deum* for a Free French victory in Libreville.[82] The victorious invaders kept Tardy imprisoned for almost a year in Lambaréné before releasing him.[83]

Self-sacrifice by missionaries continued to be one of the bishop's hallmarks, even in defeat. Tardy rebuffed any reconciliation with the Gaullists but swore political neutrality during the rest of the war. From house arrest he wrote a note to all Gabonese Catholic missionaries asking them to submit to the new government. "We ask first," he asserted, "the respect of conscience of our missionaries who from the beginning believed they had the duty to affirm their loyalty to the legitimate government of their country."[84] Jean-Baptiste Fauret, a priest who had taught in the Saint Jean seminary with Lefebvre, was assigned to oversee the day-to-day operations of Catholic clergy in Gabon, and Tardy ordered him to stay out of politics.[85] Yet Tardy never broke from the Vichyist orbit or escaped condemnation from supporters of the Allies. Despite the ban on political involvement, Tardy continued to record Pétain's speeches broadcast from Dakar.[86] A copy of a small Gaullist settler manifesto fell into Tardy's hands in 1943, and the bishop scrawled, "Lies!" next to the group's claim that in 1941 the ill-fated Gaullist governor of Gabon, Colonel Parrant, who died in a plane crash several months after taking office, had planned to force Tardy to make a public apology for his attachment to Vichy.[87] Soon after the end of the war, some settlers told a newly arrived priest in Libreville that a firing squad ought to have dispatched the Pétainist prelate.[88] Illness forced Tardy back to France, where he died in 1947.

Marcel Lefebvre shared Briault's right-wing orientation and Tardy's Pétainist allegiances, which both owed much to discourses of heroism expressed by missionaries during the Gabonese revival. Over forty years later Lefebvre told some of the nuns of the Saint Pius X order about the Vichy–Free French battles of 1940. Tardy's arrest had brought Communists and Freemasons to power and "scandalized the poor black people."[89] His frustration still can be seen in the fading ink of the Donguila mission journal that he kept from 1940 to 1943. The defeat of the Vichy administration in Gabon did not sit well with him. "After having killed Frenchmen of much better blood than their own, [the Free French] have finished by fixing our convictions of who they are—robbing factories, imprisoning Frenchmen. . . . These convicts, murderers, Russians, Czechs, [all] do not speak French," Lefebvre groaned. He finished by declaring that all the upheaval "will never remove us from the Marshal, the true standard of France." Gabon had, through its fight against these atheistic invaders, now become "a true part of France."[90] Because he was never interned by the Free French government in Gabon, Lefebvre never faced any government pressure to renounce Pétain publicly.

The traditionalist positions of Briault, Tardy, and Lefebvre did not represent the full spectrum of views about the rise of Catholicism in Gabon or about Vichy. Unfortunately, correspondence by priests in the Holy Ghost Fathers archives makes very few explicit references to politics or explanations for the revival. There are indications, however, that some priests did not agree with Tardy's program. Father Jean-Jérome Adam supported the Free French in his Franceville mission in southern Gabon; he even flew the Cross of Lorraine flag next to his church.[91] Still others expressed their dislike for the high-handed treatment of missionaries by the French administration without showing any admiration for Vichy. André Raponda Walker, the first Gabonese priest and a gifted historian and ethnologist, was expelled from his mission in Southern Gabon in 1941 at the age of seventy after celebrating Mass with Pétainist prisoners.[92] Jean-Baptiste Fauret became bishop of Pointe Noire in 1946. Fauret did not lament the fall of Vichy after 1945. He ultimately promoted the reforms of Vatican II and backed independence for French Congo.[93] A French Holy Ghost Father recalled Lefebvre's name mentioned as a successor to Tardy in 1947, but the embarrassment of Vichy helped lead to the choice of Adam over other candidates.[94]

Lefebvre followed Tardy's example of right-wing politics and authoritarian manners. Images of valiant and lonely missionaries, exploited by Lefebvre in the 1970s and 1980s, were certainly a part of clerical identities between

1918 and 1945 in Gabon. The site of hundreds of rural Gabonese lining up for baptisms was proof, at least for Tardy and Briault, that their model of hierarchical order and heroic action was the correct approach to follow. It is little wonder that some priests openly sided with Vichy in 1940, based on the attitudes expressed by Briault and others. Lefebvre did not make a dramatic break with his traditionalist orientation, which had been associated with the revival. He continued to espouse the kind of ideas about Christianity and colonialism that were presented as the norm in interwar Gabon well after they fell out of favor in Africa and Europe.

Marcel Lefebvre's Memories of Colonial Gabon

Lefebvre's loyalty to the ideals of conservative order and manly virtue continued well after 1945, even as French Catholics tried to distance themselves from the choices made by church leaders in the Vichy era. Lefebvre's choices were not supported by the majority French clergy who had begun their careers in Africa during the same period. Jean-Jérôme Adam, a priest born one year before Lefebvre, introduced masses in African languages and supported decolonization in the 1960s after he became the bishop of Libreville. Another French missionary in Africa who diverged from Lefebvre's path toward challenging Vatican II was Léon-Etienne Duval. Duval went through the same education offered at the French Seminary in Rome as Lefebvre in the 1920s, in which teachers such as Father Le Floch attacked liberalism and democracy as threats to the whole of Catholic tradition.[95] Duval eventually became a Holy Ghost Father missionary in Cameroon, but he celebrated Vatican II rather than damning it.[96]

Lefebvre, on the other hand, presented his life in Gabon as proof of the superiority of unchanging Catholic traditions. He occasionally wove vignettes from his stay in central Africa as evidence for his ideas about the nature of Christianity and civilization. Lefebvre's nemesis, Pope Paul VI, held great hope for the rise of African Christianity.[97] So did Lefebvre, albeit for quite different reasons. One theme that underlies much of Lefebvre's work was his steadfast conviction that allowing religious liberty was a dangerous error, and he pointed to Gabon to defend his position. In They Have Uncrowned Him (1988) Lefebvre railed against the idea of religious tolerance. John Paul II's willingness to watch indigenous religious ceremonies in Togo in 1985 prompted Lefebvre to declare, "If a [Gabonese] Christian were caught while participating in such rites, he would be suspect of apostasy and excluded from a mission for a year."[98] Gabonese Catholics often participated in ceremonies run by members of indigenous religious practices, especially *bwiti* temples, and indeed priests such as Lefebvre sanctioned them for doing so. The battle against *bwiti* also enters in other ways into his anti–Vatican II works. He recalled the joy of burning a "sorcerer's hut" with African children cheering him on and compared his own acts favorably to John Paul II's refusal to sanction destruction of other religious practices outside the faith.[99]

Implicit in Lefebvre's invocation of his African life is a critique of Vatican II Catholicism based on conflicting notions of masculinity. Lefebvre himself repeatedly characterized himself as aggressive in the defense of the faith, unlike the supposedly weak-kneed priests of later generations. He described modern priests as confused, unable to handle the rigors of celibacy, and willing to abandon their mission to evangelize so they might better conform to modernity.[100] Older missionaries were cut from a different, and apparently more durable, cloth. "In Africa, where I spent the major part of my life, the missions fought against the scourges of polygamy, homosexuality, and the contempt [in which] women were held," he noted in *Open Letter to Confused Catholics*.[101] Illnesses, early death, and hardship awaited missionaries, but their duty to spread the Gospel and the sure knowledge of the Catholic faith inspired them to sacrifice.[102] Lefebvre himself nearly died from fever and remembered looking at the tombstones of other missionaries cut down in the prime of their lives in Gabon.[103] The same celebratory images of tough-minded French priests guiding their flocks, despite the suffering that emerged from other missionaries in Gabon in the 1930s, comes to the fore in Lefebvre's discourse.

His aggressiveness and willingness to use rough measures comes out in discussions of African women. Lefebvre's intervention in Gabonese gender relations extended to convincing Fang chiefs to sign an agreement, apparently never enforced, to lower bride-prices and ban arranged marriages.[104] Yet he did not just settle for paper decrees. Lefebvre taught a course on papal encyclicals that did not fit with Vatican II principles, and his teaching featured a discussion of Christian marriage.[105] Lefebvre asserted that he had even recaptured women whom he believed had fled their husbands at the behest of their families. Some Fang families wished to break up marriages so that they could extort higher bride-prices from other suitors. Lefebvre derided Fang marriage arrangements as merely slavery in disguise and presented himself as a hardy missionary willing to use strong measures to defend the family.[106] His conviction that he acted correctly to reshape Gabonese marriages fit well with his more general stance that Catholics had every right to constrain others from propagating errors.[107]

Lefebvre's missionary life did more than demonstrate his own energy in comparison to the empty-headed tolerance of Vatican II priests; it also allowed him to transfer the idea of Gabon as a mission field to France itself. The civilizing enterprise of missionaries in central Africa applied to pagan Paris as well. Those Catholics who wished to participate in the Tridentine Mass in France in the 1980s were, like Christians in "missionary countries," only able to go to Mass several times a year.[108] His 1979 homily revolved around the idea of sacrifice providing the foundation for Christian civilization. The sacrifice of Christ in the Mass that inspired missionaries to teach the faith to Africans and that led Gabonese to forsake indigenous beliefs was, for the prelate, the means to constructing a new Christian order in France itself. "I have seen this grace at work in Africa—there is no reason why it will not work as well in [Europe]," he preached.[109]

Lefebvre wove together his work with his previous experience in Gabon in discussions of decolonization and civilization. At his traditionalist seminary he taught a course on papal encyclicals that cited Pius X's assertion that "there is no true civilization without the true religion."[110] True civilization was Saint Louis serving at Mass two times a day, Lefebvre concluded, echoing Father Barreau's knighting of his African manservant.[111] France's double game of trying to civilize without upholding Catholicism explained postcolonial troubles in Africa. He told his listeners in 1979, "The fault [for Africa's problems] does not so much lie in the Africans themselves as with the colonial powers, which did not understand how to avail themselves of this Catholic faith which rooted itself among the African peoples."[112] French republican nationalism was a dismal failure in France for Lefebvre, so he constructed a Catholic identity that went beyond the boundaries of Europe. Secular colonization had failed, but Lefebvre hoped his supporters would act in France in the same way that he labored in Gabon.

Lefebvre's own skills as a missionary were still sharp after 1970, when he set about organizing an international traditionalist movement based out of

Switzerland, and his stay in Gabon had prepared him for this role. He was used to inspecting catechists in rainforests, establishing new churches—such as Saint Marcel of Kango, which still overlooks the Como River in Gabon today—and directing evangelization efforts. His reputation for coordinating mission efforts in interwar Gabon is no mere invention of his supporters. "The whole world is devastated by the departure of our dear father [Marcel]. He was universally loved and admired," wrote the priest who succeeded him at Donguila in 1943 before listing Lefebvre's accomplishments in building construction, placing catechists, and creating new fields to feed students.[113] One elderly Donguila resident interviewed in 2004 asserted that he thought Lefebvre was called to war because he spent so much time in the villages and setting up a church in Kango.[114] These sentiments were echoed by other Gabonese along the Ogooué River, who praised him as a teacher, a master of logistics, and an engineer par excellence.[115]

Images of docile Africans and strong missionaries pervaded Lefebvre's discussion of his early career. He believed that prayers in Latin and the Tridentine Mass inspired loyalty and devotion to the church among the Gabonese. "The simple peoples of Africa and of Asia love the Gregorian chant and that one sacred language, the sign of their belonging to Catholicism," observed Lefebvre.[116] Good Catholic Gabonese demonstrated the value of older traditions undermined by Vatican II. "The village began to be trans-formed little by little, under the influence of grace—under the influence of the grace of the Holy Sacrifice of the Mass, and soon all the villages were wanting to have one of the fathers visit them. Oh, the visit of a missionary! They waited impatiently to assist at the Holy Mass, in order to be able to confess their sins and then to receive Holy Communion," Lefebvre said in 1979.[117] Instead of skeptics and liberal Catholics, the Gabonese were becom-ing a loyal flock under the guidance of pre–Vatican II Catholicism.

A minority of Gabonese Catholics hold similar sentiments. A 1985 article in Lefebvre's Congregation of Saint Pius X magazine, *Angelus*, described happy throngs of well-wishers who remembered the bishop from his early days.[118] Lefebvre's biographer Bernard Tissier de Mallerais found Lambaréné residents who, over five decades after the fact, wept recalling when Lefebvre went to France in 1945, and the present Saint Pius X mission in Lebreville draws crowds for its services.[119] When Lefebvre initially considered setting up a mission in Gabon in 1985, some older Catholics welcomed him with opened arms. Father Groche, the present head of the Saint Pius X mission in Libreville, recalled services held at Donguila: "They sang the Mass of the Epiphany just like that, with no preparation. Just 15 minutes before the Mass they asked the Archbishop: 'Which Mass would you like to sing?' And they sang practically by heart the Mass of the Epiphany. Amazing!"[120] The reasons why Lefebvre would find these images favorable are obvious—they furnish evidence for his contention about the Latin Mass and the success of pre–Vatican II theology.

Why some Gabonese would disdain Vatican II reforms deserves a study all its own, but the disappointments of everyday life in postcolonial Gabon certainly would be a starting point. One elderly man recalled in 1988 how happy he was to be attending a Latin Mass. He derided the use of drums in African masses by noting how one woman, an initiate in a female secret society, became possessed by a spirit during church services. Acculturation to African music had made the Mass into a spirit possession ceremony.[121] Jean Obame, a village chief at Donguila, snickered about the lack of a priest at the mission in 2004. "In the old days, we had the Latin mass," he said, "and now it is the Polish mass."[122] A Polish congregation now sends a priest to hold services from time to time, but Obame might have also been referring to Pope John Paul II.

The old man had reasons to lament. Donguila has endured rough times since independence. Once extensive fields now are covered by brush, and the rusted relics of machinery used for training carpenters and processing cocoa lie strewn about the mission grounds. The pull of the capital has led hundreds to abandon surrounding villages for Libreville, and neighbors even perform bwiti dances with the tacit acceptance of clergy near the church.[123] Local politicians such as Casimir Oye Mba rebuilt the church itself after it nearly collapsed. The patronage and dominance of Marcel Lefebvre's generation of colonial priests is a distant memory, but some older rural people wax nostalgic for the material aid and order they represented. Some elderly Gabonese are as taken with the representation of manly colonial missionaries in his promotion of traditionalism as Lefebvre himself was in his final years.

Marcel Lefebvre's missionary career, in its initial stages, did not distinguish him from most priests in interwar Gabon. The confidence engendered by

an expanding church and a resurgence of French Catholic influence intoxi-
cated a fair number of clergy in the 1920s and 1930s. After years of disap-
pointment for French priests, a Gabonese Catholic Church was thriving.
Foreign missions renewed faith in conservative French Catholicism. Maurice
Briault and others lionized the heroic priest battling evil and African superstitions. Yet other priests shed the trappings of interwar triumphalism
that Lefebvre displayed throughout his later traditionalist period. Bishop
Adam's endorsement of translating the liturgy into African languages set
the model for contemporary Gabonese Catholicism. The formation of a
traditionalist church in Libreville emerged not from African demand but,
rather, from Lefebvre's own will that his movement have a place in Gabon.
What happened?

First, Lefebvre was a member of the interwar Catholic revival that was
upended by World War II. Democratic tendencies within French Catholicism
flourished in the postwar period, from the worker-priest movement to the
espousal of Vatican II. Many French missionaries in Africa after 1945 welcomed the current of reform that had begun to flow after World War I. Not
Lefebvre. His initial experiences in Gabon allowed him to form a model
of traditionalism that—combined with his earlier training at the French
seminary in Rome, his opposition to independence and socialism as archbishop of Dakar, and finally his woes in managing the Holy Ghost Fathers
as superior general in the 1960s—brought him to the point of commenc-
ing his own project of renewing pre–Vatican II teachings. Colonial settings
were fertile ground for inspiring ideas of French Catholic renewal, whether
on the left or the right.

Lefebvre's confidence in traditionalism stemmed in part from his work in
colonial Gabon, but it would be a mistake to consign his movement as simply a product of hidebound missionaries in Africa cut off from changes in
metropolitan France. French Holy Ghost priests in Gabon often proved more
interested in adapting to the winds of change in the church than Lefebvre in
Senegal or in Europe. Some of Lefebvre's former colleagues endorsed African
nationalism rather than French imperialism in the 1950s, just as Lefebvre produced a Catholic traditionalist international identity that considered Gabon
as much a part of Christendom as his homeland itself. Lefebvre forsook his
colonial origins to imagine a worldwide struggle between liberalism and
tradition in which central African Catholics set the trends that metropolitan

French Catholics should follow. Few observers of reactionary Catholicism in Europe, or the United States for that matter, have considered how imperial visions of Christian crusades in Africa could come back home to roost. The interwar dream of rebuilding a greater Catholic France had, after the turbulent 1960s, invaded France itself. The rise of traditionalism thus must be placed in a colonial and international context. If this colonial background is ignored, one might miss how Lefebvre's vision came to be in the first place.

Notes

I would like to thank the following people, who provided comments and assistance with this essay: the organizers and participants of the conference held in memory of William Cohen at Indiana University in December 2003, where a draft of this essay was presented, Sarah Curtis, Kevin Callahan, Owen White, J. P. Daughton, Father Gérard Morel, Congregation of the Holy Ghost Fathers, Spiritans (cssp), the library staff of Cabrini College, Brother François at the Donguila mission, Meyo M'Obiang Moise, and Jean Obame.

1. William Dinges, In Defense of Truth and Tradition: Catholic Traditionalism in America (South Bend IN: University of Notre Dame Press, 1986); Mary Jo Weaver and R. Scott Appleby, eds., Being Right: Conservative Catholics in America (Bloomington: Indiana University Press, 1996); Michael Cuneo, The Smoke of Satan: Conservative and Traditionalist Dissent in Contemporary American Catholicism (Baltimore: Johns Hopkins University Press, 1997).
2. Marcel Lefebvre, "The Sermon of His Grace the Most Reverend Archbishop Marcel Lefebvre, 23 September 1979," Angelus 2, no. 12 (1979), www.sspx.org/SSPX_FAQs/appendix_iv_sermon.htm.
3. Philip Jenkins, The Next Christendom: The Rise of Global Christianity (New York: Oxford University Press, 2002).
4. Marcel Lefebvre, Open Letter to Confused Catholics, trans. Michael Crowdy (Kansas City: Angelus Press, 1986), 8.
5. Barbara Kingsolver, The Poisonwood Bible (New York: HarperCollins, 1998).
6. Philip Nord, "Catholic Culture in Interwar France," French Politics, Culture, and Society 21, no. 3 (2003): 1.
7. Nord, "Catholic Culture," 5.
8. W. D. Halls, Politics, Society and Christianity in Vichy France (New York: Berg, 1995).
9. J. P. Daughton, An Empire Divided: Religion, Republicanism, and the Making of French Colonialism, 1880–1914 (New York: Oxford University Press, 2006). Owen White and Troy Feay, among others, are conducting research on missionaries and colonialism as well.

10. Here I agree with Frederick Cooper and Ann Laura Stoler's call for examining the complicated interactions between metropole and empire in a single analytic field. Frederick Cooper and Ann Laura Stoler, "Between Metropole and Colony: Rethinking a Research Agenda," in *Tensions of Empire: Colonial Cultures in a Bourgeois World*, ed. Frederick Cooper and Ann Laura Stoler (Berkeley: University of California Press, 1997), 1.

11. Bernard Tissier de Mallerais, *Marcel Lefebvre* (Paris: Clovis, 2002), 100.

12. Raymond Girod, *Couleurs d'aventure africaine: une vie missionnaire* (Geneva: Éditions à la Carte, 2001), 36–37; Marcel Lefebvre, *The Little Story of My Long Life* (Browerville MN: Sisters of the Society of St. Pius X, 2002), 45.

13. Tissier de Mallerais, *Marcel Lefebvre*, 109.

14. Henry J. Koren, *To the Ends of the Earth: A General History of the Congregation of the Holy Ghost* (Pittsburgh: Duquesne University Press, 1983), 414–15.

15. Bengt Sundkler and Christopher Steed, *A History of the Church in Africa* (Cambridge: Cambridge University Press, 2000), 626–29, 719–21, 755–57, 828–31; Adrian Hastings, *The Church in Africa, 1450–1950* (Oxford: Clarendon Press, 1994), 559–67.

16. General works on colonial Gabon after 1900 include Catherine Coquery-Vidrovitch, *Le Congo au temps des grandes compagnies concessionaires, 1898–1930* (Paris: Mouton, 1972); Anges François Ratanga-Atoz, "Les Résistances Gabonaises à l'impérialisme, 1870–1914" (PhD diss., Université de Paris, 1973); Ralph Austen and Rita Headrick, "Equatorial Africa under Colonial Rule," in *History of Central Africa*, ed. David Birmingham and Phyllis Martin (New York: Longman, 1983), 2:27–94; John Cinnamon, "The Long March of the Fang: Anthropology and History in Equatorial Africa" (PhD diss., Yale University, 1998); Christopher Gray, *Colonial Rule and Crisis in Equatorial Africa: Southern Gabon ca. 1850–1940* (Rochester: University of Rochester Press, 2002); Michael Reed and James Barnes, eds., *Culture, Ecology, and Politics in Gabon's Rainforest* (Lewiston NY: Edwin Mellen, 2003).

17. The following discussion on the war, the famine, and the timber industry is drawn from Gilles Sautter, *De l'Atlantique au fleuve Congo* (Paris: Plon, 1966), 2:761–74, 2:852–64; Louis de Dravo, "L'Exploitation forestière du Gabon, 1896–1930" (Mémoire de Maîtrise, Université de Reims, 1979); Christopher Gray and François Ngolet, "Lambaréné, Okoumé, and the Transformation of Labor along the Middle Ogooué (Gabon) 1870–1945," *Journal of African History* 40 (1999): 87–107; Gray, *Colonial Rule*.

18. The best source on early Catholicism in Gabon remains David Gardinier, "The Beginning of French Catholic Evangelization in Gabon and African Responses," *Proceedings of the French Colonial Historical Society* 2 (1978): 49–74.

19. Interview, Zimbé Michel, Lalala, Libreville, Gabon, January 5, 2000; interview, Ndoutoume Nkobe Justin, Kango, Gabon, August 6, 2004.

20. Interview, Meyo M'Obiang Moise, Lalala à Gauche, Libreville, Gabon, August 18, 2004.

21. Wolfgang Schivelbusch, *The Culture of Defeat: On National Trauma, Mourning, and Recovery* (New York: Henry Holt, 2003).

22. American and French Protestants also noted dramatic gains in the 1930s, although historians have yet to examine seriously this outburst of fervor. See André Perrier, *Gabon: un réveil religieux, 1935–1937* (Paris: Harmattan, 1988); David Thompson, *Beyond the Mist: The Story of Donald and Dorothy Fairley* (Camp Hill PA: Christian Publications, 1998).

23. James Fernandez, *Bwiti: An Ethnography of the Religious Imagination in Africa* (Princeton NJ: Princeton University Press, 1982); Stanislaw Swiderski, *La Religion Bouiti*, 5 vols. (Ottawa: Legas, 1989); René Bureau, *Bokaye! essai sur le Bwiti Fang du Gabon* (Paris: Harmattan, 1996); André Mary, *Le Defi du syncretisme: le travail symbolique de la religion d'Eboga (Gabon)* (Paris: EHESS, 1999).

24. Jeremy Rich, "Troubles at the Office: Clerks, State Authority, and Social Conflict in Gabon, 1920–1945," *Canadian Journal of African Studies* 35, no. 1 (2004): 58–87.

25. Bishop Louis Martrou to Archbishop, April 4, 1921, Boîte 4J1.7a, Lettres 1921–24, Lettres Gabon 1921–47, Archives of the Congregation of the Holy Ghost Fathers, Chevilly-Larue, France (hereafter cited as ACSE).

26. On Mba, see Florence Bernault, *Démocraties ambiguës en Afrique Centrale: Congo-Brazzaville et Gabon, 1945–1965* (Paris: Karthala, 1996), 131–46.

27. Interview, Ndong Felicien, Atong Abé, Libreville, February 27, 2000; interview, Jean Ondo, km 12, Libreville, Gabon, March 1, 2000; Tissier de Mallerais, *Marcel Lefebvre*, 114–18.

28. Lefebvre, *Little Story*, 48.

29. Maurice Briault, *Sur les pistes de l'AEF* (Paris: Alsatia, 1945), 142–50.

30. Maria Rohrer and Gérard Morel, *Sur la route de la sainteté: Mère Cécilia* (Libreville: Éditions du Bosquet, 1994), 84.

31. Priests sheltered women seeking to escape polygamous marriages. Affaire Nkoé, March 3, 1938, Registre 104, Registres, Deuxième Tribunal Indigène de la Commune de Libreville, ANG.

32. Tissier de Mallerais, *Marcel Lefebvre*, 135–36. Fang marriage practices in the early twentieth century required men to exchange a substantial amount of money and goods with the wife's family. These multiple payments, or bride-price, bedeviled missionaries throughout colonial and postcolonial Africa.

33. Bishop Adam to Archbishop, September 6, 1893, Boîte 4J1.3b, Correspondance 1891–1920, ACSE.

34. Tissier de Mallerais, *Marcel Lefebvre*, 142–43.

35. Interview, Soeur Benedicta, Donguila, Gabon, March 11, 2000.

36. "Journal de la Mission 1928–1940," entry for April 28, 1929, Donguila Archives, Donguila, Gabon.

37. André Raponda Walker, *Souvenirs d'un nonagénaire* (Paris: Classiques Africaines, 1993); Rohrer and Morel, *Sur la route de la sainteté*.

38. Lefebvre, "Sermon."

39. "Journal de voyage: voyage en Rembwé," entries for September 12–20, 1932, Donguila Archives; "Journal de voyage: voyage en Rogolie," entries for September 11–25, 1944, Donguila Archives; "Journal de Voyage: voyage à Kango," entries for November 5–29, 1945, Donguila Archives.

40. Tissier de Mallerais, *Marcel Lefebvre*, 121–24.

41. "Mission de Saint Hilaire de Franceville," *Bulletin de la Congrégation du Saint Esprit* 32 (1925–26): 786.

42. Maurice Briault, *Une soeur missionnaire: la Soeur Saint-Charles* (Paris: Téqui, 1914); Maurice Briault, *Sous le zéro équatoriale* (Paris: Bloud et Gay, 1927); Maurice Briault, *Dans le fôret du Gabon* (Paris: Bernard Grasset, 1930); Maurice Briault, *Récits sur le verandah* (Paris: Bloud et Gay, 1939); Maurice Briault, *Les sauvages d'Afrique* (Paris: Payot, 1943); Maurice Briault, *Sur les pistes de l'AEF* (Paris: Éditions Alsatia, 1945).

43. André Raponda Walker, a Gabonese priest who wrote scores of publications, including histories and dictionaries, for the Catholic mission in Gabon between 1910 and 1965, regularly quoted Briault. Copies of Briault's works were kept at mission stations such as Donguila and Libreville, where they still can be found today. During my visits to Donguila in 2000 and 2004 Briault's books clearly had been brought to the mission before 1950.

44. Sundkler and Steed, *History of the Church*, 629.

45. Briault would occasionally tour Gabonese missions, often in the company of Bishop Tardy. Briault, *Sur les pistes*, 130–33.

46. The information on Barreau in this paragraph and the one that follows is drawn from Briault, *Sur les pistes*, 239–85.

47. Briault, *Sur les pistes*, 272–73.

48. Briault, *Sur les pistes*, 271–72.

49. Nord, "Catholic Culture," 5.

50. Briault, *Sur les pistes*, 271–72.

51. John Hellman, *The Knight-Monks of Vichy France: Uriage, 1940–1945* (Montreal: McGill-Queen's University Press, 1993).

52. Briault, *Sur les pistes*, 260–70.

53. Briault, *Sur les pistes*, 41–44.

54. Briault, *Les sauvages*, 16.

55. Briault, *Sur les pistes*, 98.

56. Briault, *Sur les pistes*, 133.

57. Excerpted from Rohrer and Morel, *Sur la route de la sainteté*, 125.

58. Briault, *Dans la forêt*, 99–106.

59. Briault, *Sous les zéro*, 143–54.

60. The following information on Dahin is a summary of the discussion in Marcel Sauvage, *Secrets de l'Afrique noire* (Paris: Denoel, 1937), 94–114.

61. Sauvage, *Secrets*, 100.

62. Information and quotations in this paragraph are drawn from Sauvage, *Secrets*, 106–9.

63. Varied attitudes toward officials were common among missionaries in nearby Moyen Congo (Congo-Brazzaville). See Phyllis Martin, "Celebrating the Ordinary: Church, Empire, and Gender in the Life of Mère Marie-Michelle Dédié (Senegal, Congo, 1882–1931)," *Gender and History* 16, no. 2 (2004): 297.

64. Bishop Louis Martrou, n.d. [1919], Boîte 4J1.6a, Dossier Autorités civils 1919, Divers Gabon 1920–49, ACSE; Martrou to Archbishop, April 28, 1923, Boîte 4J1.7a, Martrou Lettres 1921–24, Lettres 1921–24, Lettres Gabon 1921–47, ACSE.

65. Louis Tardy to Maurice Briault, March 14, 1926, Boîte 4J1.6a, Dossier Tardy, Divers Gabon 1920–49, ACSE.

66. Father Mesange to Archbishop, September 15, 1925, Boîte 4J1.7a, Lettres 1925–27, Lettres Gabon 1921–47, ACSE.

67. Briault, *Sur les pistes*, 139–50.

68. Gov. Gen. Raphael Antonetti to Lt. Gov. Gabon, October 31, 1928, 3B641, Correspondance du Gouverneur Général de l'Afrique Équatoriale Française avec le Lt. Gouverneur du Gabon, October 1928, ANSOM.

69. "Mission de Saint Francis Xavier de Lambaréné," *Bulletin de la Congrégation de Saint Esprit* 32 (1925–26): 771.

70. "Journal de la Communauté 1928–1932," entries for April 19–20, 1929, Donguila Archives.

71. "Journal de la Communauté 1922–1940," entry for July 1, 1922, Donguila Archives.

72. Jean Bénilan, *Coup de bambou 1940* (Paris: Office Colonial d'Édition, 1947), 54.

73. Charles de Gaulle was one of the leaders of the Free French movement that wished to continue fighting the Axis powers, while Henri-Philippe Pétain, a famed general during World War I, formed a government that collaborated with the Nazi occupation.

74. Éboué was one of the first administrators to rally to de Gaulle against Vichy and the Germans in 1940 and was celebrated as a hero in the war against fascism. Brian Wienstein, *Éboué* (New York: Oxford University Press, 1972).

75. René Labat, *Le Gabon devant le gaullisme* (Bordeaux: Delmas, 1941), 32.

76. Material from the following paragraph is taken from Louis Tardy, "Extrait de l'allucation de 30 septembre 1940," Tardy papers, Archdiocese of Libreville, Libreville, Gabon (hereafter cited as TP).

77. Eric Jennings, *Vichy in the Tropics: Pétain's National Revolution in Madagascar, Guadeloupe, and Indochina, 1940–1944* (Stanford: Stanford University Press, 2002), 95–97.

78. In the unorganized Tardy papers the bishop's notes on at least ten articles from French periodicals in 1940 survive.

79. General Tetu to Tardy, November 6, 1940, TP.

80. Captain of *Bougainville* to Tardy, November 5, 1940, TP.
81. Telegram, Governor-General of French West Africa Boisson to Tardy, October 13, 1940, TP.
82. Tissier de Mallerais, *Marcel Lefebvre*, 130.
83. Pierre Mantreaux to Father Fauret, November 16, 1940, TP.
84. Bishop Tardy, "Circulaire 34," March 17, 1941, TP.
85. Tardy to High Commissioner of Free French Africa, March 16, 1941, TP.
86. Notes of Pétain speech, August 12, 1941, TP.
87. "Comité de la France Combattante, Libreville," n.d. [1943], TP.
88. Girod, *Couleurs*, 31.
89. Lefebvre, *Little Story*, 53.
90. Journal of the Mission, entry for November 1940, Donguila Archives. The author does not identify himself by name, but the handwriting appears to match Lefebvre's.
91. Girod, *Couleurs*, 37.
92. Raponda Walker, *Souvenirs*, 53.
93. Guy Pannier, *L'Église de Pointe-Noire: évolution des communautés chrétiennes de 1947 à 1975* (Paris: Kathala, 1999), esp. 39–54, 104.
94. Girod, *Couleurs*, 35–37.
95. On Le Floch, see Tissier de Mallerais, *Marcel Lefebvre*, 39–80.
96. Desmond O'Grady, "A Tale of Two Prelates," *Commonweal*, January 31, 1997, 20–24.
97. Sundkler and Steed, *History of the Church*, 1018.
98. Marcel Lefebvre, *They Have Uncrowned Him: From Liberalism to Apostasy; The Conciliar Tragedy* (Kansas City MO: Angelus Press, 1988), 177.
99. Lefebvre, *They Have Uncrowned Him*, 179.
100. Lefebvre, *Open Letter*, 50–56.
101. Lefebvre, *Open Letter*, 79–80.
102. Lefebvre, *Open Letter*, 74; Marcel Lefebvre, *Against the Heresies* (Kansas City MO: Angelus Press, 1997), 218–19.
103. Lefebvre, *Little Story*, 50–51.
104. Tissier de Mallerais, *Marcel Lefebvre*, 135–36.
105. Lefebvre, *Against the Heresies*, 92–94.
106. Lefebvre, *Against the Heresies*, 92–93.
107. As detailed in Marcel Lefebvre, *Religious Liberty Questioned*, trans. Jaime Pazat de Lys (Kansas City MO: Angelus Press, 2002), 55–64.
108. Lefebvre, *Open Letter*, 29.
109. Lefebvre, "Sermon."
110. Lefebvre, *Against the Heresies*, 289.
111. Lefebvre, "Sermon."

112. Lefebvre, "Sermon."
113. "Journal de Mission 1942–1946," entry for April 27, 1943, Donguila Archives.
114. Interview, Jean Obame, village chief of Donguila, Donguila, Gabon, July 22, 2004.
115. Tissier de Mallerais, *Marcel Lefebvre*, 131–47.
116. Lefebvre, *They Have Uncrowned Him*, 226.
117. Lefebvre, "Sermon."
118. "Archbishop Honored by Africa," *Angelus*, March 1985, www.angelusonline.org.
119. On Lambaréné, see Tissier de Mallerais, *Marcel Lefebvre*, 147. The author has attended a mass at the Libreville mission.
120. "An Interview with Fr. Patrick Groche, Superior of Gabon," *Angelus*, February 2005, www.angelusonline.org.
121. Government of Gabon, *Témoinages de notre temps: les trésors de la mémoire* (Geneva: SIED, 1988), 120–21.
122. Interview, Jean Obame, Donguila, July 22, 2004.
123. A *bwiti* dance took place next door to the church in March 2000.

STEPHEN L. HARP

3

Marketing in the Metropole
Colonial Rubber Plantations and
French Consumerism in the Early
Twentieth Century

Stephen L. Harp focuses on the divergence between the realities of rubber production—notably the establishment of exploitative rubber plantations in "primitive" Indochina—and the "modern" tourist identities propagated by Michelin advertising and tour guides in the metropole. In responding to changes in the world rubber commodity market and France's economic weakness after the devastation of World War I, Michelin promoted a vibrant tourist culture in which wealthy French consumers could experience a sense of Frenchness by utilizing their leisure time to learn about their homeland's splendid regional culture and attractions. At the same time, such consumers were kept from knowing about the conditions in Michelin rubber plantations, which made the development of modern automobile tourism with regional guides covering the French provinces possible in the first place. In the case of Michelin, Harp argues that this willful forgetfulness depended on government officials, leaders of public opinion, journalists, and experts involved in world's fairs, not to mention consumers themselves. By examining rubber from the point of production to that of consumption, his essay demonstrates that historians cannot neatly separate the presumed periphery of the colonies from the presumed core of metropolitan France.

✧ ✧

In 1926 the Michelin tire company published a guide to Brittany, the company's first regional touring guide. A precursor of the oblong green guides, Michelin's new regional guide offered some background information and then traced various itineraries, allowing automobile tourists to find the noteworthy tourist sites by following the more picturesque routes. Similar guides soon covered much of the French countryside. Like the earlier red guide and Michelin's other tourist initiatives, the regional guides strongly encouraged well-heeled French to take their automobiles and see France, to taste regional gastronomy, to savor fine wines, and to appreciate how regional differences came together to make a richer national culture. A veritable master of advertising in the early twentieth century, Michelin sold a lifestyle of consumption to early tourists, not simply tires. Although interwar American advertisers normally get the credit for selling lifestyle rather than just products and supposedly set a trend ultimately followed by the Europeans, Michelin was well ahead of the curve. Michelin fashioned tourist identities while avoiding much mention of the dynamics of rubber production.

In 1926 Michelin also bought its first rubber plantation in the French colony of Cochinchina, part of southeastern French Indochina at the time and southern Vietnam today. Michelin soon purchased two additional planta- tions, in the process becoming not only a major landowner but also a major employer in Indochina. On the plantations Michelin intended to grow rub- ber for its metropolitan tire manufacturing factories. But whereas Michelin offered a tourist lifestyle to wealthy French in the metropole, in Indochina the company offered substandard living conditions, brutal labor conditions, and low wages. There seemed to have been almost two different worlds: one was the world of Western consumption, particularly for the rich; and one was the world of Indochinese production, undertaken by poor Vietnamese. Yet they were not two different worlds but, rather, two parts of a single global economic system (the term *globalization* may have been new to the 1990s, but the reality most certainly was not), one in which Western consumerism already relied heavily on cheap non-Western production.

A major blind spot of twentieth-century Western consumerism is at issue: how did twentieth-century consumers learn to ignore (in both the sense of not knowing and the sense of not really wanting to know) the condi- tions of production? In reality there was a close connection between French consumerism in the metropole, in this case the development of tourism in particular, and Euro-American exploitation of non-Western labor in the colonies. The link is a broad, global one: without large quantities of cheap rubber produced on plantations by non-European labor in Southeast Asia, pre–World War II automobile tourism would not have been possible. The big picture is that of the history of rubber, a commodity that is as revealing of international production and consumption as the histories of bananas, coffee, salt, and sugar.[1] Taking a cue from Arjun Appadurai's concept of the "social history of things," the history of rubber offers a case study of the development of modern Western consumerism.[2]

This essay focuses on Michelin for several reasons. First, Michelin was a leading world producer of tires in the early twentieth century. Second, by the late 1930s it was one of the three largest rubber plantation owners in French Indochina, thus a significant force in the production of rubber. Third, and more practically, because of several labor uprisings on Michelin plantations, we have a better paper trail for Michelin plantations than for other French, British, or Dutch ones. Finally, because Michelin's production and marketing are better known than those of its American or British competitors, study of the plantations can be better contextualized. Nevertheless, we have no reason to believe that Michelin was an outlier; rather, the company should be seen as a case study of the connection between Southeast Asian production and Western consumption more generally.

This is not the first effort to tie the development of French consumer culture to the colonies. In *Fast Cars, Clean Bodies* Kristin Ross has argued that the devastating loss of the colonies after World War II caused the French public to plunge into consumerism, almost as a sort of salve for wounded national pride.[3] Ross is right that there was a link between colonies and consumerism, but she has that connection reversed: French consumerism, like Euro-American consumerism generally, was made possible by the exploitation of people and resources in the non-Western world. Even after the loss of colonies in the wake of World War II, the global economic structure remained dominated by Americans and Europeans; there is an important continuity between the imperial and postimperial eras. Consumerism may appear to be a flight from this geopolitical and geoeconomic reality, while in fact it rests solidly on that reality. Moreover, the discursive strategies of "forgetting" non-Western production were well in place before World War II. This essay illustrates how Western consumers learned to avoid the dynamics of production in the headlong rush to collective consumption—that is, how consumers in the center learned to know what not to know about the periphery.

Automobilism and Identity in Modern France

Michelin, the first company to produce a pneumatic tire for the automobile in 1895, led world tire production until World War I. Although during the war Michelin lost market share to the Americans, the company continued to dominate the French market in the interwar years.[4] Until after World War II, the primary problem for Michelin was that the automobile remained a luxury of the upper, and then the middle, class. Unlike in the United States, where Ford's Model T quickly led to a mass rural market for tires, demand for tires in France had to be created and fostered.

As a result, well before World War I Michelin launched a series of initiatives to convince wealthy Frenchmen that they should buy automobiles and thus the expensive tires on which they rode. Advertising, particularly in the form of posters, newspaper ads, and racing sponsorship, generally reaffirmed the rich, white, and male identities of tire purchasers.[5] The company focused particular attention on sponsoring automobile tourism by rich Frenchmen. Just before the war, it led a drive to institute road signs and began to offer touring maps. And the small, gratis red guide to garages and hotels, launched in 1900 to show motorists where to buy Michelin tires (given their fragility and an average longevity of no more than a couple thousand miles in the first decade of the twentieth century, early tires were a constant preoccupation) and where to sleep, gradually metamorphosed into a guide for hotels and restaurants, with tire dealers taking a secondary role.

In the interwar years Michelin established a veritable tourist network in France. The red guide named the appropriate hotels and restaurants for the well-heeled tourist, which one could find by using Michelin maps that covered the entire French countryside. In the early 1930s the red guide ranked restaurants across France at a time when regional cuisine was all the rage, as (mostly Parisian) automobile tourists drove to the provinces to find the emerging regional specialties that have since become seemingly immutable "traditional" culinary treats.[6] The regional guidebooks to tourist destinations further complemented this network. The guides offered itineraries, much like the AAA's route books in the United States, which listed the precise turns, road markings, and sights between various cities and towns.

Even after a close examination of the maps, or guides, be they regional or red, and other forms of advertising, one would never guess that Michelin owned rubber plantations in Indochina. Michelin did a great deal to define French identity, mostly through defining tourism, in the twentieth century. But the world of automobile consumption described by the company never made reference to the realities of the world labor market that made such consumption possible in the first place. Instead, the company could rely on an emerging cultural divide between production and consumption, one that allowed companies to focus on the lifestyle their products offered without reference to the production that made consumption possible.[7]

Colonial Plantations in the Global Context

Michelin rubber plantations were part of a much longer-term development of the global rubber industry and Western consumption. In the nineteenth century France, like other European countries, had imported wild rubber from Brazil, the Congo "Free State," and the French Congo. Although Leopold II's systems of exploitation in the Congo—directly resulting from the rapid development of the Euro-American bicycle and automobile tire markets— were the best-known abuses at the turn of the century, callous exploitation of indigenous labor also existed in both Brazil and the French Congo.[8] In short, in this age of imperialism a pattern of non-Western exploitation and Western consumerism was not new.

British traders and scientists recognized very well the superior qualities of the latex from Brazilian hevea trees for use in the production of rubber as well as the virtual monopoly of the rubber trade Brazilians enjoyed until the 1890s. Thus, as part of the great transplantation of flora sponsored by European science in the nineteenth century, Henry Wickham successfully took rubber seeds from Brazil to Kew and thence to Ceylon and Singapore. By the first decade of the twentieth century, as rubber prices climbed quickly with the advent of the automobile, planters who had planted hevea trees in South and Southeast Asia found themselves sitting on gold mines. Soon plantations grew in size and quantity across Malaya and increasingly the Dutch East Indies as well.[9]

The first rubber plantation in French Indochina did not appear until 1904.[10] And while the cultivated area grew quickly, rubber planting remained here as elsewhere risky business because it took six years from the planting of a seedling until the first year of production, in addition to the time it took to clear the land for the plantation. It required a good ten years before hevea trees reached peak production levels. When rubber prices were high, up to 1919, capacity quickly rose. But then oversupply caused prices to crash in the early 1920s. In 1922 the British, who controlled about two-thirds of world rubber production, imposed the Stevenson Restriction Scheme. The scheme managed to bolster the price of rubber, which peaked in the mid-1920s.[11]

Once British rubber restriction caused rubber prices to rise, and simultaneously sent the message that economic autarky might be the best means of survival, other imperial powers responded by establishing their own plantations. In the Dutch East Indies both European plantations and indigenous smallholdings rapidly expanded their acreage. The United States, by far the largest consumer of rubber, absorbing about two-thirds of the world's supply, responded by having the Bureau of Foreign and Domestic Commerce investigate where the United States might establish its own plantations.[12] The U.S. Congress appropriated millions of dollars for the purpose. The U.S. State Department supported Harvey Firestone in his negotiation of a concession of one million acres from the Liberian government.[13] In this context French investors looked to Indochina, where the growing conditions had been found to rival any rubber-growing areas of the Malay Peninsula or of Sumatra.

There was a veritable rubber boom in French Indochina after 1910 that peaked in the late 1920s, as companies attempted to create plantations as quickly as possible. In 1926 there were 367 plantations in French Indochina comprising 166,818 hectares and roughly 13.5 million hevea trees planted. By 1931 there were 559 plantations, covering 311,446 hectares, of which 126,653 had already been planted with nearly 29 million hevea trees. But fewer than 9 million trees were old enough to be in production, a reminder of how recent the plantings were.[14] To an even greater extent than in British or Dutch possessions, ownership was heavily concentrated in the hands of a small number of Europeans. Plantations with two hundred or more hectares produced virtually all of the rubber in Indochina.[15] The three largest plantation owners—Société des Terres Rouges, Société Indochinoise des Plantations de Hévéas, and Michelin—held over 50 percent of land planted with rubber trees.[16] By the 1930s rubber was a very important agricultural commodity in Indochina, second only to rice.

In addition to significant state subsidies in the early 1920s and the elimination of restrictions on the size of concessions granted in the late 1920s,[17] European plantation owners received state support in the movement of labor from the heavily populated province of Tonkin, what is today northern Vietnam, to the lightly populated "jungle" of northern Cochinchina

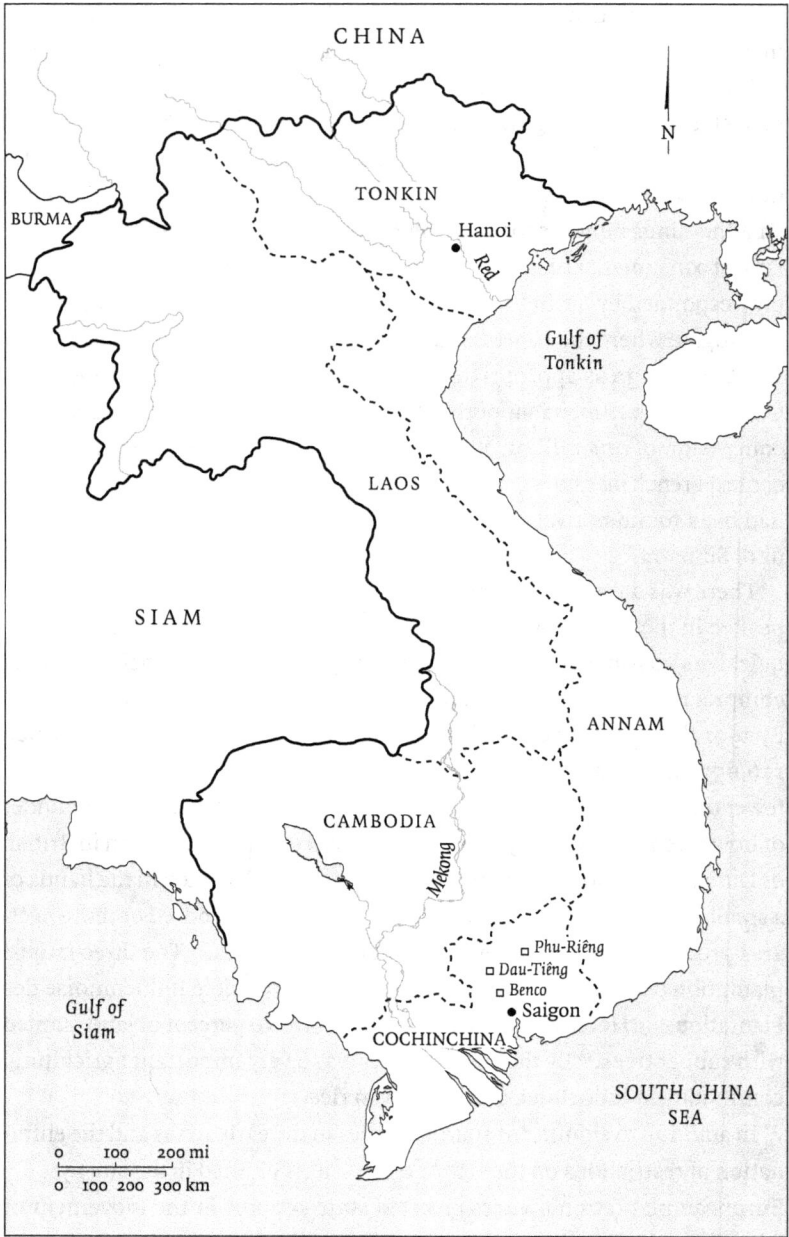

Map 3.1. French Indochina

and eastern Cambodia. In an era before earthmoving equipment the arduous clearing of land and then the actual planting of rubber trees required significant manual labor. Until the 1920s local (Viet, from Cochinchina) workers did most of the plantation labor, but better pay and much better working conditions in Saigon offered more attractive employment options. When French planters could not recruit coolies from China, Java, or India, they focused on the northern province of Tonkin, where the population was both numerous and destitute. In 1922, 3,242 coolies from Tonkin and Annam (central Vietnam today) had been engaged by contract to work on rubber plantations. Their number climbed to 29,168 in 1926 and 41,750 in 1928.[18]

Contract laborers lived a life akin to indentured servitude, having signed contracts in which rules of work and of living were determined by the employer. In essence they signed away their right to reject harsh working conditions for the three-year term. Having been recruited with promises of high wages, generous benefits, and good working conditions until they actually signed the contract, these laborers had little recourse once they arrived on plantations and learned that their promised ten-hour days often did not include an hour-long morning reveille, up to one and a half hours' walk from barracks to the workplace, or the return trip.[19] They learned that neither numerous (unpaid) holidays nor (unpaid) sick days counted toward the three years, thus extending terms to almost four years. Potable water was in short supply. Promised healthy conditions, coolies instead arrived in a jungle that quickly became infested with malaria during the initial clearing. At Michelin's Phu-Rîeng plantation 17 percent of coolies died in 1928, mostly from malaria. Given that coolies were adult men in their prime, this rate of mortality is astounding.[20]

Like the British and Dutch plantations taken as models for the French, Indochinese rubber plantations had an elaborate hierarchy reflecting perceived racial and ethnic differences. Europeans, or "whites," were at the top, usually dressed in white, and they gave orders to have work done but did very little manual labor.[21] Under the manager was an array of European assistants. Below assistants were "native" overseers (surveillants and caïs, the French equivalent of British/Indian kanganis), who directly supervised the coolies' work, kept order, and administered any beatings to coolies who did the tapping and weeding of hevea trees. On plantations, and frequently even in government reports, coolies were referred to by their assigned number on the plantation, not their names. They were generally called "coolies" (even in French) or "labor" (*main d'oeuvre*), not "workers" (*ouvriers*) or "personnel," a term usually reserved for European employees but occasionally used for indigenous overseers.[22]

From the beginning, and again like their British and Dutch counterparts, French plantations relied on the direct and daily threat of violence to get coolies to plant the trees, eliminate the stubborn lalang (cogongrass), tap the trees, gather the latex, produce the smoked or crepe sheets of rubber needed for shipping, and perform every other plantation function. Coolies attempting to escape were fined, beaten, and locked up. Tardy coolies were fined and beaten. And of course, any coolies who did not follow orders were beaten, sometimes with fists, sometimes with rattan canes or other objects.[23]

Michelin Plantations

In 1926, as rubber prices were reaching their interwar peaks, Michelin acquired Benco, its plantation near Saigon. The plantation had just 150 hectares, of which 110 had already been planted in heveas by 1931. By 1927 Michelin had established two more plantations on land granted in concessions. Dau-Tiêng, in the province of Thudaumot, consisted of 8,700 hectares, of which 7,500 had been planted by 1931. The third, Phu-Riêng, was in the province of Bienhoa and consisted of 5,500 hectares, of which 1,800 were planted in heveas by 1931. By 1931 Michelin employed more than four thousand coolies on its various plantations, most of whom were three-year contract laborers hauled in from Tonkin.[24]

Michelin plantations were disproportionately well represented in government reports that made their way to Paris. In part this may have resulted from the fact that the Ministry of the Colonies was in direct communication with Michelin headquarters in Clermont-Ferrand about the plantations (given this paper trail, one should not doubt that Michelin management in the hexagon knew very well what was happening on its distant Indochinese plantations). Equally important, Michelin plantations had a disproportionately large number of coolie revolts, leading to better documentary evidence from the plantations, via Saigon, then on to Paris. French preoccupations with Communists in Indochina meant that each revolt, from its causes to its denouement, was carefully analyzed for the national government. Michelin or other planters' misdeeds, government officials feared, might inadvertently jeopardize the whole imperial project. Michelin plantations thus drew administrators' attention on a very regular basis in the late 1920s and 1930s. A chronological account of the various incidents reveals the profound gap between actual coolie lives on Michelin plantations and the lifestyles Michelin promised automobilists in the metropole.

In September 1927, during the initial clearing of the plantation of Phu-Riêng, as malaria killed workers in droves, coolies physically attacked and killed a European named Monteil and then went after the director and the European assistants generally until they were stopped by European arms. As was the case in other incidents, the government showed no mercy for the coolies: one was condemned to death, two to forced labor for life, and three to forced labor for twenty years (sixteen others were acquitted). Governor-General Varenne (the highest-ranking government official in Indochina) noted, however, that this incident confirmed the need to regulate the employment of manual labor as well as the need for the newly formed Labor Inspectorate (Inspection du Travail). The Labor Inspectorate, by regulating recruitment and employment of contractual labor, could reduce abuses that threatened to damage the long-term control of the colony.[25]

In February 1930 at least three hundred coolies at Phu Riêng stopped working in order to attend the burial of a fellow worker. By the end of the day at least 1,300 coolies were demanding an eight-hour workday, the removal of two assistants known for their brutality, and the freeing of an overseer accused of theft by the plantation.[26] Leaders were arrested. Michelin blamed the incident on Communist agitators and demanded that additional police be assigned to the area.[27] Colonial officials were less sure; by August 1930 the governor-general noted that Michelin had since then replaced the director of the plantation as well as his assistants and that there had been no further incident, in essence denying that the work stoppage was Communist in inspiration.[28] Moreover, Michelin was reported to have instituted an eight-hour day, appearing to legitimate the fairness of coolies' original demands.[29]

In the early 1930s economic crisis hit the rubber industry particularly hard. Declining demand for new cars and even for replacement tires caused the price of rubber to fall below the price of production. In Malaya and Indonesia planters stopped rigorous weeding and planting new trees, reduced production, sometimes halting it altogether, and sent many Javanese, Chinese, and Indian coolies back to their native countries. In Indochina some coolies from Tonkin were also sent back, but because French plantations received hefty governmental subsidies that their British and Dutch counterparts did not receive,[30] few planters reduced production significantly. Nevertheless, French planters faced pricing pressures, and with the value of rubber dropping, they looked for ways to cut their costs.

In this context coolies working for Michelin once again found cause to protest unfair treatment; the incident reveals much about the lopsided nature of their work contracts. In May 1932 the important French planters' association the Union des Planteurs de Caoutchouc en Indochine notified the government that it wished to reduce coolie wages from forty cents to thirty cents for a male coolie, thirty cents to twenty-three cents for a female coolie (the union worked with the government to avoid competing wage rates). The government agreed that contract renewals and new contracts would be for a lower wage rate than existing contracts, which would allow French plantations to produce at the same cost as British and Dutch plantations.[31] In December 1932 Michelin, which remained aloof from the organization, reduced coolie wages across the board and cut rice rations, even issuing a poster claiming that the government required the wage cut. At Dau-Tiêng approximately one thousand coolies decided to take their grievance (of course on foot) to the local administrator at Thudaumot, but they were stopped at a guard post around midnight. Spooked and given no warning by plantation management that coolies were on the march, the guard quickly fired into the air to disperse the crowd and then fired on the crowd, killing four coolies and wounding several others. According to French government reports, the coolies were neither armed nor aggressive; the guards had merely lost their "sang-froid."[32]

The government placed most of the blame on the Michelin plantation for having undertaken wage cuts in violation of existing contracts (though there is no evidence that either Michelin or guard members were prosecuted). Labor Inspector Beneyton had been summoned by Michelin to Dau-Tiêng to approve the cuts two days before the announcement and ensuing uprising, and he had clearly told Michelin management that the government only supported wage cuts for renewals and new contracts. Yet more disturbing, the director of the Michelin plantation, M. Planchon, later tried to intimidate Beneyton by letting him know that he "could count on all of the support of Michelin, powerful enough in France to have him named governor of Cochinchina," letting it be understood that Beneyton should avoid being critical of the plantation.[33] Similarly, Planchon told work inspector J.-P. Rougni that the "administration should not forget the power of Michelin" or the political and social hierarchy more generally: "Administrators [and] inspectors have the governor as their boss. The governor has the governor general above him, and above the governor general is Michelin et Cie in Paris. . . . Remember that Michelin can ruin a functionary, just as it can advance those it is happy with."[34] Given the pressure that the plantation did not hesitate to place on French bureaucrats, we should have little doubt about the director's dealings with coolies who might dare to protest their working conditions. The governor-general, in disbelief that Michelin in France would support such suggestions, urged the minister of colonies to approach Michelin management. There is no archival record of their exchange, but it is noteworthy that Planchon and his staff remained in place at Dau-Tiêng for several more years.[35]

Incidents of coolies' mistreatment continued through the 1930s. In October 1936 a coolie identified as "folio 14,436 du village 6" appeared late for reveille with his head bleeding from a small wound approximately one centimeter long. Passing the house of the overseer Thanh, Thanh had hit him in the head. The coolie claimed the blow was with a rattan cane, while Thanh said it was only his fist. Fellow coolies threw down their buckets (for the latex) and refused to go to work, though the assistant persuaded them ultimately to work. At the end of the day, however, 130 tappers set off marching for the director's (Planchon's) office, some six kilometers away. Planchon was away, and to placate the coolies the assistant promised that Thanh would no longer accompany coolies to work. The next day, after Thanh had disappeared, the coolies demanded that another overseer known for his brutality be dismissed. The work inspector found little evidence of brutality during the incident. Only "folio 13,988" (thus a different coolie than the original folio 14,436) said he had received blows with a rattan cane. "Folios 13,985, 13,988, 13,996, and 13,549," accused of leading the march, each received five days in prison. Although following the usual government policy of repressing coolies daring to demonstrate, in his confidential report the inspector nevertheless placed primary blame on the overseer, who had clearly been brutal during the eight months that he had been on the plantation. Moreover, he noted the fact that Michelin had consistently employed overseers of particularly "bad quality" and "inferior value."[36] The governor of Cochinchina Pagès (the highest-ranking government official in Cochinchina, who reported to the governor-general of Indochina) agreed completely and wrote Michelin's office in Saigon that "conflicts at Dau-Tiêng appeared to result, at least in part, from acts of brutality of which the overseers are guilty." Pagès urged much greater care in the selection and training of its indigenous overseers.[37]

In May 1937 approximately 300 coolies at Dau-Tiêng, eventually joined by about 1,200 more, claimed that their daily wage should be raised to the forty cents they charged was paid on other plantations and that their rice ration should be restored to the 1932 level of eight hundred grams. While the government noted that the planters' association (of which Michelin was not a member) had indeed raised salaries on April 1 to thirty-two cents for male workers, it was not true that plantations were paying forty cents. After two days of protest the workers were willing to accept truck transportation back to their villages (part of the usual practice for placating men who had walked miles to get there, sometimes after a day's work, and who were ravenously hungry).[38] Eight coolies ultimately received prison terms.[39] At the same time, however, officials communicated serious concerns about Michelin's treatment of workers. The workers' demands for higher pay for experienced coolies, a larger rice ration, sufficient potable water for drinking and washing, more equitable distribution of work, and more humane treatment all seemed reasonable. The governor-general went so far as to threaten that if the management of Dau-Tiêng failed to continue to respect the work contracts, he would not hesitate to suspend its recruitment of contract labor.[40] In his own confidential report the governor of Cochinchina was yet more critical. He noted that "there exists on Michelin plantations a 'planter's' spirit that is particularly appalling," that there was serious neglect of even a minimal infrastructure available for coolies' well-being, that "Michelin was the last to transform barracks [for coolie habitation] into individual houses, but even the latter were sordidly cheap." He accused both Planchon and his successor as having a "feudal spirit," of ignoring the real life of the coolies, and of relying on condescending French assistants. Above all, he claimed that the coolies at Dau-Tiêng always appeared to him "to be treated like prisoners, like poor wrecks" brutalized by the assistants.[41]

Even if Michelin plantations were, as Governor Pagès and his colleagues asserted, particularly brutal, it was in fact simply at the harsh end of a fundamentally brutal spectrum. Several protests and work stoppages broke out on other Indochinese plantations, and there is abundant evidence of brutality.[42] Moreover, while one British historian has claimed that the French planters were more brutal than British or Dutch counterparts, such an assertion has yet to be proved.[43] It does seem very possible, however, that Michelin plantations were indeed more abusive than most other French plantations, given French officials' own assessments.

Public Knowledge of the Colonies in the Metropole

The gap between the reality of the plantations and the lifestyles proffered by advertising was also made possible by the paucity of other public information about the plantations, resulting from the lack of concern about non-Europeans inherent in the racial hierarchies of the imperial era. Government officials and the mainstream press offered little more information than Michelin did. After all, the governmental sources cited earlier were intended for the consumption of fellow administrators; some were not accessible for historians or the general public until the 1990s.[44] The single printed Vietnamese memoir of coolie life on a Michelin plantation, Tran Tu Binh's *The Red Earth*, did not appear until the 1960s.[45]

There were a few other sources of information, but they were not central to public discourse in France. Given the sheer size of plantations and their workforces, information about plantation practices seems to have been widespread among Vietnamese, by word of mouth, and within French planting circles. In Tonkin Vietnamese outrage at the stories told by coolies who had successfully escaped, combined with employers' concerns within Tonkin about the loss of cheap labor; in the North the abuses on southern plantations were no secret.[46] Theoretically, information could also have been available in metropolitan France, as French newspapers picked up stories from Vietnamese ones, had government censorship of the Vietnamese press not been so effective and had tales of abuses actually fit the dominant colonial narrative. Several inspectors' reports were leaked to the local press, including the French-language *La Résurrection*, but early issues of the newspaper were seized by the government and then production abruptly halted.[47] A few French authors did manage to repeat Vietnamese criticisms of conditions on French plantations, but it is unclear how many readers they actually reached; Paul Monet's passionate condemnation of plantation abuses in Indochina went through at least two editions, but we have no numbers on its distribution. And there were also popular publications that defended the plantation system.[48] Equally significant, even when abuses were condemned, criticisms were overwhelmingly portrayals of bad practices by individuals or individual companies and not of a fundamental, systemic problem with the structure of a colonial capitalism that assumed "yellow" lives to be less valuable than "white" ones.[49] Much like British complaints about King Leopold and his men at the turn of the century, critics condemned individuals but not the world colonial structure that made such abuses almost logical.[50]

In retrospect it is remarkable how little information about Indochina was available in metropolitan newspapers. The most visible critics of plantations were the Communists, because both they and the Right attributed coolie uprisings to Communist insurgents. In 1933 Communist deputy Monjauvis used his position in the National Assembly to press the minister of the colonies for direct explanations of the living and working conditions borne by coolies in Indochina, a demand that subsequently appeared in the *Journal Officiel*.[51] The Communist newspaper *L'Humanité* also made charges, but they were rare, as Indochina was rarely mentioned in the newspaper's pages in the interwar era.[52] When the mainstream dailies mentioned the incidents in Indochina at all, they usually relayed issues as questions of governmental control and anti-Communist insurgency; coolies per se did not seem to merit attention.[53]

World's fairs offered another opportunity for the French public to learn about rubber plantations, but there the message was overwhelmingly that of the progress that French planters were bringing to Indochina. The Syndicat des Planteurs de Caoutchouc de l'Indochine had an exhibit at the Colonial Exposition of 1931, in which rubber appeared as part of the economic exhibit in the copy of the Temple of Angkor. The final report leaves little doubt about what viewers were supposed to have learned: "French planters with a spirit of initiative and a perseverance that nothing has been able to discourage have developed (*mis en valeur*) 100,000 hectares . . . which already produce

12,000 tons." It was a story of how bold planters mastered an unforgiving climate to produce rubber. Coolies were never mentioned, though there was a diorama featuring rubber production.[54] E. Delamarre, the head work inspector in Indochina, prepared a booklet for the exposition. Although Delamarre had, in fact, been the author of several of the more damning reports—destined only for his superiors—about labor conditions on plantations, including the one that had been leaked to La Résurrection, the French public got a very different impression from reading the booklet. Delamarre portrayed the movement of workers from Tonkin to Cochinchina to work on plantations to have been a stunning success, a tribute to bureaucratic management.[55] The gap between the reality and the presentation for the French public could not have been wider.

The Paris exposition of 1937 was little different. Here the newly created Institut Français du Caoutchouc took charge of the exhibit, constructing a "Rubber Palace."[56] It featured four large panels illustrating world production (and the place of Indochina in it), a panorama of a plantation factory, the steps in the establishment of a plantation in Indochina, and the importance of welfare measures undertaken by plantation companies. There were models of factory machines, of latex, of smoked sheets, of rubber crepe, and of workers' houses; nothing indicated that coolies' living and working conditions were anything less than ideal.[57] At the opening of the Rubber Palace, M. Petithuguenin, the institute's man in charge of "propaganda" (which did not yet have as negative a connotation as it would have after World War II), noted that the rubber plantation offered work to a "million Asians," offering "colonial populations additional resources amounting to the equivalent of 2 billion francs."[58]

The 1937 exhibition offered an array of publications about hevea and the plantations. Most were technical treatises about chemical compositions and growing rubber. A few were more general and took up the question, at least in passing, of plantation labor. Pierre Michaux's book laid out labor legislation and then jumped to a conclusion not really proven in the text: "The ever more precise technical organization . . . has found itself completed by a considerable progress in the conditions of life of labor. The social improvements . . . consist principally of transplanting Tonkinois from overpopulated Tonkin to the south, of clothing them, of feeding them decently, of giving them little houses with gardens, of paying them double the cost of living, and of assuring them savings at the end of their contracts."[59]

A book on labor was even more direct. René Mingot, who was the general secretary of the Union des Planteurs de Caoutchouc de Indochine, began by noting that free laborers "are irregular and lack quality" (no doubt because they refused to work in conditions they considered unacceptable), so he focused on contracted labor.[60] Mingot maintained throughout that the workers were well treated, that two-thirds decided to renew their contracts in 1934 and 1935, and that labor legislation (though actually opposed by the planters in 1927, which was not mentioned in the book) resulted in good working conditions. In 1927, 4,484 coolies had broken their contracts, whereas in 1935 only 1,516 did so (out of 18,060 contractual laborers). Of those trying to escape, only 19 percent were found in 1925, but 60 percent were found by 1935, hence the reduction in the number of coolies successfully breaking their contracts. Of course, this was progress as measured by planters, not by coolies who had hoped to escape. And while the mortality rate on plantations was 5.4 percent in 1927, it was only 1.48 percent in 1935.[61] Clearly, whereas what French officials said privately was not far from what Vietnamese workers claimed, there was a huge gap between that reality and the image that the planters, fully supported publicly by the government at the exposition, projected to the French public. Michelin advertising could thus offer up lifestyles for well-heeled French, and little in the public discourse reminded tire buyers of the labor conditions that made their new lifestyles possible.

In the end there was obviously a link between modern French consumerism in the metropole and laborers in the colonies. More specifically, there was a close connection between the development of modern automobile tourism, with its regional guides covering French provinces, and Southeast Asian hevea plantations. The self-referential world of modern consumerism resulted from the fact that companies, including Michelin, have successfully, if sometimes inadvertently, helped to obscure the fundamental economic realities that make it possible; consumers generally did not have to think about the implications of their purchases. This profound, willful forgetfulness of what was done depended on government officials, leaders of public opinion, journalists, and experts involved in world's fairs, not to mention consumers themselves, accepting what one might simply call a structural racism built into economic relations in the era of imperialism;

the lives of the "natives" were simply valued less than those of Europeans or Americans.

At least in part twentieth-century consumerism was made possible by companies' advertising, which featured constructed identities to be found within Western civilization while neglecting to consider the production of these consumer goods. This interpretation goes beyond the traditional condemnation of modern consumer culture as being not good for people in the West, embodied above all by Thorstein Veblen,[62] or its glorification as the realization of identities within the West, found in a good many studies of consumerism. Western consumption cannot be fully understood without a coequal focus on the global "history of things." Like cotton, sugar, coffee, bananas, and a host of other commodities, rubber products did not fall from the sky, offering buyers the dreamed-up identities promised in advertising. They came from the sweat, even the blood, of people perceived to be inferior. In order to forget, ignore, or avoid that underlying fact, cultural constructions of seemingly free-floating Western identities, including those mass produced in the form of advertising, were indispensable.

Notes

A National Endowment for the Humanities University Teachers fellowship, combined with summer and sabbatical funding from the University of Akron, made this research possible. I would like to thank participants at the "Encountering Modern France" conference held in Bloomington, Indiana, in December 2003 in memory of William B. Cohen. I am also grateful for suggestions from the organizers and participants at the École des Hautes Etudes en Sciences colloquium "Au nom du consommateur," held in Paris in June 2004.

1. The pathbreaking anthropological study of a commodity is, of course, Sidney W. Mintz's *Sweetness and Power: The Place of Sugar in Modern History* (New York: Penguin, 1985). See also Virginia Scott Jenkins, *Bananas: An American History* (Washington DC: Smithsonian Institution Press, 2000); Michael F. Jiménez, "'From Plantation to Cup': Coffee and Capitalism in the United States, 1830–1930," in *Coffee, Society, and Power in Latin America*, ed. William Roseberry, Lowell Gudmundson, and Mario Samper Kutschbach (Baltimore: Johns Hopkins University Press, 1995), 38–64; Mark Kulansky, *Salt: A World History* (New York: Penguin, 2003); Pierre Laszlo, *Chemins et savoirs du sel* (Paris: Hachette, 1998); Marco Palacios, *Coffee in Columbia, 1850–1970: An Economic, Social, and Political History* (Cambridge: Cambridge Univer-

sity Press, 1980); and Mark Pendergrast, *Uncommon Grounds: The History of Coffee and How It Transformed Our World* (New York: Basic Books, 1999).

2. Arjun Appadurai, ed., *The Social Life of Things: Commodities in Cultural Perspective* (Cambridge: Cambridge University Press, 1986). Appardurai's concept of a commodity includes finished products as well as the traditional traded commodities. In this case rubber is both a traditional commodity and the most important component in a host of finished products, from tires to condoms. As an anthropologist, Appadurai's notion of the "social life" of a thing approximates what most cultural historians would call the "cultural life" of a thing.

3. Kristin Ross, *Fast Cars, Clean Bodies: Decolonization and the Reordering of French Culture* (Cambridge MA: MIT Press, 1995).

4. Lionel Dumond, "L'Industrie française du caoutchouc, 1828–1938: analyse d'un secteur de production" (PhD diss., University of Paris VII, 1996), esp. 43, 559, 564, 659; Lionel Dumond, "L'Arrière-plan technique et commercial," in *Michelin, Les Hommes du pneu: les ouvriers Michelin, à Clermont-Ferrand, de 1889 à 1940*, ed. André Gueslin (Paris: Editions Ouvrières, 1993), esp. 35–72; Louis Castellan, *L'Industrie caoutchoutière* (Thiers: A. Fayé, 1915), 152; Michael J. French, "The Emergence of a US Multinational Enterprise: The Goodyear Tire and Rubber Company," *Economic History Review* 40, no. 1 (1987): 64–79, esp. 69; and Michael J. French, *The U.S. Tire Industry: A History* (Boston: Twayne, 1990), chaps. 3–4.

5. Stephen L. Harp, *Marketing Michelin: Advertising and Cultural Identity in Twentieth-Century France* (Baltimore: Johns Hopkins University Press, 2001), chap. 1.

6. On the "modern" creation of a "traditional" regional cuisine, see Catherine Bertho Lavenir, *La Roue et le stylo: comment nous sommes devenus touristes* (Paris: Éditions Odile Jacob, 1999), esp. 234–35.

7. This is a global phenomenon, usually argued to be of American origin, though there is some evidence—particularly poster art—that I believe suggests that the French were selling lifestyle well before the interwar influence of American advertisers. Among the many works on early twentieth-century advertising, the clearest argument for the selling of lifestyle rather than mere products can be found in Roland Marchand, *Advertising the American Dream: Making Way for Modernity, 1920–1940* (Berkeley: University of California Press, 1985). On the American model for European advertisers more generally, see Marie-Emmanuelle Chessel, *La Publicité: naissance d'une profession, 1900–1940* (Paris: CNRS, 1998); and Victoria de Grazia, "The Arts of Purchase: How American Publicity Subverted the European Poster, 1920–1940," in *Remaking History*, ed. B. Kruger and P. Mariani (Seattle: Bay Press, 1989), 221–57.

8. The literature on the exploitation of indigenous peoples is particularly vast in the cases of the Congo Free State and Brazil. See, for example, Adam Hochschild, *King Leopold's Ghost: A Study of Greed, Terror, and Heroism in Colonial Africa* (Boston: Hough-

ton Mifflin, 1998); Jules Marchal, *E. D. Morel contre Léopold II: l'histoire du Congo,
1900–1910*, 2 vols. (Paris: Editions L'Harmattan, 1996); Daniel Vangroenweghe, *Du
sang sur les lianes* (Brussels: Didier Hatier, 1986); Richard Collier, *The River That God
Forgot: The Story of the Amazon Rubber Boom* (New York: E. P. Dutton, 1968); Michael
Edward Stanfield, *Red Rubber, Bleeding Trees: Violence, Slavery, and Empire in Northwest
Amazonia, 1850–1933* (Albuquerque: University of New Mexico Press, 1998); Barbara Weinstein, *The Amazon Rubber Boom, 1850–1920* (Stanford: Stanford University
Press, 1983). On the French Congo, see Catherine Coquéry-Vidrovitch, *Le Congo au
temps des grandes compagnies concessionnaires, 1898–1930* (Paris: Mouton, 1972).

9. For the broader history of rubber production in Southeast Asia, see Colin Barlow,
The Natural Rubber Industry: Its Development, Technology, and Economy in Malaysia
(Kuala Lumpur: Oxford University Press, 1978); Colin Barlow and John Drabble,
"Government and the Emerging Rubber Industries in Indonesia and Malaya,
1900–40," in *Indonesia Economic History in the Dutch Colonial Era*, ed. Anne Booth, W.
J. O'Malley, and Anna Weidemann (New Haven CT: Yale University Southeast Asia
Studies, 1990), 187–209; Austin Coates, *The Commerce in Rubber: The First 250 Years*
(Singapore: Oxford University Press, 1987); J. H. Drabble, *Rubber in Malaya, 1876–
1922: The Genesis of the Industry* (Kuala Lumpur: Oxford University Press, 1973); J. H.
Drabble, *Malayan Rubber: The Interwar Years* (London: Macmillan, 1991); James C.
Jackson, *Planters and Speculators: Chinese and European Agricultural Enterprise in Malaya,
1786–1921* (Kuala Lumpur: University of Malaya Press, 1968).

10. Vaxelaire, *Le Caoutchouc en Indochine* (Hanoi: Imprimerie d'Extrême Orient, 1939).

11. Henri Tard, *Economie et politique du caoutchouc: le plan Stevenson* (Paris: Les Presses
Modernes, 1928); Charles R. Whittlesey, *Governmental Control of Crude Rubber: The
Stevenson Plan* (Princeton NJ: Princeton University Press, 1931).

12. P. W. Barker and E. G. Holt, *Rubber: History, Production, and Manufacture* (Washing-
ton DC: U.S. Department of Commerce, Bureau of Foreign and Domestic Commerce, 1940); Herbert Hoover, "Foreign Combinations to Control Prices of Raw
Materials" (U.S. Department of Commerce and Bureau of Foreign and Domestic
Commerce, Trade Information Bulletin no. 385, copy at Hoover Presidential
Library); Herbert Hoover, *Memoirs*, vol. 2, *Cabinet and Presidency* (New York: Macmillan, 1952), 81–85; David M. Figart, *The Plantation Rubber Industry in the Middle
East*, Department of Commerce, Trade Promotion Series no. 2, Crude Rubber Sur-
vey (Washington DC: Government Printing Office, 1925).

13. Frank Chalk, "The Anatomy of an Investment: Firestone's 1927 Loan to Liberia," *Canadian Journal of African Studies* 1 (1967): 12–32; J. Pal Chaudhuri, "British
Reaction to the Firestone Investment in Liberia," *Liberian Studies Journal* 5, no. 1
(1972–74): 25–46; Arthur J. Knoll, "Firestone's Labor Policy, 1924–1939," *Liberian
Studies Journal* 16, no. 2 (1991): 49–75; Arthur J. Knoll, "Harvey S. Firestone's Liberian Investment (1922–1932)," *Liberian Studies Journal* 14, no. 1 (1989): 13–33; Emily

S. Rosenberg, "The Invisible Protectorate: The United States, Liberia, and the Evolution of Neocolonialism, 1909–40," *Diplomatic History* 9, no. 3 (1985): 191–214; I. K. Sundiata, *Black Scandal: America and the Liberian Labor Crisis, 1929–1936* (Philadelphia: Institute for the Study of Human Issues, 1980); Wayne Chatfield Taylor, *Firestone Operations in Liberia* (N.p.: National Planning Association, 1956).

14. *Annuaire du Syndicat des Planteurs de Caoutchouc de l'Indochine* (n.p., 1926), 83–84; *Annuaire du Syndicat des Planteurs de Caoutchouc de l'Indochine* (n.p., 1931), 33.

15. Martin J. Murray, *The Development of Capitalism in Colonial Indochina (1870–1940)* (Berkeley: University of California Press, 1980), 266–67.

16. "Le Caoutchouc," *Cahiers Coloniaux* (February 1944), carton 59, dossier 7, Affaires Economiques Indochine, Centre des Archives d'Outre-Mer (hereafter cited as CAOM).

17. Murray, *Development of Capitalism*, 260–65; "Soutien au planteur," FM AGEFOM 189 105, CAOM.

18. Ferdinand de Montaigut, *La Colonisation française dans l'Est de la Cochinchine* (Limoges: Imprimerie Commerciale Perrette, 1929), 35–36. Numbers would decline then fluctuate during the economic crisis of the 1930s.

19. See the report of the inspector of political affairs, which originally appeared in the December 1928 edition of *La Résurrection*, reprinted in Paul Monet, *Les Jauniers: histoire vraie*, 2nd ed. (Paris: Gallimard, 1930), 321–33.

20. Report from the governor in Saigon to the Ministry of Colonies, June 10, 1930, FM INDO NF 2614, CAOM. The rates fell in the 1930s, as few new areas were cleared, coolies' tasks changed to tapping and weeding instead of clearing, quinine was distributed, and hospitals were built.

21. On the racial (and sexual) hierarchies in Southeast Asia, see Ann Laura Stoler, *Capitalism and Confrontation in Sumatra's Plantation Belt, 1870–1979* (New Haven CT: Yale University Press, 1985); and Ann Laura Stoler, *Carnal Knowledge and Imperial Power: Race and the Intimate in Colonial Rule* (Berkeley: University of California Press, 2002).

22. I use the term *coolie* in this essay in the contexts that contemporaries used it, in order to give readers a feel for the mental categories that helped Europeans justify their treatment of Asian and Southeast Asian laborers.

23. Evidence of physical violence runs throughout the archival files dealing with rubber plantations. For overviews, see Pierre Brocheux, "Le Prolétariat des plantations d'hévéas au Vietnam méridional: aspects sociaux et politiques (1927–1937)," *Mouvement Social* 90 (January–March 1975): 54–86; and Murray, *Development of Capitalism*, chap. 6. On the Netherlands East Indies, see Stoler, *Capitalism and Confrontation*; Ann Laura Stoler, "Rethinking Colonial Categories: European Communities and the Boundaries of Rule," *Comparative Studies in Society and History* 31 (January 1989): 134–61; Madelon Lulofs, *Coolie*, trans. F. J. Renier and Irene Clephane (New York: Viking Press, 1936); and Madelon Lulofs, *Rubber: A Romance of the Dutch East Indies*, trans. F. J. Renier and Irene Clephane (London: Cassell, 1933).

24. *Annuaire du Syndicat des Planteurs de Caoutchouc de l'Indochine* (Saigon, 1926); *Annuaire du Syndicat des Planteurs de Caoutchouc de l'Indochine* (Saigon, 1931), esp. 17, 20, 27, 55, 85.

25. "Note pour le Ministre sur deux incidents survenus sur la plantation Michelin, dans la région de Phu-Riêng," June 5, 1930, FM INDO NF 2614, Ministère des Colonies, Direction des Affaires Economiques, 2e Bureau, CAOM.

26. Report by J. G. Hérisson, February 28, 1930, FM INDO NF 2625, CAOM; "Note pour le Ministre sur deux incidents survenus sur la plantation Michelin," June 5, 1930, FM INDO NF 2614, CAOM.

27. Michelin et Cie., Clermont-Ferrand, to the Minister of Colonies, March 31, 1930, FM INDO NF 1839, CAOM.

28. Governor-General of Indochina to the Ministry of the Colonies, August 12, 1930, FM INDO NF 1839, CAOM.

29. Report by J. G. Hérisson, February 28, 1930, FM INDO NF 2625, CAOM.

30. "Soutien au Planteur," carton 189, dossier 195, FM AGEFOM, CAOM; and Murray, *Development of Capitalism*, 263–65.

31. Union des Planteurs de Caoutchouc en Indochine to the Governor General, May 26, 1932; and return letter from the Governor General, June 9, 1932, both in FM INDO NF 2616, CAOM.

32. Governor-General of Indochina to the Minister of the Colonies, January 7, 1933; "Note pour le Ministre," sent along with the governor-general's memorandum; and Governor-General of Indochina to the Minister of the Colonies, February 9, 1933, all in FM INDO NF 2616, CAOM.

33. Résident Supérieur Eutrope to the Governor General of Indochina, December 24, 1932, FM INDO NF 2616, CAOM.

34. J.-P. Rougni to the Labor Inspectorate, forwarded to the Ministry of the Colonies, December 23, 1932, FM INDO NF 2616, CAOM.

35. Governor-General to the Minister of the Colonies, February 9, 1933, FM INDO NF 2616, CAOM.

36. Contrôleur du Travail Lespinasse to the Labor Inspectorate, October 14, 1936, forwarded through the governor of Cochinchina and the governor-general to the minister of the Colonies, FM INDO NF 2404, CAOM.

37. Governor of Cochinchina to the Director General of Michelin in Saigon, October 19, 1936, FM INDO NF 2404, CAOM.

38. Governor-General of Indochina to the Minister of Colonies, June 24, 1937, FM INDO NF 2404, CAOM.

39. Governor-General of Indochina to the Minister of the Colonies, July 28, 1937, FM INDO NF 2404, CAOM.

40. Governor-General of Indochina to the Minister of the Colonies, June 24, 1937, FM INDO NF 2404, CAOM.

41. Rapport confidentiel by Pagès, May 27, 1937, in the private holdings of Daniel Hémery, as cited by Brocheux in "Le Prolétariat," 75.

42. FM INDO NF 2404, CAOM; Brocheux, "Le Prolétariat"; see also Monet, Les Jauniers.

43. Karen Adler, presenting a paper on Michelin plantations in Indochina at the annual meeting of the Society of French Historical Studies, Toronto, April 2002.

44. Several of the CAOM dossiers cited previously were "non-communicable"—as still marked on the dossier covers themselves—until sixty years had passed.

45. There are apparently several Vietnamese accounts of life on rubber plantations. To my knowledge, only Tran Tu Binh's The Red Earth: A Vietnamese Memoir of Life on a Colonial Rubber Plantation, trans. John Spragens, ed. David G. Marr (Athens: Ohio University Center of International Studies, 1985), has been translated from Vietnamese. Tran Tu Binh later became a Communist leader, and The Red Earth reads a bit like a Vietnamese Communist Bildungsroman. It is astounding how closely his firsthand account of life on a Michelin plantation coincides with government records.

46. Goudal for the Bureau International du Travail, Geneva, Problèmes de travail en Indochine (Geneva: Bureau International du Travail, 1937), 50–65, app.

47. La Résurrection, nos. 1 and 3 (nos. 2 and 4 were not allowed to appear at all). Excerpts of both issues are printed in Monet, Les Jauniers, 321–38. No. 3 also appeared more recently in Félicien Challaye, Un Livre noir du colonialisme: souvenirs sur la colonisation, ed. Marc Ferro (Paris: Les Nuits Rouges, 1998), 162–65.

48. Georges LeFèvre, Démolisseurs et bâtisseurs (Paris: André Delpeuch, 1927).

49. See, for example, Monet's Les Jauniers, esp. 21–33, 202–27, and 321–28. Ilya Ehrenbourg, 10 CV (Paris: Les Revues, 1930), offers a critique of the plantations as part of a broader critique of capitalist automobile production, but he portrays the white planter and not just the coolies as victim (103–11).

50. See, for example, the most visible and vocal critic of Leopold and his men: E. D. Morel, Red Rubber: The Story of the Rubber Slave Trade Flourishing on the Congo in the Year of Grace 1906 (1906; repr., New York: Haskell House Publishers, 1970). Even Adam Hochschild's popular and quite good King Leopold's Ghost (1998) tends to focus on him as an individual and not on the colonial context that could so easily lead to such abuses.

51. On January 26 and October 17, 1933, for example, Deputy Monjauvis demanded to know what the minister of the colonies was doing about reports of abuses at Michelin's Dau-Tiêng plantation. Chambre des Députés, Questions écrites, FM INDO NF 1839, CAOM.

52. "Comment Pasquier 'fait régner le calme' en Indochine," L'Humanité, February 18, 1933.

53. See, for example, "Le Mouvement communiste," Le Temps, March 16, 1930.

54. "Rapport sur la participation de l'Indochine, Exposition Coloniale Internationale de Paris, 1931," carton 533, dossiers 53 and 54, FM AGEFOM, CAOM.

55. E. Delamarre, *L'Émigration et l'immigration ouvrière en Indochine* (Hanoi: Imprimerie d'Extrême Orient, 1931), esp. 28–29.

56. The Institut Français de Caoutchouc was founded in 1936 as part of French implementation of the rubber restriction scheme. In the short term the strategy limited rubber production in Malaya and Indonesia; French Indochina got an exemption until French rubber production matched the level of the country's rubber consumption, which was not attained until the eve of World War II. In the long term, taking a page from the very active British Rubber Growers' Association, all of the major imperial producers focused on building demand by sponsoring both research centers that found new uses for rubber and propaganda offices to encourage new uses for rubber.

57. "Institut Français de Caoutchouc, deuxième rapport annuel," 34–35, carton 201, dossier "Rapports 1937," FM AGEFOM, CAOM.

58. "Annexe 6: activité du Centre de Propagande," 5, carton 201, dossier "Rapports 1937," FM AGEFOM, CAOM.

59. Pierre Michaux, *Caoutchouc: l'hévéaculture en Indochine; son évolution*, Institut Français du Caoutchouc, Délégation française à la Propagande (Paris: Exposition Internationale de Paris, 1937), 39.

60. René Mingot, *Caoutchouc: l'hévéaculture en Indochine; la main d'oeuvre; la main d'oeuvre contractuelle sur les plantations de caoutchouc* (Paris: Exposition Internationale de Paris, 1937), 5.

61. Mingot, *Caoutchouc*, 28–32.

62. Thorstein Veblen, *The Theory of the Leisure Class* (New York: Macmillan, 1899).

4

Exorcising Algeria

French Citizens, the War, and the Remaking of National Identity in the Rhône-Alpes, 1954–1962

Lee Whitfield explores regional identity against the backdrop of the centralizing imperial policies of France. In this instance the leading politicians of the Fourth Republic
prosecuted a military policy to combat autonomist and separatist forces in France's most
prized imperial possession: Algeria. The citizens of the Rhône-Alpes were in the process of
developing their own distinct identities anchored in regional revival and economic vitalism
when the central government's imperial nationalism disrupted the fabric of Rhône-Alpes
society. Events in the empire tangibly spilled over into the homeland, and vice versa, as
the Rhône-Alpes citizenry's reaction to the Algerian crisis affected policies promulgated
in Algeria. As the citizens of the Rhône-Alpes resisted forcefully the unpopular wartime
measures of the central government, local elites encouraged a pragmatic solution to end
the war and an alternative notion of national identity, which stood in opposition to the
central government's imperial vocation. Yet the diversity in the Rhône-Alpes, as in other
regions, in no way impeded the unity of France. On the contrary, this trend helped the
public to transcend the war and permitted the fundamental cohesive structures of the
nation to prevail. While national identity was recast and preserved, the leaders of France's
Fourth Republic were not; they were staunchly rejected, precipitating a political crisis in
the core of France, leading to the toppling of the Fourth Republic and Charles de Gaulle's
creation of the Fifth Republic in 1958.

⊷ ⊷

In William Cohen's study of modernization in five provincial cities in nineteenth-century France, he found that city dwellers often were drawn into
the intense battles between local and national interests as the urban facade
yielded to unprecedented change. Citizens inevitably went along with their
civic leaders' advice for renewal and rejected counsel that was nationally

based. As Cohen writes, "To be sure, cities were not insular. Their inhabitants increasingly were swept up in the national ideologies and movements. Yet municipal leaders were able to forge and maintain a sense of unity that lent the regional city significance."[1] In this light consider the more recent tug between the nation and its diverse regions over the prosecution of the Algerian War. As disagreement between the nation and the region worsened, certain French citizens disavowed the acts of their national leaders. They sought alternative stewards of the Republic among municipal authorities, and together the alliance of local elites and citizens formulated a different concept of national identity based on references to their own region.

This essay explores the question of how the Algerian War affected French national identity. The region of the Rhône-Alpes provides the evidence for the themes I seek to examine. There citizens responded to *les événements* in distinctly communal ways. This study of national identity in wartime places the eight-year conflict within the broader context of citizens' ongoing burden of Vichy memories, attempts to honor the patrimony of the Rhône-Alpes, and exigencies of redemption and recovery in the region. Fought between 1954 and 1962, the Algerian-French conflict resulted from the Algerian majority's determination to gain independence in France's largest and oldest North African possession and its most important French settlement overseas. The French government's zeal to repress the nationalists' fight for independence came at a high cost to the nation. The prosecution of war destroyed the French Fourth Republic and national morale. The Algerian crisis brought Gen. Charles de Gaulle out of political exile in May 1958. De Gaulle's domestic and international goals required the termination of France's imperial vocation. Instead, he set the nation on a new course at home and abroad.

Historians such as John Ruedy and Alistair Horne have taken to be axiomatic that the majority of the French public only shifted against the government's military campaign when President de Gaulle led them there.[2] New evidence of regional attitudes has shown that claim to be inaccurate. By late 1956, in the Rhône-Alpes region, the majority of citizens had repudiated the war policy of their leaders, well in advance of de Gaulle's changing direction for France. At the outset of the conflict Prime Minister Pierre Mendès-France and his minister of the interior, François Mitterrand, had pledged, "Never will any French government yield on the principle that Algeria is France.

. . . In Algeria, the only possible negotiation is war."[3] No subsequent leader revised this position. Even so, the 1956 Suez Canal crisis marked the turning point for public opinion in the Rhône-Alpes, as citizens saw the conflict in Algeria take on new significance within the international conflict of the Cold War. The consequences of the Suez debacle finally crystallized the attitudes of most Rhône-Alpes citizens. They saw in the aftermath of Suez that the prolongation of the Algerian War was undermining the governance of the nation and France's international position. War costs were reversing the positive direction of the economy. Military policies in Algeria were tarnishing the universal values and mocking the laws of France. Military service was poisoning the mental and moral health of young soldiers. The public in the Rhône-Alpes rejected the unconscionable and irrational war policy to defend French imperial identity. Instead, municipal politicians, businessmen and women, and diverse civic leaders refashioned their own French national identity rooted in regional pride and revival.[4]

The Creation of Regional Identity in the Rhône-Alpes, 1944–54

After the humiliation of Vichy and the burden of Nazi German and Fascist Italian occupation, the citizens of the Rhône-Alpes tied their hopes for a resurgent France to the restoration of the French Republican heritage and the ambitious five-year plans launched by the economic modernizers. Civic leaders in the region articulated with great success the distinctive identity of the Rhône-Alpes.[5] This revitalized Rhône-Alpes identity represented a blend of pride in its residents' sacrifice for the Republic; their self-proclaimed excellence in gastronomy and eco-friendly tourism; technological, commercial, and intellectual vigor; youthfulness and adaptability; and the abundance of their natural resources. Notable among such leaders' persistent postwar projects were those to memorialize the Rhône-Alpes patrimony. Among them were two major tragedies of the resistance—March 1944, when the Germans and French Milice destroyed a unit of 450 men on the Glières Plateau above Annecy, and in July 1944, when the Wehrmacht and ss killed over 800 partisans and villagers on the plateau of the Vercors near Grenoble.[6] Such commemorative monuments were completed in the immediate aftermath of the Algerian War.[7]

Since 1945 the Rhône-Alpes had lured newcomers because of its poten-

Map 4.1. Rhône-Alpes

tial for growth, and the region had blossomed into one of the most densely populated locales in France. Among the waves of migrants seeking to benefit were numerous Algerians and other North Africans. The universities at Grenoble and Lyon played a significant role in the development and expansion of the regional economy; education and research ventures lured talent and investment, which in turn spurred innovation and international trade, affluence and jobs. Since 1945 student enrollment had multiplied five- to tenfold at both institutions. In the arts a major cultural revival drew young and progressive artists, musicians, and actors to the region.

Long an axis of commercial activity, the Rhône-Alpes enjoyed a tradition of international networking. Second only to Paris, the Rhône-Alpes was the greatest pole of population growth and economic development.

Hydroelectricity, produced in the Alps since 1860, expanded significantly from the 1930s under the impetus of the electrometallurgy and electrochemical industries. Oil pipelines that passed through the region generated new industries linked to oil refinery and petroleum by-products. In the mid-1950s nuclear research further invigorated the regional energy production, elevating the Rhône-Alpes to the leading electricity producer for France. Mechanization of the rich agricultural production expanded the local economy, as did greater specialization and farmer cooperatives. Greater efficiency among producers of Côtes-du-Rhône and Beaujolais wines, cheeses and dairy products of the Savoie and Haute-Savoie, and local beef lifted the Rhône-Alpes agricultural economy to one of the most prosperous in Europe. Developments in the tourism industry also added growth and vitality to the region. Winter and summer sports in the Alps were a substantial source of revenue. Ski-mania and camping grew affordable in the 1950s with the extended vacation and small family cars.[8]

These advances, in turn, bred further success. They stimulated investments from domestic and foreign sources and attracted international commercial contracts. Grenoble in particular had a reputation for entrepreneurial innovation that made it a pacesetter in France. This urban magnet of prosperity exemplified the region's harmonious blend of nature and nurture. In the valley of the Isère tourism and economic dynamism thrust Grenoble ahead of more conventional Dijon or Bordeaux, luring energetic migrants to the foremost industries in Europe—electrochemicals, electrometallurgy, heavy machinery, and nuclear research. Seven people in ten were immigrants to the area; one in eight was a student or scientist.[9]

The Impact of the Algerian Conflict in the Rhône-Alpes, 1954–55

Like other French citizens, the Rhône-Alpes public was accustomed to thinking of the French Empire as reassurance of their national prestige around the world. Compulsory republican education had etched the value of imperialism in the minds of schoolchildren with great success.[10] When the violence broke out in Algeria and the North African empire, a rare few questioned the prevailing gospel. As journalist Claude Bourdet explained, "Few citizens knew the history of the conquest of North Africa—the atrocities, the massacres, and the scorched earth policies. This and the brutal repression and the theft of the land were conveniently ignored in our textbooks. The French public had hardly noticed the repression at Sétif in 1945. . . . Many of our errors and our slow and difficult route to shed Algeria can be explained by our conditioning."[11] Because Algeria had a special status within the French Empire, even those citizens with anticolonial views, would not have imagined applying the same criticisms to Algeria as they did to other parts of the empire. Moreover, Algiers, as the capital of de Gaulle's Free French government, counted as a powerful symbol for the nation. "After all, unlike the British case of India, Churchill had not directed the war from Bombay," explained former Senator Robert Verdier.[12]

The national war propaganda to salvage Algeria aimed at one overarching goal: to unite the home front with the battlefront. The objective was to forge solid popular backing for the military to defend the indivisible French Republic—metropolitan France, Algeria, and the overseas territories. The inbred reflex of "Algeria, it is France" held sway in the Rhône-Alpes from November 1954 until the point in 1956 when the professional army no longer was able to repress the insurgency on its own. Even so, when the official sirens from Paris blasted those "Algerian outlaws who are enemies of France," the Rhône-Alpes public refused to capitulate to the national agenda. Instead, these independents continued their long-established traditions of charity, especially to outsiders. Nearly two years into the Algerian conflict, for example, the North African refugee community remained the beneficiaries of Annecy residents' acts of kindness. In the national climate of hostility Catholic and Protestant groups saw even greater reason to aid Algerian immigrants. The largely male factory workers were alone, separated from their families in Algeria, who relied heavily on the young men's wages. These groups proudly undertook repairs to the immigrants' dilapidated quarters and provision of food, clothes, and medicine. Generous charity funds meant the groundbreaking for new housing for North African immigrants was slated for the spring of 1956. Indicative of the deeply held appeal of local tradition, residents refuted national propaganda and instead distinguished their own refugees from the violent acts that Algerians committed in Algeria.

It is fair to claim that the lobbying efforts for the national war policy failed to produce results in the Rhône-Alpes in large part because of the region's relative success, which translated into a tangible pride and loyalty among the Rhône-Alpes citizenry. Locals were profoundly conscious of the need to safeguard this image. They embraced their balance of tradition and modernity and strongly identified with it as their own. The war propaganda of chauvinism from the national government and attendant hostility was potentially lethal to that identity. So strong was its pull that twelve months into the war, there was little popular interest in this part of France.

Imperialist Nationalism versus Regional Identity

In the first six months of 1956 Rhône-Alpes leaders recognized that the Fourth Republic's war policy was draining attention and funds. Projects to renew France in the Rhône-Alpes were put on hold while Paris escalated the war in Algeria. Instead of construction and growth, the destruction of war was pervasive in every dimension of life in the Rhône-Alpes. The national government's shift to an all-out military effort required five hundred thousand young men from the Rhône-Alpes to fight alongside the eventually five million–strong forces in Algeria. Hence, the national war policy depleted schools and universities of their teachers and students and hospitals, factories, and farms of their workforce. It stripped shopkeepers and artisans of their consumers and tourism of its clients both at home and abroad. This was hardly the first instance in which the Rhône-Alpes public distrusted the centralizing national agenda. They had previously equated Paris with the notion of runaway modernity, interference, and paralysis—a relationship mixed with optimism and distrust. In this case the Algerian conflict threatened to reverse the region's robust postwar recovery and its significant role in the renewal of the nation. As a consequence, the citizenry in the Rhône-Alpes looked to the informal power of respected business and commercial elites, local politicians, and municipal councils to forge a different patriotic narrative framed by referents to the Rhône-Alpes in opposition to the national one.

In the early spring of 1956 the economic forecast looked bright for the region. The national government's extension of paid vacations to three weeks was good news for a region whose resplendent tourist attractions had much to gain from the measure. But the Algerian conflict soon eclipsed this bright forecast. Late March saw the national government's passage of emergency war measures that subjected the Rhône-Alpes to an unprecedented peacetime civilian draft. Still in denial that France was at war in Algeria,

Paris abruptly drained three hundred million francs from the Treasury. The effects were profound for the public; in creating a gross imbalance of foreign payments, the military policy immediately triggered inflation.[13] In the Rhône-Alpes region lower-income families, farmers, butchers, artisans, small shopkeepers, and fledgling industries were struck especially hard. Draft notices arrived in the mail along with bank notices announcing that one's savings were being depleted rapidly to satisfy bills no longer covered by income. The cost of living for a family of four had already jumped by 3 percent in May, 3.4 percent in June, and 3 percent again by August. Yet local officials were constantly being urged by Paris to mobilize popular support for the war. Local officials were not circumspect in telling national leaders that Algeria was a tough sell. It was not easy to convince a hardworking public to pay for a war when their leaders seemed incapable of controlling the consequences at home. The soaring costs to the home front were lethal to popular morale.

The Algerian crisis disrupted personal and national economic stability. And its tentacles eventually reached into and poisoned the collective psyche of ethnically diverse communities in metropolitan France. From 1956 the strategy of the National Liberation Front (FLN), the dominant organization in Algeria's fight for independence, aimed to spread its nationalist struggle to France and to the Rhône-Alpes. Resident Algerian immigrants were tracked, coerced to finance the FLN, or assassinated if suspected of being loyal to Messali Hadj and his followers.[14] Militants of all stripes took refuge in the mountainous hideouts and isolated villages of the Rhône-Alpes. These individuals included members of the FLN; the "porteurs des valises," or militants in the clandestine organization of French citizens who smuggled funds to the FLN; and radicals from the Secret Army Organization (OAS), a French terrorist group unwavering in its commitment to defend France's colonial empire. The locals watched as these combatants were hunted down by officials and gunned down by their enemies. Underground warriors managed their escape and reentry to France via the permeable frontiers of the Alps. And beyond the rural areas cities such as Evian, Lyon, and Grenoble paid hefty tolls as a result of the war. The OAS bullets felled Evian's popular Mayor Camille Blanc in retribution for his offer to aid peace, by hosting negotiations between the French and FLN delegations. The FLN was particularly malicious and deadly in Lyon and Grenoble, where Algerian immigrants made up a significant percentage of the industrial workforce.

These circumstances subdued the philanthropic legacy of the region. Charitable groups concluded that solicitation of funds for the Algerian workers was awkward, at best, in light of local youth being drafted into combat in Algeria. The Reformed Church council and other charities voted to postpone indefinitely the construction of new housing for the Algerians. In communities close to the Swiss border where Algerians were known to come and go, the anxiety of locals led to erecting barbed wire fences to isolate the Muslim quarter from the rest of the neighborhoods.[15] The attendant decline in relations left Algerians vulnerable to FLN propaganda, and many workers returned to Algeria.

Municipal courts became the site of divisive trials that mirrored the deep split in public opinion and became the focus of national attention. The March 1958 trial of Pastor Étienne Mathiot and his codefendant Françoise Rapiné drew national attention to the critical debates over the imperiled Republican legacy. Key Protestants such as Professor Paul Ricoeur, Pastor Georges Casalis, and André Philip testified on behalf of the defendants. In sheltering young Si Ali, to protect the Algerian boy from certain torture or worse, Mathiot told the court, "I tried to convert an enemy into an open-minded human being. . . . I know that, in contrast with acts of violence, any gesture of love brings with it the potential for change." Ricoeur pleaded indulgence for the defendants, who were "guilty yet pure, pushed to their action by the government's perverse policy and use of the law."[16] The courtroom battles in the Rhône-Alpes brought the public closer to the Fourth Republic's imperial national identity through the testimony that revealed its content. Through the revelations about the war being waged to maintain Algeria's long-established system of massive brutality, greed, and racism came evidence of the government's current complicity with the widespread atrocities and military misconduct. "Is there a Gestapo in Algeria?" demanded journalist Claude Bourdet.[17] The net effects of the Algerian conflict were to put this region's citizens at the forefront of repudiating the war policy.

Paris expected and urged local authorities in the region to bolster support for the military effort. But a propensity for distance from the national agenda in favor of a regional one made that task difficult for them. In the Haute-Savoie and the Savoie fierce regional loyalty was a familiar pattern that distinguished this population annexed to France less than a century earlier. Reactions to the Nazi occupation had served to reinforce the strong regional identity. In its wake the monuments on the Glières, in the Vercors, and elsewhere to the *maquisards'* heroic resistance were intended to etch such memories into the regional landscape itself for generations to come. These and other regional markers of humanity and tradition indelibly forged the collective memory of the residents and helped to build a strong regional identity. Hence, when the government propaganda of pacification commenced, citizens here viewed it as an unwelcome intrusion on their positive psyche and fulfilling agenda. Beyond verbal attacks against the policy of the national government, young and old took up serious engagement, acting on their objections to the war in Algeria. Reactions to the draft among local factory workers were immediate and strident. They devised schemes to sabotage production of war supplies, which posed a serious threat to the military, given that a significant percentage of production came from the industrialized Rhône-Alpes.[18] By the late spring of 1956, in Grenoble and in the surrounding towns, many of the hundreds of thousands of draftees boarding trains, along with their supporters, revealed what they thought of the Fourth Republic's war policy by rioting and pulling emergency brake cords along the way.[19]

Demonstrations in this locale were particularly well organized. Since the 1950s there had been a consolidation of interests in concentrating energies upon regional development. The war policy further forged this unusual coalition of business, university, and factory leaders even among Communists, Protestants, and Progressive Catholics. In light of these revelations, prominent leaders urged the circulation of literature in which the message was hard to ignore: "You ought to know the truth about the methods of repression in North Africa."[20] Christian groups warned, "To all men of good faith, of all races, of all religions, of all parties: We launch a solemn call for stopping this horrible course of violence and hate before it is too late. This appeal must be heard."[21] Resistance also emerged in early April in the form of widespread spontaneous strikes, the dissemination of antiwar materials, and the organization of meetings to educate the public and to galvanize local discontent.[22] This political opposition was generally peaceful. Resistance in the cheese cooperatives of the Haute-Savoie took the form of unified work stoppage throughout the day. After hours workers would parade in line through their local streets to protest the summons to Algeria; in the commune of Vauvert 1,500 men and women took part in demonstrations, and in Mans about 200 joined the march.[23] Despite orders from Paris to suppress the demonstrations, local authorities disregarded them. In May, when the first draftees were scheduled to depart for Algeria, hundreds of protestors encouraged a spontaneously assembled crowd of onlookers to block the train tracks for six hours. They succeeded in preventing the area's youth from leaving the depot until authorities were compelled to arrest a handful of demonstrators.[24] The demonstrations in Grenoble and the surrounding communities were among the largest in France, and they helped to initiate a process of criticism about the national war policy and how to stave off further damage.

Crisis of Conscience: The Soldier's Experience

For many of the Rhône-Alpes young men who were called up to serve in Algeria, their chief worries concerned their crisis of conscience. Any number of distressed young people turned to their pastors and priests or youth counselors in their anguish about having witnessed the sadism, torture, unorthodox police methods, and summary executions routinely practiced by the French military. Sources attest to Protestant and Catholic ministers and youth leaders articulating grave concerns about the young men compelled to follow orders in a dirty war.[25] Privy to the anguish of many draftees, these religious and community leaders and their equivalents in leftist organizations were early critics of the military policy. The testimony of one soldier from a village near Samoëns suggests that their concerns were not unfounded:

> I just returned from Algeria where I was stationed for more than two years. Under the false pretext of looking for weapons, our soldiers took liberty to plunder and steal. I saw men strip eight young girls until they were completely naked because they might hide a pistol or a machine gun under their long dresses. One of the women was raped by twelve soldiers, a fact that became known to the officer of the reserve. He ignored it, claiming it appeared that the woman had fully consented. It was always this response when a husband complained to the commander of the company who rejected the complaint on these grounds. Among the men that we rounded up, I remember three that we held for three weeks.

They did forced work sustaining kicks and punches. This sequestration was perfectly arbitrary and illegal, to the point where when a superior officer came to inspect us, we hid the men.[26]

Orders to carry out illegal acts of war were not made in writing; instead, the officers disseminated them in the form of oral commands. Even for soldiers who only witnessed such methods, in their eyes the illegal character of the orders turned them into accomplices. Those who were ordered to carry out tortures and summary executions had only two choices: to refuse or to obey. Refusal took various forms, from the more benign to the more serious, from verbal protest to desertion. In 1957 an example came from the highest level by Gen. Paris de Bollardière, who refused to apply the directives of police operations and the destruction of all the mosques in his sector.[27] But to refuse was to expose the soldier to charges of treason and an attack on the honor of the military. The case of a young Catholic second lieutenant, M. Le Meur, demonstrates that the worries of those who did refuse were not exaggerated. His decision elicited the charge of "participation in organizing the demoralization of the army for having criticized an order of the commander stating 'I don't want any prisoners.'"[28] But in the milieu of a fighting army his humanitarian decision, one that honored the constitution of France, came at a high price. His closed military trial in June 1959 resulted in a guilty sentence of two years in prison.[29]

The perspective of young soldiers from the Rhône-Alpes region suggested the extent of the burden of the war experience. They were struck by the ways the military methods seemed to be harming the stature of France among ordinary Algerians. As one soldier stated:

I arrived there before 20 August 55 when the Muslim population still showed no inclination to follow the orders of the FLN. They kept to their own affairs but the ways in which we conducted our operations led to their hostility toward us. Many of my fellow soldiers did not show respect for the people and their property or the customs, values, or religion of a population extremely susceptible to shock. They awakened the men from sleep, and the people had difficulty regaining their normal work and daily life. Certain soldiers made a game of the massacres, destroying the people's belongings, their beds, breaking the jars of grain and throwing the food on the floor, ruining the stores of flour on which the people depended. Sometimes, the men took as booty, scarves and bracelets. The pillage did not stop there; they even slaughtered the chickens to enrich their boring rations.[30]

Such military strategies were perplexing for young men from the region. In his letter of May 23 one Lyon teacher home on leave wrote to Le Monde, "At this moment when the blood runs from one part of Algeria to another, where the rebels terrorize each other in a chain reaction of horror, it is difficult to understand why we hurl ourselves against the Muslims' resistance to integration."[31] Such reactions reveal the confusion of many civilian soldiers called to combat in Algeria. When the draftees served in Algeria, they generally retained their civilian outlook.[32] Especially troubling to them was the indiscriminate treatment of Algerians—men, women, and children—and the explicit racial nature of the officers' orders.[33] The nightly army raids, the mop-up operations, and the discriminate brutality gave much aid to the rebel cause. For what soldiers reaped in return for their methods of pacification was the conversion of neutral Algerian peasants into the enemies of France. What is most striking in all of the testimony of these young Rhône-Alpes soldiers is their sense of the folly of the pacification policy in Algeria. It visited misery nearly everywhere, and it did not serve France.

Public Opinion against the Backdrop of the Cold War

The Algerian conflict unfolded in a climate of troubling news splashing across the front pages of the region's newspapers. The media delivered the unmistakable impression that the rebellion had spun out of control, describing the FLN guerrillas' tirade of escalating violence and atrocities, evidently unchecked by the French Army. Moreover, journalists relayed that the rebels had successfully been converting greater segments of the indigenous population to the nationalist cause. Villagers were hiding the rebels, nourishing them, and signaling enemy tactics to them. The assessment, though avoiding any direct criticism of the army, amounted to a revelation that the French forces were floundering. Why this was so, the media did not yet ponder. The journalists simply conveyed the official version of events, assessing that a jihad of Manichaean proportions was being played out between the Arab outlaws and the Christian peacemakers.[34]

In the spring of 1956 an international angle in the conflict surfaced in reports of events taking place in Algeria, elevating it into a fresh stake in the Cold War. Apparently, the French Army had intercepted caches of Soviet and American weapons crossing the borders between Algeria and Tunisia and Morocco.[35] The intrusion of international elements led politicians and journalists to speculate on the potential escalation of Algeria into a global war. In the wake of this barrage of disturbing reportage, French public opinion polls in April revealed a shift in war attitudes among the electorate in the Rhône-Alpes. Pollsters learned that the percentage of voters clinging to the status quo in Algeria had dropped to 40 percent, down from 49 percent of two months earlier. Questioned in positive terms, voters found the concept of looser links between France and Algeria more acceptable, increasing to 33 percent in April, from only 25 percent two months prior.[36]

The evolving portrait of popular opinion suggests an electorate more pragmatic than stubborn. Technological and modernization imperatives at home were prompting the public to reconsider Algeria's importance. The majority of voters in the Rhône-Alpes had grown up with the principle of the unity of Algeria and France. They were, nonetheless, increasingly uncomfortable with the precipitous and unpredictable consequences of the military campaign. Citizens did not approve of the current policy, nor did they have confidence in the current government to settle the problem, which a significant segment viewed as getting worse despite the military buildup. In fact, a growing number were open to a reformed relationship between France and Algeria.

The national war policy had a special provenance for the public in the Rhône basin. Its audiences were among the most frequently sought by national figures mindful of the region's importance to the fate of France. Pierre Cot, staunch critic of torture and the government's betrayal of the Republic, was Haute-Savoie deputy and former minister of war. He aimed to tug opinion to accept Algeria's autonomy.[37] Counterattacks to the Cot school were the purview of Rhône deputy and former resident governor of Algeria Jacques Soustelle. Soustelle relentlessly pitched the paramount geopolitical importance of Algeria in the defense of the free world. His rationale effectively linked Algeria to the international agenda of the Cold War. This approach differed from the dominant thread of national war propaganda that framed Algeria and its oil as vital to France's resurgence as a global economic power. The latter contention ran afoul of public awareness in the Rhône-Alpes because increased evidence pointed to the fallacy of the claim. In 1956 economic interests in Algeria were on the wane in the region; the greatest markets for growth were found in collaboration and trade with European partners. The noteworthy vigor in the regional economy came from cooperative relations in research and commerce between Lyon and Grenoble with Milan, Turin, and Geneva. Related growth in the chemical, electrical, and machine industries was far more significant than the role Algeria played for the Rhône-Alpes population.[38]

These factors encouraged an international perspective that was open to Soustelle's rationale for the Algerian military policy. His thesis found frequent and ample coverage in the regional press organs, *La Dernière heure lyonnaise* and *Le Progrès*. Statements in the press such as "Danger to national security with the weakening of French power in North Africa" and "From Moscow to Algiers . . . it is the Soviets who . . . aim to remove France from her overseas territories," echoed the military education of young recruits.[39] By this logic they were in Algeria not only to preserve French soil but to serve as cold warriors to save the free world. Certainly, not everyone accepted this argument, but evidence confirms that the Rhône-Alpes public found the warnings credible.[40] The geopolitical rationale for backing the national war policy played well among this population because it helped France's image in the Western world as a strong partner in the defense against the Soviet Union.

The certainty with which Soustelle spoke also served to pump up the popularity of right-wing populism in 1956 among a different constituency. Pierre Poujade, the antitax shopkeeper champion of the foundering old-time business types, finally secured a wedge for his movement, thanks to the springtime gift of war-triggered inflation. Unlike Soustelle's constituency, the following for the Poujadist movement barely existed until he had enlarged his doctrinal base to Algeria in 1956. Reluctance to part with their protected colonial markets converted this sector to hard-line colonialism.[41] He held on to a small constituency of those segments among the small-time watchmakers, the tiny textile factories, fashion jewelers, and family operations. For them Poujade's right-wing populism linked their fate to Algeria.[42] Poujade's message acquired new legitimacy for this minority of the Rhône-Alpes citizens in the broader platform of diehard colonialism to protect the little man forsaken by Paris and modernity.[43] A retired army officer from Aix-les-Bains agreed with the hardline Poujadists: "All honest citizens must denounce the fifth column and its cowardly talk, in particular, those 'pacifists' of Grenoble, who commit a murderous chain of antinational acts."[44]

But by June 1956 a better informed public in the Rhône-Alpes was revising its views about the national war policy in light of disturbing developments. It was the job of government-appointed officials to monitor war opinion for the Ministry of the Interior, and their reports speak to the popular assumptions about the links between the war and the negative signs in the local economy. The labor shortages created by the draft were a big cause for alarm among business and commercial elites. This was particularly applicable to the heavily unionized automobile, machine tools, and farm equipment plants, in which the war was already having disruptive effects on production. The lack of skilled machinists was forcing considerable cutbacks in production. Certain sectors of the economy—chemicals, metallurgy, and hydroelectrical development—evidenced less decline, but overall growth in all sectors was less robust. The inflationary effects of the war costs on the family pocketbook especially annoyed the public, irrespective of social class. Officials noted that it was increasingly difficult to convince their hardworking voters to support a government that appeared oblivious to the Algerian policy's hemorrhagic impact at home. Complaints from all quarters spoke to the interrelated concerns of the nation's money, men, and resources being funneled into Algeria instead of metropolitan France, with no end to the drain in sight.[45] A letter of June 15 to *Dernière heure lyonnaise* is noteworthy in its disenchantment: "An army of 400,000 soldiers cannot stop the terrorism, so send our guys back home to work. We need them."[46] The commentary is indicative of the government's failure to forge a solid mobilization for the war policy between the home front and the battlefront.

The evidence makes clear that no single pattern of wartime opinion emerged at this phase of the conflict. The diversity of attitudes in the Rhône-Alpes exemplifies the range of wartime opinion across France in the spring and early summer of 1956. The Rhône-Alpes citizenry recognized Algeria's legacy to the nation, but in June *Le Dauphiné Libéré* made a sober assessment of the national war policy in an effort to secure it: "The discontentment hardens against a policy in disarray, a system disorganized and wasteful."[47]

Men and women in the Rhône-Alpes were increasingly less hesitant about challenging their national leaders. The reasons that citizens gave for rejecting the imperial identity of France were most often related to the malignant impact of the war at home—the perversion of national values, the political instability, military insubordination, and most of all, the derailment of national renewal. In their forthright repudiation of national leaders they contributed to the eventual collapse of the Fourth Republic in May 1958 and the ushering in of de Gaulle's Fifth Republic.

The Suez Canal Crisis

Historians share the view that the Suez venture was the only popular war, let alone policy, that the Fourth Republic managed to carry out.[48] New evidence on popular reactions in the Rhône-Alpes offers a less sanguine view. There is no question about the success of the Fourth Republic in its rallying of popular support for the Suez campaign. The French government viewed as an opportunity Egyptian colonel Abdel Gamel Nasser's grandstand seizure of the British and French–owned canal operation (on Egyptian soil) in July 1956. Within days official propaganda was crafted to correlate Egyptian aggression with the Algerian struggle. Plagued by dissension over the war, the French leadership sought to convince the public that toppling Nasser was tantamount to a quick victory in Algeria. The new angle was based on the alleged new evidence that Nasser was orchestrating the Algerian insurgency to serve his Pan-Arabist ambitions, an anti-Western goal bolstered by Moscow. And the government's tactic buoyed the regional population's confidence in Paris. Complaints about the war relented considerably in July and August. Even those soldiers on leave in this period expressed an uncharacteristic optimism that this tactic would cause an outright collapse of the Algerian insurgency.[49] This summertime surge of respect for the Fourth Republic policy effectively dissipated the opposition between the center and the periphery.

The aggressive Fourth Republic stance on Suez sustained this upbeat emotional climate in the Rhône-Alpes through the early autumn.[50] The army's capture of the Athos, a small ship smuggling Egyptian arms to the FLN, bolstered the case against Nasser. But the public was less certain whether to praise or criticize the army for its hijack of a Moroccan plane. On the one hand, they had captured the FLN delegation, but on the other, the Algerian leaders were en route to diplomatic talks with French delegates, under the auspices of Moroccan and Tunisian leaders. Even if Prime Minister Mollet pretended not to notice the military subversion of his authority, the riots in the Arab world and the resignation of Mollet's minister of affairs for Morocco and Tunisia, Alain Savary, exposed to the public the perilous disharmony between the army and the government.[51] As a result of the fiasco, the Moroccan and Tunisian governments threw their support behind the Algerian rebels and an independent Algeria. "My confidence in France has been destroyed. It can only be renewed when men of good faith—de Gaulle, Mendès-France—are again in charge," stated President Habib Bourguiba.[52] In France, François Mauriac's column "Bien joué" in the late October issue of L'Express warned of lasting damage to a nation that had betrayed the goodwill of its own allies: "When a [future] policy depends . . . on our word, we have no defense if our allies state they cannot trust us. With this act we have destroyed the foundations of the Franco-Muslim community we dreamed of erecting."[53]

The Rhône-Alpes tourism industry immediately felt the anti-French backlash of the Suez crisis. The traditional Middle East clientele canceled winter skiing on the French alpine slopes. The drop in winter sales dealt a severe hardship to local families. By 1957 they were experiencing the damaging consequences of the national military policy in North Africa. Moreover, opinions showed awareness of widespread Muslim animosity toward the French. The wholesale massacre of French families in rural Morocco testified to the bitterness felt by the Arab and Berber populations in the former empire.[54] A reader's letter of October 25 to Le Dauphiné Libéré observed that France was no longer trusted or welcome in North Africa.[55] Rhône-Alpes elites revised their predictions about sustained growth and redevelopment in light of the internationalization of the Algerian conflict. They reasoned that because the national leadership had produced failed policies and unmanageable hostility to France in the Maghreb, the French had virtually no chance of achieving lasting peace in Algeria.

In November, when the French and British military finally launched their military venture against Egypt, ordinary citizens witnessed the worldwide condemnation of the attack. Along with the British and the Israelis, the French were criticized around the globe as willful imperialists and reckless provocateurs, whose aggression risked a third world war. The reactions abroad left no doubt in the Rhône-Alpes that the fate of Algeria and France rested on the world situation. After Suez, Algeria became a pawn in the international competition between Cold War forces. One reader of *Le Monde* from Chambéry pointed out, "The results of the French policy are certainly very different than that expected by our leaders. It is up to them to explain to us the mistakes of a policy of suicide and, to settle completely the urgent problems the national war policy and broken promises are not settling. We have had enough killing."[56] In Lyon, Soustelle's base of support for the war soon subsided. His argument that France must fight for "our" Mediterranean bulwark against Moscow proved rather fragile in light of the fact that both the United States and the Soviet Union condemned the French, British, and Israeli incursion of Egypt. A Lyon reader of *Le Monde* articulated why the Suez situation had become more problematic: "At the moment of the nationalization of the Suez canal in July, all of us considered it an affront, a disloyalty, a unilateral break of a contract consummated in an aggressive and scornful manner. Everyone spoke of 'taking off the gloves' and everyone knew the preparations were taking place. Still August passed, then September, and nothing happened. We were stupefied that France had still not reacted to the nationalization of the canal for three months. We gave Egypt and its friends the impression of not being hostile."[57] Faced with the French government's lethargy, the disappointing military outcome, and the consequent Arab oil embargo to punish France, the will of the Rhône-Alpes public to stay the course in Algeria evaporated. Ordinary citizens blamed the humiliation of France on none other than their own leaders, despite the anti-American vitriol in the media. "After this, shame covers the face of France," wrote one Annecy reader to *Le Dauphiné Libéré*.[58] The irony, reluctantly grasped by ordinary citizens, was that the decisive moves in the latest global poker game in Suez and Algeria revealed the new American view that French interests were expendable.

In the early months of 1957 war opinions in the Rhône-Alpes registered embarrassment about the conduct of France in Egypt and in Algeria. The chief cause of their impressions came from worldwide media reports from Algiers. Journalists portrayed the French Army in Algeria carrying out potential war crimes through systematic torture against the Algerian people. The media indicated that France was so determined to suppress the nationalist liberation that the government was willing to condone the violation of international law. "It is with profound anger and stupefaction that I learn about our military's conduct in Algiers," wrote a Lyon reader and an engineer from Grenoble to the editor of *Le Monde*. "The army works against France."[59] In the early months of 1957 citizens in the Rhône-Alpes suspected the military's subversion of civilian authority. The army had progressively engaged itself and the entire nation in a "hyperbolic war" in which the action was no longer a means to achieve an end.[60] The Algerian War overwhelmed Paris, and the Republic was clearly at risk.

That winter the public appeared less mired down by the Algerian crisis as swarms of local skiers joined tourists in the Alps. Locals immersed themselves with renewed interest in the winter festivities of their hamlet, village, and city. With tensions in the Middle East reduced, at least temporarily, the Saudis and Jordanians returned to their favorite French tourist sites. Everyone seemed relieved to focus less on national problems. Nevertheless, this period gave way to uncharacteristic pessimism in the Rhône-Alpes. The mood within the business communities and among industrial leaders was prompted by Nasser's uniting an Arab alliance to block oil supplies to France. Oil restrictions could have none other than a sobering effect on the regional economy and in every dimension of the harsh winter life. At first the public had shown its customary stoicism about the fuel rations. But the chaotic supply of rations, the arbitrariness of their allotment, and the uncertainty of the extent of the shortage led even the most patient among them to conclude that the mounting incompetence in the national government had made a bad situation worse. The oil crisis posed serious challenges for tourism; the government allotment of fuel for the Savoie and Haute-Savoie departments covered only 78 percent of their need.[61]

The historic events of late 1956 brought about firm opposition to the military policy among Rhône-Alpes citizens. Citizens had been disappointed initially by the fateful decision of Paris to impose its imperial national identity by submerging France in a full-scale war effort. But that attitude had changed to outright opposition once the public recognized that the Suez conflict had developed into an international one. The outcome of the Suez invasion confirmed public opinion, as the French saw the demise of their ability to create an independent foreign policy. The Arab oil embargo made this reality especially poignant for the Rhône-Alpes public. For citizens of the region what was important in each of these events was the failure of the leadership in Paris. The regional population thus sought alternative leadership in the behind-the-scenes authority of its more trusted business and commercial leaders, politicians, and municipal councils. Together with regional authorities, the population turned its attention to building a different national identity. It framed its ideas based on references to the Rhône-Alpes, renouncing the imperial national identity of France embodied by the war policy of the Fourth Republic.

Aftermath of the Suez Crisis

Reassessment of the war campaign in the aftermath of Suez crystallized opinions in the first quarter of 1957. These months marked the point of no return in the collapse of support for the national war policy in the Rhône-Alpes. The notion of refocusing on their own regional revival grew increasingly attractive in the bifurcation between the Fourth Republic's agenda for the nation and the rejection of it among those living in the Rhône-Alpes. Successive French generations had undergone a period of renewed fascination with tradition and an idealization of the past at moments of upheaval and uncertainty. The public's choices in this phase of the Algerian War exemplify that process noted earlier, one that has been seen at other such historic moments of acute dislocation. In the early winter communities in the Rhône-Alpes region sought to reinvent their idea of France, and for guidance they turned to familiar leaders, their municipal councils, their mayors and cultural elites, and their own commercial and business leaders. With them and in the comfort of reinvigorating their own local rituals and traditions, the population found new anchorage.

The great strength of this counternarrative of regional revivalism was that the logic fit with the self-stated goals of French modernizers. They aimed to construct a strong modern nation that commemorated and integrated a rich and complex patrimony. During the 1950s the promotion of tourism in the Rhône-Alpes had been built around the thesis of its distinctive regional culture—featuring, for example, the dukes of Savoy; the Savoyard way of life; the expansion of sites named to honor François de Sales; making a museum of the chateau of François de Menthon; processions by the lake in Savoyard costume; fireworks at the lake; brochures promoting local historic contributions in music, theater, dance; plays about the area's history; folkloric festivals with dance and cuisine; and the resurrection of the local patois in the mountain villages. In Lyon these energies played out in the form of plans ranging from urban renewal of the historic medieval and Renaissance quarter to revival of the city's museum, which documented Lyon's rich silk and printing histories and the arts. Such interest had been there before, but these local customs and sites became the objects of education and the focus of tourism under the direction of local elites. The invigorated promotion of authentic regional culture accompanied the area's extraordinary postwar commercial and industrial growth. During the Algerian War this tendency was strengthened under the concerted efforts and allied cooperation of communities across the region.[62]

There was always a self-conscious identity for the residents in relationship to the Rhône-Alpes. Their own particular region exercised a powerful influence upon their concept of France. In this regard the mechanisms regional elites advanced to intensify their attachment to the revival of their own communities were appealing. Being citizens engaged in reconstructing their own environment and reinventing their French identity in the balance, they found relief from the turmoil of the nation as defined by the national government. As Madame Blanc of Menthon-Saint Bernard explained,

> Even when my own parents ran their hotel here before World War II, Lake Annecy drew international tourists among wealthier families especially from Northern Europe. But in those months right after the Suez crisis, different families enjoyed the leisure of the Rhône-Alpes. Since the government had extended the vacation period to three weeks, the mayor, the municipal councils, and local citizens were successful in drawing different sectors of the populations to the area. We were all content to promote tourism and welcome new development as long as the growth kept the balance between preserving our tradition and advancing modern comforts.[63]

Among the ideas for promotions attendant to local patrimony that communities laid out over subsequent months, local farmers, artisans, and artists eagerly welcomed the renewed attention to their traditional expressions.[64] The point is not that the concerted focus on regional affairs isolated the public, nor was the regional population immune to the disconcerting events of the Algerian War. But the reordering of priorities was welcomed as psychological comfort for an untenable situation not subject to their control.

Local authorities carefully parsed any negative reference to the war when they dispatched their monthly reports about war attitudes to Paris. They had no alternative in light of civic leaders and citizens' intensified focus on their communities and, conversely, a dip in interest in Algeria. But the unpopularity of the war even without explicit antiwar activity was undeniable: "It could be a mistake to assume residents of the Rhône-Alpes still back the military solution in Algeria, given their state of morale."[65] More and more, disgruntled soldiers encouraged their families and neighbors' negative attitudes about the military campaign. The returning soldiers' gloom about the prospects for peace was reflected in public opinion in the Rhône-Alpes. Monsieur B, for example, a restaurateur of Les Coches, recalled, "I did not serve in the war, but my brother served in the war and so my friend from Montchavins, the village below. He died in Algeria. My friends who were drafted from here served in the Kabylie, in the mountains, which was an especially dangerous area because of the ambushes. None of them knew the territory. For us, it was a terrible war, so sad."[66]

Competing constructions of what it meant to be French were at work in this region. Regional revivalism in the Rhône-Alpes shows the way these citizens aimed to rebuild Frenchness on the basis of regional pride and economic expansion. To this end they revalued local traditions and paid tribute to the shared memory of the regional population. Renewed hope and confidence among Rhône-Alpes residents came from their unity around renewing their regional identity. Their orientation away from the national imperial identity toward revival of the Rhône-Alpes as integral to the renewal of France was affirming for the citizenry. The citizens demonstrated that they were able to play a role in the remaking of a strong republic even while they repudiated the Fourth Republic's imperial concept of France.

Finally, the commitment of the Rhône-Alpes citizens to the regional revival provided an alternative goal for them to restore the nation. They chose this goal rather than the war cause of the national government. As Eric Hobsbawm has argued, any number of societies have shown an aptitude in the past two hundred years for inventing traditions and rituals at moments of acute disruption.[67] Such strategies in the 1950s Rhône-Alpes in no way aimed to impede the synthesis of the nation; rather, they helped ensure that the fundamental cohesive structures of France would prevail despite the loss of Algeria.[68] The Algerian War, like the burden of Nazi defeat and Vichy, prompted such loyal French citizens to strengthen their own patrimony as a pillar in the redemption of the Republic. The work of historians Pierre Nora and Henri Rousso helps to explain the ways in which shared memory among Rhône-Alpes citizens not only compelled them to reject the national war policy; memory also served to propel the restoration of the nation in the region: "Memory is blind to all but the group it binds. . . . Memory takes root in the concrete, in spaces, gestures, images, and objects. . . . It is an organic unity, a natural expression of the bonds within a coherent community."[69] Against the centralized state and its war to retain French Algeria, these citizens chose to redeem national identity in the Rhône-Alpes.

Notes

1. William B. Cohen, *Urban Government and the Rise of the French City: Five Municipalities in the Nineteenth Century* (New York: St. Martin's, 1998), 256.
2. John Ruedy, *Modern Algeria: The Origins and Development of a Nation* (Bloomington: Indiana University Press, 1992); Alistair Horne, *A Savage War of Peace: Algeria 1954–1962* (London: Macmillan, 1977).
3. Quoted in Horne, *Savage War of Peace*, 99.
4. For studies that explore the process of the inventing of French national identity at the local level, see Sara B. Pritchard, "Reconstructing the Rhône: The Cultural Politics of Nature and Nation in Contemporary France, 1945–1997," *French Historical Studies* 27, no. 4 (Fall 2004): 765–99; Stephen L. Harp, *Marketing Michelin: Advertising and Cultural Identity in Twentieth-Century France* (Baltimore: Johns Hopkins University Press, 2001); Heinz-Gerhard Haupt, Michael G. Müller, and Stuart Woolf, introduction to *Regional and National Identities in Europe in the XIXth and XXth Centuries* (The Hague: Kluwer Law International, 1998); and Stéphane Gerson, "Une France Locale: The Local Past in Recent French Scholarship," *French Historical Studies* 26, no. 3 (Summer 2003): 539–59.
5. Maryse Fabriès-Verfaillie, Annie Jouve, and Pierre Stragiotti, *La France des régions* (Paris: Bréal, 1992), 24–25. Between June 1955 and June 1960 the Fourth and Fifth Republics transformed the departmental infrastructure of the Republic into twenty-two regions, one of which became the Rhône-Alpes.
6. H. R. Kedward, *Occupied France: Collaboration and Resistance, 1940–44* (Cambridge: Blackwell, 1985), 72.
7. Jean-Louis Crémieux-Brilhac, "Bilan de la bataille des Glières," *Revue d'Histoire de la Seconde Guerre Mondiale* (1975): 99.

8. Fabriès-Verfaillie, Jouve, and Stragiotti, *La France des régions*, 328–30.

9. John Ardagh, *The New French Revolution* (New York: Harper and Row, 1968), 163–64.

10. Jean-Pierre Rioux, "Vivacité du récit français des origines," *Vingtième Siècle: Revue d'Histoire* 76 (October–December 2002): 131.

11. Interviews, Claude Bourdet, May 4, 1979, Fonds Odile Rudelle, Centre d'Histoire de l'Europe du Vingtième Siècle (hereafter cited as CHEV).

12. Interviews, Claude Bourdet, May 4, 1979, Fonds Odile Rudelle, CHEV.

13. Jean-Pierre Rioux, *The Fourth Republic, 1944–1958* (Cambridge: Cambridge University Press, 1987), 281.

14. Mohammed Harbi, "Le FLN et l'opinion française," in *La Guerre d'Algérie et les français*, ed. Jean-Pierre Rioux and Jean-François Sirinelli (Paris: Fayard, 1990), 50.

15. Rapport sur la situation dans l'Haute-Savoie (June–August 1956), F1cIII 1320, Archives Nationales (hereafter cited as AN).

16. Geoffrey Adams, *The Call of Conscience: French Protestant Responses to the Algerian War, 1954–1962* (Waterloo, Ontario: Wilfrid Laurier University Press, 1998), 114.

17. Claude Bourdet, "Votre Gestapo d'Algérie," *France-Observateur*, January 13, 1955.

18. Rapport sur la situation dans l'Isère (July–August 1956), F1cIII 1357, AN; Rapport sur la situation dans le Rhône (July–August 1956), F1cIII 1316, AN.

19. Matthew Connelly, *A Diplomatic Revolution: Algeria's Fight for Independence and the Origins of the Post–Cold War Era* (New York: Oxford University Press, 2002), 105.

20. "Committee for the Action of Intellectuals for the Defense of Liberties," France 4D880, Bibliothéque de Documentation Internationale Contemporaine (hereafter cited as BDIC).

21. "Appeal from Christians against Violence," signed Abbé Pierre, J. M. Domenach, Pasteur de Purey, Paul Ricoeur, and Madame Emanuel Mounier, July 1956, France 4D880, BDIC.

22. Rapport sur la situation dans l'Isère (April–July 1956), F1cIII 1277, AN.

23. Rapport sur la situation dans l'Isère (April–July 1956), F1cIII 1277, AN.

24. Danielle Tartakowsky, "Les Manifestations dans le rue," in Rioux and Sirinelli, *La Guerre d'Algérie et les Français*, 133.

25. Pierre Bolle, "Le Protestantisme français et la guerre d'Algérie," in *La Guerre d'Algérie et les Chrétiens*, ed. François Bédarida and Étienne Fouilloux (Paris: Institut d'Histoire du Temps Présent, 1988).

26. Guerre d'Algérie: witnesses, 1956–61, RGI, CHEV.

27. Raphaëlle Branche, *La Torture et l'armée pendant la guerre d'Algérie, 1954–1962* (Paris: Gallimard, 2001), 91–92.

28. Branche, *La Torture*.

29. Branche, *La Torture*.

30. Guerre d'Algérie: witnesses, 1956–61, RGI, CHEV.

31. Letter to the editor of *Le Monde*, Hubert Beuve-Méry, May 23, 1956, BM 137, CHEV.

32. Martine Lemalet, *Lettres d'Algérie, 1954–1962: la guerre des appelés, la mémoire d'une génération* (Paris: J Clattès, 1992), 178.

33. Jean-Pierre Vittori, preface to *Nous les appelés d'Algérie* (Paris: Stock, 1977).

34. Michel Winock, *La République se meurt* (Paris: Seuil, 1978), 28.

35. "La Guerre ne se terminera pas même si le gouvernement français envoie 500,000 hommes en Algérie, déclare Messali Hadj," *Le Monde*, March 16, 1956, FIcIII 1254, 1263, 1272–77, AN.

36. Connelly, *Diplomatic Revolution*, 105.

37. See, in particular, the speech of Pierre Cot in *Journal Officiel*, debates in the National Assembly, November 12, 1957.

38. Ardagh, *New French Revolution*, 124.

39. Rapport sur la situation dans le Rhône (April 1956), FIcIII 1316, AN; *Dernière heure lyonnaise*, February 7, 1956.

40. Elie Kedourie, *Islam in the Modern World and Other Studies* (New York: Holt, Rinehart and Winston, 1980), 213.

41. Connelly, *Diplomatic Revolution*, 97.

42. Connelly, *Diplomatic Revolution*, 97.

43. Stanley Hoffmann, *Le Mouvement Poujade* (Paris: Librarie Armand Colin, 1956), 92–93.

44. Letter to the editor of *Le Monde*, Beuve-Méry, August 14, 1958, BM 139, CHEV.

45. Rapport sur la situation dans l'Isère (July–August 1956), FIcIII 1357, AN; Rapport sur la situation dans le Rhône (July–August 1956), FIcIII 1316, AN.

46. *Dernière heure lyonnaise*, June 15, 1956.

47. *Le Dauphiné Libéré*, June 4, 1956.

48. Alfred Grosser, *La IVe République et sa politique extérieure* (Paris: Librairie Armand Colin, 1967), 373; Charles-Robert Ageron, "L'Opinion française devant la guerre d'Algérie," *Revue Française d'Histoire d'Outre-Mer* 63, no. 231 (1976): 263–64; Jean-Pierre Rioux, "L'Opinion publique dans l'affaire de Suez," *L'Histoire* 38 (October 1981): 35–37.

49. Grosser, *La IVe République*, 373; Ageron, "L'Opinion française," 263–64; Rioux, "L'Opinion publique," 35–37.

50. Grosser, *La IVe République*, 373; Ageron, "L'Opinion française," 263–64; Rioux, "L'Opinion publique," 35–37.

51. SV 54, 1956–58, CHEV.

52. Jean Lacouture, *Cinq hommes et la France* (Paris: Seuil, 1961), 174.

53. François Mauriac, "Bien Joué?" *L'Express*, October 26, 1956.

54. Simone Lacouture and Jean Lacouture, *Le Maroc à l'épreuve* (Paris: Le Seuil, 1958), 339.

55. *Le Dauphiné Libéré*, October 28, 1956.

56. Letter to the editor of *Le Monde*, Beuve-Méry, December 12, 1956, BM 50, CHEV.

57. BM 50, CHEV.

58. *Le Dauphiné Libéré*, November 6, 1956.

59. Letter to the editor of *Le Monde*, Beuve-Méry, May 18–19, 1958, BM 139, CHEV.

60. Raphaëlle Branche, *La Torture et l'armée pendant la guerre d'Algérie, 1954–1962* (Paris: Gallimard, 2001), 92.

61. Rapports sur la situation dans le Haute-Savoie (December 1956), FIcIII 1320, AN.

62. Emmanuel Le Roy Ladurie, *Histoire de France des régions: la périphérie française, des origins à nos jours* (Paris: Seuil, 2001), 267–69.

63. Interview, Madame Blanc, hotel owner, Menthon-Saint Bernard, July 5, 2002.

64. *Guide de Tourisme Michelin Alpes du Nord: Savoie-Dauphiné* (Paris: Pneu Michelin, 1996).

65. FIcIII 1254, 1263, 1272–77, AN.

66. Interview, Monsieur Broche, Les Coches, Commune de Bellentre, Rhône-Alpes, July 17, 1996.

67. Eric Hobsbawn, "Introduction: Inventing Traditions," in *The Invention of Tradition*, ed. E. Hobsbawn and T. Ranger (Cambridge: Cambridge University Press, 1983), 4–5.

68. John Higham, *Hanging Together: Unity and Diversity in American Culture*, ed. Carl J. Guarneri (New Haven CT: Yale University Press, 2001), 3.

69. Pierre Nora, "Between Memory and History: Les Lieux de Mémoire," *Representations* 26 (Spring 1989): 9. See also Henry Rousso, *The Vichy Syndrome: History and Memory in France since 1944* (Cambridge MA: Harvard University Press, 1991).

5

Autonomy or Colony

The Politics of Alsace's Relationship
to France in the Interwar Era

Samuel Huston Goodfellow's essay on the regional identities in Alsace shows how the concepts of empire and imperialism also has application within France's territory. In this instance the residents of Alsace sought to redefine their identity from peripheral to central during the interwar years. Newly integrated into France as a result of France's victory in World War I, both Alsatians and the French government were initially optimistic about this prospect, as Alsace had been subjected to a quasi-colonial status in Germany from 1871 until 1918. Then the imposition of French republican imperial policies emanating from Paris in Alsace provoked turmoil on the margin. Although Alsatians differed over how to redefine Alsace's relationship to France, the majority of Alsatians agreed that the region should craft its own distinctive ethnic cultural identity and not adopt wholesale France's nationalistic core identity, as reflected in policies such as language uniformity and the separation of church and state.

Consequently, a myriad of Alsatian political groups emerged to resist French encroachment on their autonomy, some even describing Alsace as a colony. Likewise, French and German right-wing political actors entered the fray, using Alsace as a cause to further their own antirepublican political agendas. The perception of difference, at odds with the French trope of Alsace as essentially French, infused politics with a deeply divisive tenor and polarized debate between pro-French and pro-German factions over the identity of Alsatians. Alsatian resistance to the centralizing force of French republican nationalism was initially successful, but ultimately its regional identities were subsumed in the larger national narratives of France and Germany in the 1930s.

↔ ↔

Emblematic of the complexity of Alsatian identity and its role as a border area between Germany and France is an Alsatian folk ditty that goes, "Hans in Schnockeloch has all that he wants. And what he has he doesn't want, and what he wants he doesn't have. Hans in Schnockeloch has all that he wants."[1] A pro-German, pro-Nazi folklorist, Karl Roos, popularized this piece of doggerel during the 1920s as part of an anti-French movement.[2] The expression of ambivalence—simultaneously desiring inclusion and chafing at external control—aptly characterizes Alsatian identity throughout the 1920s, 1930s, and into World War II. Alsatians had their own sense of identity as a Rhenish province, but in the overheated nationalistic atmosphere of the twentieth century, they were increasingly prepared to conform to the larger nationalistic entities of France and Germany.

On its face Alsace presents a clear example of the relationship between a peripheral border region and its core counterpart. The terms *core* and *periphery* usually describe a lopsided power relationship between a more advanced, more powerful, and more culturally hegemonic center and an outlying, dependent frontier. In a sense the distinctions between *core* and *periphery* describe a fundamentally imperialistic set of relations, even when the terms are applied to regions commonly considered by the core as integral to the country. The relationship between Paris and Alsace, however, demonstrates how thin this simplistic relationship actually is. Alsatians, Frenchmen, and even Germans manipulated and constructed the relationship between Alsace and France. The negotiation, really a conflict, over Alsace's identity reflected a profound transience in the identity of all the participants. In a sense Alsatians constituted a core of their own, or at least they thought themselves as such. Whereas the French and the Germans both viewed Alsace, at least rhetorically, as an essential part of their respective national cores, Alsace struggled, ultimately unsuccessfully, to play the two against each other in order to avoid marginalization and retain its distinctiveness and some degree of self-rule. Karl Roos's evocation of Alsatian folklore was only a single volley from one perspective in a cultural war over Alsace.

In the interwar era Alsace's relationship as a periphery to the Parisian core unfolded over the course of two stages, divided by the Colmar trial of 1928. The first stage was what the French called the "Alsatian malaise," which began in 1924, when virtually all of Alsace, apart from a minority of francophiles and French-Alsatian immigrants, protested the particular conditions of French sovereignty.[3] A clear attempt to assert and negotiate an independent Alsatian identity, the Alsatian malaise resulted in conflicting outcomes. On the one hand, the French government agreed to some distinct legal practices in Alsace. On the other hand, the debate got hijacked by the extreme nationalist politics of both Germany and France. The political emphasis on regional uniqueness gave way to a stark choice between France and Germany that increasingly emanated from French and German fascist ideologies.

The watershed occurred in 1928 during the Colmar trial of the most notorious Alsatian autonomist leaders. Autonomism was the political manifestation of Alsatian malaise. Alsatians' cultural insistence on the use of German, their espousal of secession from France, and their close but underground ties to Germany opened the autonomists to the charge of treason. The trial inflamed the French sensibility, which was shocked at the whiff of rejection of all that France had to offer. Competition with German culture so soon after the war only exacerbated the problems. At the same time, it brought to a head the simmering tensions within Alsace as the locals could both sympathize with the defendants and recognize their excesses.

After the Colmar trial in 1928, most Alsatians moderated their stance. Although not yet at the stage where it was "chic" to speak French, Alsatians accepted being part of France for lack of a better alternative. The separatists' protestations against French rule grew increasingly marginal, and thus more rabid, and the pro-German Unabhängige Landespartei für Elsaß-Lothringen, or Landespartei (Independent Regional Party for Alsace-Lorraine), a separatist, pro-German party, turned to Nazism. This move was still not radical enough for the young hotheads in the party's youth group, the Jungmannschaft, who developed ties to the Nazi ss. The pro-French fascists also drifted into a myriad of conflicting and transitory groups until they were collected into the more mainstream fascist Parti Social Français in the late 1930s.[4] World War II merely confirmed the tacit acceptance of France.

Traditionally, Alsatians identified with the rich Rhenish culture of the region running from Switzerland northward to the North Sea, not with a specific nationality. Dating back to Roman times, the Rhine was a major cultural nexus. Before the Treaty of Westphalia in 1648, Alsace belonged to the Holy Roman Empire, and the people living there spoke a Germanic dialect. After 1648 Alsace increasingly came under the aegis of the French. Consequently, Alsatian identity and its situation vis-à-vis its neighbors has been complex—neither fully separate nor fully integrated but always with

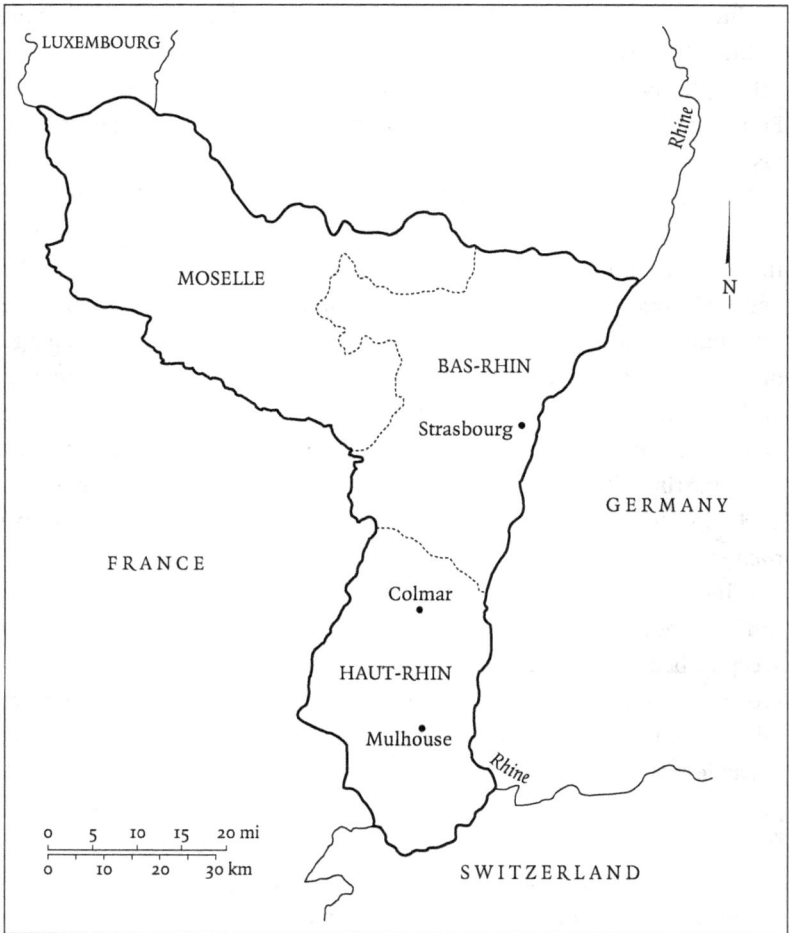

Map 5.1. Alsace

a distinctive sense of importance based on the historic, economic, and cultural centrality of the Rhineland.

Almost unconsciously, however, the historiography of Alsace shows a bias toward the nationalist aspirations of France and Germany and drowns out the independent voice of Alsace. Modern Alsatian in-between-ness has been characterized as "duality" by the French scholar Frédéric Hoffet or as "culturally German but politically French" by the German historian Karl-

Heinz Rothenberger.[5] Indeed, the struggle between the hegemonic nation-alisms of Germany and France on one side and Alsace on the other was what was at issue in the turbulence of the 1920s. The commonly accepted designation of the region as "Alsace-Lorraine" is symptomatic of the prob-lem: Alsace-Lorraine was an artificial construction created in 1870, when Germany administered the two provinces as one. Before then Alsace had never been closely tied to Lorraine.

France and Germany tossed Alsace back and forth four times over the past 140 years. In 1870 Germany took Alsace and Lorraine from France as part of the price for its devastating victory in the Franco-Prussian War, thereby creat-ing the peculiar entity known as Alsace-Lorraine. Motivated by "revanche," the French wrested Alsace and Lorraine back in 1918. The fall of France in 1940 saw the Nazi regime attach Alsace and Lorraine to the German admin-istrative districts of Baden and Saarland, respectively, following its even more convincing victory over the French. The French won Alsace back again in 1945, and so it has remained ever since. Although Alsatians attempted throughout this period to voice their perspectives, they were silenced by the power of the dominant German and French nationalist narratives. Not coincidentally, the seesawing from 1870 to 1945 corresponded to a period of intense nationalism across the Continent. Eventually, Alsatians found it more expedient to ally themselves with whomever constituted the lesser of two evils (usually the country that did not have control over Alsace)—hence, Hans in Schnockeloch. The French-German dominance over the issue of identity deeply divided Alsatian society after World War I, forcing upon each individual an unnatural either/or choice and channeling political activity into highly divisive and extremist political parties.[6]

But Alsace cannot simply be characterized as having a solely dual nature, subject only to either German or French narratives. Alsatians retained strong vestiges of their ancestral sensibilities and actively negotiated their cultural and political status during the interwar period. Indeed, beginning in the late nineteenth century, Alsatians began to appropriate the language of national-ism for Alsace much as other marginalized European ethnic groups such as Brittany and the nations of Central Europe did. Poetry, drama, and folklore emphasized Alsatian distinctiveness to the point of publishing works in dialect.[7] Negotiating from a position of weakness, many Alsatians viewed themselves both as victims of imperialism and as members of a superior culture after 1918. They initially succeeded in mobilizing against key French policies, especially in education and religion, but eventually came to accept inclusion in France.

At the end of World War I the victorious allies rewarded France with the return of Alsace-Lorraine. The initial stages of its reintegration posed particular problems for both Alsace and France. Both sides had high expectations. The Alsatians showed every sign initially of embracing France, to the point that even before the war ended, Abbé Haegy, a staunch autonomist, admitted to a German colleague that Alsace-Lorraine would vote overwhelmingly in favor of joining France.[8] Alsatians enthusiastically cheered the entry of the French Army under General Joseph-Jacques-Césaire Joffre and embraced their "definitive" return to France.[9] The Alsatians hoped that France would be more accepting of Alsatian distinctiveness than Germany had proven to be. For their part the French had scored a significant symbolic victory over Germany and reaffirmed France's territorial integrity, honor, and identity through the reacquisition of Alsace. Especially after such a protracted and violent war, which drained an entire generation of Frenchmen, the French needed to believe in the righteousness of liberating Alsace. The French assumed that the Alsatians were going to be thankful for freedom and content to be French. They interpreted Alsatians' enthusiasm in 1918 as a repudiation of German rule and as a permanent endorsement of French culture, not as a temporary expression of relief at the end of the war. The two parties thus had different expectations and hopes for the future, and both believed that they controlled, or would control, the relationship. France imagined Alsace simply as an extension of itself and remained insensitive to the ways in which reality did not match. The Alsatians expected that they would be able to cultivate their Alsatian identity under the freer auspices of France. The Alsatian malaise emerged out of the mutual recognition, acknowledged sooner in Alsace than in France, that the expectations were unrealistic.

Despite the frictions inherent in shifting Alsace from one country to another, public dissent at first was limited as a result of a tacit agreement by the French government to defer the introduction of French anticlerical legislation, which separated church and state and also secularized education. In General Joffre's words, spoken as he led the French Army into Alsace in 1918, "The values, customs, and traditions which you treasure so much . . .

should not only not be disturbed, but should flourish."[10] As a practical matter, Germany did not seem to be such a great option because of the political instability of the fledgling Weimar Republic and the hyperinflation of 1923. Nevertheless, reality gradually set in when the problems of reintegration in the 1920s generated widespread resistance. The first symptoms of the Alsatian malaise appeared as early as December 1918, when the French government issued identity cards that distinguished between Alsatian-French, half-Alsatian, foreign, and German residents.[11] These *commissions de triage* signaled the French government's serious intention to purge the region of German influence. Alsatians resented the discriminatory policies defined by the identity cards, and many left.[12] Thousands of Germans clogged the bridge across the Rhine in their exodus to Kehl, so the policy was somewhat successful. On the negative side families were divided, and expatriate Alsatians whose families had left in 1871 triumphantly returned in 1918, to the disadvantage of those who had spent the last half-century in Germany. Shifting markets from a German to a French orientation further strained many Alsatian enterprises.[13] As the autonomist leader Dr. Eugene Ricklin put it, could France really expect that Alsace, "which is racially German due to its language, which has survived nearly fifty years under the German regime, to which it owes its prosperity, can become French from one day to the next?"[14]

A key issue that plagued Alsace was education. In January 1920 the French government introduced the "direct method" of instruction, which meant that all students, regardless of their linguistic background, would be taught only in French. Students only received three hours per week of German instruction, beginning in their fourth year; before then, they used no German, except for some oral religious instruction when children could not understand French.[15] From the French perspective this was the most efficient way to assimilate Alsatians fully into French culture. Alsatians viewed it differently. The majority of the population spoke Alsatian on an everyday basis; one author estimates that in 1918 only 2 percent of Alsatians used French regularly.[16] A precise estimate of Alsatian, French, and German speakers in the region is impossible to calculate because Alsatian and German are often conflated, and many Alsatians were bilingual. Non-Alsatian Germans did not easily understand their dialect. In short, for about 80 to 90 percent of the population French was not the lingua franca, which meant that essentially the entire region was to be educated in a foreign language.[17] In the long run children would inhabit a completely different cultural world from their parents or risk being economically marginalized. The parents were already sensitized to the issue by the fact that all bureaucratic and legal business was no longer conducted in German but only in French. In the short term many Alsatian children received inadequate education; by the mid-1920s the Chambre des Métiers (Chamber of Trades) lamented the fact that students entering the workforce knew neither German nor French adequately.[18] Moreover, the purging of school officials and teachers necessary for implementing the direct method left many educated teachers and bureaucrats unemployed and unemployable. Trained in what many would consider the superior German educational system, this cohort of unemployed teachers, along with other jobless government workers, became a significant core of opposition to the centralizing French project and tended to articulate their rebellion in cultural terms.

Alsatians recognized that total immersion in the French language denigrated their language and culture. Yet language in the region was a muddle because no clear consensus on language usage existed and, ultimately, there were advantages to educating the entire population in the national language. The reality was that the autonomist movement tapped into a deep well of discontent about language. Alsatians clearly understood the deep French discomfort with the Alsatian dialect and were not fully satisfied by the pretense of bilingualism when all cultural and business affairs were suddenly being conducted in French. They were accustomed to this conflict from the German era. Most interwar political publications were written in both French and German, particularly if their orientation was francophilic, and political rallies often had to be held in dialect, French, and/or German. Alsatian was a language of resistance under both the French and the Germans. Writers such as Gustave Stoskopf had already begun writing plays in dialect during the Wilhelmine period because, according to Karl-Heinz Rothenberger, "the alternative to Germany was no longer France . . . but Alsace."[19] Virtually everything became a symbolic battlefield, from the busts of German intellectuals on the library to the striking memorial to Alsatian combatants of both sides of the war in the Place de la République in Strasbourg.

Karl Roos asserted that he became an autonomist "for cultural reasons."[20] The sense of relentless pressure to give up their indigenous culture permeated

Alsatian society. Many of the newspapers openly talked about the cultural imperialism of the French, and comparisons to the colonies were common. Caricaturing France's treatment of Alsace as a racially foreign colony, some argued facetiously that Alsace might as well have been taken over by the Chinese. This allusion to Asian culture conveyed, in the stereotypes of the time, a sense that the Alsatians were superior to the French and, moreover, that the French were needlessly barbaric and cruel. The implication was that the Alsatians could rule themselves in a more civilized way than the French and that even the Germans were more cultivated.

In another instance a cartoon showed an African woman in traditional feminine Alsatian dress with the caption that this was "an Alsatian woman who has become black as a result of the colonial method."[21] Although it might have been acceptable to exterminate the culture and language of Africans (and this cartoon implicitly acknowledges that such was the case at the time), it was cultural blasphemy to extinguish a European ethnic group and language, especially for those who believed that Alsace was fundamentally German. Another cartoon, titled "Die Wacht am Rhein" (The Watch on the Rhine) featured an Alsatian woman in traditional garb being informed by an armed African soldier that he was defending her from the "barbaric German."[22] Although this cartoon was from 1935, it stressed the same point that Alsace should not be considered comparable to the traditional colonies. Alsace was European and not some tropical white man's burden, and the punch of the cartoons rested on the contrast between Alsatians and other races. They were in one sense expressions of Alsatians' racial and cultural equality, but in another they reflected a fear that Alsace could share the treatment meted out in the empire.

Although Alsatians were increasingly conscious of the cultural war that the French were waging against them, resistance remained background noise until the national elections in 1924, which were won by the Cartel des Gauches, an alliance of left-wing and republican parties. Édouard Herriot, the new prime minister, maladroitly, at least from the Alsatian point of view, exacerbated fears of an imposed centralized republic by promising to "introduce into Alsace and Lorraine the republican legislation in its entirety."[23] The most important part of the republican legislation were the anticlerical laws of 1905, which had resulted in the separation of church and state in France. As part of the German Empire in 1905, Alsace underwent no such separation, and the state paid the salaries of church officials and supported religious instruction in the schools. After 1918 the French government maintained the German laws regulating church-state relations. The sudden imposition of the anticlerical laws in 1924 threatened religion in Alsace, on top of the other cultural strains regarding language and economics. All hell broke loose.

On July 20, 1924, less than a month after Herriot's declaration, about fifty thousand Alsatian Catholics held a massive demonstration in Strasbourg against the proposed introduction of French anticlerical laws into the region.[24] The Alsace-Lorraine deputies to the National Assembly protested vigorously that the new government was repudiating "the promises made during the war in the name of the French nation."[25] These promises included the retention of state support for the churches, along with other cultural privileges. The bishop of Strasbourg, Monsigneur Charles Ruch, urged the local chapter of the Catholic League to protest, while the Protestant churches—mostly Lutheran—also opposed the government's new direction.[26] Ruch also called for a school strike, writing that the new government would "make Catholic schools disappear and make you bow down under the yoke of sectarianism."[27] Ruch, it must be said, was no autonomist. The national deputy Camille Bilger explained, "God has the right of domicile [Heimatrecht] with us in Alsace. ... If God is not allowed to participate in our life, then in the name of God, we will remain outside and make ourselves a new home."[28] One cartoon depicted Herriot as a frog spitting on the Crucifix.[29] The spontaneous and nearly unanimous opposition to the perceived threat to Alsatian religious organizations points to the importance of religious identity and the way it brought together the threads of resistance.

Regional resistance to the centralized ideal of a Frenchified Alsace grew even more radical, and support for separation from France, or at least for a minimum of the sort of privileged status that Alsace had enjoyed under the Germans, became more open. The autonomist weekly Die Zukunft (The Future) disseminated its first issue in May 1925. The editors of Die Zukunft drew support from across the party spectrum and articulated a sharp cultural critique of France. Although Die Zukunft only printed about nine thousand copies by August 1925, it grew to thirty-five thousand copies in 1926, and its symbolic significance was enormous.[30] For the French the notion that Alsace could repudiate French culture instead of merely opposing specific policies was shocking; for the Alsatians it was empowering. By moving past the shared criticism of the anticlerical movement, however, the autonomists lost whatever opportunity they might have had to work out an early accommodation with the French government.

Emboldened, on June 8, 1926, 101 prominent Alsace-Lorrainers signed the *Heimatbund* (Homeland Alliance) manifesto calling for Alsace-Lorraine to develop a political organization to defend its rights.[31] The following year the Landespartei was founded with the mission of creating "a free Alsace-Lorraine belonging to the United States of Europe that bridges France and Germany."[32] Such separatist language stressed a European, rather than either French or German, identity. European in this context, however, meant more than just greater regional autonomy; it also meant separation from France, which in turn favored a pro-German agenda. Indeed, one editorial in the *Elsass-Lothringische Zeitung*, the Landespartei's newspaper, espoused the idea of Europe because it "solved the modern *Staatsproblem* of the twentieth century in a fascist sense."[33] Not surprisingly, most of the core of the Landespartei turned to Nazism in the 1930s.[34] Alsatian response to the hegemonic discourse of assimilation into France and Germany first took the form of autonomism, which called for limited self-determination over cultural and political issues, and then separatism, which went a step farther and demanded complete independence from France. As the language of autonomism increasingly became separatist through the growth of the Landespartei, the argument over Alsace became a vehicle for German and French nationalism. The Alsatians were heavily influenced by the pervasive nationalism of the late nineteenth and early twentieth centuries, and they tried to adapt nationalist approaches to their regional needs. Ultimately, they were unsuccessful because the language of nationalism suited Germany and France better.

Each political party in Alsace had to respond to the pressing question of autonomism or risk marginalization. At best ignoring the issue was a statement of pro-French assimilationism. Each party, however, was deeply divided over the issue, causing them to divide. The Union Populaire Républicaine (UPR), a conservative Catholic party, split between its French nationalist wing and its *heimatrechtliche* (homeland rights) wing.[35] The Lutheran pastor Georges Wolf, for example, departed the Radical-Republican Party to form the Elsäßische Fortschrittspartei (Alsatian Progressive Party), railing that assimilationism was "inimical to Kultur and immoral."[36] In short a realignment of Alsatian politics took place not along a traditional left-right ideological axis but between autonomist and assimilationist factions. Except for the relatively small leftist parties, both factions were highly critical of France.

On August 22, 1926, a rally protesting France's cultural imperialism took place in Strasbourg that clearly revealed the new alliances. Autonomists from the conservative Catholic UPR led by Dr. Eugène Ricklin demonstrated "shoulder to shoulder" with the Communists in a shocking symbolic violation of existing ideological taboos.[37] For the autonomists August 22 became "Bloody Sunday" as a result of the violence that erupted between the autonomist Catholics and Communists on one side and the assimilationists, led by the Action Française (AF), an extreme-right-wing, royalist group, on the other. The shedding of blood further hardened the existing positions. By mid-1928 a formal electoral alliance known as the Volksfront (Popular Front, not to be confused with the 1936 French Popular Front) emerged that collected the support of the autonomist factions against the National Front that coordinated the efforts of the assimilationists. The Volksfront did well in the October cantonal elections and in the municipal elections of 1929, winning decisive control in Strasbourg's municipal council.[38] The Alsatian Communist and staunch advocate of autonomism Charles Hueber became mayor of Strasbourg in 1929.

The breadth of the Alsatian rejection of France deeply shocked the metropole. When Charles Hueber, deputy to the National Assembly in Paris, brazenly addressed the body in German, telling the deputies that "German is my mother tongue and that of the majority of Alsace-Lorrainers," the outraged deputies of the National Assembly expunged much of his speech from the record.[39] This move was the national government's attempt to deny that there even was a problem. As denial became less tenable, policy shifted toward repression. The government monitored subscribers to Die Zukunft.[40] An obscure 1895 law provided the legal grounds for banning Die Zukunft along with two other autonomist journals because they were published in a foreign language.[41]

Censorship was not enough. The French saw the Alsatians' malaise as treason, especially after the bloody sacrifice that France had endured during the Great War to liberate Alsace. This treason had to be exposed in order to purify the nation, so the government arrested twenty-two autonomists from across the political spectrum and put them on trial in Colmar in May 1928, alleging that they were working for the German government. Although some evidence indicated that the autonomists did have German financial support, ultimately it was irrelevant whether the French accusations were accurate because the trials enflamed Alsatian public opinion. Just before the trial, Alsatians thumbed their noses at the French by electing two of the arrested autonomists to the National Assembly. Flexing its muscle, the National Assembly invalidated the election results, which elicited the election of two other defendants. The Colmar trials became a showdown, and the trial itself was tense. Large crowds threatened the courthouse, and when the court decided that only four of the defendants were guilty and sentenced them to one year in prison and five years banishment from Alsace, the crowd responded by singing a regional anthem.[42] French policy was a failure, the premises of laicization or secularization were unraveling, and the Alsatians were unified in their desire to maintain their culture.

If Paris did not understand that it needed a new approach to Alsace after the Colmar trials, the fact was inescapable in the 1929 trial of Karl Roos, erstwhile folklorist and founder of the Landespartei. Roos returned voluntarily from self-exile in Switzerland to stand trial for treason. Bloodied by the experience of holding the 1928 autonomist trials in Alsace, the government moved the trial site to Besançon. From the beginning Roos dominated the proceedings by arguing that his opposition to the government was justified, a defense that the prosecution never convincingly rebutted. As a result, Roos was acquitted.[43] Triumphant, Roos returned to Strasbourg and addressed a mass rally.[44] It is worth noting that the French government got the last word in his case when it arrested and executed Roos for treason shortly after the outbreak of World War II.

The moderate national deputy Camille Bilger called the Alsatians "Bedingungsfranzosen" (conditional French). They were willing to be French but on their own terms. The Alsatian malaise revealed the broad dimensions of the conditions that were acceptable to the Alsatians. Language, culture, and above all, religion were to be preserved to some degree. Too much stress on Alsatian unanimity, however, would be misleading. Although there were broad areas of agreement, no absolute consensus existed. Some found France to be better than Germany, some wanted a little bit of autonomy, some were solely concerned with protecting religion, others envied the success of the German working-class movement, and still others were wholly pro-German. Alsace also had regional differences, with Strasbourg more solidly German and Mulhouse to the south more French. People living in rural districts tended to be more religious and more likely to speak Alsatian than those living in the cities. Insofar as the Alsatian malaise had any sort of consistency, it drew from the same ideological sources that fed the growth of nationalism in Germany and France as well as Europe in general. French heavy-handedness and the vigorous action of the autonomists, especially those associated with the Landespartei, shaped the Alsatian end of the debate.

Because Alsace was not something that mattered intrinsically to all French men and women, it is a bit harder to get a clear view of the French position. So far we have seen the Alsatians refusing to accept unconditional cultural dissolution into France. What did the French people and the French government want Alsace to be? Did the majority of the French really expect Alsatians to become indistinguishable from other French citizens, as the Cartel des Gauches clearly did? One way to look at assimilationism and its relation to French attitudes is to examine the positions of the most vociferous proponents of French nationalism, the French fascists. Part of the reason for this choice is because they mirror the pro-German autonomists who eventually embraced Nazism and also because the extremes formulated the political debate. It is no accident that the malaise resulted in a split between the autonomist Volksfront coalition and the assimilationist National Front coalition. The most prominent French fascist groups in the 1920s included the Action Française and the Faisceau and in the 1930s the Francistes and the Croix de Feu/Parti Social Français.[45] These groups yield insight into the general views of France toward Alsace because, like the separatists from the Alsatian side, they controlled the pro-French discourse, wielding a decisive influence on the political views of those who tended to favor France. Moreover, the French fascist groups were quite active in the region and were the most public face of assimilationism in Alsace. Additionally, these groups publicized Alsace's discontent to the rest of France.

The Action Française played a significant role in shaping France's view of Alsace and Lorraine. In 1905 Maurice Barrès' popular novel *Colette Baudoche* presented Alsace-Lorrainers as loyal francophones, who suffered under the oppression of the heavy-handed Germans.[46] The image of Catholics in the eastern departments suffering under the yoke of the German *Kulturkampf*, a conflict in which the German state persecuted German Catholics, highlighted the church's centrality for French identity. The effects of this novel included the important goal of stimulating the French memory of the defeat in the Franco-Prussian War and at the same time reminded the French of the key pillars of France—nation, language, and church. This book broadly, and incorrectly, shaped the French view of Alsace before, during, and after the war as belonging in spirit to France. The cartoons of the popular francophile Hansi also reinforced the stereotype of clumsy Germans ruling a francophile territory.[47] Alsatians gleaned some advantage out of this image in the 1920s because it established that they deserved fair treatment as the French. The danger, of course, came when the French learned that the Alsatians may not have been as thoroughly Gallic as they imagined.

After the war the AF's use of Alsace turned into a vitriolic attack on the Third Republic. Whereas before the war Alsace had represented positive Catholic and patriotic virtue, in the 1920s Alsace evoked the evils of republicanism. The AF characterized the Third Republic as "the government of the foreign powers," a charge that the German-speaking separatists in the Landespartei appeared to substantiate.[48] The argument, presumably, was that the Third Republic was too weak to counter German influence effectively. Another editorial in Action Française's local weekly, the *National d'Alsace* (Alsatian National), wrote, "We do not confuse France with the present government."[49] Alsace, of course, did not control the Third Republic, but the AF was promising francophile and fence-sitting Alsatians that they needed only to jettison the Republic to solve the malaise. Perhaps more important, the AF associated the German influence (and the AF hated the Germans) with the Third Republic. An extreme version of this tactic was the Action Française's accusation that "the laic laws, ostensibly from the Republic, are in reality of *boche* origin," meaning that they were socialist. Karl Marx, after all, was German.[50]

In attacking the Republic through Alsace, the AF sought to increase its membership. Virtually nonexistent in the region in 1918, the election of the Cartel des Gauches breathed life into the AF as much as it did the autonomist movement. Both Alsatians and French expressed disgust with the goals of the leftist government, which AF editor Jacques Denisane wrote "attacks above all the Catholics."[51] By 1926 the local Ligue d'Action Française had between 2,000 and 2,500 members inscribed on its membership rolls, and Alsace and Lorraine constituted one of the strongest regions in the national AF.[52] Its success reflected the growing credibility and intellectual influence of the AF's assimilationist views. In general the extreme nationalist parties did well in Alsace, as they often do in border regions, because they addressed identity. Neither liberal nor Marxist parties had much to say about identity, which was a critical error in a region where the primary political fissure after 1925 was autonomism versus assimilation and the question of Alsace's orientation was up in the air.

In many ways the fundamental assumptions of the French radical Right and the pro-German separatists were the same. Both objected to what they perceived as the liberal and socialist agenda of the Third Republic. Adherents of both the Volksfront and the National Front placed identity rather than material issues at the top of the agenda. Even the Alsatian Communists, who were supposed to be inheritors of Karl Marx's materialism, joined ranks with the autonomists in the *Volksfront*. Alsatian resistance to the Cartel des Gauches initially resonated with the conservative and right-wing spectrum of French politics. The Left's threat to religion in Alsace reminded the French Right that the 1905 anticlerical laws marked a threat to the role of religion not just in Alsace but in France. Thus, the French Right and the Alsatians shared a hostility to the 1905 anticlerical laws. Still somewhat blind to the depth of the critique of France levied by the autonomists, the French Right preferred to see the Alsatians as privileged speakers of truth about France's decadence rather than as an independent culture. The French Right could not quite fathom the Alsatians' rejection of the French language, but it could rally around the cause of the Catholic Church. As journalist Henry de Jouvenel put it, "Each French politician was able to believe that the Alsatians were on his side."[53] This patronizing view of the malaise exacerbated the problem because many Alsatians tended to see assimilationism as being compromised by political ideology—either it was part of a leftist agenda or the Right used the malaise to further its own ends, not the welfare of Alsatians.

Perhaps the most striking convergence is that both autonomists and assimilationists advocated the importance of region, although in slightly different ways. In other words, both French and German extreme nationalists accepted and embraced, at least rhetorically, the maintenance of an Alsatian identity. Although the AF rejected autonomism because it would lead to "detachment from France," it called on local members to reject "centralization, in order to fully re-liberate the provincial uniqueness and customs for the good of the whole land."[54] Regionalism was acceptable; separation was not. Similarly, the AF was the first to commit itself to support of the German language, despite its leader Charles Maurras's dislike of Germany. Allowing Alsace to be bilingual would preserve the linguistic and cultural community while binding Alsatians more tightly to France.[55] The AF's growth was predicated on the AF's ability to present itself as the most persuasive voice for a national (French) defense of Alsatian rights.

The AF was not unique among the French nationalist parties. Like all fascist movements, the AF believed in a hierarchy of identity. Fascism was not, as is often argued, simply hypernationalism, but instead it advocated integrally linking local, and even familial, identity and regional identity with national identity.[56] The Faisceau, under the leadership of Georges Valois, emerged in 1926 as a descendant and competitor of the AF.[57] Valois clearly advocated a "unitary state, which has one leader."[58] But this position was not inconsistent with a clearly articulated regionalism. At a Faisceau rally in Mulhouse, Philippe Barrès argued that the party opposed "the overly rapid assimilation of Alsace-Lorraine."[59] Barrès implied that the end goal of assimilation was still appropriate but that regional sensibilities should be considered—an appeal that worked best with French nationalists. The head of the Strasbourg chapter, Edmond Schiffmacher, went further and called for a "regionalism based on a pervasive decentralization."[60]

Another fascist proponent of regionalism for Alsace was Marcel Bucard, whose career was virtually a history of the French fascist movement. A courageous veteran of World War I, after the war Bucard turned to fascism. He is most famous for founding his own group, the Francistes, in 1933, in which he expressed his solidarity with the international fascist movement. Regionalism was an important part of the Francistes's ideology. Provincial autonomy would complement bureaucratic centralization by stimulating local economies and nurturing what Bucard called "the symphony of their [regional] traditions."[61] Francisme insisted on "absolute political loyalty" to France based on a reciprocal respect for Alsatian culture.[62] Thus, party activists in Alsace demanded the "protection of the mother tongue, culture, morals, and customs in addition to the local legislation."[63] Although the

national party remained small, Alsace was one of Bucard's most successful departments, complete with its own German-language newspaper, *Le
Franciste*.

Much of the emotive appeal of fascism stems from a visceral sense of
belonging and of community, which is then connected to the rather abstract idea of nation or race. Despite urbanization and modernization, many
Europeans still retained an almost tangible sense of regional community.
But as Celia Applegate puts it when writing about the German idea of *Heimat*
(homeland), "In reality, of course, *Heimat*'s nostalgic evocation of a closed
and close-knit community reflected its replacement by these larger and less
personal forms of political and territorial belonging."[64] At the same time,
the spread of national and international economies, national military service, and demographic changes were gradually eroding popular culture and
with it the traditional ways of expressing and acting out local identity.[65] The
demographic changes taking place threatened regional sensibility. The rise
of nationalism undermined the individual's finely honed sense of place by
simply bypassing regionalism. In the interwar period the discourse of a sense
of place was up for political grabs. Nationalism needed to be regrounded in
concrete identity. Fascists recognized the power of place, and they stepped
into the vacuum by utilizing a rhetoric that appeared to empower the region
by connecting traditional popular cultural symbols to nationalist ones.

The French fascist parties not only imagined Alsace as a pro-French region;
they tried to make it so. Although somewhat unrealistic at first, and slow to
react to the unfolding malaise, the French nationalists co-opted Alsace as
an example of fascist regionalism that cultivated local traditions in order to
strengthen the whole. Their critique of the Third Republic's inability to solve
the Alsatian question dovetailed with their national push to undermine the
liberal and socialist elements increasingly evident in modern France. The
influence of the French fascists was pernicious because it did nothing to
reconcile Alsace with French rule, opting instead to further stimulate local
discontent. By channeling Alsatian resistance against the Third Republic,
they hoped to gain more local and national converts to their ideology.

Obviously, the Landespartei at one end of the spectrum and the francophile
fascist parties at the other did not agree on the specifics of Alsace's identity;
the former sought a return to Germany, and the latter insisted on some
degree of assimilation into France. They agreed that Alsace should be either

German or French. Ironically, given the emphasis on Alsatian identity, both of the extremes shaped the political discourse in Alsace toward accepting inclusion in one of what Lewis Namier called the "master nations."[66] They also agreed that the best way to encourage Alsatians in the short term was to cultivate local culture. If Alsatians duly accepted their absorption into the larger national entity, then both autonomists and assimilationists thought that they could permit a degree of regional identity.

Regrettably, Alsatians did not have much choice in the interwar period, largely because their political options shrank. Even though Alsatians were ostensibly voting about Alsatian culture, they were actually voting about whether France was better for them than Germany. In 1924, when massive crowds appeared in Alsace to protest the heavy hand of the Cartel des Gauches, the reaction was spontaneous and nearly universal. The majority of the local population objected to existing French policy and most likely saw themselves as a unique culture, regardless of whether they were culturally oriented toward France or Germany. In their view Alsace was the core, and Paris was the periphery. The formation of the Landespartei and the intrusion of the French fascists, however, channeled local opposition into a set of two choices. Rather than remain Alsatian, the region had to accept a definition of itself as having a dual identity.

Karl Roos's trial in 1929 was the high point of the autonomist movement's success. In April 1929, only six months after the prefect of Bas-Rhin had characterized the mood of Alsace as "troubled," he predicted a "more tranquil period" for the region.[67] Ironically, the Colmar and Besançon trials, although heavily publicized by the autonomists, had the effect of exposing the separatist agenda and the extent of German financial and moral support.[68] The autonomist movement degenerated over the course of the 1930s and into World War II into an arm of the German Nazis. The government eased its repressive policies, as was evident when it pardoned the convicted Colmar defendants in July 1928. The Alsatian malaise subsided, and the pragmatic Alsatians generally accepted being part of France.

The Alsatian malaise posed the quintessential twentieth-century problem of identity. Hans in Schnockeloch did not necessarily want to be either French or German, but Alsatian attempts to assert their distinctiveness resulted in an even more vociferous assertion of both German and French identity. Ironically, the extremes of the autonomists and the assimilationists channeled the malaise into a choice between Germany and France under the guise of supporting Alsatian traditions. On the whole Alsatians accepted inclusion into France as the best of a bad set of choices, but they continued at times to want what they did not have. As a result of the turbulence of the mid to late 1920s, Alsace's regional character came to be defined as a duality, a combination of German and French attributes, and not as a unique and independent entity.

Notes

1. Quoted from Frédéric Hoffet, *Psychoanalyse de l'Alsace* (Colmar: Éditions Alsatia, 1973), 14.
2. For more on Karl Roos, see Philip Bankwitz, *Alsatian Autonomist Leaders, 1919–1947* (Lawrence: Regents Press of Kansas, 1978); and Samuel Goodfellow, *Between the Swastika and the Cross of Lorraine: Fascisms in Interwar Alsace* (DeKalb: Northern Illinois University Press, 1999), chap. 6.
3. For general information on the Alsatian malaise, see Karl-Heinz Rothenberger, *Die elsaß-lothringische Heimat-und Autonomiebewegung zwischen den beiden Weltkriegen* (Frankfurt am Main: Peter Lang, 1975); François G. Dreyfus, *La Vie politique en Alsace, 1919–1936* (Paris: Armand Colin, 1969); and Bankwitz, *Alsatian Autonomist Leaders*. *Alsatian malaise* is the term adopted by the francophile factions; the autonomists preferred to call it the "autonomist crisis." I use the term *malaise* as shorthand for the period and not as an endorsement of the French position.
4. See William D. Irvine, "Fascism in France and the Strange Case of the Croix de Feu," *Journal of Modern History* 63 (June 1991): 271–94; Robert Soucy, "French Fascism and the Croix de Feu: A Dissenting Interpretation," *Journal of Contemporary History* 26 (January 1991): 159–88; and Goodfellow, *Between the Swastika and the Cross of Lorraine*, chap. 8.
5. Hoffet, *Psychoanalyse*, 16.
6. See Samuel Goodfellow, "From Germany to France? Interwar Alsatian National Identity," *French History* 7, no. 4 (1993): 450–71.
7. Jack G. Morrison, "The Intransigents: Alsace-Lorrainers against the Annexation, 1900–1914" (PhD diss., University of Iowa, 1970).
8. Untitled "Memoire" on post-1918 Alsace, 2, 2J.226.1, n.d., ca. 1927–28, Collection Fernand-J. Heitz, Colmar.
9. David Schoenbaum, *Zabern 1913: Consensus Politics in Imperial Germany* (Boston: Allen and Unwin, 1982), discusses the German attitude toward Alsatians. General Joffre cited in Paul Schall, *Elsaß gestern, heute und morgen* (Filderstadt-Bernhausen: Erwin von Steinbeck Stiftung, 1976), 154.

10. Cited in Geneviève Baas, *Le Malaise alsacien, 1919–1924* (Strasbourg: Imprimé par Developpement et Communauté Alsagraphie, 1972), 119.

11. David Allen Harvey, "Lost Children of Enemy Allies? Classifying the Population of Alsace after the First World War," *Journal of Contemporary History* 34, no. 4 (October 1999): 537–54.

12. Irmgard Grünewald, *Die Elsaß-Lothringer im Reich, 1918–1933: Ihre Organisation zwischen Integration und "Kampf um die Seele der Heimat"* (Frankfurt am Main: Peter Lang, 1984), discusses the lives of these Alsatians and Germans who had settled in Alsace following their return to the Weimar Republic.

13. Michel Hau, *L'Industrialisation de l'Alsace, 1803–1939* (Strasbourg: Associations des Publications près des Universités de Strasbourg, 1987), is an excellent discussion of the economic issues facing Alsace.

14. Rapport, September 24, 1929, Mulhouse, F7.13396, Archives Nationales (hereafter cited as AN).

15. Stephen L. Harp, *Learning to Be Loyal: Primary Schooling as Nation Building in Alsace and Lorraine, 1850–1940* (DeKalb: Northern Illinois University Press, 1998), 196.

16. Pierre Magué, *Le Particularisme alsacien, 1918–1967* (Paris: Presses d'Europe, 1970), 47.

17. Paul Lévy, *Histoire linguistique d'Alsace et de Lorraine* (Paris: Société d'Edition, 1929), 2:477.

18. Joseph Rossé et al., *Das Elsass von 1870 bis 1932* (Colmar: Alsatia Verlag, 1932), 4:528–30.

19. Rothenberger, *Die elsaß-lothringische Heimat-und Autonomiebewegung*, 23.

20. *Der Komplott-Prozeß von Besançon vom 10. Juni bis 22. Juni 1929: Gesammelte Verhandlungsberichte* (Colmar: Alsatia Verlag, 1929), 26.

21. *Volkswille*, August 8, 1929.

22. Christian Hallier, *Vom Selbstbehauptungskampf des deutschen Volkstums im Elsass und in Lothringen, 1918–1940* (Bühl-Baden: Verlag Konkordia AG, 1944), table 22.

23. Rossé, *Das Elsass*, 4:422.

24. Rothenberger, *Die elsaß-lothringische Heimat-und Autonomiebewegung*, 53.

25. Rossé, *Das Elsass*, 4:422.

26. Rossé, *Das Elsass*, 4:425–26.

27. Rothenberger, *Die elsaß-lothringische Heimat-und Autonomiebewegung*, 87.

28. Rothenberger, *Die elsaß-lothringische Heimat-und Autonomiebewegung*, 84.

29. Robert Heitz, *Petite histoire de l'autonomisme* (Strasbourg: National d'Alsace et de Lorraine, 1928), 21.

30. Rothenberger, *Die elsaß-lothringische Heimat-und Autonomiebewegung*, 93.

31. Dreyfus, *La Vie politique en Alsace*; Rossé, *Das Elsass*, 4:50.

32. Rothenberger, *Die elsaß-lothringische Heimat-und Autonomiebewegung*, 135, quoting the party program.

33. "Im IX.Jahre faschistischer Zeitrechnung," *Elsaß-Lothringer Zeitung*, November 5, 1930.

34. Goodfellow, *Between the Swastika and the Cross of Lorraine*, chap. 6.

35. Christian Baechler, *Le Parti catholique alsacien, 1890–1939* (Paris: Éditions Ophrys, 1981), is a thorough analysis of the UPR.

36. *Das neue Elsaß*, April 14, 1927.

37. Jean-Paul Mourer, *Heraus aus der Sackgasse! Warum elsäßische Arbeiter-und Bauernpartei?* (Strasbourg: Solidarité, 1935), 30.

38. Dreyfus, *La Vie politique en Alsace*, 147–48.

39. Charles Hueber, *Elsaß-Lothringen in der Kammer* (Strasbourg: Imprimarie Solidarité, 1927), 10.

40. Commissaire Special à M. le Préfet du Bas-Rhin, Strasbourg, October 29, 1925, D286, 351, Archives départementales du Bas-Rhin (hereafter cited as ADBR).

41. Rossé, *Das Elsass*, 4:449; Hermann Hiery, *Reichstagswahlen im Reichsland* (Dusseldorf: Droste, 1986), 45.

42. *Der Komplott-Prozeß von Colmar vom 1.–24 Mai 1928* (Colmar: Alsatia Verlag, 1928), provides a pro-autonomist overview. Bankwitz, *Alsatian Autonomist Leaders*, had access to the court documents of the trial.

43. *Der Komplott-prozeß von Besançon* provides a useful, if biased, overview of the trial.

44. Autonomisme Alsacien, 1929–31, Rapport, June 25, 1929, Strasbourg, F7 13398, AN.

45. For more information on these groups, see Robert Soucy, *French Fascism: The First Wave, 1924–1933* (New Haven CT: Yale University Press, 1986); Robert Soucy, *French Fascism: The Second Wave, 1933–1939* (New Haven CT: Yale University Press, 1995); Zeev Sternhell, *Neither Right nor Left: Fascist Ideology in France*, trans. David Maisel (1986; repr., Princeton NJ: Princeton University Press, 1996).

46. Maurice Barrès, *Colette Baudoche: The Story of a Young Girl of Metz* (New York: George H. Doran, 1918).

47. Jean-Jacques Waltz, *Mon village: ceux qui n'oublient pas* (Paris: Floury, 1913).

48. "Im Dienst des Auslandes," *Le National d'Alsace*, December 11, 1926.

49. Henri d'Halys, "L'Opposition fantôme," *Le National d'Alsace*, February 25, 1926.

50. Léon Daudet, "Salut au National d'Alsace," *Le National d'Alsace*, December 24, 1924.

51. Commissaire Spécial, Gare de Strasbourg à M. le Préfet de Bas-Rhin, March 2, 1925, Strasbourg, AL 121.862 (AF 1919–1925), ADBR.

52. Commissaire de Police à M. le Commissaire Central, June 27, 1926, Strasbourg, D286.349, ADBR; Commissaire Spécial à M. le Préfet du Bas-Rhin, June 28, 1926, D286.349, ADBR.

53. Quoted in David Allen Harvey, *Constructing Class and Nationality in Alsace, 1830–1945* (DeKalb: Northern Illinois University Press, 2001), 156.

54. Jean Pictave, "Regionalismus und Autonomie," *Le National d'Alsace*, June 21, 1925.

55. "Die Sprachenfrage in der Zukunft," *Le National d'Alsace*, September 12, 1925. Note that this article is in German.

56. Roger Griffin, *The Nature of Fascism* (London: Pinter Publishers, 1991), 26, is fairly typical in listing one of fascism's key characteristics as "ultranationalism."

57. For general information on the *Faisceau*, see Soucy, *French Fascism: The First Wave*.

58. Georges Valois, *Le Fascisme* (Paris: Nouvelle Librairie Nationale, 1927), 39.

59. Commissaire Chef de la Sûreté à M. le Commissaire Central à Mulhouse, April 15, 1926, Mulhouse, F7.13210, AN.

60. Commissaire Spécial à M. le Préfet du Bas-Rhin, October 5, 1926, Strasbourg, F7.13210, AN.

61. Marcel Bucard, *Les Tyrans de la IIIe* (Paris: Éditions du Coq de France, 1937), 66.

62. "Der Francisme u. die ElsaB-Lothringische Frage," *Le Franciste*, November 1935, German language ed.

63. "Wir wollen," *Le Franciste*, April 1936, German language ed., lists these issues as "special for Alsace-Lorraine."

64. Celia Applegate, *A Nation of Provincials: The German Idea of Heimat* (Berkeley: University of California Press, 1990), 10.

65. Eugen Weber, *Peasants into Frenchmen: The Modernization of Rural France, 1870–1914* (Stanford: Stanford University Press, 1976).

66. Lewis Namier, *1848: The Revolution of the Intellectuals* (New York: Proceedings of the British Academy, 1946).

67. Cabinet du Préfet, Bas-Rhin, Questions d'Alsace et de Lorraine, IIe volume commencé le 1. janvier 1925, Strasbourg, April 16, 1929, Préfet du Bas-Rhin à M. le Président du Conseil, D 286, 348, ADBR.

68. Jean Dumser, *Bekenntniße eines waschechten els.-Loth. Autonomisten: Das Hauptquartier der elsäßischen Autonomiebewegung: Berlin-Frankfurt* (Strasbourg: Berger-Levrault, 1929).

6

The "True" French Worker Party

The Problem of French Sectarianism and Identity Politics in the Second International, 1889–1900

Kevin J. Callahan takes up the theme of identity politics and the contested processes of identity creation in his survey of the sectarian politics of the French Left in the movement of international socialism from 1889 to 1900. The essay disputes the standard view of the relationship between a hegemonic and doctrinaire German Marxism at the core of the Second International and a weak and reformist French socialism at its periphery. A critical reexamination of the events at party congresses shows that it was really the French periphery as opposed to the German core that engendered conflict within the international socialist movement. The disputes within the French Left emerged primarily from a contest over national identity, in which socialist factions asserted their own notion of national identity and internationalism in contradistinction to an international socialist movement perceived to be dominated by a Germanic socialist imperialism. Thus, identity markers revolved around the axis of French/other in multiple forms such as French/non-French, French/Germanic, and French/international. Elements of the French Left insisted that they alone represented the "true French worker party" while labeling their contenders as foreign/German worker parties. Paradoxically, Callahan demonstrates, it was the French disorder at the margins of the international socialist movement that prompted the Second International to establish a strong core political culture based on promoting fraternity and containing sectarianism.

◁ ◁

The international socialist and labor movement of Europe was the largest global social movement in the pre–World War I era. Uniting diverse socialist and labor parties under a loosely knit organization known as the Second International (1889–1914), it stood as the model for political mobilization and social change. At its height the Second International encompassed labor and socialist organizations in more than twenty countries across Europe and even had links with organizations in North America, South America, Africa, and Asia. The success of the movement was rooted in an evolving political culture centered on mass-based political performances such as demonstrations and carefully orchestrated international socialist congresses.[1]

Yet in its formative years, from 1889 to 1900, the Second International was hardly a movement worthy of imitation. It was plagued by divisions and factional strife, and its periodic congresses created an image of indiscipline and futility rather than solidarity and unity. Commenting on the 1896 London congress, for example, the English delegate John Burns called it a "ghastly failure,"[2] and his Scottish comrade Keir Hardie concurred that "a Congress on the present lines is largely a farce."[3] The French liberal newspaper *Le Temps* added that the French delegation gave "the example of indiscipline, disorder and pugilism,"[4] and even the venerable German socialist Wilhelm Liebknecht, whose words carried much weight in socialist circles, offered the sober opinion, "Thus, we were obligated [to spend] day long and unfruitful discussions that were forced upon us in order to discredit the congress and to ruin the negotiations so that the enemies could triumphantly [exclaim]: 'Look at the men that want to create a new world, [they] cannot even keep order in their own congresses.'"[5]

Many contemporaries and subsequently historians have explained the source of such discord within the Second International as an ideological struggle between a hegemonic and doctrinaire German Marxism at its core versus a weak and reformist French socialism at its periphery.[6] James Joll has even made the dubious claim that the Second International forced an unhealthy union upon the disparate elements of the French Left, with tragic consequences.[7] While examining this phenomenon from the perspective of core and periphery can be fruitful, the relationship between the putative German-dominated core and the vulnerable periphery as embodied by the French Left as well as the source of their conflict (namely ideology) are in need of critical reexamination. This essay disputes the standard view in two ways. First, it argues that it was really the French periphery as opposed to the German core that engendered conflict within the international socialist movement. Second, the source of this dispute was driven not solely by ideology but also by identity politics.[8]

French sectarianism from 1889 until 1900 was the primary instigator of division within the Second International, challenging and at times directly sabotaging international socialist unity. The disparate groups within the French Left were embroiled in fierce battles of identity politics in three distinctive ways. First, they sought to define themselves as the "true" French worker party to their domestic constituencies and international comrades.[9] They presented themselves as the rightful heirs to French socialist traditions, thus implying that other factions were illegitimate. Second, non-Marxist French factions constructed their political identities as the true French worker party in opposition to a foreign "other." What made them French was in part the fact that they were not affiliated with the foreign other. In this case the foreign other was defined as an aggressive and imperialistic German socialist movement rooted in Marxist ideology. Unsurprisingly, non-Marxist French factions not only defined themselves in opposition to the "German menace," but they also accused French Marxists as being non-French and the mere pawns of German socialism. In both cases, however, French sectarian groups created their identities—similar to French society's general preoccupation and "crisis" with Germany as a whole—in strong reaction to the perceived influence of German socialism.[10] Third, all French factions attempted to use the Second International as an instrument to legitimize their political views while simultaneously defaming their contenders. They wanted the International to validate the correctness of their version of internationalism to their domestic constituencies. The reverse side of this coin was to discredit the International if it endorsed policies or fashioned a form of internationalism antithetical to a particular faction. In either case French groups foisted their own sectarian interests upon the International time and again, and the International did its best to avoid or reconcile the confrontation.

Paradoxically, French divisiveness indirectly strengthened international socialism because the Second International responded by creating a new political culture aimed at promoting fraternity and solidarity. French sectarians were ineffective in advancing their agendas within the international socialist movement, but they did prompt the Second International to reform itself, in part as a result of their disruptive actions. After the 1900 Paris congress, international socialist congresses were transformed from venues of intense bickering, partisanship, and public embarrassment to impressive political spectacles that united the disparate elements of the international socialist movement. The seeds of the Second International's future success were thus sown in the turbulent years of the 1890s.

This essay is organized into four sections. The first section covers the battle over identity politics from the 1880s to the early 1890s, which pitted mainly the Fédération des Travailleurs Socialistes de France (FTSF, Federation of the Socialist Workers of France) against the Marxist Parti Ouvrier Français (POF, French Workers Party). The second section describes the years 1893 to 1896, highlighted by the 1896 London international socialist congress. In this period non-Marxist groups within the French Left—mainly anarchists, the Parti Socialiste Révolutionnaire (PSR, Revolutionary Socialist Party), and the Parti Ouvrier Socialiste Révolutionnaire (POSR, Revolutionary Socialist Worker Party)—aided the cause of international anarchism against the so-called German-dominated International. As such, militants of these factions imagined themselves as defenders of an authentic French socialism against a foreign menace. The third section discusses the realignment of French socialist groups in the years 1896 to 1900 in reaction to the Dreyfus Affair and the entrance of the socialist Alexander Millerand into a bourgeois government. At this juncture the militants within the French Left were preoccupied with each other until the 1900 Paris international socialist congress presented each of them with another opportunity to exploit the International for their own sectarian purposes. The essay concludes with a brief discussion of the aftermath of the 1900 Paris congress until 1905, when the French Left, with the assistance of the International, was finally able to reconcile its differences and move beyond its contest over identity politics.

French Sectarianism in the 1880s and Early 1890s

French sectarianism had direct repercussions for the Second International from its inception in 1889 because the conflicts between Marxism and anarchism in the First International (1864–72) were carried over into the French political milieu in the 1880s and 1890s. The Russian-born anarchist Mikhail Bakunin successfully popularized the belief that the First International was a centralistic authoritarian institution dominated by a German, Karl Marx. The term Marxist was first used in France in 1872 as an adjective to describe the actions of the "Marxist" conspiracy to root out "anarchist" tendencies within the First International. Marxists of the First International employed

TABLE 6.1 Overview of Socialist Groups within the French Left and the Second International, 1889–1900

Name of Party/Political Affiliation	Principal Leader(s) (relevant to this essay)	Ideology
Anarchists	August Hamon Malatesta (Italian) Nieuwenhuis(Dutch)	Anti-Marxist, rejection of all authority
Parti Ouvrier Français (POF, French Workers Party)	Jules Guesde Paul Lafargue	Doctrinaire French version of Marxism
Fédération des Travailleurs Socialistes de France (FTSF, Federation of the Socialist Workers of France)	Paul Brousse	Anti-Marxist socialist reformers
Blanquists	Paul Argyiadès Victor Jaclard	Eclectic mix of followers of the deceased August Blanqui, who advocated the violent overthrow of the existing order; some gravitated toward violence and anarchism
Parti Socialiste Révolutionnaire (PSR, Revolutionary Socialist Party)	Eduard Vaillant	Followers of the deceased August Blanqui and the legacy of the Paris Commune, who sometimes allied themselves with the POF
Parti Ouvrier Socialiste Révolutionnaire (POSR, Revolutionary Socialist Worker Party)	Jean Allemane	Anti-Marxist socialists who emphasized worker militancy, autonomy, and the tactic of the general strike
Independent Socialists	Jean Jaurès Alexander Millerand	Reform-oriented socialist republicans committed to parliamentary democracy
Social Democratic Party of Germany (SPD)	Wilhelm Liebknecht August Bebel Karl Kautsky Paul Singer	Marxist party, mix of revolutionary rhetoric and political reformism
Belgium Workers Party (POB)	Émile Vandervelde	Reform-oriented socialist republican
Independent Labour Party, Britain	Keir Hardie	Scottish socialist reformer

the injurious epithet *anarchist* to stigmatize Bakunin's supporters. Thus, as historian David Stafford has argued, "Neither the term 'anarchist' nor the term 'Marxist' was endowed with much theoretical content; both originated with the struggles within the International between the General Council and the national federations."[11] French anarchists in turn conflated the term *Marxist* with *German* so that the Marxist-anarchist struggles of the First International were understood in a French-German national framework.

With French socialism in a state of disarray after the defeat of the Paris Commune in 1871 and the dissolution of the First International in 1872, Jules Guesde and Marx's son-in-law Paul Lafargue were able to spread their own version of Marxism in France in the late 1870s and early 1880s.[12] Guesde and Lafargue often looked to the German Social Democratic Party (SPD) as a model party and with good reason. The SPD, which was founded in 1875, experienced remarkable growth and electoral success in Germany in spite of facing persecution from Otto von Bismarck's authoritarian government from 1878 to 1890. Guesde and Lafargue were also influenced by the advice of Friedrich Engels, who was Karl Marx's compatriot living in London and who, since Marx's death in 1883, had assumed the role as the doyen of international socialism. In spite of these connections to German socialism, Guesde and Lafargue were stubborn individuals who ran their POF as a distinctly French Marxist party.[13] Nevertheless, the POF's Marxism was interpreted by opponents on the French Left—and prominent historians such as Edward Berenson—as a Germanic import devoid of French socialist traditions.[14]

Guesde and Lafargue's rigid definition of socialism brought them into conflict with militants who were critical of the adoption of Guesde's version of Marxism as the basis of the POF. The non-Marxist French Left consisted of several groups, including followers of the deceased August Blanqui, or Blanquists; anarchists inspired by the political philosophy of Pierre Proudhon and Bakunin; and the FTSF. Although an eclectic group, Blanquists advocated mainly for the violent overthrow of the existing order, while FTSF adherents supported whatever reforms proved possible under the existing republican system. Anarchists wanted the eradication of all forms of authority in society and, as such, rejected vehemently the POF platform of Marxian socialism.

Paul Brousse, a one-time anarchist and most prominent leader of the

FTSF, deserves credit for popularizing derisive stereotypes about German socialism in his fervent campaign against the POF in the early 1880s. In his 1882 polemic, *Le Marxisme dans l'Internationale et dans le Parti Ouvrier*, Brousse revitalized the Marxist-anarchist vitriol of the 1870s and described the activities of Guesde and Lafargue in the POF as an extension of the behind-the-scenes political machinations of Karl Marx. Brousse's strategy to discredit French Marxism by associating it with a foreign non-French ideology found considerable resonance within socialist circles.[15]

The FTSF had staked its claim to be the authentic French socialist party in contradistinction to the "German-tainted" POF. Its leader, Brousse, also attempted to differentiate the party from the POF by seizing the initiative to create a new Socialist International in the late 1880s. Unsurprisingly, the two central components of the internationalism of the FTSF were its anti-Marxism and its insistence that it be the only internationally recognized worker party of France.[16] Taken together, the FTSF was forging a political identity based on three pillars: anti-Marxism, which included a strong anti-German strain; internationalism; and its assertion of being the only genuine French worker party.

The FTSF proceeded to make preparations to hold an international socialist congress in Paris in 1889 and invited only non-Marxist socialists of other European countries. Fearing they would be upstaged by their FTSF contenders, the POF leadership responded by drafting up plans to convene its own international socialist congress in Paris. In this initial identity contest to lay sole claim to represent French socialism, the FTSF had an early publicity advantage over the POF because of Brousse's personal connections with socialists in Belgium, Denmark, England, and Holland and a socialist newspaper at his disposal. The POF did not have a national socialist newspaper in operation with which to create publicity. Furthermore, the POF had strong organizations in the provinces, but it wielded little influence in Paris, which foreigners considered the heart of the French socialist movement. Engels conveyed the inauspicious scenario of the POF to Lafargue when he stated,

> But do not forget that the Possibilists [FTSF] have managed to appear as the official representative of French socialism; that they are recognized as such by the English, Americans and the Belgians; that they have fraternized with the Dutch and the Danish at the London congress . . . If you

do nothing to announce and prepare your congress of 1889, the whole world will go to the Broussist one [congress], because one does not run behind those who renounce. Announce your congress, make a little noise in the socialist press of all countries, so that the others notice that you are still there.[17]

In order to outflank the FTSF congress, the POF leaders sought to emphasize the international character of their congress. In this effort they enjoyed the support of Engels, who explained to Lafargue that the precise wording of the invitation to the POF congress was not paramount but, rather, the "signatures [from foreign delegates] make the music."[18] The success of this strategy rested in large part on the actions and international reputation of the SPD. As early as November 1888, Wilhelm Liebknecht was contacted by the POF leadership in order to solicit his unqualified support for the POF-organized international socialist congress. Equally important, Liebknecht was asked "if at the same time you could write to them [other socialist parties] in order to launch the idea of the congress of Paris in 1889, [since] you will make it with a greater authority than we."[19]

At this juncture it is evident that the two leading figures of German socialism—Wilhelm Liebknecht and August Bebel—were reluctantly being drawn into a French sectarian affair, with which they felt uncomfortable. In essence they saw before them factions within the French Left wrestling over the mantle of internationalism for their own advantage. Initially, Liebknecht played the role of mediator, attempting to reconcile the FTSF and POF but to no avail. August Bebel was mainly concerned about the embarrassment that having two separate international socialist congresses would bring to international socialism. In a letter to Engels dated a few months before the impending congresses, Bebel expressed his sentiment forcefully: "That two congresses convene in one year appears already very ridiculous and gives the enemies ample chance for mockery. The immaturity of the leaders of a movement, who are not able to agree on a question that is so important for the working class of the whole world, comes with this to light."[20]

Two international socialist congresses were, therefore, set to convene in Paris in July 1889 largely due to the division between the FTSF and POF. Most foreign socialists in attendance at the two rival congresses were driven by the motivation to have a united international socialist movement. The leaders of Belgian, Danish, and Italian socialism in particular dreaded the impending schism, and they all played active roles at the 1889 Paris and future congresses to bring socialists of different stripes together. Other groups, mainly non-French Marxists, were averse to the appearance of disunity but were willing to live with a divided International until they were able to set it up on their own terms.

The central question at the rival congresses in Paris was the topic of unity. On the first day of the "Marxist" congress, delegates from several countries such as Germany and Italy announced their intention to do everything possible to unite the two bodies. Liebknecht argued that Marxists had already made overtures to the FTSF leadership in the past months but without success. Therefore, Liebknecht felt it was incumbent upon the FTSF congress to seize the initiative. Belgian socialists made a reconciliation attempt by directing a letter written by the executive committee of the Belgian socialist party (POB) to the Marxist congress. The POB letter implored the congress to move for the sake of unity beyond the French factional strife that had resulted in the current debacle, as the International should never give the capitalist class the chance to "applaud at the spectacle of the division of the working class."[21]

French sectarianism, however, undermined all attempts at mediation. The French delegate Duprés, for example, maintained that the so-called Marxist congress should under no circumstances associate itself with "bourgeois politicians" in the FTSF camp.[22] When Liebknecht put forth a resolution that would declare the congress ready to seek an understanding if its rival would pass a similar resolution of reciprocity, the disgruntled French delegate Tressaud proposed a counterresolution that precluded any negotiation with the "dissidents" of the other congress. Other French delegates submitted their own resolutions, worded in less harsh terms than Tressaud's but containing essentially the same idea. Three resolutions were finally put to a vote: the Liebknecht resolution endorsed reluctantly by the POF, Tressaud's acerbic resolution, and the Dutchman F. Domela Nieuwenhuis's resolution calling for immediate union. With the vast majority of national delegations supporting the Liebknecht resolution, the matter appeared to be settled; there would be no union unless the FTSF-organized congress took the next step. Displaying his sectarian intent, Eduard Vaillant, who was the leader of the PSR, felt it necessary to express that all French delegates were really in favor of Tressaud's resolution, but for the "dignity of the congress" and respect for the foreign delegates, the French delegation decided to support Liebknecht's resolution.[23] It must be added that the Possibilist congress was no less forthcoming in its deliberations on the prospect of union.

The inescapable conclusion to draw about the disunity of international socialism in Paris in 1889 is that the sectarian attitudes within the French Left, rather than unbridgeable ideological differences, produced division. In fact, virtually all of the resolutions passed by the two rival congresses were the same, and both congresses were united in their contempt for anarchism. The real issue at stake for the various factions of the French Left was their common struggle to present themselves as the "true" worker party of France to their domestic constituencies and foreign comrades. French Marxists were thrilled because they were able to boast that their congress played host to the vast majority of international delegates. In effect they had stolen the thunder of the FTSF by claiming legitimacy as being France's authentic worker party, armed with the support of the International. The FTSF plan to resurrect a new International devoid of Marxists had thus backfired.

The FTSF challenge in the International was seriously debilitated after the summer of 1889. Jean Allemane and his cohort of supporters were critical of Brousse's emphasis on reformist and parliamentary politics and wanted to direct the attention of the movement to the economic front. The upshot of Allemane's campaign against Brousse was the schism from the FTSF at the Châtellerault congress of 1890; thereafter, Allemane established his own party, the POSR.[24]

The leaders of other socialist movements were measured in their opinion of the Paris congresses. German socialists such as Liebknecht and Bebel were content with the course of events in Paris because they had stood their ground against the FTSF. The patent divisions displayed in Paris disappointed Belgian delegates. Distraught by the sectarianism of their French brethren and its negative influence on the unity of international socialism, leaders of the POB took it upon themselves to rectify the situation at the next international socialist congress, which they hosted in Brussels in 1891. Their task was made easier by the loss of influence of the FTSF and the absence of prominent POF leaders such as Paul Lafargue (who was serving a prison sentence). The 1891 Brussels congress witnessed provocations from anarchist hecklers, some of them from France. They were minor interruptions, however, and did not impede the goal of the

POB to avoid the patent division of international socialism as symbolized in separate congresses at Paris.

Two years later the most direct challenge to unity at the 1893 Zurich international socialist congress came from anarchists. This time French sectarians did not dominate the stage; nevertheless, their presence—or absence, in the case of Marxists—served to exacerbate rather than mitigate the Marxist-anarchist confrontation. The Dutchman Domela Nieuwenhuis, who had decided to convert from Marxism to anarchism after the 1891 Brussels congress, was able to strike fragile alliances throughout Europe with opponents of the SPD in an effort to strengthen the "revolutionary" and antiparliamentary wing of the International.[25] In this attempt Nieuwenhuis had much success in France, particularly within Allemane's POSR and Blanquist circles. The POF facilitated Nieuwenhuis's task, its leaders stubbornly refusing to attend the congress when the Zurich organization committee denied their request to change the date of the congress on short notice.[26] Their absence in turn allowed delegates from the POSR and Blanquists to establish a majority in the French delegation that was hostile to the SPD and sympathetic to the anarchist cause.

The first order of business of the Zurich congress, achieving a majority vote on a verification procedure to determine eligible delegates, turned into a public debacle. The sticking point was a clause that stipulated that congress delegates had to recognize the importance of "political action."[27] Realizing that the litmus test of political action would exclude anarchists, a French delegate proposed immediately to strike the phrase. The stalwart Marxist Charles Bonnier, speaking for the French minority, made his contribution to the uncivil discourse by exclaiming that all anarchists were either imbeciles or agents provocateurs. August Bebel put forth an amendment to clarify its meaning in the attempt to expedite the process of excluding anarchists from the congress. Most delegations supported Bebel's amendment. To no surprise, the Dutch delegation led by Nieuwenhuis voted against it, while the French delegation abstained from voting. After the vote several minutes of chaos and pandemonium ensued when disgruntled anarchists protested vociferously, prompting sturdy stewards to remove them forcefully from the meeting.

The public fiasco at Zurich had not yet reached its peak. Anarchist hecklers continued to find ways to interrupt congress proceedings. The majority in the French delegation assisted the anarchist cause and took opportunities to launch invectives against the French minority and POF leaders not in attendance. Paul Argyriadès, for example, acting as chair of the congress on the third day, used his authority to make a critique of the POF when he employed the true French worker party rhetorical strategy. The French delegation in attendance, Argyriadès stated, represented all parts of French socialism and above all "the working France, the real proletariat."[28] The French delegate Amilcare Cipriani, who implored the chair to read aloud a protest letter addressed to "the Delegates of the Marxist Congress of Zurich," left the congress in an act of personal protest, condemning the International for its intolerance and exclusivity. Cipriani was not allowed to read his letter before the congress so he responded by printing pamphlets of it and having them thrown down from the galleries into the main meeting hall.

Few, if any, delegates were satisfied with the course of the Zurich congress. The multitude of anarchist interruptions—in large part facilitated by the French and Dutch delegations—marred the International's reputation in the public sphere. Prominent leaders such as the Belgian Émile Vandervelde exhorted the delegates to display unity: "We had debates in the beginning of this congress, which allowed the enemies to hope, as if no unity prevailed among us; there were scenes that evoked the impression, as if individual nations were glad when another nation suffered a small defeat. Let us erase this impression, we [can] show the world of the enemies that we are united, that we know only one enemy, and we proclaim this unity the best and most clearly through a unanimous acceptance of the submitted resolution."[29]

The reaction to the Zurich congress among the French Left reflected little concern over the embarrassment the congress had meant for the International but, rather, showed a preoccupation with its consequences for individual factions. The POF organ, Le Socialiste, called the French delegation at Zurich "reactionary" and "bourgeois" because it had flirted with Nieuwenhuis and the interests of anarchism.[30] Delegates of the POSR such as Allemane had left the congress early in protest. Blanquists such as Victor Jaclard felt offended that the SPD had ostensibly dominated the congress. Jaclard and many French anarchists portrayed the events of the Zurich congress with essentialist stereotypes about German socialism and the German race. Explaining the orderliness of the pre-congress demonstration, Jaclard wrote, "In this, it is the German who appears, with his instincts of discipline and obedience, his love of rules—that intolerable thing to the French character."[31] The Zurich congress was, according to Jaclard, "the consecration of German hegemony," a "brutal force" against which French socialism must protest.[32] In defining their identity as defenders of French socialism against the "Germanic menace," Jaclard and like-minded delegates committed themselves to combating the "German hegemon" on two fronts: in the International as well as in their own country, as embodied by the "Germanic socialism" of the POF.

In the formative years of the Second International from the 1880s until the early 1890s, French sectarianism served as a force of division and disruption. The most visible consequence of French divisiveness was the convening of two rival congresses in 1889 in Paris. In response Belgian socialists—supported in spirit by many other movements—took up the challenge to bring the movement together without the intention of imposing conformity, aside from excluding anarchists. Four years later, at Zurich, the containment of French disunity became untenable because members of the French delegation were eager to undercut each other. The anarchist-Marxist tension served as a vehicle through which French factions continued their quarrels over identity politics. As at the Paris and Brussels congresses, they were not successful in shaping congress resolutions or persuading foreign delegates that their opinions were valid. But the fledgling International still lacked a strong core and was reacting haphazardly to the peripheral forces of French sectarianism and anarchism. It would take the catastrophes of two more international socialist congresses dominated again by forces on the periphery to usher in full-fledged changes in the nature and purpose of the International.

Sabotaging Unity and Enforcing Conformity at the 1896 London International Socialist Congress

As a result of the chaos in the French delegation at Zurich, all strands of French socialism were eager to outmaneuver each other at the 1896 London international socialist congress. The key for each faction was to maximize the number of delegates it could send to the congress in order to achieve a majority within the delegation. Trade unions allied with the POF encouraged their members to organize public reunions and festivals and to start a collection drive to raise money.[33] POF leaders found an uneasy ally with Independent Socialists because both embraced parliamentary politics. Independent Socialists, who tended to be reformist socialist republicans, had emerged as a bloc in the Chamber of Deputies following the 1893 national elections. Opposing them, French anarchists, disaffected Blanquists, and the POSR forged an alliance to discredit the leaders of the POF and their supporters in the "German-dominated" International.[34]

The commotion of the French delegation in London began immediately in the delegate verification session. The Marxist Gabriel Deville insisted that all potential delegates publicly declare that they support political action. Deville's proposition was rejected because it would have meant that genuine trade union representatives would have been excluded. Independent Socialists such as Alexander Millerand and Jean Jaurès added to the discord when they refused to show their credentials to the verification committee, claiming that their status as members of the Chamber of Deputies was sufficient for them to participate in the congress. While the French delegation deliberated, the rest of the London congress waited impatiently until the Englishman Edward Cowey decided to commence the congress without the participation of the French delegation.

The French delegation finally joined the congress. Having arrived from unresolved negotiations, delegates were anxious to voice their opinion on the questions of when and whether anarchists would be allowed to participate. It was generally understood that the provisional orders of the congress— including the adoption of Bebel's Zurich resolution or a political litmus test—would be moved en bloc before the congress adjourned for the day. A majority vote in favor of the provisional standing orders would have meant the official exclusion of anarchists. Upon the suggestion of an English delegate, the congress decided to postpone a vote until the following morning. But at that moment the Italian anarchist living in London, Errico Malatesta, demanded to speak. It is possible that Malatesta would not have had the opportunity to provoke the congress without the cooperation of the French delegation given that he had managed to acquire a mandate from the metallurgical syndicate of Amiens (presumably a POSR organization), after his attempts to be recognized as a delegate of the Spanish and Italian delegations had failed.[35] It is certain that the entire congress and spectators from the gallery reacted to Malatesta's provocative action with approving shouts matched by condemnation. The English chairman attempted to establish order with his bell but to no avail. Excited French delegates hurled themselves—figuratively and literally—into the pandemonium, as the English version of the congress proceedings vividly captured:

> It was Babel and Bedlam rolled into one. Christ Cornelissen, Dutch Socialistenbund and editor of Recht Voor Allen, went to speak from the platform, but was denied. Returning to his place in the hall beside Domela Nieuwenhuis, he addressed the Congress in three languages. While he was speaking there was comparative quiet, but a disturbance at the platform stairs made matters wild as before. Delesalle, a French delegate for the Société en Instruments de Precision (mathematical instrument makers), having a weak voice, went to ask if he could be allowed to speak from the platform. Before he had received time to put his question Bouillon, a French interpreter, pale to the lips with excitement, hurled him down the stairs. A storm raged, and developments might have been more complex had not Mr. Cowey, who had become comparatively helpless in the chair, announced the adjournment of Congress till Tuesday morning. Much resentment was shown at the brutal treatment of Delesalle, though it is but fair to add Bouillon afterwards apologised.[36]

The French delegation met later that afternoon and swiftly rejected another POF proposal designed to impose the litmus test of political action. The intransigence of POF adherents was reinforced by the actions of French anarchists, who were creating negative publicity for Guesde by passing around a disparaging pamphlet titled *Variations Guesdistes* to foreign delegates.[37] After further debate, the French delegation held an important vote on the so-called Zurich resolution of the standing orders. By a slim margin of fifty-seven to fifty-six, the majority, consisting mainly of POSR and Blanquist delegates, voted against upholding the Zurich resolution, for its meaning was interpreted to exclude trade union delegates. The POF faction of the minority, or about forty-four to forty-six delegates, refused to recognize the validity of the vote and left the session. POF delegates were unwavering in their belief that anarchists in their delegation were illegitimate. Some POF militants ostensibly threatened to use violence on other members of the French delegation. That evening the POF and a group of Independent Socialists deemed it necessary to write a manifesto to the "socialist delegates of the congress of London" explaining why they would no longer be able to stay in the French delegation if it continued to reject the Zurich resolution.[38] The usage of the term *socialist* was intentional and left no room for ambiguity. POF and Independent Socialist delegates were insisting on a political identity in which true socialists were only those individuals who recognized political action.

The disagreements between French factions on Monday were for the most part kept within the confines of the delegation itself; from Tuesday onward they required the attention of the entire congress in plenary session. Rumors swirled around the congress that if the Zurich resolution were upheld, a large section of the French delegation would have to be physically forced to leave the congress. POF delegates likewise intimated that they would leave the congress if the Zurich resolution were rejected.[39] The London congress finally voted to uphold the Zurich resolution, but the matter was far from settled.

During the afternoon session each delegation was to read its country report and explain how many delegates were admitted to the congress. The congress first heard from several countries until a member of the French delegation indicated that he was ready to deliver a report. Here is where the next controversy began, although what exactly transpired is difficult to say. The position of the French majority is that the German Paul Singer deliberately ignored the French request as long as possible, knowing that it would lead to a contentious public debate. A French delegate finally received the opportunity to speak, explaining that even though three Independent Socialists had not furnished any credentials, the French delegation would nevertheless accept their mandates as a gesture of tolerance.[40]

Jean Jaurès responded by reiterating that members of the Chamber of Deputies were not obligated to show their credentials. Jaurès had effectively exposed his own sectarianism because he and his Independent Socialist counterparts had simply refused to show their credentials to the French delegation in order to generate a public confrontation, in which they could publicize the need for political action.[41] After at least two attempts to hold a vote on the question, Singer finally adjourned the proceedings until the next day. The French majority interpreted the adjournment of the congress as another Marxist ploy to delay the vote in order to "win over several leaders and obtain the following day a favorable vote."[42] The reality is that Singer and the majority of other congress delegates wanted the French delegation to settle its own internal affairs and to spare the congress further embarrassment.

If the third day of the London congress was not an outright disaster, it was certainly close. Upon the insistence of the Scottish labor leader Keir Hardie, the congress agreed to relegate the credential dispute of the Independent Socialists back to the French delegation. Jaurès and company were finally compelled to show their credentials because members of the English delegation threatened to leave the congress if they did not. This dispute, once settled, gave way to the next French predicament. A forty-seven-member-strong French minority submitted a declaration to the congress stating that it sought recognition as a separate section in light of the presence of anarchists within the French delegation. French anarchists and their supporters in other delegations protested the audacity of the motion; disorder reigned once again in the congress hall. When given the opportunity to explain the intent of the declaration, Millerand made a scathing attack against the anarchist delegates and their specious organizations. The French minority, Millerand asserted, could never give the impression to the International and to the working class of France that the majority of French socialism was sympathetic to anarchism. After more vitriolic speeches by French and foreign delegates against a backdrop of frequent insults and interruptions, the congress finally put the issue to a vote. Fourteen nationalities supported Singer's suggestion to recognize two autonomous French delegations, while five delegations voted against it. The congress was then adjourned until Thursday morning, all delegates hopeful that the congress could finally move on to productive business.

The rest of the London congress transpired in an orderly fashion, but the damage had already been done. Each faction of the French Left came to London prepared to engage in a fierce battle of identity politics, committed to do whatever was deemed necessary to publicize its own inflexible definition of socialism. The tactics used to undercut their challengers were varied: distributing damaging pamphlets to foreign delegates; questioning the validity of delegates and the organizations they represented; denying the legitimacy of a vote if the result was not satisfactory; withholding credentials deliberately to make a political statement; threatening to leave the congress in an act of protest; threatening to use physical intimidation;

insisting on being recognized as a separate delegation; and last but not least, an actual episode of one delegate tackling another in order to prevent him from speaking. There is no doubt that differences of opinion over ideology drove a wedge between the various factions, but their undignified actions at London attested to a deeper problem: their insistence on their own faction being the only valid voice of French workers and, likewise, their inability to respect the legitimacy of their contenders.

The fallout of the London congress was considerable back in France, where the battle over identity politics continued with vigor. The French factions engaged in vigorous propaganda wars to impugn their rivals, and in this contest the illegitimacy of the International was a dominant theme. Some members of the French majority regarded the congress as further evidence of "Germanic imperialism" in the International. The publicist and anarchist August Hamon, for example, could not contain his racism when he wrote,

> The Germans aspire for hegemony everywhere; they want to impose their tactic and their viewpoint. Very militarized by their education, very feudal, in this above all, their spirit has not conquered independence as we find among the most developed political people, such as the inhabitants of Great Britain, the Belgians, the French. This desire to dominate in everything and the entire socialist world is also perhaps due in part to race. If one studies the leaders of German Social Democracy, one will find without a doubt the trace of influence of the conquering race of the Aryans, the blond dolichocephelans.[43]

Meetings were held throughout Paris and in the provinces at which militants voiced their recriminations against each other. To give a few from many possible examples, the Comité Central de Propagande Révolutionnaire, a Blanquist organization, organized a meeting on August 22 in Paris. Argyriadès, the same man who had made public his contempt for the POF at the Zurich congress, exclaimed, "One found there Frenchmen, citizens Deville and Guesde, more reactionary than capitalists."[44] Militants at another meeting even went so far to assert that Guesde, the founder of France's Marxist party, could no longer claim to be a true Marxist as a consequence of his sectarian behavior in London.[45] At a public assembly held in late August in Lyon, the Marxist Guiat addressed a crowd of about six hundred people. Upon walking up to the podium to speak, Guiat was verbally assaulted by restless anarchists in the crowd. Anarchist hecklers ignored the speaker's plea for civility and intensified their vociferations. In a diplomatic move Guiat ceded the podium to one of his hecklers, Monnier. This time Monnier spoke, but he was prevented from concluding his speech because POF stalwarts mocked him. Anarchist and POF militants threatened to inflict violence on each other, at which point the local police dissolved the meeting.[46]

The 1896 London congress showed once again how disruptive French disunity could be because French factions willingly brought their internal feuds before the International. Even after the expulsion of anarchists, the body was forced to confront the problem of French division in a public forum that tarnished its reputation in the public sphere. The headlines of the Parisian daily Le Matin, for example, captured vividly the folly of international socialism at London. To list but a few, some of the more descriptive headlines read "Like at the Tower of Babel," "A Schism among the French Delegation," "Indescribable Tumult," and "The Quarrel Continues."[47]

As early as the 1889 Paris congress, the International had been committed to the policy of excommunicating anarchists, and it was finally able to enforce this rule at the London congress in 1896. Anarchism was clearly a disruptive force irrespective of the problem of French sectarianism. The International had dealt successfully with one peripheral force, but French divisiveness continued to be a major source of disruption. French factions such as the POF were adamant that they truly represented the French workers while denying the legitimacy of other French socialist factions. These other factions in turn called into question the legitimacy of the International, perceiving it to be under the yoke of German socialism. As was the case at Zurich, the same groups abetted greatly anarchist efforts of sabotage at London. And yet the International's firm resolve in its treatment of anarchists was a marked contrast in its repeated attempts to handle French division without imposing conformity. Diverse leaders of the International ranging from the German Paul Singer to the Belgian Émile Vandervelde to the Scot Keir Hardie sought deliberately not to intervene in French factional strife over who constituted France's true worker party. Their actions at London—relegating credential and mandate disputes back to the French delegation and then accepting de facto two separate French delegations—were defensive in nature and certainly not evidence of Germanic imperialism. Leaders of the International were increasingly coming to the realization, however, that the venue of an international socialist congress was in a state of crisis and needed an overhaul.

Hijacking Unity and Containing Sectarianism at the 1900 Paris International Socialist Congress

In the wake of the disaster of the London congress the leaders of international socialism looked toward future congresses with little hope and optimism. At this juncture more than a few socialists seriously questioned the wisdom of holding international socialist congresses that hurt more than aided the international cause. The fact that French sectarianism continued to plague the International from 1896 to 1900 did not help matters either.

The marriage of convenience between the POF and the Independent Socialists at London was a tenuous relationship that collapsed under the pressure of the Dreyfus Affair and the entrance of the Independent Socialist Alexander Millerand into a bourgeois government in 1899. Independent Socialists such as Jean Jaurès joined the coalition in defense of Dreyfus in order to protect the French Republic. POF leaders such as Guesde and Lafargue distanced themselves from the conflict, arguing that it diverted the workers' movement's attention away from the class struggle. The decision of Millerand to enter a bourgeois government offended doctrinaire Marxists such as Guesde and old Communards such as Vaillant, serving to forge a common pact between the POF and PSR. In the years from 1896 to 1900 the POSR continued to sympathize with the anarchist agenda, especially the general strike.

In December 1898 the German socialists announced that they would be unable to host the next international socialist congress, so the responsibility fell into the hands of the French socialist movement. The five major socialist groups in France—the FTSF, the Independent Socialists, the POF, the POSR, and the PSR,—formed the Comité d'Entente (Committee of Understanding) in order to organize the congress. As its name suggests, the Comité d'Entente was an attempt to reconcile the differences within the movement for the sake of hosting an impressive congress. Some socialists were initially optimistic about this awkward construct. In late 1898, before the Millerand Affair, Jean Longuet stated, "In spite of everything, I am certain that they [the POF and Independent Socialists] will unite more and more and for the international congress of 1900, the foreign comrades can be tranquil. One will not see take place again the scandal of London."[48] The position of the POSR was the most complicated. Because of their expulsion at London, French anarchists sought to contest the International by convening their own "revolutionary" counter-congress. Urged by French anarchists to join their cause, Allemane and some Blanquists threatened to leave the Comité d'Entente and join the antiparliamentarian international congress if the issue of the general strike was not placed on the agenda.[49]

In retrospect it appears miraculous that not a single group from the Comité d'Entente made good on threats to leave. Two reasons explain this pecu- liarity. First, the leaders of French socialism took seriously the mandate to organize the next congress of the International and the moral persuasion it carried. Second, French factions sought to use the international socialist congress as an instrument to legitimize their own entrenched position with respect to the Millerand Affair. Simply put, they were intent on resuming their identity politics armed with the sanction of the International. It was certainly no coincidence that the POF and Independent Socialists scheduled a congress of "unity" to be held in Paris immediately after the international congress convened. Both groups wanted to gain momentum by attending the congress with a supportive resolution directly from the International.[50] To make matters worse, Paul Lafargue even gave his foreign comrades false assurances when they expressed that the International should not be forced to intervene in the quarrels of French socialism.[51]

As was the case in London four years earlier, the 1900 Paris congress was forced to commence later than planned due to extended deliberations within the French delegation. The respective organizations of French socialism had already met earlier that morning in cafés near the congress hall to discuss the actions they would take at the congress. There was considerable confu- sion in the French delegation over when credentials were to be verified and who would represent the French delegation in the congress bureau. The POF and PSR expected that the French delegation would elect members to represent France on the bureau after the verification of all credentials.[52] The FTSF, Independent Socialists, and POSR wielded a majority and motioned to elect temporary bureau members so as not to delay further the convoca- tion of the congress. Jaurès was elected president. The majority applauded this decision, while the minority denounced it. In order to achieve some sense of parity, Vaillant and Allemane were named as assistants to Jaurès and were to sit on the congress bureau. Vaillant refused his nomination out of protest. More tumult and debate ensued.

When the French delegation finally made its way into the main hall of the congress, its very entrance, according to each group's ideological affinity, symbolized the division of French socialism.[53] The POF delegates took up positions on the left side of the hall, as if marking out their territory across from the "reformist" socialists on the other side. Jaurès delivered the convocation speech, admitting publicly the disunity of French socialism. Jaurès also invited the foreign delegations to send representatives forward to serve in the congress bureau. At this gesture some delegates of the POF and PSR left the hall in an act of protest.[54] Determined to make another political statement, Lafargue, surrounded by militants of the POF, appeared at the podium and delivered a long diatribe, affirming that Jaurès and Allemane did not have the right to "speak in the name of the French delegation."[55] The battle over speaking for the true French worker party was continued. The session dragged on another full hour until it was adjourned.

The question of which delegates would represent France in the congress bureau was still unresolved when the meeting reconvened the following day. The bureau from the previous day had met earlier in order to offer its assistance in working out the conflict, but the best it could do was to recognize the current bureau as provisional and to let the French delegation meet once again that afternoon to come to a conclusive solution. After clarifying a few procedural questions, the Belgian Léon Furnemont informed the congress that the issue of the general strike had been added to the agenda on the demand of the POSR. In order "to prevent any contestations on the regularity of this addition," Furnemont implored the congress to accept the change.[56] The inclusion of the general strike in the agenda might have been a strategic consideration on the part of the congress to avoid further public spectacles such as the Lafargue outburst. Allemane clearly sought to put this contentious issue on the agenda, and he probably would have made the POSR's further participation in the congress contingent on this factor. Later that afternoon the French delegation finally accomplished some semblance of a cease-fire. When the chairman Singer announced this result with pride before the congress, foreign delegates responded with thunderous applause.[57]

Because the question of whether a socialist should be allowed to enter a bourgeois government remained the centerpiece of the congress agenda, the International was still confronted with the unenviable situation of having to adjudicate the Millerand Affair. The congress first debated the issue of ministerialism in a commission and then Émile Vandervelde, speaking on behalf of the majority resolution, and Enrico Ferri, speaking in defense of the minority resolution, summarized the debates before a plenary session. Vandervelde first made it known that few disagreed that a socialist, under exceptional circumstances, should be able to enter into an alliance with a bourgeois party against a common enemy. The sticking point revolved around the question of how a socialist was to enter such an alliance. The German Marxist theoretician Karl Kautsky proposed a resolution, supported by a vote of twenty-four to four within the commission, stating that a socialist could (under exceptional circumstances) enter a bourgeois government but only with the consent of the party. The Kautsky resolution was lenient in the sense that it did not criticize Millerand's action as a transgression of socialist principle; rather, it faulted Millerand for having proceeded without the sanction of his party. Vandervelde was careful to emphasize that the Kautsky resolution "should neither be envisioned as a condemnation nor a tacit approbation of the conduct of French socialists."[58] Through Vandervelde's and Kautsky's leadership the International was trying to play the role of honest broker.

Ferri defended his resolution; it did not prohibit the participation of a socialist in a bourgeois government but only affirmed this course of action when a socialist party had achieved a majority within a political institution. Jaurès and Guesde followed and stated their positions. The Jaurès-Guesde discourse resembled more a clash of personalities than a conflict over principles,[59] with both speakers preaching the need to respect the other in deference to their international guests, implying that their spirited disputes over identity politics in other venues were acceptable (and perhaps even natural). In spite of their lip-service respect to their comrades and the setting of the international socialist congress, the temptation to advance their cause in a public forum proved too great. Guesde, now with the support of Ferri, succumbed to a sectarian attitude by proposing his own resolution that forbade unequivocally the participation of a socialist in a bourgeois government. Nevertheless, the Kautsky resolution was adopted over the Guesde-Ferri resolution by a vote of twenty-nine to nine. Each delegation was given two votes, yet another impromptu procedural change meant to accommodate the division in French socialism.

The Millerand Affair presented the International with an important tactical question that needed clarification. Had the issue been addressed under different circumstances in a nonpartisan environment, the International might have engaged in a productive and stimulating debate. Most foreign delegates, however, understood the question first and foremost as a "French" problem foisted upon the International. This motivation best explains the vagueness and ambiguity of the much criticized Kautsky resolution that satisfied no one. Even Ferri, who ardently supported the POF position out of principle, commented that it was necessary for French socialism to move beyond this stage of personality politics.[60] The comments of the German delegate Ignaz Auer reflected the viewpoint of foreign delegates: "We wish that after our negotiations that have been imposed on us here, the French would like to draw the lesson that they have to sort out such things among themselves and in their own house . . . We wish that the French exit the hall not as victor or vanquished, but rather shoulder to shoulder with us as fighters for the cause of the international proletariat. (Thunderous applause, in which the Guesdists do not participate.)"[61]

The diplomatic gymnastics the International undertook to achieve the Kautsky resolution were not the actions of a heavy-handed center seeking to impose uniformity or assert a "German hegemony" on a defenseless periphery. Rather, they were impromptu efforts to prevent the further deterioration of internecine strife within the French Left and to spare the International the unenviable situation of having to take sides in what it considered another episode of French sectarianism. The Kautsky resolution was nothing more than a hollow tract laced in Marxist jargon that allowed the International to avoid the dilemmas of French socialism. A reporter of the organ Le Temps put it best: "The international socialist congress has to decide on one question [ministerialism]: it has left it entirely [unsettled]. Invited to say yes or no, it has responded; 'Yes and No,' which equates exactly to neither yes nor no."[62]

The International was successful in that it did not take a firm position on the Millerand Affair that would allow a French faction to claim victory. The strategy of the French factions to manipulate the International to gain an upper hand in its domestic quarrels ultimately failed. And to no surprise, the so-called congress of unity the French factions had scheduled to take place just days after the Paris international socialist congress unraveled even before it began. Unable to muster a majority, the POF and PSR made a quick exit, demonstrating once again the inability of the groups within the French Left to overcome their identity politics for the sake of unity.

The Aftermath of the Paris Congress and Beyond

Before it adjourned, the 1900 Paris congress undertook a significant step toward reforming and redefining the purpose of international socialist congresses by passing a resolution to create a permanent organizational structure. The delegates in attendance wisely wanted to prevent the next congress from falling prey to the problem of French disunity and in general to the whims of peripheral forces. In short the International resolved to establish some semblance of an institutional core. Set up in Brussels under the capable auspices of Belgian socialism, the International Socialist Bureau (ISB) was inaugurated in early 1901 in order to help organize future congresses and to offer assistance in mediating factional disputes among its members. The ISB would periodically offer to play the role of honest broker in the internal affairs of socialist movements—most notably the Bulgarian, English, French, and Russian—in the goal of promoting unity. Furthermore, by setting the agenda of future congresses and helping to finance them, the ISB was able to take the politics out of congress organization committees. These committees were then empowered to devote their undivided attention to staging spectacular congresses full of fanfare and festivities conducive to the promotion of socialist unity. At all subsequent international socialist congresses after 1900, mass demonstrations, elaborate inaugural and closing ceremonies, intricate congress decoration and symbolism, and entertaining excursions became staples.

The ISB was left with the arduous task of containing French division for the benefit of socialist fraternity. In these efforts the ISB was remarkably successful, as it demonstrated at the 1904 Amsterdam congress. The backdrop of this congress was the revisionist challenge to Marxism within German social democracy. Eduard Bernstein sought to revise some of the sacred tenets of classical Marxism in an effort to bring socialist theory into accordance with the social reality of turn-of-the-century Europe. In a nutshell Bernstein's revisionism, if adopted, would have resulted in an evolutionary and reformist brand of German socialism. The SPD grappled with the Bernstein controversy for five wrenching years, until finally Kautsky's Marxist orthodoxy emerged victorious at the 1903 Dresden national party congress. The resulting Dresden resolution condemned the revisionist viewpoint, reinforced the principle of class struggle and forbade the participation of a socialist in a bourgeois government. In contrast to the French Left, the SPD was able to resolve its own internal ideological challenges, safeguard party unity, and spare the International the burden of its internal feuds.

Unlike the German case, however, the continuing divisiveness among French socialists made yet another appearance in Amsterdam in 1904. The Parti Socialiste de France (the unification of the POF and PSR, producing the PSF), losing the battle against Jaurès in French national politics, wanted to capitalize on the Dresden resolution by having the issue of socialist tactics debated at the Amsterdam congress.[63] The sectarian intent of the PSF was on full display when it adopted the Dresden resolution in an unaltered form at its national party congress at Reims in 1903 and then informed the ISB that it would make the case for this resolution at Amsterdam. In essence the PSF knew that this ploy would ensure the unconditional support of the SPD because the reputation of German socialism would be on the line. The PSF action also illustrated the continuing preoccupation of French factions with the developments of their German brethren on the other side of the Rhine River.

At the Amsterdam congress Jaurès deftly exploited this knowledge by brilliantly shifting the terms of the debate from a Jaurès-Guesde sectarian dispute to a German-French ideological and national confrontation. Instead of focusing on Guesde, Jaurès made the case that the SPD and specifically its leader, August Bebel, were attempting to impose rigid tactics on the International to the detriment of French socialist traditions. In doing so, Jaurès skillfully evoked the support of other delegations, which were now willing to defend the revisionist position because it was a legitimate debate about socialist ideology, not simply squabbles among French socialist factions. At the same time, Jaurès presented himself as the defender of an indigenous and authentic French socialism in contrast to the Germanic socialism of the SPD and by implication the PSF's putative non-French/

foreign ideology.[64] Jaurès's rhetoric merely reinforced the stereotypes about German socialism and French Marxists that had been in circulation in the non-Marxist French Left since Paul Brousse had propagated them twenty years earlier, in the 1880s.

The orthodox Marxist standpoint prevailed by a slim margin at Amsterdam, but James Joll's "German hegemony" interpretation of these events does little to explain what was really at stake. First, the SPD did not even propose to bring the Dresden resolution for debate before the International. Second, on the eve of the Amsterdam congress both Bebel and Kautsky expressed their concerns about the agenda item on socialist tactics, afraid that yet another congress could once again be marred by French sectarianism.[65] Third, even though SPD leaders felt compelled to defend the Dresden resolution out of national pride for their own socialist principles, the German delegation showed itself willing to grant concessions in order to make the resolution sound less denunciatory and derisive.[66] The aforementioned reasons cast serious doubt on the thesis that a hegemonic center as embodied by the SPD imposed its will on a weak periphery, namely the French Left. The 1904 Amsterdam congress showed that in reality the periphery continued to exert influence on the center, but this time the center was able to handle peripheral forces in a dignified manner that did not tarnish the reputation of the International in the public sphere.

In sharp contrast to the previous congresses, the Amsterdam congress exceeded the expectations of its participants. Delegates were enthused by the Bebel-Jaurès duel on socialist tactics; it was comparable to a heavyweight boxing match that offered real drama and theater. The Amsterdam congress became a template upon which all future international socialists congresses in the era of the Second International would build. The ISB at Amsterdam had finally succeeded in its objectives of promoting fraternity while containing sectarianism. The force of French sectarianism did not altogether disappear in the International, but it would no longer sabotage or severely threaten international unity. The French Left continued to be influenced by German socialism, although a new cast of characters emerged as defenders and opponents of the SPD and its putative influence in the International.[67] After decades of internecine strife, French factions left the Amsterdam congress determined to overcome their personal and ideological differences for the sake of unity. The result was swift and remarkable. Not only did

French factions come together and form a single socialist party less than a year after the Amsterdam congress in 1905, but perhaps in gratitude to the role the International had played, they called their party Section Française de l'Internationale Ouvrière (SFIO), bringing to an end, at least until the rise of French communism in the 1920s, their fierce battles of identity politics over who constituted the true French worker party.

Notes

I would like to thank the organizers and participants of the conference held in memory of William B. Cohen at Indiana University in December 2003, at which I first presented a draft of this essay. I am especially grateful for the comments and input of George Alter, Sarah Curtis, and Irwin Wall.

1. This statement is the central thesis of a larger research project I am conducting on international socialism in Europe in the era of the Second International. Aspects of the thesis can be found in Kevin Callahan, "Performing Inter-Nationalism in Stuttgart in 1907: French and German Socialist Nationalism and the Political Culture of an International Socialist Congress," *International Review of Social History* 45 (April 2000): 51–87; and Kevin Callahan, "The International Socialist Peace Movement on the Eve of World War I Revisited: The Campaign of 'War against War!' and the Basle International Socialist Congress in 1912," *Peace & Change* 29 (April 2004): 147–76.

2. "Mr. John Burn's Criticism," *Daily Chronicle*, August 3, 1896, in Michel Winock, ed., *Le Congrès de Londres devant la presse* (Geneva: Minkoff Reprint, 1980), 11:41.

3. International Socialist and Trade Union Congress, *Illustrated Report of the Proceedings of the Workers Congress Held in London in July 1896* (London, 1896), 95.

4. *Le Temps*, July 31, 1896.

5. *Verhandlungen und Beschlüsse des Internationalen Sozialistischen Arbeiter und Gewerkschaftskongresses zu London, 1896* (Berlin, 1896), 31.

6. The standard works on the Second International contain implicitly or explicitly this bias. The key works are G. D. H. Cole, *A History of Socialist Thought: The Second International, 1889–1914* (London: Macmillan, 1956); Julius Braunthal, *Geschichte der Internationale*, vol. 1 (Hannover: Dietz, 1974); and Milorad M. Drachkovitch, *Les Socialismes français et allemand et le problème de la guerre, 1870–1914* (Geneva: Librairie E. Droz, 1953).

7. James Joll, *The Second International, 1889–1914*, 2nd ed. (London: Routledge and Kegan Paul, 1974), 3.

8. On identity politics, some key works are Jane F. Fulcher, *The Nation's Image: French Grand Opera as Politics and Politicized Art* (New York: Cambridge University Press,

1987); Jerrold Seigel, *Bohemian Paris: Culture, Politics, and the Boundaries of Bourgeois Life, 1830–1930* (New York: Penguin, 1986); Marc Antliff, *Inventing Bergson: Cultural Politics and the Parisian Avant-Garde* (Princeton NJ: Princeton University Press, 1993); Robert Nye, *Crime, Madness, and Politics in Modern France: The Medical Concept of National Decline* (Princeton NJ: Princeton University Press, 1984); Herman Lebovics, *True France: The Wars over Cultural Identity* (Ithaca NY: Cornell University Press, 1994); Philip Nord, *The Republican Moment: Struggles for Democracy in Nineteenth-Century France* (Cambridge MA: Belknap Press, 1994); and Kolleen M. Guy, *When Champagne Became French: Wine and the Making of a National Identity* (Baltimore: Johns Hopkins University Press, 2003).

9. Although my analysis of the creation of French national socialist identity is mainly in relation to the Second International, it would be equally interesting to explore how this created identity in turn played out in French politics beyond the French Left's immediate constituency to ascertain its marginality in a broader domestic setting. Such analysis is, however, beyond the scope of this essay.

10. See Claude Digeon's seminal work *La Crise allemande de la pensée française (1870–1914)* (Paris: Presses Universitaires de France, 1959); and most recently, Allan Mitchell, *A Stranger in Paris: Germany's Role in Republican France, 1870–1940* (New York: Berghahn Books, 2006).

11. David Stafford, *From Anarchism to Reformism: A Study of the Political Activities of Paul Brousse within the First International and the French Socialist Movement, 1870–1890* (London: Weidenfeld and Nicolson, 1971), 15–16.

12. Claude Willard, *Les Guesdists: le mouvement socialiste en France (1893–1905)* (Paris: Éditions Sociales, 1965).

13. Jutta Seidel, *Deutsche Sozialdemokratie und Parti ouvrier 1876–1889* (Berlin: Akademie-Verlag, 1982).

14. See Edward Berenson's comments in *Populist Religion and Left-Wing Politics in France, 1830–1852* (Princeton NJ: Princeton University Press, 1984), 238.

15. Stafford, *From Anarchism to Reformism*, 196.

16. Stafford, *From Anarchism to Reformism*, 213–18.

17. Friedrich Engels to Paul Lafargue, December 4, 1888, in *Werke: Karl Marx; Friedrich Engels* (Berlin: Dietz, 1967), 37:124.

18. Friedrich Engels to Paul Lafargue, May 24, 1889, in *Werke*, 221.

19. Raymond Lavigne to Wilhelm Liebknecht, November 15, 1888, 221/1, Liebknecht Collection, International Institute of Social History, Amsterdam (hereafter cited as IISH).

20. August Bebel to Friedrich Engels, March 31, 1889, in *August Bebels Briefwechsel mit Friedrich Engels*, ed. Werner Blumenberg (The Hague: International Institute of Social History, 1965), 353.

21. *Protokoll des Internationalen Arbeiter-Congresses zu Paris. 1889* (Nuremberg, 1890), 11–12.

22. *Protokoll des Internationalen Arbeiter-Congresses zu Paris*, 14.

23. *Protokoll des Internationalen Arbeiter-Congresses zu Paris*, 22–23.

24. Thomas Moodie, "The Reorientation of French Socialism, 1888–1890," *International Review of Social History* 20 (1975): 347–68, 361–66.

25. Markus Bürgi gives a magnificent account of this opposition in several countries. Markus Bürgi, *Die Anfänge der Zweiten Internationale* (Frankfurt am Main: Campus, 1996), 191–238.

26. Charles Bonnier to Jules Guesde, including a note by Klara Zetkin, August 2, 1893, 229/1, Guesde Collection, IISH.

27. *Protokoll des Internationalen Sozialistischen Arbeiterkongresses. Zürich 1893* (Zurich, 1894), 5.

28. *Protokoll des Internationalen Sozialistischen Arbeiterkongresses*, 11.

29. *Protokoll des Internationalen Sozialistischen Arbeiterkongresses*, 43.

30. "Le Congrès de Zurich," *Le Socialiste*, August 20, 1893.

31. Victor Jaclard, "Le Congrès Socialiste International de Zurich," *La Revue Socialiste* (September 1893): 295.

32. Jaclard, "Le Congrès Socialiste International de Zurich," 301, 311.

33. Police report dated June 10, 1896, Paris, F7/12494, Archives Nationales (hereafter cited as AN).

34. Police report dated July 3, 1896, Paris, F7/12494, AN.

35. Liste des Membres de la Délégation Reguliére Française, 633/7, Guesde Collection, IISH.

36. International Socialist and Trade Union Congress, *Illustrated Report*, 17–18.

37. Emile Pouget, ed., *Variations Guesdistes* (Paris, 1896).

38. Musée Social, ser. B, circ. no. 3, Quatrième Congrès Socialiste International (Paris, 1896), 83–84, in Winock, *Le Congrès de Londres*, 11:161–62.

39. International Socialist and Trade Union Congress, *Illustrated Report*, 16.

40. Eugène Guérard, *Le Congrès de Londres* (Paris, 1896), 13, in Winock, *Le Congrès de Londres*, 11:463.

41. International Socialist and Trade Union Congress, *Illustrated Report*, 19.

42. Guérard, *Le Congrès de Londres*, 14, in Winock, *Le Congrès de Londres*, 11:464.

43. August Hamon, *Le Socialisme et le Congrès de Londres, étude historique* (Paris, 1897), 71–72.

44. Police report dated August 23, 1896, Paris, F7/12494, AN.

45. Police report dated August 23, 1896, Paris, F7/12494, AN.

46. Police report dated August 31, 1896, Paris, about the prefecture du Rhône, F7/12494, AN.

47. *Le Matin*, July 25–August 3, 1896.

48. Jean Longuet to Wilhelm Liebknecht, November 2, 1898, 241/3, Liebknecht Collection, IISH.

49. Police report dated May 4, 1899, Paris, F7/12494, AN.

50. Police report dated September 13, 1900, Paris, F7/12494, AN.

51. Paul Lafargue to Jules Guesde, August 12, 1900, 313/6, Guesde Collection, IISH.

52. *Cinquième Congrès Socialiste International tenu à Paris du 23 au 27 Septembre 1900. Compte rendu analytique officiel* (Paris, 1901), 13–14.

53. Marie-Louise Goergen, "Les Relations entre socialistes allemands et français à l'époque de la deuxième Internationale (1889–1914)" (PhD diss., Saint-Denis, Paris, 1998), 75.

54. *Internationaler Sozialisten-Kongress zu Paris. 1900* (Berlin, 1900), 7.

55. *Cinquième Congrès Socialiste International*, 20–21.

56. *Cinquième Congrès Socialiste International*, 24.

57. *Internationaler Sozialisten-Kongress zu Paris*, 8.

58. *Cinquième Congrès Socialiste International*, 61.

59. *Cinquième Congrès Socialiste International*, 72–84.

60. *Cinquième Congrès Socialiste International*, 66.

61. *Internationaler Sozialisten-Kongress zu Paris*, 25.

62. "Un Congrès qui ne se compremet pas," *Le Temps*, September 29, 1900.

63. "Compte rendu de la quatrième réunion de B.S.I., February 7, 1904," in *Bureau socialiste international, comptes rendus des réunions, manifestes et circulaires*, vol. 1, 1900–1907, ed. Georges Haupt (Paris: Mouton, 1969), 103.

64. For this bias, see *L'Humanité*'s extensive coverage of the congress from August 20–28, 1904, esp. the editorial by Gustave Rouanet on August 21, 1904.

65. Karl Kautsky, "Der Kongreß zu Amsterdam," in *Die Neue Zeit*, vol. 2, 1903–1904 (Stuttgart: Dietz Verlag, 1904), 673.

66. *Internationaler Sozialisten-Kongreß zu Amsterdam 1904* (Berlin, 1904), 47.

67. Interestingly, after the Amsterdam congress Jaurès became the SPD's strongest supporter, while French syndicalists and specifically the socialist Gustav Hervé led the charge to combat "German socialist imperialism."

7

Sex and the Citizen

Reproductive Manuals and
Fashionable Readers in Napoleonic
France, 1799–1808

Sean M. Quinlan explores the fascinating nexus between sex and citizenship identity constructions proffered by marginal medical writers against the backdrop of the instability of the early Napoleonic years. Medical outsiders—some of whom had been upended by the French Revolution—penned an extraordinarily popular and salacious medical literature on human sexuality, reproductive strategies, and child rearing.

These manuals appealed to a core reading public whose members wanted to raise new French citizens attached to the principles of 1789 but who were opposed to radical Jacobinism, reactionary royalism, and religious revivalism. Consequently, contrasting sexual identities tinged primarily with republican political ideologies were up for grabs in the early Napoleonic years. The readers (primarily women, if contemporary critics are to be believed) hoped to express their national identity by raising their children within the context of particular civic and moral values. Medicine provided a common, "objective" language to discuss divisive political and social questions. Quinlan's essay offers a poignant critique of Michel Foucault's theory of hegemonic power by arguing that medical outsiders and the marketplace were propagating civic identities unattached to the hegemonic ideological objectives of the French government and medical establishment. Likewise, this essay shows the fluidity of gender identity and citizenship prior to the consolidation of the bourgeois separate sphere ideology.

⊷ ⊷

In the early years of the Napoleonic regime (1799–1815) a new craze hit Paris high society: a vogue for self-help manuals that taught readers the art of having gifted, healthy, and beautiful children—preferably boys. These bestsellers included the anonymous On the Propagation of the Human Species (1799), J.-A. Millot's The Art of Procreating the Sexes at Will (1800), L.-J.-M. Robert's

An Essay on Mega-Anthropogenesis (1801), J.-J. Virey's *On the Public and Private Education of Frenchmen* (1802), and A. G*** de B. S. O.'s *Philopaedia, or the Art of Having Children without Passions* (1808).[1] Indeed, observers hailed this bizarre corpus as a kind of publishing event, and the books were widely debated in the literary and popular press. As one critic complained, with tongue planted firmly in cheek, "Paris is truly a fertile source of new inventions."[2]

This literature, though rarely discussed by historians, marks a significant departure in medical and lay writings about sex and family hygiene.[3] Before 1789 French doctors usually wrote about sex in two ways: either they informed readers about basic sexual mechanics and self-help methods, or they warned against libertinism and self-pollution and thus sought to change moral behavior. Like other domestic manuals, these books were meant to be read and to be used (to borrow Charles Rosenberg's phrase)—though, as many historians have cautioned, we know little about how people understood such books, much less used them in their daily lives.[4]

The sex manual craze of the Napoleonic period opens a different view upon this process of diffusion, suggesting a complex and confused dialogue between doctors and their readers, as both groups used the medium to exploit political and professional agendas. Instead of reinforcing more general standards of morality, doctors now told readers that they could use sex and domestic hygiene to attain specific ideological agendas. Sex and child rearing, they wrote, could become self-conscious political acts. In so doing, doctors tailored these books for an engaged readership, teaching targeted groups how to use medical knowledge about reproduction and heredity to help them raise their children with particular political and moral values. At the same time, these doctors—all outsiders to the Paris medical establishment—also advanced their own professional and ideological agendas, hoping to use their books not just for profit but also to align themselves with possible patrons and political networks. Sex, medicine, politics, and interest, as we shall see, combined in unstable and unusual ways. Working and practicing on the periphery, doctors entered into a dialogue with a core reading public and toyed with official ideologies about moral values and sexual difference.

These medical sex manuals significantly challenge key historiographical assumptions regarding the relationship between biomedical science, political power, and the creation of gender identities in post-revolutionary France. On one level these writings provide an important counterpoint to philosopher

Michel Foucault's controversial but influential studies on modern medicine and sexuality, in which he claims that medicine became a tool of social control, as bourgeois elites tried to impose rationality and control upon the French polity—all with the hopes of creating a fertile, productive, and nonseditious population. On a second level these writings also played with official ideas about sexual identities and practices and in some cases deliberately undermined what might be construed as more normative models of human sexual behavior. This interplay between intended male and female reading audiences suggests that gender polarities—often perceived as one of the key elements of revolutionary ideology—were potentially less rigid and monolithic than has been described in much recent historiography. Seen in this light, the making of modern French identity, especially in terms of sexuality, was still up for grabs in the late revolutionary years.

The post-Terror sex manuals developed from an earlier tradition. Starting in the seventeenth century, large numbers of sex books rolled off the printing presses in England, France, Holland, North America, and the German-speaking states. These works ranged from medical advice such as Nicolas Venette's *Conjugal Love; or the Pleasures of the Marriage Bed* (1685), popular treatises such as *Aristotle's Master-Piece* (1690) and *The Admirable Secrets of Albert the Great* (1722), verse poetry such as Claude Quillet's *Callipaedia* (1655), and a whole range of erotic, smutty, and obscene books written by the Grub Street hacks.[5] A number of these works, such as Venette's *Conjugal Love* and *Aristotle's Master-Piece*, continued to appear well into the nineteenth century. The tone of the books needs emphasis. In *Conjugal Love* Venette provided his readers with all sorts of practical advice about conception, how to tell whether a woman was a virgin or whether she was pregnant, how to cure sterility, and whether or not female orgasm mattered. As a writer steeped in Renaissance humanism, Venette thought that readers could use their knowledge of nature to help control sex and fertility. Significantly, he did not view sex problems in terms of personal identity or mental inhibitions (sex problems, for him, were always mechanical problems); and he celebrated marriage and childbearing without pushing an explicit theological or political agenda.[6]

This earthy approach in sex manuals contrasts with a new literature that began to appear in France during the 1750s. Written largely by doctors, the later works denounced libertinism and luxury among the upper classes and promised that a hygienic regimen could reform debauched manners and morals. This medical activism was driven by a large-scale panic about degeneracy and population decline.[7] Among the upper classes, said moral critics, sexual free living, philosophic skepticism, and consumerism had caused nervous degeneracy and thus infertility. To cure luxury and debauchery, prominent medical crusaders—such as Antoine Le Camus, Charles Vandermonde, and Samuel Tissot—proposed systems of moral hygiene in which "high-risk" groups (fashionable women) could learn family values and self-restraint.[8] In particular these doctors stressed that the family could regenerate moral values because it provided a healthy and natural environment in which to nurture and socialize the individual.[9]

The moral hygienist agenda was intensified by the French Revolution. Inspired by clinical breakthroughs and hospital reform in the 1790s, revolutionaries hoped that medical science could regenerate a sick and decayed population and thus make a "New Man" for the French nation.[10] Medicine and millenarianism thus converged in revolutionary politics. These dreams permeated all levels of political thinking. In his book *The Progress of the Human Spirit* philosopher A.-N. de Condorcet proposed that sexual hygiene and sanitary science could one day perfect the human race in body and spirit.[11] Needless to say, the Reign of Terror dealt a heavy blow to this radical optimism, causing many people to question whether rational laws could promote a greater good in society. But these revolutionaries did not entirely abandon plans for regeneration. Following the Reign of Terror, moderate republicans wanted to regenerate public order and hoped that domestic law and public instruction could contain radicalism within the family. The Idéologue philosophers provide a case in point, as they tried to combine Enlightenment beliefs with conservative republicanism.[12] Prominent doctors, such as Pierre Cabanis and Xavier Bichat, contributed to this discussion. Although inspired by the philosopher Condorcet's call to perfect society, doctors doubted that all citizens could improve themselves in body and mind. Rather, they urged parents and physicians to use domestic hygiene to push morals and discipline in the family.[13] Official taste supported this medical ideology, yet these ideas clashed with the cynicism, hedonism, and crass materialism associated with post-Terror elites.[14] As a result, doctors gingerly balanced official moralism and perceived decadence. In the end they created books that mixed, in bizarre ways, sexual know-how, patriotism, and family values.

Within this context *On the Propagation of the Human Species* was first published in 1799. The book advertised itself as an "indispensable manual for those who wanted beautiful children" and promised to teach parents how to conceive male or female babies at will.[15] The book, like others in this genre, was derivative: the author plagiarized large sections of Quillet's *Callipaedia*, attached Johann Heinrich Meilbron's piece on flagellation (which had been translated two years earlier), and included two pieces by Juliette Offray de La Mettrie, *The Art of Enjoying* and *Man a Plant* (the latter of which had been banned under the old regime).[16] The book also discussed sex and astrology, conveniently updating the zodiac to reflect the new revolutionary calendar. Overall, the author assumed that his buying public wanted to learn about conception, not erotica, and he thus took sex as a physical, not a psychological, issue. Largely addressed to men, the book offered topical "know-how" advice about sexual timing, diet, wine selection, orgasm, impotency, sterility, phimosis, and genital size, and it offered solutions that ranged from surgery for women to bizarre mechanical contraptions and cataplasms for men.

On the surface, then, *On Propagation* fit into the traditional corpus of sex writings (not least because it plagiarized them), but it emphasized two things that made it novel on the self-help market: first, the book advertised how to conceive boy children; and second, it connected sex and domestic hygiene with revolutionary regeneration. This fad for having boys—and *On Propagation* was not the last word on this subject—is striking. Since the Counter-Reformation, moralists had cautioned parents against having girls, although women were clearly needed to propagate the species. Girls, they said, were an emotional and financial drain on the family: emotional, because girls were jealous and fickle and caused all sorts of discord and mischief; financial, because girls could not assume a lucrative trade and their dowries emptied the family purse.[17] But the French Revolution introduced two new factors into the boy craze. The first was military. By 1799 France had experienced seven years of civil and foreign war, and although French armies were on the offensive, the demographic losses weighed upon the public mind. Many observers recognized that the nation simply needed to replace a lost generation of men (not least for future wars, if necessary). The second factor was cultural. The French Revolution created a cult of male virtue, public life, and beauty that informed official taste and iconography (especially in neoclassical paintings and sculpture).[18] Given this emphasis on masculine prerogative and sociability, mothers and fathers perhaps concluded that only male children could benefit from this new world of careers open to talent. Later, this belief appears in Gustave Flaubert's *Madame Bovary* (1856), in which the protagonist, Emma, mourns the birth of her daughter because she too will stay disadvantaged in French society ("a male child was like an anticipated revenge for the powerlessness of her past. A man, at least, is free").[19]

Beyond these sexual concerns, moral politics also entered *On Propagation*. Procreation was, as the legislators preached, a patriotic duty. According to the book's author, the old regime had suffered from degeneracy and depopulation, but the Revolution had aroused patriotic sentiment and made people think about their domestic duties. His book, he said, would appeal to these upstanding citizens. And he warned that ill-advised marriages bred sickly children, who were incapable of fulfilling their moral and civic duties. For these reasons prospective partners should avoid mates with gout, epilepsy, and melancholic or consumptive temperaments. In particular older men should not marry young women because these unions were sterile or at best produced degenerate children. In other instances female "negligence and imprudence" caused physical degeneration. Pregnant women should thus exercise and avoid "violent movements" (such as dancing); moreover, women should keep their emotional life under control because the maternal imagination—a powerful force in reproduction and growth—caused monstrous births.[20]

The moral didacticism aside, *On Propagation*'s author juiced up his text. He was subversive and titillating: the book broached such taboo subjects as occultism, flagellation, and philosophic materialism in a tradition that harked back to mid-Enlightenment pornography such as *Thérèse philosophe* and *Dom Bougre*.[21] Throughout the author assumed that his readers engaged in nonprocreative sex for carnal self-satisfaction and spoke about men and women as though they were naturally libidinous and sexually indulgent. When a couple hoped to conceive, however, different rules applied. Under those circumstances men and women should become less physical in their lovemaking; frenzied passion, for example, dissipated the vital energy needed for procreation (note that the author did not view women as frigid or passive). Nevertheless, in *On Propagation* male sexuality is posed as a universal norm. The author insisted, for example, that women's sexual needs were "without measure and without order" and caused diseases such as hysteria and nymphomania. He then went on to tell readers that men felt greater physical pleasure because their genitals were more sensitive. Despite these disparaging remarks, the author wished to placate both his male and female readers: a healthy sex life, he said, promoted personal happiness, well-bred children, and good family life. The couple should change their sexual behavior only when they wanted to conceive.[22] Overall, then, *On Propagation* fits into an entire genre of post-Terror writings dealing with Mesmerism, magical medicine, and eroticism (such as Dr. François-Amédée Doppet's wildly successful writings on occult healing and the therapeutic value of the whip).[23]

On Propagation set the stage for Jacques-André Millot's *The Art of Procreating the Sexes at Will or the Complete System of Generation*, which appeared in 1800. The *Art of Procreating* was Millot's first self-help book, and although he penned three others, none of them achieved the same success or notoriety (the book had undergone six editions by 1828).[24] Before the French Revolution Millot had been a highly respected doctor in Paris high society. He had delivered babies for Marie Antoinette and the duchess of Orléans; he was personal physician to the comte d'Artois (the future Louis XVIII); and he famously saved the newborn duc d'Enghein from a nursery fire.[25] Because of these past aristocratic associations, Millot lost everything during the Reign of Terror, and he later squabbled with the republican doctors at the new Paris clinics: a quintessential insider had been reduced to practicing on the periphery. For a time he still wrote about his special expertise in obstetrics and pediatrics, publishing studies on caesarians and vaccination. Frustrated by poverty and professional neglect, Millot turned to writing pulp medical books on sex and domestic hygiene, which allowed him to vent his professional, political, and religious conservatism (views that his readers may have also shared). In these works Millot denounced radical and opportunistic republicans as murderers and thieves; he praised Napoléon Bonaparte for restoring order and morality; and he attacked the Paris medical faculty for its philosophic skepticism, materialism, and cliquishness.

His conservatism notwithstanding, Millot understood that sex sells, and he tailored his books to suit the lifestyle, political sensibilities, and sexual needs of new Consulate elites (indeed, a bookseller who called the book "crazy, extravagant, and immoral" admitted that he had sold over a thousand copies).[26] To his first self-help book Millot brought a gallant wit; sly discussions of hermaphrodites, monsters, and sterility; and even testimonials from satisfied female patients. As his main sales pitch, he promised to teach readers the proper way to conceive boys. "Everyone knows how to make babies," he said, "but no one knows how to conceive a boy or a girl at will."[27] For his part Millot argued that the ovaries contained the preformed germs of young boys and girls: boys on the right, girls on the left. Depending upon which ovary the male's semen permeated, a child of one or the other sex would result.

The process, however, was tricky. Following naturalist Lazarro Spallanzani, Millot argued that the male semen had a "spirituous" quality—an *aura seminalis*—that caused it to permeate the womb, rather like a miasma spreading in a dense thicket. During coitus, therefore, the man should lean on his partner's left side; at the moment of climax he should gently reach down and pull up the woman's right buttock—making an angle of twenty-five or thirty degrees—so the *aura seminalis* can permeate the proper ovary. While Millot recommended the missionary position, he claimed that partners could use this technique no matter what their preferred sexual positions might be; the man simply had to adjust the woman's right buttock and discharge his "life canon" (*canon de la vie*) at the proper angle.[28] Like *On Propagation*, then, Millot assumed his readers practiced both procreative and recreational sex, but he seemed forced to remind them that they should have vaginal sex when they wanted to conceive (in veiled terms he alluded to various sexual activities, including sodomy).[29]

At first glance Millot was not terribly novel. Nicolas Venette's *Conjugal Love* and Michel Procope-Couteau's *Art of Making Boys* (1750), for example, had debated similar techniques; and *On Propagation* had covered the problem just two years earlier and may have inspired Millot's book.[30] But Millot was different. In the earlier books writers discussed generation in an ancillary fashion, either to indulge the reader's curiosity or to give the books a scientific veneer. By contrast, Millot opened by discussing generation theory, and the discussion consumed three-quarters of his four hundred–page work (Venette had opened his book by graphically describing the male genitalia). At the same time, Millot attacked the new obstetric curriculum at the Paris clinics, violently lashing out at prominent faculty doctors such as J.-L. Baudelocque, who had revolutionized obstetrical approaches.[31] More than vulgarization was going on here. Recall that Millot, the former court physician, lacked a formal academic appointment in the 1790s, a professional embarrassment accentuated by his financial distress. Perhaps he hoped his book would create a demand for his medical services amongst Consulate high society or even improve his professional status by showcasing a rival embryological system. In this sense Millot may have imitated Pierre Maupertuis's *Physical Venus* (1745), which had used a gallant dialogue to make complex arguments about generation theory.[32] At least one critic took Millot seriously on this point.[33] By promoting a professional agenda in a self-help book, however, Millot took a calculated risk because well-respected doctors such as Philippe Pinel had begun criticizing medical popularizers, especially William Buchan and Samuel Tissot.[34]

In this book Millot was trying to make an argument for ovist preexistence. By the late Enlightenment doctors and naturalists had two theories to explain generation: preformation and epigenesis. The first, influenced by rationalist philosophy, saw the embryo (called a homunculus) as preformed in the mother's or father's seed; following fertilization, it expanded in a purely mechanical fashion. A version of this theory, called preexistence, believed that God had encased all possible beings in the germ, so that the embryo was "the simple evolution of what was already engendered," as naturalist Charles Bonnet put it.[35] By contrast, the epigenetic view, expounded by P.-L. de Maupertuis and G.-L. de Buffon, claimed that the embryo developed from a mass of organic molecules that arranged itself through chemical attraction or the species' interior mold. By emphasizing how both parents contributed material qualities to their offspring, epigenesis explained a wider range of biological variations, suggesting that reproduction was a dynamic process that did not need the agency of a creator. Historians usually portray the shift from preformation to epigenesis as having occurred in the 1740s and 1750s—despite resistance from Charles Bonnet, Albrecht von Haller, and Lazarro Spallanzani—with epigenesis triumphing in medical and naturalist circles by 1800.[36]

In post-Terror France, however, the medical faculties rejected epigenesis. By the 1790s Spallanzani's experiments on animal reproduction in frogs, toads, salamanders, silkworms, snails, and dogs—later confirmed by Pierre Rossi in Pisa and John Hunter in London—convinced Paris doctors of Haller's and Bonnet's theories of ovist preexistence.[37] These physicians praised Spallanzani's experiments as "one the most precious discoveries ever made upon Earth" and then tried to artificially inseminate human couples.[38] In 1803 Michel-Augustin Thouret, a professor at the Paris medical school, announced that he had impregnated a twenty-four-year-old woman by "purely mechanical means." With graphic detail Thouret reported how the husband had manually stimulated his wife, ejaculated into a syringe, and then injected his semen into her vaginal canal. With help from a doctor, the couple repeated these experiences every two weeks before the woman successfully conceived and gave birth to a child who resembled both parents. Following this "great and important experiment," Thouret promised that doctors could now cure all impediments, or "vices," that "opposed the consummation of the conjugal act."[39]

Millot contributed to this public discussion about ovist preexistence, introducing his readers to the prevailing theories and offering his own pointed reflections on the subject. Rejecting epigenesis, Millot argued that reproduction was not an open-ended process. As he explained, "Generation does not suppose the production of new [organic] parts; it is only a new modification of already-existing elements."[40] Nature endlessly created new individuals but still conserved the species: variation occurred without evolution. Yet Millot rejected Bonnet's strict encasement theory. Doubting that the womb contained all these encased germs, Millot instead suggested that the ovaries formed embryonic germs throughout the female life course (a process called "germification"), and only the male seminal fluid could cause these embryos to grow into a full individual.[41] Millot thus rejected hermaphroditism and parthenogenesis in humans (in which an unfertilized egg cell develops into a fully formed individual). Satiric writings such as Abraham Johnson's (Henry Hill's) *Lucina sine concubitu* and Richard Roe's *Concubitus sine Lucina* (both published in 1750) had explored this possibility, and they had been recently republished in post-Terrorist France.[42] Lest readers take these theories seriously, Millot told them that only two sexes existed— one for each ovary—and only a large amount of semen could inseminate both ovaries and produce twins. He therefore tried to bridge epigenesis and preformation; he kept the ovist model but acknowledged the obvious epigenetic inference that children inherited material qualities from both parents. As he saw it, his theory of ovist preexistence, which stressed germ formation and a "mode of aggregation" between sexual partners, was more likely than "that famous preexistence since the creation of our world."[43]

As historians have argued, religious and philosophic belief often informed generation theory, causing naturalists to embrace either the deterministic preformation theory (Calvinists) or the more open-ended epigenesist (Catholics).[44] During the French Revolution new political ideologies replaced philosophy and theology as an influence upon generation theory. This trend clearly emerges in Millot's writings. When discussing reproduction, Millot addressed a reading audience whose members valued the political gains provided by the French Revolution and who still wanted to create a regenerated New Man for the French nation.[45] While somewhat sympathetic, Millot gently told his readers that they might want to lower their expectations. As the embryological evidence suggested, preformed embryos could not inherit much in terms of genius or work ethic; when children received anything from their parents, it seemed limited to negative traits such as anomalies, sicknesses, and mental debilities. Talent was thus innate, forming a neo-Kantian "sixth sense"—"a natural inequality in physical and intellectual faculties amongst men." Education could not overcome these born inequalities. Millot doubted therefore whether public instruction could transform morals and manners, and he indirectly criticized philosophers such as Condorcet who believed that future generations could inherit progressive adaptations. But Millot did not abandon regeneration. Like conservative republicans (such as the Idéologue philosophers at the National Institute), Millot promised that the family could inculcate morality and civic virtue. In this case parents, doctors, and educators should combine pedagogy and sexual hygiene to improve society. Given social limitations, however, citizens faced a stark choice: they could reform the present generation or focus upon the yet unborn.[46]

Other doctors were more enthusiastic about human breeding. The year after Millot's Art of Procreating appeared, J.-L.-M. Robert, a young medical student from St. Tulle, entered the self-help sex market with his short book, An Essay on Mega-Anthropogenesis (1801).[47] Dedicating the work to the Institut National, Robert hoped to teach readers and administrators how to make people healthy in body and spirit and thus promote population growth. Quite simply, Robert promised to inform his readers about how to breed "great men" (grands hommes) in the neoclassical style, suggesting that citizens could make France into a living pantheon.[48] Beyond his opening essay—original if not bizarre—Robert was crassly derivative, plagiarizing large sections of Millot's *Art of Procreating* and adding chapters from Johann Lavatar's recently published *Essay on Physiognomy* (1781).[49] Some reviewers even confused Millot and Robert or thought they were playing an elaborate hoax upon Paris high society.

According to Robert, the government and the people must work together to breed a future race of republicans. The Revolution had inspired citizens to regenerate themselves; the government must now take this political capital and invest it in the next generation. To perfect the human race, education was the first step; it liberated people from ignorance and superstition and imparted the abstract values of liberty, equality, and fraternity. Yet education was not enough. Robert rejected the philosopher C.-A. Helvétius's controversial claim—"man is only a product of his education"—and claimed instead that biology made human destiny.[50] Individuals could only do so much with the bodies and brains that they had received at birth. But all was not lost, according to Robert. Geniuses were born and then refined; when forming bright minds and beautiful bodies, good pedigree and good schooling went hand in hand. And Robert promised to make such people. "Mega-anthropogenesis," he bragged, could breed a great race of republicans by educating the French people and then marrying the best and brightest men and women. In contrast to Condorcet and Cabanis, who tried to convince legislators that biological engineering could perfect humanity, Robert marketed these utopian projects to a broad reading public. Through their private sex lives ordinary readers could breed the "New Atlantis" in the revolutionary present.

Robert's plan was simple. The government should create two primary schools, or Atheneums, for regenerating citizens: one for men at the Paris military school, the other for women at the palace of Versailles. Using physiognomic techniques (as provided in Robert's book), the Ministry of Interior could identify promising children and place them in advanced schools until a national jury declared their education complete. The young women learned science, literature, home economics, and good mothering; after graduation, they would marry their male schoolmates and receive a state pension based upon merit. Adolescent males would learn the arts and sciences, too, but in contrast to the young women, their teachers should emphasize the classics and natural philosophy, and their education should inculcate a patriotic, militaristic attitude. Finally, at the annual Festival of the

Republic, the first consul (Napoléon) would give a national award to the six best male and female students of the Atheneum, and the youngsters would celebrate their mega-anthropogenetic marriages with solemn dignity. Robert concluded, "Oh, government of France! It is you who must calculate the happy influence of mega-anthropogenesis and its effect upon the Republic and the well-being of nations."[51]

Like Millot, Robert found an audience. In response, he published a brief synopsis, defended a medical thesis on this subject (directed by obstetrician Alphonse Leroy), and soon issued a greatly revised edition. The book was also translated into German.[52] Not surprisingly, Robert attracted angry critics. In a poor move he used his own characterization as the book's epigraph—"my century might call me crazy"—and hostile reviewers gleefully agreed with him. One anonymous critic said that Robert's plagiarism taught readers not the art of making children but, rather, the art of making books ("c'est un faiseur de livres faits"); another quipped that Robert's parents should have learned mega-anthropogenesis before they had children.[53] In 1807 the Théâtre de Vaudeville performed a one-act satire called The Island of Mega-Anthropogenesis. The play staged an overrefined "world turned upside-down" in which inbred social elites had forgotten how to work.[54] The play was so successful that theater companies imported it to northern Italy, where translators replaced French caricatures (such as an autistic gastronomer) with Italian objects of ridicule (such as an autistic politician).[55]

Robert hit a nerve. Unlike On Propagation or Millot's The Art of Procreating, Robert identified with the "principles of 1789," and he claimed the French Revolution had regenerated the nation's health. In so doing, he plugged into a medical debate about the health consequences of the French Revolution. Predictably, political outlook often determined how doctors thought about the Revolution's physical side effects. For conservatives such as J.-A. Alibert the French Revolution had destroyed self-control, political order, and, ultimately, personal health. To improve health and public safety, he thought, legislators had to use public hygiene and paternal authority. In this sense Alibert connected political radicalism with dirt and disease.[56] By contrast, moderate doctors such as M.-A. Petit (a leading surgeon in Lyons, a city devastated during the Reign of Terror) believed that freedom and patriotic virtue had revivified a moribund population. Jacobinism and popular violence were aberrations that obscured the Revolution's healthy benefits. Petit thus followed Idéologues such as Cabanis and Pinel, who believed that the Revolution had improved both medicine and social well-being.[57]

In his writings Robert made it clear that he supported the political and clinical program of the Idéologue doctors.[58] Although he opposed Jacobinism, he believed that the French Revolution had rejuvenated the nation's health and thus its fertility—and fertility, as Robert quoted Lucien Bonaparte, was the mother of all victory, the safeguard of liberty. Using well-known revolutionary iconography, Robert claimed that freedom and medical reform had made "every Frenchman [into] a Hercules, so great is the influence of the spirit of liberty on the population."[59] Still, the government had more work to do—such as prenuptial marriage checks, midwifery regulations, breastfeeding, and so on—in order to improve the nation's health. Nevertheless, Robert cautioned against radical social engineering. Following Cabanis and Bichat, he believed that inequality had a biological basis; people could not improve themselves beyond their born abilities. Social engineering was therefore ineffective, and only selective breeding could improve society. Although perfection was an instinct, human nature could not be totally changed.[60]

At the same time, Robert advocated striking ideas about female education and emancipation. For many doctors and legislators ovist preexistence suggested that women did not actively contribute to conception; rather, they were simply passive receptacles for the animating male semen. Yet ovist preexistence also showed that the child's physical well-being was first and foremost a maternal duty. As doctors explained, women contained the preexisting germs of all future citizens in their wombs: their blood nourished the fetus, molding its temperament and passions; the maternal imagination potentially influenced gestation and could cause anomalies; and breastfeeding transmitted vice and virtue. Because of these maternal influences, doctors such as Pierre Cabanis and J.-L. Moreau de la Sarthe concluded that women should forget intellectual or public life and instead focus upon their natural domestic duties.[61] These sentiments were largely shared by Millot, even though he wanted to placate female readers.[62]

By contrast, Robert drew different conclusions from embryological science.[63] To breed a regenerated New Man, he argued, the republic must first create a great woman of spirit as well. Robert criticized the government for failing to educate women, and he even implied that legislators deliberately kept women ignorant and subdued. According to him, women were not physically and morally inferior; rather, they had a number of sublime qualities that included wit, sentiment, virtue, and intelligence. His mega-anthropogenetic Atheneums, he thought, could cultivate these innate faculties and thus promote regeneration. By refining their minds and bodies, doctors and educators could make women into better wives and mothers. Most important, children eventually inherited these acquired qualities, thus internalizing progress in their bodies.[64] Not surprisingly, some critics alleged that only women bought Robert's books—and indeed Robert wrote constantly about women's health, on matters ranging from breast cancer to music therapy.[65]

Political pressures began to change the sex self-help market. Beginning in 1801, the Consulate became increasingly authoritarian and militaristic. That same year, after reconciling the French government and the papacy in the Concordat, Napoléon began to use religion for social control. Earlier in 1800 the government had also adapted new censorship laws, and the revolutionary book trade soon experienced severe financial difficulties.[66] Taking their cue, sex writers adopted a more conservative tone and explicitly rejected what they viewed as Millot's flamboyance or Robert's radicalism. This shift emerges in J.-J. Virey's On the Public and Private Education of Frenchmen (1802). Steeped in Rousseauian primitivism (associated with writers such as Bernardin de St. Pierre and L. S. Mercier), Virey thought that education should create "honest and virtuous men," not Robert's great men or intellectuals (savans).[67] His ideological differences notwithstanding, Virey nevertheless believed that citizens could breed virtuous citizens and thus make "a new Utopia in which everyone will be perfectly happy and content"[68]—though he often emphasized the limits of regeneration and rejected women's education out of hand.[69]

Virey had a novel approach. In his writings he distinguished between the organism's cerebral and genital poles, claiming that people needed to balance both extremes in order to experience normal biological functions (including mental aptitude and fertility). When a person used one pole to excess—as seen with intellectuals and libertines—they drained the body's sensibility and sapped procreative energy. Great men thus rarely begot distinguished children or could not reproduce at all.[70] The best example was Isaac Newton himself: while his fertile mind had penetrated the cosmos, his body proved sadly sterile in the earthly world.[71] Virey thus rejected Robert's mega-anthropogenesis because it favored social mobility over rustic virtue and religious sentiment, two things needed to maintain a hierarchical, patriarchal society. As he saw it, mega-anthropogenesis simply appealed to a cynical new aristocracy that embraced decadent materialism rather than sentimental virtue.[72]

The fullest expression of this conservative worldview appeared in 1808, with the anonymous *Philopaedia, or the Art of Having Children without Passions*. Moving beyond Virey (who never disavowed his republicanism), the author—who described himself as a twenty-nine-year-old bachelor—wanted to create a self-help manual to cure "hypersensibility" and radicalism. Hoping to appeal to former aristocrats and nostalgic émigrés, the author adopted a pious and sentimental tone.[73] After the French Revolution, he said, society must breed and educate a new generation of sensible, loving, and responsible subjects. Unlike Millot and Robert, who advertised their knowledge of clinical pathology and embryological science, this author returned to an explicit Cartesian dualism. As he saw it, the individual was made of two substances: one material and corruptible (the body), the other pure and immaterial (the soul). As an emanation of God, the soul was perfect; its impurities only came from its union with the body's flesh. By perfecting the body, then, individuals could eradicate physical vices and thus bring them closer to God. "A moral *evil* is only an organic vice susceptible to being rectified," the author explained, and he literally localized sin in the body's physical drives—what moral hygienists called the "passions of the mind."[74]

Indeed, passion was society's biggest problem. An impassioned person often lacked pity and empathy, two things that a just and harmonious society always needed; in times of political crisis excessive passion caused anarchy, violence, and civil war. Fortunately, parents could teach their children how to control their passionate sensibilities by imparting moral values and self-discipline. As the author put it, a man without passions could find a peaceful harmony and inner feeling of satisfaction and happiness. In creating passionless offspring, parents were not simply raising unreflective or misanthropic children. Quite the contrary, the man without passions was a man who could distinguish between vice and virtue, private charms and public dignity. This person was constant but faithful, compassionate but not weak, religious but not fanatical, patriotic but not ferocious. For their part doctors and educators imparted the self-reliance and moral values that guided citizens in all moral and civic duties, recognizing that they should not try to fit citizens into preconceived "rational" molds; rather, education should form them "according to the state adapted to their tastes, character, and liking."[75]

To cure themselves of passion, parents and children needed sexual hygiene. As the author saw it, both vice and virtue had material attributes. Given current medical understanding, he believed that children might inherit physical vices and that mothers might communicate (or incubate) these debilities in their wombs. He was particularly struck by recent reports about crime and madness in particular families, evidence that suggested that children inherited deviant tendencies.[76] Nevertheless, the author did not believe that biology determined moral behavior, and he cautioned against materialist sophisms. In his view the Supreme Being might give individuals innate ideas about vice and virtue, but sensory experience and education always shaped moral autonomy. Individuals could always improve (or degrade) their minds and bodies. In this sense degeneracy was a constitutional vice and not caused by "an organic necessity."[77] As a result, readers should reject luxurious and libertine trappings, such as philosophic freethinking, sexual free living, gambling, popular novels, fashionable clothing, wet-nursing, coffee, tea, and tobacco, among other things. By altering their lifestyle, citizens could cure physical degeneration, and he especially encouraged women to educate themselves and implement these reforms in the nursery.

Self-help sex manuals were more than a simple craze, a garish fancy that appealed to fashionable elites in the confused and anarchic world of late revolutionary France. Rather, these books stand at the crossroads of significant changes in the making of modern French identity. As such, they raise three important historiographical questions about medical power, gender relations, and mass politics during the French Revolution. The first question concerns the relationship between medicine and ideology. Over the past two decades Michel Foucault's provocative "biopower" model has influenced historians of sexuality and medicine. Foucault used the term to describe how society tried to control all elements of human life. For him biopower took two forms: one an "anatomo-politics" to control the individual body; the other a "bio-politics" to regulate the population as a species.[78] Foucault's chosen word was *governmentality*. He thus identified an ideological or "discursive" partnership between the state, professions, and social elites; in turn these disciplines and technologies worked together to exercise power upon a given polity.[79]

Given the emphasis on sexuality and population in post-Terror sex manuals, Foucault's biopower model seems to offer a fruitful approach. Indeed, historians have often characterized Millot, Robert, and Virey as odd but sinister precursors to modern eugenics.[80] In this case, however, it is unclear what "interests" these self-help doctors served beyond their own, given that they were not serving an overarching government or professional agenda. Rather, they wrote from the margin. They were quintessential outsiders, strangers to new social elites, political power, and the medical establishment itself (indeed, this alienation may have motivated their bombastic style and fanciful plans). In their writing they advocated less a broad agenda than they tried to calculate their readers' desires and political sensibilities. Like the empiricists and mountebanks who hawked their cures on Quack Street, these doctors competed in the medical marketplace—but in this case they sold not remedies but the keys to sexual happiness.[81] As such, they tried to appeal to particular demographic groups and distinguish themselves by offering titillating or bawdy subject matter. In this manner medical writers diluted any broad hegemonic program or simply reinforced their reader's existing political and religious views. Given their underlying tone, they were closer to the saucy and subversive world of Enlightenment pornography than Foucault's "political technologies of governmentality."

Second, these books cast substantial light upon the so-called sexual panic of the 1790s, a panic that forced contemporaries to embrace bourgeois views about separate spheres and sexual incommensurability.[82] According to Londa Schiebinger and Thomas Laqueur, modern ideas about sex difference were born sometime at the end of the eighteenth century. During this period science and medicine shifted from a "one-sex model" to a "two-sex model" of sexual dimorphism.[83] Accordingly, contemporaries no longer saw men and women as anatomically homologous, distinguished simply by humoral qualities. Rather, they thought men and women were sexually distinct beings and thus inscribed sexual difference throughout the body, from the genitalia to the skeleton.[84] At the same time, doctors and naturalists moved from the old Galenic model of conception, which emphasized the ways in which both partners contributed to procreation, to the new ovist model, which devalued sexual activity in generation. In so doing, doctors elided female orgasm from medical texts and now claimed that women were sexually passive and frigid beings.[85] These sexual theories had political ramifications. During the French Revolution, for example, legislators used biomedical science to justify pushing women out of public life and enshrine the separate spheres ideology in the Civil Code of 1804.[86]

The sex manuals published between 1797 and 1808 complicate this picture. Although a whole generation of doctors learned disparaging theories about ovist preexistence and female physiology, they did not draw consistent political views from biomedical science.[87] Among their authors Virey was perhaps the most systematic misogynist, but his malevolence was distinctive. Robert, for instance, criticized legislative action against women, even pushing for a relative equality between the sexes, especially in terms of education. Although he was a political conservative, Millot hoped to placate his female readers: he emphasized female education and treated them as active agents in political regeneration. Even *Philopaedia* criticized the current rage for having boys and tried to flatter women readers by likening their new civic duties to the spiritual call of Joan of Arc. These writers were not feminists in the current understanding of that word. None of them argued for sexual equality or a change in women's legal status. When compared to the antifeminist violence of many revolutionaries, however, these self-help writers were clearly pro-women: they advocated some forms of female agency and addressed women as self-motivated actors in revolutionary change.[88] They also saw women as inherently libidinous, sexual beings and stressed that couples should restrain their sexual behavior only when they wanted to conceive. The reason was less enlightened than calculated. Doctors understood that women routinely bought books and medical services, and they might resent sustained misogyny in their reading selections. In this case the medical marketplace finessed biological models of sex difference.

Most strikingly, these books suggest the ways in which medicine became a mediating voice in French politics after the Reign of Terror. For many people traditional French society fell apart (to use the line from William Butler Yeats, the "center could not hold"), and all the old values and all the old stories—rooted in king, church, and nobility—no longer gave people a sense of meaning and place. In the absence of these old values and stories, people looked elsewhere to explain a rapidly changing world. For many elites medicine provided one such answer. Medicine gave them a whole new way of explaining mind, body, and society. It was both scientific and dispassionate, intimate and tactile, no doubt owing to its closeness to the body and private experience. It gave them an objective language to talk about revolutionary change and helped them make sense of the disparate and dislocating events in their lives.

These post-Terror sex manuals underscored the new cultural sensibility, teaching readers new tools and new language—ideas about hygiene, physiology, embryology, and heredity—to explain bewildering changes in society and, perhaps more important, to justify moral values and political interests in scientific and objective terms. But these writers also assumed that their readers had already formed their political and moral views. Like English Newtonians after the Glorious Revolution, these doctors tried to reinforce particular beliefs rather than modify them.[89] On Propagation, for example, addressed sartorial and freewheeling elites; Millot appealed to fashionable conservatives and chastened former aristocrats; Robert targeted moderate republicans and Napoleonic technocrats; Virey appealed to Rousseauian pastoralists; and Philopaedia addressed traditional Catholics and nostalgic aristocrats.

Despite these ideological differences, the books preached a common message: men and women, these doctors taught, could use their private homes as a specially controlled environment—a kind of affective laboratory—in which they could raise their children according to chosen values. In many ways their books underscore how contemporaries withdrew into private life following the Reign of Terror, preferring the intimate associations found in family and civil society over the collective sociability of the radical republic. In the authoritarian Napoleonic state, then, these writers exploited official efforts to direct personal energies away from the public arena back into the private realm. By being devoted spouses and loving parents, individuals could still think of themselves as engaged and patriotic citizens, even after a dictatorial regime had stripped them of active political rights. Doctors thus encouraged readers to abandon revolutionary activism and use their energies to mold a generation yet to come. A better future would come by organic means. But the doctor could always give nature a helping hand in the process.

Notes

1. For helpful surveys of this literature, see P. Darmon, *Le Mythe de la procréation à l'âge baroque* (1977; repr., Paris: Seuil, 1981), 134–41, 150–54; and A. Carol, *Histoire de l'eugénisme en France: les médecins et la procréation XIXe–XX siècle* (Paris: Seuil, 1995), 20–26. Summaries can also be found in Dubuisson, *Tableau de l'amour conjugal, édition remise à la hauteur des connaissances d'aujourd'hui*, 4 vols. (Paris, 1812); and A. Debay, *Histoire des métamorphoses humaines et des monstruosités, stérilité, impuissance, procréation des sexes, calligénésie* (Paris, 1845).

2. Review of L.-J.-M. Robert, *Essai sur la mégalanthropogénésie*, in *Le Décade Philosophique, Littéraire et Politique*, no. 9 (30 frimaire, Year X): 549–50.

3. The closest parallel was the upsurge of erotic literature in the 1740s, an event that Robert Darnton calls the "double explosion" of writings about sex and nature; see *The Forbidden Best-Sellers of Pre-Revolutionary France* (New York: Norton, 1996), 90.

4. See C. Rosenberg, "Medical Text and Social Context: Explaining William Buchan's *Domestic Medicine*," in *Explaining Epidemics and Other Studies in the History of Medicine* (Cambridge: Cambridge University Press, 1992), 32–56. On medical popularization, see especially J. Poirier and J.-L. Poirier, "La Vulgarisation médicale: considérations philosopho-historiques," *Revue d'Éducation Médicale* 6 (1983): 184–90; L. J. Jordanova, "The Popularisation of Medicine: Tissot on Onanism," *Textual Practice* 1 (1987): 68–79; and R. Porter, *Patients and Practitioners: Lay Perceptions of Medicine in Pre-Industrial Society* (Cambridge: Cambridge University Press, 1985). Matthew Ramsey provides an excellent overview in "The Popularization of Medicine in France, 1650–1850," in *The Popularization of Medicine 1650–1850*, ed. R. Porter (London: Routledge, 1992). On the general problem of diffusion and the "popular" and "elite" spheres of print culture, see R. Chartier, *The Cultural Uses of Print in Early Modern France*, trans. L. G. Cochrane (Princeton NJ: Princeton University Press, 1987).

5. A. McLaren, *Reproductive Rituals: The Perception of Fertility in England from the Sixteenth Century to the Nineteenth Century* (London: Methuen, 1984); R. Porter, "Mixed Feelings: The Enlightenment and Sexuality in Eighteenth-Century Britain," in *Sexuality in Eighteenth-Century Britain*, ed. Paul-Gabriel Boucé (Manchester: Manchester University Press, 1982); R. Porter, "'The Secrets of Generation Display'd': *Aristotle's Master-piece* in Eighteenth-Century England," in *'Tis Nature's Fault: Unauthorized Sexuality during the Enlightenment*, ed. R. P. Maccubbin (Cambridge: Cambridge University Press, 1985); and most recently, Mary E. Fissell, "Making a Masterpiece: The Aristotle Texts in Vernacular Medical Culture," in *Right Living: An Anglo-American Tradition of Self-Help Medicine and Hygiene*, ed. Charles E. Rosenberg (Baltimore: Johns Hopkins University Press, 2003), 59–87.

6. R. Porter, "Spreading Carnal Knowledge or Selling Dirt Cheap? Nicolas Venette's *Tableau de l'amour conjugal* in Eighteenth-Century England," *Journal of European Studies* 14 (1984): 233–55.

7. J. J. Spengler, *French Predecessors to Malthus: A Study in Eighteenth-Century Wage and Population Theory* (Durham NC: Duke University Press, 1942), 78–103; J. C. Riley, *Population Thought in the Age of Demographic Revolution* (Durham NC: Carolina Academic Press, 1985), 52–57; R. Favre, *La Mort dans la littérature et la pensée françaises au siècle des Lumières* (Lyons: Presses Universitaires de Lyon, 1978), 275–331; H. Chisick, *The Limits of Reform in the Enlightenment: Attitudes toward the Education of the Lower Classes in Eighteenth-Century France* (Princeton NJ: Princeton University Press, 1981), 185–97; and most recently, C. Blum, *Strength in Numbers: Population, Reproduction, and Power in Eighteenth-Century France* (Baltimore: Johns Hopkins University Press, 2002).

8. "Recueil d'observations tant de médecine que de chirurgie, avec un traité de la génération de l'homme et la manière de perfectionner l'espèce humaine et un recueil de plantes propres à chaque maladie," October 1756, MS 5116, Bibliothèque de la Faculté de Médecine de Paris (hereafter cited as BFMP); and S.-A.-A.-D. Tissot, *Avis au peuple sur sa santé* (Lausanne, 1761), 7. Of this literature, see especially Antoine Le Camus, *Médecine de l'esprit* (n.p., 1753); C.-A. Vandermone, *Essai sur la manière de perfectionner l'espèce humaine* (n.p., 1756); N. Brouzet, *Essai sur l'éducation médicinale des enfans* (n.p., 1759); and Samuel Tissot, *L'Onanisme* (n.p., 1760).

9. For biomedicine and the family, see L. J. Jordanova, "Naturalizing the Family: Literature and the Medical Sciences in the Late Eighteenth Century," in *Languages of Nature: Critical Essays on Science and Literature*, ed. L. J. Jordanova (London: Free Association, 1986), esp. 95–105; J. Donzelot, *The Policing of Families*, trans. R. Hurley (New York: Pantheon, 1979), 9–47; and A. S. Benzaquén, "Childhood, Identity and Human Science in the Enlightenment," *History Workshop Journal*, no. 57 (2004): 35–57. On Enlightenment views of childhood and the family, see D. G. Charlton, *New Images of the Natural in France: A Study in European Cultural History, 1750–1800* (Cambridge: Cambridge University Press, 1984), 135–53.

10. See the classic analyses in E. H. Ackerknecht, *Medicine at the Paris Hospital, 1794–1848* (Baltimore: Johns Hopkins University Press, 1967); M. Foucault, *Naissance de la clinique*, 4th ed. (Paris: PUF, 1994); and D. M. Vess, *Medical Revolution in France, 1789–1796* (Gainesville: University Presses of Florida, 1975). For excellent overviews of the "medical revolution" and the historiographical debates, see esp. E. A. Williams, "The French Revolution, Anthropological Medicine, and the Creation of Medical Authority," in *Re-Constructing Authority in Revolutionary France*, ed. B. T. Ragan Jr. and E. A. Williams (New Brunswick NJ: Rutgers University Press, 1992), 79–97; and C. C. Hannaway and A. F. La Berge, eds., *Constructing*

Paris Medicine (Amsterdam: Editions Rodopi B.V., 1998). On general thinking about regeneration, see M. Ozouf, "La Révolution française et l'idée de l'homme nouveau," in *The Political Culture of the French Revolution*, ed. K. M. Baker (Oxford: Pergamon, 1988), 2:213–32; A. de Baecque, "L'Homme nouveau est arrivé: la 'régénération' du français en 1789," *Dix-huitième Siècle*, no. 20 (1988): 193–208. On science and regeneration, see N. Rattner Gelbart, "The French Revolution as Medical Event: The Journalistic Gaze," *History of European Ideas* 10 (1989): 417–27; E. C. Spary, *Utopia's Garden: French Natural History from Old Regime to Revolution* (Chicago: University of Chicago Press, 2000), 99–102; A. C. Vila, *Enlightenment and Pathology* (Baltimore: Johns Hopkins University Press, 1998), 296.

11. A.-N. de Condorcet, *Esquisse d'un tableau historique des progrès de l'esprit humain*, ed. A. Pons (Paris: Flammarion, 1988), 80; and *Cinq mémoires sur l'instruction publique*, ed. C. Coutel and C. Kintzler (Paris: Flammarion, 1994), 70–71. See also Spary, *Utopia's Garden*, 127–28.

12. See M. S. Staum, *Minerva's Message: Stabilizing the French Revolution* (Montreal: McGill-Queen's University Press, 1996); L. J. Jordanova, "The Authoritarian Response: The French Revolution and the Enlightenment," in *Nature Displayed: Gender, Science, and Medicine* (London: Transaction, 1999), 86–100; and C. Hesse, *The Other Enlightenment: How French Women Became Modern* (Princeton NJ: Princeton University Press, 2001), 104–29. On this general context, see L. A. Hunt, *The Family Romance of the French Revolution* (Berkeley: University of California Press, 1992), chap. 5; S. Desan, "Reconstituting the Social after the Terror: Family, Property, and the Law in Popular Politics," *Past and Present*, no. 164 (1999): 81–121; E. Lajer-Burcharth, *Necklines: The Art of Jacques-Louis David after the Terror* (New Haven CT: Yale University Press, 1999); and S. Moravia, *Il pensiero degli Idéologues: scienza e filosofia in Francia (1780–1815)* (Florence: La Nuova Italia, 1974).

13. P.-J.-G. Cabanis, "Considérations générales sur l'étude de l'homme et sur les rapports de son organisation physique avec ses facultés intellectuelles et morales," *Mémoires de l'Institut National des Sciences et Arts: 2e Classe, Sciences Morales et Politiques* 1 (Year VI): 64; and P.-J.-G. Cabanis, *Rapports du physique et du moral de l'homme*, 2 vols. (Paris, Year XI [1802]), 1:287, 2:79–80, 2:81–82, 2:250–51, 2:444–45; X. Bichat, *Physiological Researches upon Life and Death*, trans. T. Watkins (Philadelphia, 1809), 63, 70–75, 109–10, 112–13, 115; C.-L. Dumas, *Principes de physiologie, ou introduction à la science expérimentale, philosophique et médicale de l'homme vivant*, 4 vols. (Paris, 1800–1803); and B.-A. Richerand, *Nouveaux élemens de physiologie*, 2nd ed. (Paris, 1802). On post-Thermidorean medical ideas about regeneration, see S. M. Quinlan, "Physical and Moral Regeneration after the Terror: Medical Culture, Sensibility, and Family Politics in France, 1794–1804," *Social History* 29 (2004): 139–64; M. S. Staum, "Volney et l'idée d'une science morale à l'institut," in *L'Héritage des Lumières: Volney et les Idéologues*, ed. J. Roussel (Angers: Presses de l'Université, 1988), 131–40.

14. On the myths of late-revolutionary decadence, see R. Schechter, "Gothic Thermidor: The *Bals des victimes*, the Fantastic, and the Production of Historical Knowledge in Post-Terror France," *Representations*, no. 61 (1998): 78–94.

15. *De la propagation du genre humain, ou manuel indispensable pour ceux qui veulent avoir de beaux enfants de l'un ou l'autre sexe* (Paris, 1799), vii–viii.

16. R. Darnton, *The Corpus of Clandestine Literature in France, 1769–1789* (New York: Norton, 1995), 91.

17. Darmon, *Le Mythe de la procréation*, 142–45.

18. A. Potts, "Beautiful Bodies and Dying Heroes: Images of Ideal Manhood in the French Revolution," *History Workshop Journal*, no. 30 (1990): 1–20; A. Solomon-Godeau, "Male Trouble: A Crisis in Representation," *Art History* 16 (1993): 286–312.

19. G. Flaubert, *Madame Bovary, Provincial Lives*, trans. G. Wall (Harmondsworth: Penguin, 1992), 70.

20. *De la propagation*, 115.

21. See esp. Darnton, *Forbidden Best-Sellers*; M. C. Jacob, "The Materialist World of Pornography," in *The Invention of Pornography: Obscenity and the Origins of Modernity, 1500–1800*, ed. L. A. Hunt (New York: Zone Books, 1993), 198–99; and R. L. Dawson, "The *Mélange de poésies diverses* (1781) and the Diffusion of Manuscript Pornography in Eighteenth-Century France," in Maccubbin, *'Tis Nature's Fault*, 237–38.

22. *De la propagation*, 178.

23. Ramsey, "Popularization of Medicine," 106.

24. Millot's work was replaced in 1829 by J. Morel de Rubempré, *Les Secrets de la génération, ou l'art de procréer à volonté des filles ou des garçons, de faire des enfants d'esprit, de les orner du bon de la beauté, de les avoir sains et robustes*, 12th ed. (1829; repr., Paris, 1840). Morel de Rubempré packaged these revolutionary writings for middlebrow taste in Restoration society.

25. Darmon, *Le Mythe de la procréation*, 258; Carol, *Histoire de l'eugénisme*, 24–25.

26. *Journal des débats* (18 nivôse, Year X).

27. J.-A. Millot, *L'Art de procréer les sexes à volonté, ou système complet de génération*, 2nd ed. (1800; repr., Paris, 1801), 301.

28. Millot, *L'Art de procréer*, 315, 317.

29. On the possible shift toward vaginal sex, see T. Hitchcock, "Redefining Sex in Eighteenth-Century England," *History Workshop Journal*, no. 41 (1996): 73–90.

30. M. Procope-Couteau, *L'Art de faire des garçons ou nouveau tableau de l'amour conjugal* (Montpellier, 1755).

31. Millot, *L'Art de procréer*, 196–97ff. On childcare and obstetrics at the Paris clinics and hospitals, see D. B. Weiner, *The Citizen-Patient in Revolutionary and Imperial Paris* (Baltimore: Johns Hopkins University Press, 1993), 191–222.

32. M. Terrall, *The Man Who Flattened the Earth: Maupertuis and the Sciences in the Enlightenment* (Chicago: University of Chicago Press, 2002), 218–21.

33. Guilhermond, *Lettre à Millot sur son système de la génération et sur l'art de procréer les sexes à volonté* (Paris, 1802).

34. H. Mitchell, "Rationality and Control in French Eighteenth-Century Medical Views of the Peasantry," *Comparative Studies in Society and History* 21 (1979): 101; Ramsey, "Popularization of Medicine," 113–14.

35. Charles Bonnet, *Considérations sur les corps organisés*, 2 vols. (Neuchâtel, 1779), 1:120.

36. On generation theory, see Jacques Roger, *Les Sciences de la vie dans la pensée française au XVIIIe siècle: la génération des animaux de Descartes à l'Encyclopédie*, 3rd ed. (Paris: Albin Michel, 1993); Elizabeth B. Gasking, *Investigations into Generation, 1651–1828* (Baltimore: Johns Hopkins University Press, 1967). For helpful analysis, see esp. P. J. Bowler, "Bonnet and Buffon: Theories of Generation and the Problem of Species," *Journal of the History of Biology* 6 (1973): 259–81; and M. H. Hoffheimer, "Maupertuis and the Eighteenth-Century Critique of Preexistence," *Journal of the History of Biology* 15 (1982): 119–44.

37. L. Spallanzani, *Expériences pour servir à l'histoire de la génération des animaux et des plantes, avec une ébauche de l'histoire des êtres organisés avant leur fécondition* (Geneva, 1785). On eighteenth-century ovism, see J. Farley, *Gametes and Spores: Ideas about Sexual Reproduction, 1750–1914* (Baltimore: Johns Hopkins University Press, 1982), 25–29; and W. Bernardi, *Le metafisiche dell'embrione: scienze della vita e filosofia da Malpighi a Spallanzani (1672–1793)* (Florence: Olschki, 1986), 309–486.

38. M.-A. Thouret, *Application sur l'espèce humaine des expériences faites par Spallanzani sur quelques animaux, relativemenet à la fécondation artificielle des germes, ou résultat d'une expérience qui prouve que l'on peut créer des enfans avec le concours des deux sexes, mais sans leur approche* (Paris, 1803), 11. For the early history of artificial insemination, see F. N. L. Poynter, "Hunter, Spallanzani, and the History of Artificial Insemination," in *Medicine, Science, and Culture: Historical Essays in Honor of Oswei Temkin*, ed. L. G. Stevenson and R. P. Multhauf (Baltimore: Johns Hopkins University Press, 1968).

39. Thouret, *Application sur l'espèce humaine*, 24, 29–30, 36.

40. Millot, *L'Art de procréer*, 30.

41. "Personne ne doute que ce soit l'homme qui, en fécondant la femme, vivifie et animine l'homocule dont les premiers élémens sont renfermés dans l'oeuf con-tenu dans l'ovaire"; Millot, *L'Art de procréer*, 219, 338–39.

42. *Lucina sine concubitu; Lucine affranchie des lois du concours; ouvrage singulier, traduit de l'anglais de Johnson par le citoyen Moet, dans lequel il est pleinement démontré par des preuves tirées de la théorie et de la pratique, qu'une femme peut concevoir et enfanter sans le commerce de l'homme*, trans. Moet (Paris, Year III). The translator called Roe's work, in particular, "contre les loix naturelles et civiles" (73). For discussion, see Lynn Salkin Sbiroli, "Lucina sine concubitu: procreazione tra scienza e ideologica," in *Medicini e biologia nella rivoluzione scientifica*, ed. Lino Conti (Perugia: Poziuncola, 1990), 256–66; J.-L. Fischer, "La Callipédie ou l'art d'avoir de beaux enfants," *Dix-huitième Siècle*, no. 23 (1991): 141–58.

43. Millot, *L'Art de procréer*, 65.

44. K. R. Benson, "Observation versus Philosophical Commitment in Eighteenth-Century Ideas of Regeneration and Generation," in *A History of Regeneration Research: Milestones in the Evolution of a Science*, ed. C. E. Dinsmore (Cambridge: Cambridge University Press, 1991), 93, 100.

45. Millot, *L'Art de procréer*, 105.

46. J.-A. Millot, *L'Art d'améliorer et de perfectionner les hommes au moral comme au physique*, 2 vols. (Paris, 1801 [Year X]), 2:234.

47. On Robert, see Quinlan, "Physical and Moral Regeneration," 157–59; and Anne Verjus, "'L'Éminente noblesse du mérite': distinction et transmission des talents dans la pensée républicaine, 1780–1810" (paper presented at the XIe Congrès des Lumières, August 3–10, 2003).

48. L.-J.-M. Robert, *Essai sur la mégalanthropogénésie, ou l'art de faire des enfants d'esprit, qui deviennent des grands hommes; suivi des traits physiognomoniques propres à les faire reconnaître, décrits par Lavater, et du meilleur mode de génération* (Paris, 1801), 14–15, 17, 19–20.

49. J. G. Lavater, *Essai sur la physiognomie, destiné à faire connaître l'homme et à le faire aimer*, 4 vols. (La Haye, 1781–87, 1803).

50. C.-A. Helvétius, *Oeuvres complètes*, 9 vols. (Paris, 1795), 1:189–91; on Robert's response, see *Essai sur la mégalanthropogénésie*, 29; *Nouvel essai sur la mégalanthropogénésie ou l'art de faire des enfants d'esprit, qui deviennent de grands hommes*, 2nd ed., 2 vols. (Paris, Year XI [1803]), 1:ix; and *Coup d'œil physiologique et médical sur la mégalanthropogénésie* (Paris, Year XI [1803]), 39. Usually, Enlightenment and revolutionary doctors rejected Helvétius's radical environmentalism as biologically unsound. For discussion, see Moravia, *Il pensiero degli Idéologues*, 151–65.

51. Robert, *Essai sur la mégalanthropogénésie*, 33–34, 47–49, 60, 230–31.

52. L.-J.-M. Robert, *Existe-t-il un art physico-médical pour augmenter l'intelligence de l'homme, en perfectionnant ses organes, ou la mégalanthropogénésie n'est-elle qu'une erreur?* (Paris, Year XI).

53. Review of Robert, *Essai sur la mégalanthropogénésie*, in *Le Décade philosophique, littéraire et politique*, no. 9 (30 frimaire, Year X): 549–50; and [H. D.], "À l'auteur de la mégalanthropogénésie, ou l'art de faire des enfans d'esprit," *Le Décade philosophique, littéraire et politique*, no. 5 (20 brumaire, Year X): 304.

54. Barré, Radet, Desfontaines, and Dieulafoi, *L'Isle de la mégalantropogénésie, ou les savans de la naissance* (Paris, 1807).

55. *La megalantropogenesia, ossia l'isola sapiente*, trans. Luigi Bossi (Venice, 1807). Bossi reported that the Paris performance "Fu moltissomo applaudito, come una novità spiritoso: fu replicato moltissime volte, et sempre con numerioso concorso" (46); he said, however, that audiences were less enthusiastic about the earlier Turin performances and that the play smacked of French science and rationalism.

56. J.-L. Alibert, "De l'influence des causes politiques sur les maladies et la constitution physique de l'homme," *Magasin Encyclopédique, ou Journal des Sciences, des Lettres et des Arts* 5 (1795): 298–305.

57. M.-A. Petit, "Discours sur l'influence de la Révolution française sur la santé publique, prononcé à l'ouverture des cours d'anatomie et de chirurgie de l'Hôtel-Dieu de Lyon," September 30, 1796, MS 5212, fol. 68, BFMP.

58. See esp. L.-J.-M. Robert, *Manuel de santé, ou nouveaux éléments de médecine pratique, d'après l'état actuel de la science et la méthode analytiqe de Pinel et de Bichat, à l'usage des médecins, chirurgiens, curés et autres habtans de la campagne*, 2 vols. (Paris, Year XIII [1805]).

59. L.-J.-M. Robert, *De l'Influence de la Révolution française sur la population; ouvrage où l'on prouve qu'elle a augmenté depuis dix ans, où l'on en donne les causes morales et politiques*, 2 vols. (Paris, Year XI [1802]), 1:93.

60. Robert, *Coup d'œil*, 9, 39. As Robert put it elsewhere, "L'égalité des conditions et des fortunes étant reconnue aujourd'hui une chimère, il doit y avoir autant d'éducations diverses, qui'il y a d'ordres différentes dans la société" (*De l'Influence*, 2:49–50).

61. Cabanis, *Rapports*, 1:348, 1:349–50, 1:351–52, 1:353, 1:364–65; J.-L. Moreau de la Sarthe, *Histoire naturelle de la femme, suivie d'un traité d'hygiène appliquée à son régime physique et moral aux différentes époques de la vie*, 2 vols. (Paris, 1803), 2:23–31, 211, 221. On Cabanis's and Moreau de la Sarthe's views on sex and politics, see Y. Knibiehler, "Les Médecins et la 'nature féminine' au temps du code civil," *Annales: E.S.C.* 31 (1976): 824–45; and G. Fraisse, *Reason's Muse: Sexual Difference and the Birth of Democracy*, trans. J. M. Todd (Chicago: University of Chicago Press, 1994), 72–102. On general discussions about women's proper social and political roles after the Reign of Terror, see E. Colwill, "Women's Empire and the Sovereignty of Man in *La Décade philosophique*, 1794–1807," *Eighteenth-Century Studies* 29 (1996): 265–89.

62. Millot, *L'Art d'améliorer*, 2:39.

63. On Robert's ovism, see Robert, *Nouvel essai*, 1:32–57, 1:58–69.

64. Robert, *Essai sur la mégalantropogénésie*, 230–31; and Robert, *Coup d'œil*, ii, 18–19, 39.

65. L.-J.-M. Robert, *L'Art de prevenir le cancer au sein chez les femmes, qui touchent à leur époque critique, ou qui peuvent craindre cette funeste maladie, à la suite d'un dépôt laiteux ou d'une contusion* (Paris, 1812); and L.-J.-M. Robert, *De la musique considérée sous les rapports de son influence sur les moeurs, le passions et la santé* (Marseilles, 1807), 10–11. On the charge that Robert's books appealed largely to women, see *Défenseurs de la patrie* (26 brumaire, Year X).

66. See C. Hesse, *Publishing and Cultural Politics in Revolutionary France, 1789–1810* (Berkeley: University of California Press, 1991), esp. chaps. 5 and 6; and more generally, L. Bergeron, *France under Napoleon*, trans. R. R. Palmer (Princeton NJ: Princeton University Press, 1981).

67. J.-J. Virey, *De l'éducation publique et privée des français* (Paris, Year X [1802]), i, v–viii,

xiii, xiv. He later expanded these views in *L'Art de perfectionner l'homme, ou de la médecine spirituelle et morale*, 2 vols. (Paris, 1808).

68. J.-J. Virey, "La Mégalanthropogénésie," in *Dictionnaire des sciences médicales, par une société de médecins et chirurgiens* (Paris, 1812–22), 32:135.
69. Virey, *De l'éducation*, 75.
70. For further elaboration of this theory, see J.-J. Virey, *De la femme sous ses rapports physiologique, moral et littéraire*, 2nd ed. (Paris, 1825). For helpful discussion, see R. A. Nye, *Masculinity and Male Codes of Honor in Modern France* (Oxford: Oxford University Press, 1993), 59–62.
71. Robert made the same point (*Coup d'oeil*, 36–27). See A. C. Vila, "Sex, Procreation, and the Scholarly Life from Tissot to Balzac," *Eighteenth-Century Studies* 35 (2002): 239–46.
72. Virey, "La Mégalanthropogénésie," 32:143.
73. On the conventions of émigré writing, see Malcolm Cook, "The Emigré Novel," in *The French Emigrés in Europe and the Struggle against Revolution, 1789–1814*, ed. Kirsty Carpenter and Philip Mansel (Houndsmills UK: Macmillan, 1999), 151–64.
74. A. G*** de B. S. O., *La Philopédie, ou avis aux époux sur l'art d'avoir des enfans sans passions* (Paris, 1808), 2.
75. A. G*** de B. S. O., *La Philopédie*, 7–8.
76. A. G*** de B. S. O., *La Philopédie*, 25–26, 31, 34–35.
77. A. G*** de B.S.O., *La Philopédie*, 191, 198–99.
78. Michel Foucault, *The History of Sexuality: An Introduction*, trans. Robert Hurley (1978; repr., New York: Vintage, 1990), 138–39. For a similar take on the biopower theory, see Giorgio Agamben, *Homo Sacer: Sovereign Power and Bare Life*, trans. D. Heller-Roazen (Stanford CA: Stanford University Press, 1998).
79. M. Foucault, "Governmentality," in *Power*, vol. 3, *The Essential Works of Foucault, 1954–1984*, ed. James D. Faubion (New York: New Press, 2000), 219; and M. Foucault, "The Political Technology of Individuals," in Faubion, *Power*, 3:403–17.
80. Carol, *Histoire de l'eugénisme*, 20–26.
81. For the term *Quack Street*, see C. Jones, "Pulling Teeth in Eighteenth-Century Paris," *Past and Present*, no. 166 (2000): 100–145. On the medical marketplace model, see esp. H. J. Cook, *The Decline of the Old Medical Regime in Stuart London* (Ithaca NY: Cornell University Press, 1986); and for recent criticism, see M. Pelling, *Medical Conflicts in Early Modern London: Patronage, Physicians, and Irregular Practitioners, 1550–1640* (Oxford: Oxford University Press, 2003).
82. K. Binhammer, "The Sex Panic of the 1790s," *Journal of the History of Sexuality* 6 (1996): 409–35; and D. Wahrman, "Percy's Prologue: From Gender Play to Gender Panic in Eighteenth-Century England," *Past and Present*, no. 159 (1999): 1–41; but cf. L. Hunt and M. Jacob, "The Affective Revolution in 1790s Britain," *Eighteenth-Century Studies* 34 (2001): 491–521.

83. T. W. Laqueur, *Maxing Sex: Body and Gender from the Greeks to Freud* (Cambridge MA: Harvard University Press, 1990), 149–92.

84. T. W. Laqueur, "Amor Veneris, vel Dulcedo Appeletur," in *Fragments for a History of the Human Body*, ed. M. Feher (New York: Zone, 1989), 90–131; L. Schiebinger, "Skeletons in the Closet: The First Illustrations of the Female Skeleton in Eighteenth-Century Anatomy," in *The Making of the Modern Body: Sexuality and Society in the Nineteenth Century*, ed. C. Gallagher and T. Laqueur (Berkeley: University of California Press, 1987), 83–106.

85. T. W. Laqueur, "Orgasm, Generation, and the Politics of Reproductive Biology," in Gallagher and Laqueur, *Making of the Modern Body*, 1–41.

86. L. Schiebinger, *Nature's Body: Gender in the Making of Modern Science* (Boston: Beacon, 1993). On the political context, see J. B. Landes, *Women and the Public Sphere in the Age of the French Revolution* (Ithaca NY: Cornell University Press, 1988); and D. Outram, *The Body and the French Revolution: Sex, Class, and Political Culture* (New Haven CT: Yale University Press, 1989); but cf. Hunt, *Family Romance*, 193–204; and Hesse, *Other Enlightenment*, on how the French Revolution undermined patriarchy and helped mold modern feminist thought. For a nuanced appraisal of medicine and gender relations, based largely upon archival and manuscript sources, see L. Wilson, *Women and Medicine in the French Enlightenment: The Debate over Maladies des Femmes* (Baltimore: Johns Hopkins University Press, 1993).

87. See Desmormaux, "Cours de maladies des femmes et des enfants," April 11, 1820, MS 1062, t. XI, Bibliothèque de l'Académie Nationale de Médecine.

88. On pro-women thought, see D. Goodman, *The Republic of Letters: A Cultural History of the French Enlightenment* (Ithaca NY: Cornell University Press, 1994), chap. 2; and on the political consequences in 1790s England, see B. Taylor, "Feminists versus Gallants: Manners and Morals in Enlightenment Britain," *Representations* 87 (2004): 125–48.

89. A. McLaren, "Pleasures of Procreation," in *William Hunter and the Eighteenth-Century Medical World*, ed. W. F. Bynum and R. Porter (Cambridge: Cambridge University Press, 1985), 340; here he follows Margaret Jacob, *The Newtonians and the English Revolution, 1689–1720* (Ithaca NY: Cornell University Press, 1976), 15–71.

ANNE R. EPSTEIN

8

Gender and the Creation
of the French Intellectual

The Case of the *Revue de Morale Sociale*,
1899–1903

Anne R. Epstein investigates the identity politics of French republican political culture
and of the creation of the French Intellectual. Epstein shows how, during the turbulent
years of the Dreyfus Affair, marginalized women intellectuals learned to cooperate with
prominent male intellectuals through the informal intellectual sociability that characterized the turn-of-the-century Third Republic. These women were able to approach
the center of the (political) public sphere from the margins by using a moral authority
grounded in the gender assumptions of the day. In light of these findings Epstein raises
the pertinent question: why does the figure of the French public intellectual born with
the twentieth century retrospectively appear male? At issue is the heart of French national
identity because the public intellectual, one of France's most successful exports, has
come to represent a key component of all understandings of Frenchness. Epstein shows
the resilience of the French intellectual model as a masculine construct even when the
historical reality was much more complex.

✧ ✧

It is the others who declare you an intellectual, never oneself. . . . Hence
also the consoling fact that everybody can always become the intellectual
of someone. . . . Brigitte Bardot may some day be elected to the Collège
de France. Simone Signoret is virtually there already. The intellectual is
the one in whose discourse the public hears, directly or indirectly, the
echo of its ultimate ends. One is an intellectual only on the basis of elec-
tive criteria.[1]

Contemplating the future of the French public intellectual in the early
1980s, French historian, academician, and political observer Pierre Nora

acknowledged that moral authority—a symbolic resource that enables well-known thinkers and cultural figures to shape public opinion—was not a quality an individual could simply lay claim to by virtue of personal integrity, achievement, genius, or peer recognition. Rather, this critical political resource, the hallmark of the public intellectual, derived from an egalitarian and arbitrary process of social negotiation. To drive home the terrifying potential of this democratized process, Nora chose an image he knew the educated readers of his newly created moderate-Right, intellectual-political review *Le Débat* would find absurd: film star and former sex symbol Brigitte Bardot—a female icon not best known for her erudition—at the Collège de France, symbol of learned culture and hallowed "site of memory."[2] What makes this picture incongruous is not the marriage of sex and intellect (a combination that has actually worked well for male intellectuals in France). Instead, Brigitte Bardot and the Collège de France symbolize extremes, respectively, of modern French femininity and masculinity, and combining them causes immediate cognitive dissonance.

Public intellectuals occupy a special place in the French psyche that is not always easy for foreign observers to comprehend.[3] In the twentieth century the French intellectual became a matter of national pride and identity. But so did the kind of eroticized femininity the young Brigitte Bardot incarnated. In 1969, on a lark, the sculptor Aslan made a bust of Bardot as a kind of alternative Marianne, the symbol of the French Republic. This likeness of the star soon became the official prototype for statues of Marianne in public buildings across France. Thus, although the French had found Brigitte Bardot fit to embody their Republic, they could not help but chuckle at the thought of her at the prestigious Collège de France. In the traditional Republican system of values men's cultural authority has come from rational thought and words, whereas women's can only derive directly or indirectly from the female body.[4]

A second visual image brings us to the problem of the French woman intellectual, whose existence disrupts this nexus of gender, cultural authority, and national identity. In the library, while doing research some years ago, I picked up the 1986 edition of Pascal Ory and Jean-François Sirinelli's *Les Intellectuels en France, de l'affaire Dreyfus à nos jours* (Intellectuals in France from the Dreyfus Affair to the Present), then the standard textbook history of twentieth-century French intellectuals.[5] The cover photograph caught my eye: noted philosopher Jean-Paul Sartre seated at a café table reading the *Figaro Littéraire*. Next to Sartre is a woman, looking at the newspaper over his shoulder. A caption confirms her identity, as does the signature head scarf Simone de Beauvoir is wearing. Half of Beauvoir's face is obscured, however, by Sartre's newspaper. In the text Ory and Sirinelli nevertheless refer to the existentialist philosopher and pioneer feminist theorist as the third most frequent signer of petitions appearing in France's most authoritative daily *Le Monde* during the de Gaulle era—the signing of petitions representing for the authors the supreme mode of engaged intellectual intervention. Why, I wondered, did they choose this particular photograph to grace their work? Did they mean a woman could not be a "French Intellectual" in her own right?[6]

Although it begins with cultural icons and photographs, this essay is about the place of real women—and men—in French political culture. It is about the history and memory of French intellectuals, about civic engagement, about moral authority, and about gender. At the turn of the twentieth century, when historians claim that the now-"iconic" figure of the French Intellectual began to take shape,[7] educated, socially conscious Frenchwomen collaborated with leading male activists in an array of civic projects. Like the men with whom they cooperated, these women began to use their reputations, personal charisma, credentials, and cultural authority to shape public discussion about a range of current issues. Yet unlike the men, very few of these women are remembered by either historians or the public as French Intellectuals. In histories of twentieth-century French intellectuals, even the most politically engaged female thinkers have, like Beauvoir, been assigned to supporting, peripheral, or symbolic roles—in a sense reading the newspaper over famous male contemporaries' shoulders. Focusing on the *Revue de Morale Sociale* (1899–1903), an international, French-language publication of which a number of the most visible contemporary French civic activists, both men and women, were affiliates, this essay seeks to understand women's marginalization within the political history of French intellectuals by returning to the context in which intellectuals supposedly are thought to have assumed their civic vocation. Although their exclusion from full political participation and intellectual institutions should have kept women at the margins, it is my contention that informal intellectual networks and the gendered structure of the French public sphere in fact brought certain intellectual women close to the center of fin-de-siècle political culture. Is the Woman-as-Intellectual, then, a problem of memory rather than history?

Public Intellectuals, Gender, and Authority in Republican France

In France public intellectuals began to emerge as political actors with a distinct social identity toward the end of the nineteenth century. The national crisis triggered by the Dreyfus Affair—a celebrated case in which a Jewish army officer was wrongly convicted of spying for the Germans and sent to Devil's Island, to be pardoned only much later—abruptly transformed a group of well-known journalists, scholars, writers, and other cultural figures, led by the novelist Émile Zola, into ardent defenders of human rights. Thus, historians claim, both the figure and vocation of the Engaged Intellectual, above partisan politics, were "born." By connecting this figure with both the French Enlightenment and the French revolutionary heritage, history and official memory have since transformed the intellectual into a symbol of Frenchness in general and of French masculinity in particular.[8]

The ability of cultural figures to use their social—and moral—standing to shape public opinion lay at the heart of the emergent vocation of the public intellectual.[9] As an individual strategy, using the written or spoken word and one's status and reputation to influence minds was not a new phenomenon, nor was the collective mobilization of cultural notables in support of political causes a development unique to France. Traditions of social protest had long roots in France, of course. But throughout the nineteenth century civil society and the forms of social interaction it fostered had also provided means whereby democratic ideas and practices could develop, find expression, and take root.[10] Moreover, at the turn of the twentieth century many continued to regard shaping public opinion as a legitimate and viable means of exercising sovereignty, equal or even superior to the vote. As a political commentator for *La Grande Revue* observed in 1900, "The right to change governments is implicitly contained in the very principle of our political organization, national sovereignty. From the moment I am sovereign, I am free to choose the form of government I prefer. But the Constitution defines and limits the means I may use to exercise my sovereignty. These means are *spoken or written political propaganda and finally, the vote.*"[11] Indeed, at this time more people than ever—including women, who could not vote or run for office—were expressing political opinions and initiating public discussion in the flourishing mass press, in novels, in public lectures, in voluntary associations, and in scientific societies and intellectual circles of all varieties.

The Dreyfus Affair fostered an array of new opinion forums of this kind and sharpened the focus of those already in existence. Not just anyone, however, could influence minds or spread political "propaganda" effectively. The victory of meritocratic republican ideals meant that men's authority to pronounce on politics and questions of right and wrong rested on a magical combination of social capital, personal achievements, honor, charisma, and chance. As a form of symbolic capital based in contemporary values, this moral authority was clearly gendered. Throughout the nineteenth century moral virtue had been considered a female attribute, political authority the prerogative of the male citizen. When the Dreyfus Affair brought traditional political authority into question, male defenders of the Rights of Man frustrated with the political instruments at their disposal essentially appropriated an alternative, potentially womanly source of political authority and rendered it virile. They claimed that their credentials as men of science and letters gave them a moral authority with universal reach.[12]

This did not mean, however, that women's moral standing no longer had any political value. Grounded in long-held notions of gender complementarity, moral authority became a political resource to which both sexes had access. Different rules simply governed its use by women. In pre–World War I France ideals of republican womanhood and discourses of femininity with roots in the eighteenth century still grounded much of women's social power and moral status. Their identification with the family and "domestic" segments of civil society still made it nearly impossible for individual women to lay claim to the kind of personal yet unrestricted public authority that male intellectuals had begun to wield. A woman's authority was also more definitively bound to her gender than was a man's. If men felt at home in public because they were men, women still had constantly to justify their presence there because they were women. If individual women began to participate in public debate and shape politics by the turn of the twentieth century, it was always either because of or in spite of being women: they appeared as representatives of their sex or of a "female" perspective, or as exceptional, "virile" women. Their gender conditioned the sphere of their potential influence as well. Whereas men felt free to speak out as experts or moral guides not only on "masculine" subjects such as politics, international relations, and science but also on "feminine" subjects relative to the family, education, and culture, women's public authority and moral clout extended only to the latter. Women's authority thus appeared as doubly gendered, based both on their sex and also on the domains in which their authority held sway.[13]

Ideological, juridical, and customary constraints both gendered public authority and conditioned the public activities of Frenchwomen as a group. Excluded from the apparently universal, but actually masculine, concept of the individual upon which French democracy rested, women still lacked full political rights at the turn of the twentieth century. Moreover, because in practice they were still denied access to many prestigious professions and to scientific and scholarly recognition, any cultural authority that women acquired could not depend on the same kinds of intellectual and social resources as men's. Although they now had access to public primary and secondary education, women remained excluded from formal intellectual institutions, from the *baccalauréat* to the Académie Française (first female member: Marguerite Yourcenar, 1980) and the Collège de France (first female professor: Jacqueline de Romilly, 1973), and the grounds for exclusion were often just plain old masculinist tradition.[14] Men alone had access to key positions at the center of the French political, educational, and intellectual establishment and to the status these positions brought with them.

Nevertheless, Frenchwomen had never been completely smoked out of the public sphere following the French Revolution, if not for want of effort.[15] Throughout most of the nineteenth century, in addition to the very public intervention of such "exceptionally" politicized women as writers Germaine de Staël and George Sand, many women had participated actively in civil society. They engaged in activities neither fully private nor fully public such as philanthropy, charity, joining cultural and scientific societies, writing political novels, and inviting political types to their salons and dinner parties.[16]

By the end of the nineteenth century women could accumulate other forms of institutional legitimacy and expertise that conferred to them a certain public standing. Unlike the traditional forms of social and cultural "capital" that had opened the public sphere to women such as de Staël and Sand,[17] these new resources no longer derived only from a privileged background or an advantageous marriage. Women could acquire status through their own professional activities, such as working in women's education or in child welfare in a government ministry, as did nursery school inspector Pauline Kergomard and child welfare inspector Olympe Gevin-Cassal, by attending institutions such as the prestigious normal schools for women at Sèvres and Fontenay-aux-Roses, through organizational activities on behalf of women and children, or by founding or editing reviews and newspapers.[18] Women began to use their social and cultural resources in the same way men did: to advance in their careers, place articles in the press, publicize projects or causes that interested them, become members of civic associations and forums in which they could present their ideas, or gain access to the salons and meeting places where networking occurred. A kind of moral authority also came to women occupying positions of responsibility in appropriately feminine segments of public life, specifically those areas that seemed to incarnate or further women's traditional maternal role.

Republican gender ideology had always emphasized women's importance as mothers and educators of citizens, and being an exemplary mother still functioned as a credential for a woman in the Third Republic: a mark of respectability, professional aptitude, merit, and even a predictor of responsible performance of public duties.[19] A reputation as a good mother also gave one's public opinions on appropriate subjects moral legitimacy.[20] Physical attributes, feminine "charm," and other, more or less aesthetic dimensions of femininity, such as womanly (or motherly) bearing and attire, remained assets to the effective public feminine persona as well. If skillfully deployed, one's appearance and comportment might even function as moral enhancements.[21] But most often women acquired moral authority through a combination of womanly respectability and "feminine" activity outside the home: founding, running, or publicizing philanthropic organizations, popular education initiatives, or women's groups; occupying appropriately feminine positions of responsibility in the civil service; or directing women's publications. Success in these areas was acceptable and legitimate for women, who could use the moral standing they thus acquired to participate in public debate. When new associations or publications formed whose programs targeted women, their founders eagerly sought the support of these female authorities.

But would people listen to what women with this kind of authority had to say about any subject? It is revealing that only a few women even tried to speak out individually on issues beyond women's political and social role.[22] Rarely did women—even those few female writers blessed with the "virile" femininity of a George Sand—succeed in turning their womanly authority into the kind of universal moral authority that male writers and scholars had begun to claim. Prized in men, individualism was at the bottom of the hierarchy of moral values for women. Not only would a woman's manifestations of individual will or opinion not advance the causes they were meant to advance; they might actually be detrimental to the public image of the woman. That Mme Pégard, one of the only female signatories of the first 1898 petition demanding that the Dreyfus verdict be struck down, listed her credentials as "mother, Frenchwoman, and Christian" speaks volumes about the nature of women's moral authority at the turn of the twentieth century.[23]

Although restricted, however, female moral authority was by no means politically insignificant. The gendered structure of the public domain had begun to change by the beginning of the twentieth century, as seemingly feminine concerns acquired not only legitimacy but also symbolic, propaganda value within political circles and public discourse. Both Marguerite Durand's daily newspaper by and for women, La Fronde, and the Dreyfus Affair contributed to this sea change: on the one hand, as Mary Louise Roberts has suggested, helping raise the visibility and political value of the feminine by modifying the public's understanding of womanhood and femininity, and on the other hand, by enabling intellectuals to make the moral connection between women's rights, human rights, national interests, and social progress increasingly explicit. For the members of the Ligue des Droits de l'Homme (League of Human Rights), the founding board of which included several women, promoting women's rights on a limited scale bolstered the organization's credibility in defending a truly universal version of the Declaration of the Rights of Man. The lines between masculine and feminine, men's and women's, issues and interests had also blurred: birth control, maternal and child welfare, and woman's work had become national political issues in response to the government's growing alarm about French population trends, while women were increasingly concerned with war, peace, and colonialism.[24] Because these questions ultimately came down to ethics and morality, which were understood as gendered, the cultural authority of highly regarded professional women became useful to those at the French political and intellectual center despite the institutionally marginal position of such women.

Mostly upper-middle-class female intellectuals joined enlightened men of their own social background in civic education initiatives of various kinds. Lecturing to mostly female audiences on women's history or women's role in society or providing practical instruction in infant care or hygiene at people's universities gave schoolteachers, journalists, civil servants, and other female intellectuals the opportunity to join leading male intellectuals in a practical and acceptable form of *engagement*. These women became public mother-educators, responsible for the moral uplift of their sister-citizens. Politicians saw that educated women had a clear role to play in the search for a new set of secular, republican moral values, which was sorely needed to restore France's stability. In an era when so many national political issues seemed to contain a gender dimension, female authorities could be valuable allies: women were recognized as the best possible propagandists on behalf of their sex.[25] The new public interest in gender issues benefited women's advocates as well. At mixed-gender meetings of the Société de Sociologie de Paris (Parisian Sociological Society), the Union pour la Vérité (Union for Truth), and the Ligue des Droits de l'Homme, politically savvy authorities on womanly matters such as journalist Jane Misme, home economist Augusta Moll-Weiss, moral reformer and human rights activist Ghénia Avril de Sainte-Croix,[26] and suffragist Cécile Brunschvicg joined prominent academics, lawyers, and government administrators in discussions on subjects ranging from internationalism and the impact of the separation of church and state on the family to suffrage reform and depopulation. Invited to speak as female experts, they could use their status both to publicize women's causes and present a feminine perspective on other topical issues.[27] When public discussion of suffrage and depopulation heated up during the first decade of the twentieth century, male intellectuals welcomed like-minded female educators, journal editors, lawyers, and moral reformers, many of them now defenders of women's rights, to participate in discussion circles or scholarly societies or give courses on women's position in society. Women's rights and suffrage now constituted additional areas of feminine expertise and authority. As historians of French feminism have shown, women's rights activists in turn called upon certain male intellectuals to boost the legitimacy of their enterprises.[28]

The *Revue de Morale Sociale*, founded in 1899, serves as an early, and emblematic, example of this kind of cooperation between enlightened men and women. The publication provides evidence that from the outset the intellectuals at the vanguard of the campaign to exonerate Alfred Dreyfus understood that their new vocation as defenders of human rights meant drawing public attention to a range of pressing national and international moral concerns beyond the affair, including gender injustice. The collaboration of female and male authorities in this enterprise also suggests that the gendering of moral authority at the turn of the twentieth century made women necessary, rather than incidental, participants in the larger civic mobilization that produced the French Intellectual.

Gender Injustice and Human Rights in the Revue de Morale Sociale

A French-language publication founded and edited in Geneva, and published also in Paris, the *Revue de Morale Sociale* (RMS) brought leading members of the Ligue des Droits de l'Homme and French-speaking moral reformers and feminists together with like-minded intellectuals from all over Europe who wished to eradicate the sexual double standard and promote more just gender relations. Concerned with the relationship of the individual to society, with human progress, and with the tensions between moral responsibility, social order, and individual freedom, these liberal intellectuals began to find common ground in the idea of *morale sociale*, or social ethics (as the review's collaborators translated the term in a survey of international readers in 1899).[29] Contemporary social theorists generally acknowledged the importance of gender relations to social ethics, but the intellectuals grouped around the *Revue de Morale Sociale* argued that establishing justice in the moral and social relations between the sexes should be the main task for a progressive system of secular moral values. Whereas for most contemporary French readers the semantic field of the term *morale sociale* encompassed all kinds of social interaction, RMS founders and correspondents used it to refer to "the reciprocal rights and duties of man and woman, the obligations and prerogatives of each in the family and in society, and the regulation of their relations of coexistence."[30] The review's collaborators demanded the same moral standard for both sexes: "respect for the human person who must never be envisioned as a simple means for others" and "recognition and guarantee of the rights of woman, as well as the rights of man, both having to be equally free and responsible."[31]

PRO JUSTITIA, or "For Justice," the review's motto, sent out a clear signal to Francophone readers for whom promoting justice and human rights were high priorities at the height of the Dreyfus Affair. In seeking to define the new social ethics, the review's approach would be empirical and reformist: "on the one hand, in-depth study of everything concerning moral and social relations between the sexes; on the other hand, the search for the best solutions to put into practice and their enunciation in the clearest and most precise terms."[32] To establish justice between the sexes required critical, scientific analysis, "for we believe that social science, like the exact sciences, cannot do without strict examination and method. Just because morals, sentiment, honor and conscience are at stake in these delicate questions doesn't mean we can be content with vague affirmations, *a priori* precepts or oratorical ranting."[33] Thus, the search—methodical, scientific, critical— for truth about the relations between the sexes would lead to justice and progress for everyone, just as revealing the facts of the case was to lead to justice for Dreyfus.

To give legitimacy to their agenda, the review's editors rounded up a large group of internationally recognized supporters. Because they saw gender injustice as a problem with both social and ethical dimensions that must be examined scientifically, it was crucial that founding members and correspondents exhibit feminist, scientific, or reformist credentials. The group must include intellectuals of both sexes: the founding board could thus be presented as "[an] imposing group of *men and women, all thinkers and workers,* filling for the most part some important social function, who responded enthusiastically to our appeal."[34] The diversity of this founding board and the review's correspondents also reinforced the impression of what they termed the "intersexual question" as a problem of vast dimensions and infinite implications. Its study required expertise from all domains that could possibly contribute to or benefit from its resolution, from biology to pedagogy to law.[35] And because the injustice being addressed was above all that experienced by women, feminists appeared as authorities whose endorsement the project absolutely required for legitimacy. The names of the review's founding sponsors boosted the credibility of those who wrote for it, reinforcing the appeal the publication was making to its public.

The RMS was not, strictly speaking, a "French" review, but 43 of the original 166 founding members hailed from France.[36] Eleven of these were women, and about thirteen of the actual contributors from France were women, compared to approximately twenty-five men.[37] The credentials of the Frenchwomen who contributed to the RMS were impressive given the restrictions on women's access to the professions at the time: editors, well-known journalists, jurists, civil servants, and philanthropists.[38] The RMS also welcomed representatives of different currents of female activism, from Protestant philanthropy to Catholic feminism.[39] The presence in the groupe d'initiative of leaders of women's organizations and editors of women's journals from Alsace, England, Finland, Germany, Italy, Russia, Spain, Switzerland, and the United States further enhanced the feminist credentials of the RMS.

All of the French male correspondents and supporters were members of the intellectual-political establishment with impeccable credentials. The French men who wrote for the review included prominent social scientists, political economists, reformist legal scholars, theologians, physicians, leaders of the newly formed Ligue des Droits de l'Homme, and the secretary-general of the Ligue Française de la Moralité Publique (French League for Public Morality), as well as journalists, editors, and philanthropists. The French male founding members included professors from Parisian and provincial faculties of law, theology, and medicine, from the Collège de France and from the Sorbonne; politicians; directors of important scholarly reviews; and well-known journalists or publicists. Many of the academic contributors and sponsors had links to social science milieux, among them political economist Charles Gide, anthropologist Léonce Manouvrier, and social economist Alexis Delaire.[40]

As contributors to a variety of important publications and as members of diverse organizations and movements, the review's influential French collaborators also placed it within an extensive national intellectual network.[41] Ghénia de Sainte Croix, Maria Pognon, Marie Bonnevial, Jeanne Schmahl, Charles Gide, Maurice Bouchor, Ferdinand Buisson, Yves Guyot, Joseph Reinach, Gabriel Séailles, Gabriel Monod, and Frédéric Passy, for example, were all both affiliates of the RMS and active members of the Ligue des Droits de l'Homme.[42] The founding board of the review included editors and directors of several high-profile French political and scientific periodicals, including Yves Guyot (the political journal *Le Siècle*); Gabriel Monod (*Revue Historique*), F. Pillon (*L'Année Philosophique*), George Renard (who had just retired from the *Revue Socialiste*), Édouard Toulouse (*Revue de Psychiatrie*), and Louis Comte (*Le Relèvement Social*). Maria Martin, Marie Maugeret, and Jeanne Schmahl ran influential feminist-leaning publications, *Journal des Femmes*, *Féminisme Chrétien*, and *L'Avant-Courrière*, respectively. These connections enhanced the intellectual legitimacy of the RMS and provided access to very different segments of the educated public, in particular the milieux most closely associated with the Dreyfusard campaign.

Moral internationalism served three distinct purposes as an editorial strategy: it enhanced the review's local legitimacy in domains such as feminism; it permitted the review to introduce new, "foreign," and perhaps slightly provocative ideas to its French-speaking readers; and it made clear that addressing problems in gender relations was a universal moral imperative that encompassed but also went beyond the politics of local legal remedies.[43] Having assembled an impressive roster of international sponsors, the editors used various means to construct an international vision. The programmatic statement that appeared in the first issue of the review clearly defined their priorities and perspective as moral, social, internationalist, and feminist. Not only were their concerns "vital for the collectivity as a whole and for each of its members," but "the well-being or misfortune of individuals, the prosperity or decadence of nations and the very future of the human race depends on their resolution." At the core of the problem lay the "injustice of which woman is a victim" and in particular the sexual double standard. This injustice was both against nature and a threat to the global social order: in other words, it was both an international and transnational problem. Feminism, very broadly conceived, was part of its remedy.[44]

The rhetorical strategies of individual authors reinforced the editors' universalist aim of making gender injustice—a transnational moral issue—the central problem of human rights. In 1900, for example, Louis Wuarin, professor of sociology at the University of Geneva, Switzerland, contributed a review article comparing the Dreyfus case in France and the unsuccessful crusade of Swiss abolitionists to end state regulation of prostitution in the canton of Geneva. For Wuarin the Geneva "affairs" and the Dreyfus Affair, as well as Finland's valiant struggle to maintain its autonomy, the Boer War, and the massacre of the Armenians all reflected the worldwide moral threat that was in the air. Republican values were in crisis; Finland, Genevan prostitutes, and Alfred Dreyfus were all victims of grave moral wrong, as were the Boers and the massacred Armenians. French writer Émile Zola, antiregulation feminists, and other concerned internationalist intellectuals appeared as martyrs, with justice and moral right on their side. Connecting these problems, Professor Wuarin challenged any enlightened, *moral* reader not to see the relationship between national sovereignty, human rights, and gender equity.[45]

Soliciting and publishing the opinions of the review's correspondents and readers on topical gender issues served as another means of defining and legitimizing the synthesis the review was trying to achieve. During the first year the review conducted a survey that contributed directly to its project of constructing gender injustice as a transnational moral and social issue requiring international cooperation between the sexes. In it the editors asked their international founding members, in French, German, and English, "What moral mission do you attribute to the feminist movement in the evolution of contemporary society?" In the responses to this somewhat leading question,[46] French and international opinions about women's social role sometimes appeared quite conservative or ambivalent, but belief in women's potential to contribute publicly to moral and social progress together with men was strong. French cooperatist Charles Gide saw hope for more "normal" and "complete" human progress if women participated more in public life, based on his traditional conception of women as intellectually inferior but morally superior.[47] For the secretary-general of the Ligue Française de la Moralité Publique, M.-J. Gaufrès, feminism was a symptom of moral and social illness brought on partly by historical factors and partly by the newer phenomenon of industrialization, but it would disappear when this illness did, and women and men could resume their complementary functions.[48] Although correspondents' understanding of the concept and its aims varied greatly, they agreed that if feminism meant giving women a more active and equitable public role, women would exert a positive influence on humanity's moral and social development. Whether regarded as a requirement for sexual justice or a temporary evil, women's participation in public life was both justified and necessary for moral improvement.

The sociological and political positioning of the *Revue*, especially the social and cultural capital of its founders, enabled it to produce, legitimate, and circulate specific kinds of knowledge about gender issues. In their program the editors constructed the problem of gender injustice as a basic question of justice and human rights that, like the Dreyfus case, must be addressed scientifically. Presenting themselves as scientists and reformers, the review defined a feminism that could respond to a problem they understood as both moral and social. Their credentials as female experts sufficed to give women the authority to participate on an equal footing with male collaborators in this moral project of promoting just relations between the sexes. Finally, demonstrating that gender injustice was universal—an international and national concern—and backing up this claim with an impressive roster of correspondents from Europe and beyond, the review's collaborators could persuade readers at home that their program was nonpartisan and that they were acting in the interest of humanity.

The RMS bore a striking resemblance to the form of action favored by intellectuals throughout Europe at this time: the petition. Indeed, in the year the review was founded, 1899, many correspondents, including Swiss editor Louis Bridel and members of the Ligue des Droits de l'Homme Gabriel Séailles, Gabriel Monod, Charles Gide, and Frédéric Passy, had signed their countries' addresses to the Russian czar in support of Finnish sovereignty.[49] French contributors were in the vanguard of the pro-Dreyfus initiatives of the Ligue at home. In the review's pages intellectuals, not all of whom were widely known, made their cases for different types of social change and were seconded by a group of more prominent individuals whose connections, status, and authority made their name in the pages of a review a mark of legitimation.[50] Its very title, the *Revue de Morale Sociale*, evoked one of the major French concerns of the fin-de-siècle, one that preoccupied "Dreyfusards" and "anti-Dreyfusards" alike: the search for a just secular ethos that would reflect the ideals of the Revolution *and* guarantee social harmony and progress. For a brief moment, by appealing to the moral nature of their project, the founders and collaborators of the review succeeded in synthesizing these elements, making gender relations central to the new *morale sociale*. The cultural authority of female experts was vital to their project because contemporaries saw social ethics as gendered. Truly just sexual morality meant respect for the individual person, male or female, as well as choices, duties, and responsibilities on the part of individual men and women as sexed members of society. The combined social and moral capital of the intellectuals grouped around the RMS authorized them to place gender injustice on a par with the Dreyfus case, war and peace, national sovereignty, and genocide, as a subject for urgent moral intervention.

History, Memory, and Forgetting: In Search of the French Woman Intellectual

The *Revue de Morale Sociale* was one of a number of intellectual enterprises in which educated French women and men cooperated beginning in the late nineteenth century. Yet scholarly works have paid little systematic attention to the kind of interaction described here or, in general, to women's part in the civic mobilization that produced the new figure of the French Intellectual. Indeed, the preoccupations of historians of women, on the one hand, and historians of political and intellectual life, on the other, have seldom intersected with regard to this decisive period in French political history.[51]

Yet the case of the *Revue de Morale Sociale* and the intellectual milieu of which it was a part makes it difficult to ignore either male intellectuals' concern with gender injustice or women's civic engagement beyond gender-segregated associations. Raising questions about the separateness of these two phenomena, the practical collaboration of men and women in various civic projects also sheds new light on both Third Republic politics and the creation of French intellectual identity. Between 1899 and 1903 the leaders of the campaigns to obtain justice for Alfred Dreyfus, who, along with Zola, have been portrayed as prototypical public intellectuals, also fostered national and international discussion about state-regulated prostitution, birth control, Finnish sovereignty, genocide, public education, social ethics, marriage reform, and women's rights. Mapping the social networks of the *Revue's* supporters and correspondents reveals that their concern with such issues led engaged intellectual men to collaborate with a select group of like-minded women in various gender-integrated civic initiatives. Thus, even if the Dreyfus Affair lacked its token George Sand or Madame de Staël—an exceptional female counterpart to male archetype Émile Zola—the example of the RMS and similar enterprises demonstrates that enlightened women with a specific kind of cultural authority were collaborating quite publicly with the men upon whom the ideal French Intellectual would be modeled.

Moral values, civic duty, and public authority were all perceived as gendered at the turn of the twentieth century. Consequently, cooperation with female authorities on social and moral questions became crucial to male intellectuals' overarching civic aim of constructing a more just, democratic, and ethical Republic. For the women in these milieux participation in such projects offered a means of acting out the civic vocation they also felt, though they lacked the full political rights of the citizen. They could also use their connections within these groups to further gender-specific political aims. The male and female members of these intellectual networks shared social and cultural backgrounds. They also shared a commitment to the Republic and similar reservations about the direction in which it was evolving. Hence, cooperation was easy, "natural." Denied access or dissatisfied with the available formal means of expressing sovereignty, these citizens voted with their pens, pooling cultural resources and using forums such as the *Revue de Morale Sociale* to raise awareness of moral and social problems.

But a gender-sensitive interpretation of the political context that brought intellectuals—and other enlightened members of the public—to join the fray is difficult to reconcile with the timeless ideal of the Intellectual created since the Dreyfus Affair. To be sure, public intellectuals' political vocation has always been contested.[52] Yet curiously, the rigid representation of the French Intellectual as a man with a certain cultural pedigree has not been seriously challenged. Obliterating the historical role that all but a few women played in the creation of the French Intellectual, this gendered image continues to shape the history and official memory of twentieth-century intellectuals and the identity of intellectuals in France today. This state of affairs has made critical analysis challenging, ensuring that those studying French intellectuals have rarely been disinterested observers. Unlike the case of the Algerian War, in which, as William B. Cohen's work has demonstrated, reconciling popular and official memory has been a long, painful process that is still under way, scholars and the French state have collaborated to produce a vision of France's intellectual past that has been remarkably in sync with popular perceptions.[53] Themselves leading public intellectuals, social scientists and philosophers have developed models and theories of political engagement that—with the help of official ceremonies, public education, and the media (in which many academics play important roles)—connect popular beliefs about intellectuals, official sites of memory such as the Panthéon and the Collège de France, and seminal texts and events such as the Declaration of the Rights of Man and Citizen, great thinkers' funerals, and the Dreyfus Affair.[54] Historical research, much of which is publicly funded in France, both shapes and reflects popular perceptions of who public intellectuals are and have been. It is certainly going too far to suggest that any synchronization has been premeditated or that scholars have been encouraged to produce a certain vision of French intellectuality for the public and the world. It is not entirely surprising to find, however, that academic, popular, and official stories converge on key aspects of this crucial issue of national pride and identity.

The gender of intellectuality is one such area of agreement.[55] Indeed, the gap between the public intellectual's "transhistorical" status as an icon of French masculinity and his modest origins in the fluid, heterogeneous, dynamic, and above all, gender-integrated civic culture of the Dreyfus era seems to be the outcome of an almost natural alignment of history, public perceptions, national aspirations, and official memory.[56] Because the figure of the Dreyfusard intellectual appears male, in the image of those who have fashioned and refashioned it, the French woman intellectual has since the Dreyfus Affair become a historical, and historiographical, problem.[57] Feminist scholars have long pondered the marginalization or exclusion of women from various cultural canons. But the gender politics of creativity and cultural consecration are only part of the problem of the modern French woman intellectual. As Toril Moi has demonstrated in the case of Simone de Beauvoir, the association in the French mind between intellect and political engagement complicates matters for women in particular, because political authority was, and still is, so hard for women to acquire.[58] It is not entirely surprising that feminist scholarship has not placed too much emphasis on revising traditional interpretations of the rise of the French Intellectual either. The Dreyfusard ideal of the Intellectual is so much a part of popular memory that although few Third Republic women seem to fit the model, it is hard to imagine a more accommodating alternative. For some feminists masculinist structures of cultural reproduction have ensured that no "real" women Intellectuals existed until recently, anyway. Moreover, seeking such women Intellectuals of the past seems merely to reinforce and valorize the masculine norm and patriarchal values, because public intellectuality has been by definition a male prerogative, enacted via traditionally "masculine" modes of action, ways of thinking, and cultural habits. Masculinity and intellect have been so closely connected (even more so in the nineteenth century) that intellectual women appear "male identified," out of the ordinary (*pas comme les autres*), or indeed, not really even women, having deliberately or unconsciously "transformed themselves into men" (as Christine de Pizan, the first professional woman writer, put it at the turn of the fifteenth century). Some exceptional women additionally operated as lone wolves, showing little solidarity with other women and even less interest in feminism, and preferring the company of men. Finally, the figure of the public intellectual immortalized by historians and in public memory has promoted "universal" values that were never really universal. In short it is difficult to find a constructive way to approach the "problem" of the woman intellectual.

To an outside observer such excessive concern with the political role of public intellectuals, whose "power" to shape opinion seems feeble compared to that of certain movie stars and rock singers, may seem unwarranted. But intellectuals still matter in France, and the Dreyfus Affair was a defining moment in their history. Not all of the French public really cares about intellectuals, of course. Yet the amount of media attention they continue to get both in France and in Francophone circles abroad suggests that many people do care. The death of renowned sociologist Pierre Bourdieu in 2002 was front-page news, and even former French president Jacques Chirac, whose political outlook could not have been further from Bourdieu's during his lifetime, did not miss the opportunity to pronounce the latter a national hero at his death, at the same time reaffirming the French national conception of the public intellectual's political vocation: "With the passing of Pierre Bourdieu, France has lost one of her most talented intellectuals, recognized the world over. . . . A celebrated philosopher and scientist, Pierre Bourdieu experienced sociology as a science that was inseparable from civic engagement [*engagement*]."[59] Difficult as it may be for Americans to imagine, histories and biographical dictionaries of public intellectuals constitute a best-selling genre in France. History textbooks such as Ory and Sirinelli's have gone into second and third printings. Political historian Michel Winock's *Le Siècle des intellectuels* (*The Century of the Intellectuals*), a chronicle of heroic political struggles between twentieth-century thinkers that first appeared in 1997, has been revised and now exists as a pocket paperback in the popular "Points" series; and a revised, soft-cover edition of Julliard and Winock's massive *Dictionnaire des intellectuels français* appeared the same year that Bourdieu died. Thus, unlike books on intellectuals in the United States, mainly produced by university presses and with a corresponding readership, books on intellectuals in France are published by major commercial publishing houses, are read by a substantial audience, and can become popular enough to be published in pocket paperback editions.[60]

In the later twentieth century the French Intellectual, incarnated by men such as Jean-Paul Sartre, became an elite export commodity as well as a national symbol. If the "French intellectual heritage" is a key constituent of modern French identity, ideas—especially "French theory"—along with fine wines, high fashion, perfumes, and gastronomy, continue to figure among France's most prized exports. Not unlike a luxury brand, *French Intellectual* has become a signifier designating not only individuals but also a tradition, a myth, Frenchness itself.[61] Men such as Sartre and Michel Foucault personify this tradition to such a degree that it is nearly impossible to hear their names without thinking "French." Only exceptional female names, such as Simone de Beauvoir, have the power to evoke this heritage in quite the same way. That such a woman stands out as "exceptional," not only at home but also abroad, merely reinforces the core identity of the French Intellectual as a man.

Most important, the model of civic engagement identified with the (male) Dreyfusard intellectual continues to influence the activities, identity, and public personas of aspiring shapers of public opinion. An important element of French democratic culture, the notion of a civic vocation combining the disinterested pursuit of knowledge and truth with Zola-style defense of human rights, justice, and universal moral values has guided and been reinforced by successive generations of engaged writers and thinkers since the late nineteenth century. But this ideal has also empowered other men and women of diverse backgrounds, individually and collectively, to initiate or animate critical public conversation on a range of charged moral and political issues, from colonialism to abortion rights, from poverty and unemployment to secularization and the European Union. Although they do not fit the Dreyfusard model, members of social and professional groups from farmers to immigrants to high school students now routinely initiate public discussion in France.[62] Other French traditions of social protest with roots beyond the Dreyfus Affair also motivate this activism. But many people continue to see the engagement of Zola or Sartre as points of reference, testifying to the enduring political and cultural importance of a particular ideal of the public intellectual.[63]

Pierre Nora's wry comment that nowadays "everybody can always become the intellectual of someone" suggests that being excluded from the canon of "true" intellectuals should no longer really matter. But if, as the continued preoccupation with them suggests, the idea and vocation of the Intellectual are still so important in France that the label should not be so readily accessible, then the relatively high sales figures for books on French intellectuals—and the limited space these works accord women and other "marginals"—should still give pause to those interested in women's place in French political life. After all, Julliard and Winock only managed to come up with 42 women to include in their 584-member pantheon in the 2002 edition of the *Dictionnaire des intellectuels français*.[64] This should not necessarily be seen as a sign of progress since the cover of the 1986 edition of Ory and Sirinelli's text, considering the still-marginal position of women in certain intellectual institutions and the continued popular perception of cultural and political authority as masculine.[65]

To ask whether women can be French Intellectuals in their own right may be a misplaced question. Yet looking for the woman intellectuals of the turn of the twentieth century serves a purpose. It leads us beyond the contested terrains of both feminism and pro-Dreyfus activism—without questioning their critical importance in French political history—to a broader understanding of French civic engagement, which has been obscured by the same synchronization of history, collective perceptions, and official memory that reinforces the masculinity of the Intellectual.

At the turn of the twentieth century, alongside male Dreyfusards and anti-Dreyfusards, women ostensibly excluded from politics were turning their traditional and newfound social and symbolic capital into political resources: not only demanding legal and social reforms affecting women but arguing in the name of the Republic, the Nation, or humanity for moral reform, peace, social justice, and international cooperation. Their status as educated female experts and reference to womanly civic duty helped them create new public roles through which they could express their sovereignty and "act like citizens." Women's words and actions suggest that they *felt* like citizens, too, even though they lacked full political rights. Collaboration with like-minded men of similar social backgrounds and the restructuring of public discourse brought female authorities into the public sphere, close to the center of politics, although they remained excluded from political institutions. Although gender relations within intellectual milieus were seldom egalitarian and only a few women occupied leadership positions in mixed-gender projects, it is still significant that male leaders of the fin-de-siècle civic mobilization sought female cooperation.

The cooperation of intellectual women and men in enterprises such as the *Revue de Morale Sociale* demonstrates that although women have been marginalized in the history of French intellectuals, they took active part in creating modes and discourses of civic engagement that continue today to shape the identity of public intellectuals and other activists worldwide. During and after the Dreyfus Affair enlightened men and women of various backgrounds, many all but forgotten by posterity, could and did acquire a civic vocation, though not all are remembered as "real" Intellectuals. This case suggests that if the figure of the Intellectual born with the Dreyfus Affair introduced a hard-to-break link between civic engagement, intellect, and masculinity, this was but one model of intellectual identity available to contemporaries at the turn of the twentieth century. The emergence of women intellectuals also has implications for understanding the interpretation of citizenship in the Third Republic, providing a framework for analyzing the political practices of other seemingly marginal groups. By paying attention to the full range of civic enterprises in which intellectuals took part and by concentrating on practices and discourses in context, rather than on timeless ideals, we may arrive at a more historically grounded and comprehensive understanding of the meaning of the fin-de-siècle civic mobilization for the development of French democracy. Seeking the Woman Intellectual, using gender as an analytical guide, provides one rather fruitful means of doing so.

Notes

This essay originated in 1993 as a seminar paper that, at the suggestion of my late advisor, William B. Cohen, grew into a longer work, "Gender, Intellectual Sociability and

Political Culture in the French Third Republic, 1890–1914" (PhD diss., Indiana University, 2004). His guidance and belief in the project were crucial to its completion, which he sadly did not live to see. An earlier version of this essay was presented at "Encountering Modern French History: A Conference Honoring the Contributions of William B. Cohen," Bloomington, Indiana, December 5–6, 2003, and portions of it at the Twelfth Berkshire Conference on the History of Women, University of Connecticut, Storrs, June 6–9, 2002. I am grateful to Rachel Fuchs, Niilo Kauppi, Karen Offen, Christine von Oertzen, and members of the audience at both conferences for their comments on it.

1. Pierre Nora, "About Intellectuals," in *Intellectuals in Twentieth-Century France*, ed. Jeremy Jennings (New York: St. Martin's Press, 1993), 192. ("Que peuvent les intellectuels?" *Le Débat*, no. 1 [1980]: 3–19.)

2. The venerable Collège de France is the oldest institution of higher learning in France. See Christophe Charle, "Le Collège de France," in *Les Lieux de mémoire*, vol. 3, *La Nation*, ed. Pierre Nora (Paris: Gallimard, 1986), 389–424.

3. The phrase *public intellectual* is probably the closest English equivalent for the French term *intellectuel*. Rather than simply describing a highly educated member of a "thinking" or creative, rather than manual, profession, *intellectuel* has come to denote a cultural figure, usually a writer or academic, whose standing in a particular field brings the authority to initiate or shape public discussion. A recent work that places both the terminology and the public role of intellectuals, especially writers, in comparative perspective is Helen Small, ed., *The Public Intellectual* (Oxford: Blackwell, 2002).

4. For an image of this sculpture, see www.aaslan.com/english/biography/photos/Marianne_bardot.html. On Marianne and republican symbolism, see Maurice Agulhon, *Marianne into Battle* (Cambridge: Cambridge University Press, 1981); Maurice Agulhon, *Marianne au pouvoir* (Paris: Flammarion, 1989); and Maurice Agulhon, *Les Métamorphoses de Marianne* (Paris: Flammarion, 2001). On Bardot and the Mariannes who succeeded her, including actress Catherine Deneuve and Victoria's Secret model Laetitia Casta, see Suzanne Daley, "Does France's Symbol Need a Face-Lift? 'Marianne' Contest Has 5 Beauties, and Some Say That's the Problem," *International Herald Tribune*, September 28, 1999, 1, 6; and Debra Ollivier, "Liberté, Égalité, 36C," *Salon.com*, February 19, 2000, http://archive.salon.com/people/feature/2000/02/19/mkarianne/index.html.

5. Pascal Ory and Jean-François Sirinelli, *Les Intellectuels en France, de l'affaire Dreyfus à nos jours* (Intellectuals in France from the Dreyfus Affair to the Present) (Paris: Armand Colin, 1986). Removed from the 1992 edition, the photo reappeared on the 2002 edition. A copy of the cover can be found online at www.amazon.fr/gp/product/images/2200263589/.

6. I will capitalize *Intellectual* when referring to the dominant representation of the

French public intellectual from which women, and many men, have been excluded. Ory and Sirinelli, *Les Intellectuels en France*, 205.

7. Venita Datta uses this term in her work, *Birth of a National Icon: The Literary Avant-Garde and the Emergence of the Modern Intellectual* (Albany: State University of New York Press, 1999).

8. A body of recent popular and scholarly literature, including biographical dictionaries, addresses the French incarnation of the public intellectual. See, for example, Christophe Charle, *Naissance des "intellectuels," 1880–1900* (Paris: Les Éditions de Minuit, 1990); Ory and Sirinelli, *Les Intellectuels en France*; Michel Winock, *Le Siècle des intellectuels* (Paris: Seuil, 1999); and Jacques Julliard and Michel Winock, *Dictionnaire des intellectuels français: les personnes, les lieux, les moments* (Paris: Seuil, 2002); as well as innumerable articles and specialized works. For the state of the field of the history of intellectuals in France and in comparative perspective, see Michel Leymarie and Jean-François Sirinelli, eds., *L'Histoire des intellectuels aujourd'hui* (Paris: Presses Universitaires de France, 2003). On masculinity and intellectuals during the Dreyfus Affair, see John Cerullo, "The Intellectuals and the Imagination of Heroism during the Dreyfus Affair," *Proceedings of the Western Society for French History* 23 (1996); Datta, *Birth of a National Icon*; and Christopher Forth, *The Dreyfus Affair and the Crisis of French Manhood* (Baltimore: Johns Hopkins University Press, 2004). See also Annelise Maugue, *L'Identité masculine en crise au tournant du siècle, 1871–1914* (Paris: Rivages, 1987). On the public memory of French intellectuals, see, for example, Avner Ben-Amos, *Funerals, Politics, and Memory in Modern France, 1789–1996* (Oxford: Oxford University Press, 2000); Jean-Claude Bonnet, *Naissance du Panthéon: essai sur le culte des grandes hommes* (Paris: Fayard, 1998).

9. According to historians of twentieth-century intellectual life, what set new-style intellectuals apart from earlier engaged writers and thinkers was that they began systematically to use their cultural authority to speak out on moral issues not directly related to their own areas of specialization. See, for example, Jacques Julliard and Michel Winock, introduction to Julliard and Winock, *Dictionnaires des intellectuels français*, 11–18; Ory and Sirinelli, *Les Intellectuels en France*, 10.

10. See Philip Nord, *The Republican Moment: Struggles for Democracy in Nineteenth-Century France* (Cambridge MA: Harvard University Press, 1995); James R. Lehning, *To Be a Citizen: The Political Culture of the Early French Third Republic* (Ithaca NY: Cornell University Press, 2001). For a comparative perspective, see Nancy Bermeo and Philip Nord, eds., *Civil Society before Democracy: Lessons from Nineteenth-Century Europe* (London: Rowman and Littlefield, 2000).

11. Jules Cornély, "Chronique politique," *La Grande Revue*, February 1, 1900, 493. The translation and emphasis are mine. See also Pierre Rosanvallon, *La Démocratie inachevée: histoire de la souveraineté du peuple en France* (Paris: Gallimard, 2000), 333–35.

12. I thank Rachel Fuchs for the comments upon which this discussion builds.

13. On gender as a means of signifying relations of power, see Joan Scott, "Gender: A Useful Category of Analysis," *American Historical Review* 91 (December 1986): 1053–75.

14. See Karen Offen, "The Second Sex and the *Baccaulauréat* in Republican France, 1880–1924," *French Historical Studies* 13 (1983): 252–86. Pauline Savary's application to replace Ernest Renan at the Académie Française in 1893 received a response directed "in advance to all of those [women] who may similarly present themselves in the future," stating that the traditions of the institution prevented it from even considering the question. "Les Femmes à l'Académie," *Le Journal*, December 20, 1903 (press review from *Le Figaro*), Dossier Académie Française, Bibliothèque Marguerite Durand (hereafter cited as BMD). Similarly, despite excellent connections within the Ministry of Education, Anna Yon-Lampérière was told she could not be sent as an official delegate to the 1893 Chicago World's Fair because there was no precedent for sending a woman on such a mission. Lampérière mission, F17 3014B, Archives Nationales (hereafter cited as AN).

15. On women's exclusion from the public sphere and French democracy, see esp. Joan Landes, *Women and the Public Sphere in the Age of the French Revolution* (Ithaca NY: Cornell University Press, 1988); and Christine Fauré, *Democracy without Women: Feminism and the Rise of Liberal Individualism in France* (Bloomington: Indiana University Press, 1991). On feminists' recurrent difficulties framing their demands for full political rights, see Joan Scott, *Only Paradoxes to Offer: French Feminists and the Rights of Man* (Cambridge MA: Harvard University Press, 1996).

16. On these exceptional women, see, for example, Michèle Riot-Sarcey, *La Démocratie à l'épreuve des femmes: trois figures critiques du pouvoir, 1830–1848* (Paris: Albin Michel, 1994); Whitney Walton, *Eve's Proud Descendants: Four Women Writers and Republican Politics in Nineteenth-Century France* (Stanford: Stanford University Press, 2000); Claire Goldberg Moses, *French Feminism in the 19th Century* (Albany: State University of New York Press, 1984); and Claire Goldberg Moses, "Saint-Simonian Men/ Saint-Simonian Women," *Journal of Modern History* 54 (June 1982): 240–67. On women's activities between public and private domains, see, for example, Hazel Mills, "Negotiating the Divide: Women, Philanthropy, and the 'Public Sphere' in Nineteenth-Century France," in *Religion, Society, and Politics in France since 1789*, ed. Frank Tallett and Nicholas Atkin (London: Hambledon Press, 1991), 29–54; Steven D. Kale, "Women, the Public Sphere, and the Persistence of Salons," *French Historical Studies* 25, no. 1 (December 2002): 115–48; and esp. Alain Corbin, Jacqueline Lalouette, and Michèle Riot-Sarcey, eds., *Femmes dans la cité, 1815–1871* (Grâne, France: Créaphis, 1997).

17. This is very free usage of the concept developed by French cultural sociologist Pierre Bourdieu. See, for example, *La Distinction, critique sociale du jugement* (Paris: Les Éditions de Minuit, 1979); "Culture et politique," in *Questions de sociologie* (Paris:

Les Éditions de Minuit, 1980), 236–50; and "The Forms of Capital," in *Handbook of Theory and Research for the Sociology of Education*, ed. J. G. Richardson (New York: Greenwood Press, 1986), 241–58.

18. On Kergomard, Gevin-Cassal, and other female administrators, see Linda Clark, *The Rise of Professional Women in France: Gender and Public Administration since 1830* (Cambridge: Cambridge University Press, 2000); on the École Normale de Sèvres, see Jo Burr Margadant, *Madame le Professeur: Women Educators in the Third Republic* (Princeton NJ: Princeton University Press, 1990).

19. Glowing assessments of maternal character from prominent supporters, highlighting the exceptional sacrifices women had made on their children's behalf, appear frequently in letters of recommendation of female civil servants. A note from her editor on behalf of Anna Lampérière, who had requested to be sent on a second mission to the United States in 1894, referred to her heroic struggle to support her two daughters alone as a demonstration of her good character. Pauline Kergomard's recommenders earlier highlighted how well she was raising her sons. Note to the bureau chief, St. Arroman (January 24, 1894), dossier Mme Yon-Lampérière, Mission, Exposition de Chicago, 1893, F17 3014B, AN. Recommendations from Gabriel Monod, Mme Adam, dossier de carrière (Pauline Kergomard), F17 23609B, AN.

20. Nelly Roussel and her artist husband, Henri Godet, painstakingly crafted a public persona for Roussel as a respectable and "good" bourgeois mother both to temper her radical message about reproductive freedom and to give her the moral authority to get it heard. See Elinor A. Accampo, "Private Life, Public Image: Motherhood and Militancy in the Self-Construction of Nelly Roussel, 1900–1922," in *The New Biography: Performing Femininity in Nineteenth-Century France*, ed. Jo Burr Margadant (Berkeley: University of California Press, 2000), 218–61; and Elinor A. Accampo, *Blessed Motherhood, Bitter Fruit: Nelly Roussel and the Politics of Female Pain in Third Republic France* (Baltimore: Johns Hopkins University Press, 2006).

21. Journalists Marguerite Durand and Séverine were among the exceptional women who became public figures in spite of being mothers (rather than by emphasizing their motherhood). Their public authority rested on social resources, personal qualities, and a decidedly nonmaternal feminine aesthetic. See Mary Louise Roberts, *Disruptive Acts: The New Woman in Fin-de-Siècle France* (Chicago: University of Chicago Press, 2002), 58–71, 134.

22. Durand and Séverine are among the handful of Third Republic women, mostly feminists, included in Winock and Julliard's *Dictionnaire des intellectuels français*. See Laurence Klejman and Florence Rochefort, "Durand (Marguerite) 1864–1936" and "Séverine [Caroline Rémy] 1855–1929," in Winock and Julliard, *Dictionnaire des intellectuels français*, 484–85, 1283. On Durand's politics, see also Mary Louise Roberts, "Acting Up: The Feminist Theatrics of Marguerite Durand," in Margadant,

New Biography, 171–217. On Séverine's, see also Françoise Blum, "Séverine, ou la recherche d'une justice perdue," *Mil Neuf Cent* 11 (1993): 94–100.

23. Her name appears on the tenth list of signatories of the first petition to circulate, in January 1898. See "Dreyfus (affaire) 1894–1906," in Winock and Julliard, *Dictionnaire des intellectuels français*, 451. The first three protests are reproduced in Winock and Julliard, *Dictionnaire des intellectuels français*, 443–62. Focusing on the polemics of the Dreyfus Affair, Christopher Forth has suggested that Dreyfusard men actually tried to guide women to gender-appropriate manifestations of solidarity that would not discredit the cause by upsetting the traditional gender order. See *The Dreyfus Affair and the Crisis of French Manhood*, 137–55, esp. 153. On women and the Dreyfus Affair, see, for example, Julie Sabiani, "Féminisme et dreyfusisme," in *Les Écrivains et l'affaire Dreyfus*, ed. Géraldi Leroy (Paris: PUF, 1983), 199–206; Françoise Blum, "Itinéraires féministes à la lumière de l'affaire," in *La Postérité de l'affaire Dreyfus*, ed. Michel Leymarie (Villeneuve d'Ascq: Presses Universitaires du Septentrion, 1998), 93–101; Máire Cross, "Les Représentations de l'affaire Dreyfus dans le journal *La Fronde* entre décembre 1897 et septembre 1899," in *Les Représentations de l'affaire Dreyfus dans la presse en France et à l'étranger* (Tours: Université François Rabelais, 1997); Willa Silverman, *The Notorious Life of Gyp: Right-Wing Anarchist in Fin-de-Siècle France* (New York: Oxford University Press, 1995), 137–57.

24. Finally declaring full support for women's rights, the Ligue des Droits de l'Homme framed its commitment in terms of the "rights of man." See "Rapport de Mme Maria Vérone, 'Les Droits de la Femme,'" Rapports présentés au Congrès de la LDH, *Bulletin Officiel de la Ligue des Droits de l'Homme*, Année IX, no. 17 (September 15, 1909): 1094–1104. On the mainstreaming of gender in political discourse, see Karen Offen, "Depopulation, Nationalism, and Feminism in Fin-de-Siècle France," *American Historical Review* 89 (1984): 648–76; Karen Offen, "Exploring the Sexual Politics of Republican Nationalism," in *Nationhood and Nationalism in France: From Boulangism to the Great War, 1889–1918*, ed. Robert Tombs (London: HarperCollins, 1991), 195–209; and Elinor A. Accampo, Rachel G. Fuchs, and Mary Lynn Stewart, eds., *Gender and the Politics of Social Reform in France, 1870–1914* (Baltimore: Johns Hopkins University Press, 1995). On *La Fronde*'s challenges to conventional femininity and the role of nationalist anti-Semitism and Dreyfusism in bringing female journalists such as Gyp and Séverine into politics, see Roberts, *Disruptive Acts*, 73–106, 131–64. The rise of the female publicist, or *propagandiste*, and the increasing visibility of women and women's achievements in international showcases of French culture such as world's fairs also bore witness to changes under way in the gendered structure of the French public sphere.

25. Books and articles by female authorities, such as solidarist educator Anna Lampérière's *Le Rôle social de la femme* (1898) and *La Femme et son pouvoir* (1909) and Children's Services inspector Olympe Gevin-Cassal's *La Fraternité en action* (1904), offered a "feminine" perspective on topical debates.

26. Until her marriage in 1900, she was known simply as Mlle de Sainte-Croix (I thank Karen Offen for drawing my attention to the timing of this name change). See also Karen Offen, "'La Plus grande féministe de France': mais qui est donc Madame Avril de Sainte-Croix?" *Bulletin des Archives du Féminisme* 9 (December 2005): 47.

27. For a detailed discussion of women's contributions to these organizations and forums, see Epstein, "Gender, Intellectual Sociability, and Political Culture in the French Third Republic," chap. 2.

28. On the relations of feminists and suffragists with their male allies, see Steven Hause with Anne R. Kenney, *Women's Suffrage and Social Politics in the French Third Republic* (Princeton NJ: Princeton University Press, 1984); and Laurence Klejman and Florence Rochefort, *L'Égalité en marche: le féminisme sous la Troisième République* (Paris: Presses de la Fondation Nationale des Sciences Politiques/Des Femmes, 1989).

29. "De toutes parts," *Revue de Morale Sociale*, no. 2 (April–June 1899): 197.

30. "Programme," *Revue de Morale Sociale*, no. 1 (1899): 1. This and all subsequent translations are my own.

31. "Programme," 3.

32. "Programme," 2–3.

33. "À nos abonnés, lecteurs et amis," *Revue de Morale Sociale*, no. 15 (1903): 245–46.

34. "À nos abonnés, lecteurs et amis," 246; my emphasis.

35. "Programme," 2–3.

36. The rest were American, British, Finnish, German, Italian, Norwegian, and Swiss. See "Groupe d'initiative," *Revue de Morale Sociale*, no. 1 (1899): 5–8. Only one of the review's founders was French, but the director and the other founders were French-speaking Swiss with close links to France.

37. It is necessary to distinguish between founding members and those who actually wrote for the review. Although not all of the founding members of the review ever published articles in it, it is significant that they gave their support to the review and that their names were among those listed in the original *groupe d'initiative*.

38. Jeanne Schmahl, Maria Martin, and Marie Maugeret edited feminist newspapers. Jeanne Oddo-Deflou and Jeanne Chauvin had been among the first women to obtain law degrees. Olympe Gevin-Cassal served in the Interior Ministry as inspector general of children's services and wrote children's books. Ghénia de Sainte-Croix (writing in the review as "Savioz") was a widely published journalist and essayist, cofounder and secretary-general of the Conseil National des Femmes Françaises (National Council of French Women), and active in the international movement to abolish legalized prostitution and in the Ligue des Droits de l'Homme. Isabelle Bogelot, also active in the Protestant women's movement, had since 1881 directed l'Oeuvre des Libérées de Saint-Lazare, a philanthropic work aimed at aiding prostitutes. Marie Bonnevial, a schoolteacher who wrote on women's economic position and education, was involved in socialist politics, was active in the Ligue

des Droits de l'Homme, and later served as secretary-general and then president of the Ligue Française pour le Droit des Femmes (French League for Women's Rights). Maria Pognon—feminist, pacifist, suffragist—was president of the Ligue Française pour le Droit des Femmes and a member of the International Arbitration League. Pauline Kergomard, inspector general of nursery schools, was the first woman to serve on the Conseil Supérieur de l'Instruction Publique and an advocate of expanded roles for women in the public administration.

The professions or affiliations of most of these individuals appear alongside their names on the list of *groupe d'initiative* members that appeared in the first issue of the review. Additional information cited here and in the notes that follow has been gathered from a wide variety of biographical dictionaries, publishing catalogues, periodical indexes, archival documents, personal correspondence, and secondary sources. For further information, see the appendix and bibliography of Epstein, "Gender, Intellectual Sociability, and Political Culture."

39. Founded two years after *La Fronde*, a Dreyfusard daily produced entirely by women and sympathetic to feminism, the *Revue de Morale Sociale* (*RMS*) numbered among its founding members and collaborators several women who wrote for that paper, including Savioz (Ghénia de Sainte-Croix), Maria Martin, Marie Maugeret, Louise Georges-Renard, Elisabeth-J. Hudry-Menos, and Olympe Gevin-Cassal. Jeanne Oddo-Deflou contributed to both publications as well as to fellow *RMS* collaborator Maria Martin's *Journal des Femmes*. Isabelle Bogelot and de Sainte-Croix had campaigned actively against state-regulated prostitution, a cause they had in common with such male compatriots as M. J. Gaufrès, secretary-general of the Ligue Française de la Moralité Publique (French League for Public Morality), as well as with their Swiss collaborators, many of whom had been followers of Josephine Butler. Like Bogelot, Marguerite de Witt-Schlumberger had been involved with the philanthropy and the Conseil National des Femmes Françaises, an organization known to have Dreyfusard connections, and later became active in the Union Française pour le Suffrage des Femmes (French Union for Women's Suffrage). Founding member of the *RMS* Marie Maugeret represented Catholic feminism as editor of the review *Féminisme Chrétien*; fellow founding member Elisabeth Hudry-Menos was a dedicated socialist feminist. Further, in the year after the review ceased publication, Charles Gide, J. Charmont, and Olympe Gevin-Cassal all contributed to *Femme Nouvelle*, a review with which Louise Renard also was affiliated. Contributors who had published or would publish essays or books on feminism or social relations included Savioz, Isabelle Bogelot, Jeanne Chauvin, Käthe Schirmacher, Margueritte de Schlumberger, Jeanne Schmahl, Jacques Lourbet, E. Hudry-Menos, Ferdinand Buisson, J. Charmont, and Paul Robin. Significantly, these books shared the same French publisher as the *RMS*—E. Giard et Brière, Paris—which also published other books on feminism and related subjects.

40. On the Third Republic reform circles within which some of these individuals moved, see, for example, Christian Topalov, ed., *Les Laboratoires du nouveau siècle: la nébuleuse réformatrice et ses réseaux en France (1880–1914)* (Paris: Éditions de l'École des Hautes Études en Sciences Sociales, 1999); Janet R. Horne, *A Social Laboratory for Modern France: The Musée Social and the Rise of the Welfare State* (Durham NC: Duke University Press, 2002); and Collette Chambelland, ed., *Le Musée social en son temps* (Paris: Presses de l'École Normale Supérieure, 1998). Annie Stora-Lamarre, *La République des faibles: les origins intellectuelles du droit républicain 1870–1914* (Paris: Armand Colin, 2005), provides the intellectual historical context, with particular attention to the moral foundations of late-nineteenth-century reform legislation. Many French supporters and contributors of the review belonged to the Protestant minority and had contacts with French-speaking Swiss Protestants through transborder social action inspired by the French pastor Tomy Fallot. Cooperatist Charles Gide's ties with Switzerland dated to the 1870s. Independent socialist academic Georges Renard, like many former Communards, had lived in exile in Switzerland for thirty years and had married a Swiss woman, Louise Renard, another RMS contributor. See Anne-Marie Käppeli, *Sublime Croisade: éthique et politique du féminisme protestant, 1875–1928* (Geneva: Éditions Zoé, 1990); Marc Penin, *Charles Gide, 1847–1932: l'esprit critique* (Paris: L'Harmattan, 1998); Renard Papers, Bibliothèque Historique de la Ville de Paris.

41. RMS contributors who wrote for the literary-political *Revue Bleue* included Raoul Allier, Henry Bérenger, Ferdinand Buisson, Olympe Gevin-Cassal, Gabriel Monod, Auguste de Morsier, Frédéric Passy, Edouard Schuré, Gabriel Séailles, and Edouard E. Toulouse,. Dora Melegari, from Italy, contributed articles on Italian feminism to both reviews. Allier, Bérenger, Maurice Bouchor, Henry Joly, Monod, Käthe Schirmacher, Schuré, and Séailles published in the *Revue de Paris* during the same period—a review that not only included works by members of the literary establishment such as Anatole France, Henrik Ibsen, Pierre Loti, and Romain Rolland but also published fiction by noted women writers and journalists such as Marcelle Tinayre, Myriam Harry, Arvède Barine, Judith Gautier, and Lucie Delarue-Mardrus. No RMS contributors wrote for the staid *Revue des Deux Mondes* during this period, but several articles by Henri Joly on social issues and at least one by Dora Melegari on Italian feminism appeared in the Catholic review *Le Correspondant*. Bérenger, Monod, Séailles, and the neo-Malthusian Paul Robin had earlier contributed to the *Revue Blanche*. Articles by Buisson, Guyot, Monod, Gide, Manouvrier, de la Grasserie, and Lourbet also appeared in René Worms's *Revue Internationale de Sociologie*. See indexes and issues published between 1899 and 1903 of the *Le Correspondant*, *Revue Blanche*, *Revue Bleue*, *Revue de Paris*, *Revue des Deux Mondes*, and *Revue Internationale de Sociologie*; A. B. Jackson, *La Revue Blanche* (Paris: Lettres Modernes, 1960), 163–257.

42. "Groupe d'initiative," *Revue de Morale Sociale*, no. 1 (1899): 5–8.

43. Examples of potentially controversial topics included coeducation in Finland and neo-Malthusian thought, the latter of which proved too disturbing for some of the review's subscribers. See, for example, Lucina Hagman, "La Coéducation des sexes en Finlande," *Revue de Morale Sociale* (1899); Dr. Rutgers, "La Question du Néo-Malthusianisme: une question de morale," *Revue de Morale Sociale* (1901); and Dr. Drysdale, "La Ligue Malthusienne," *Revue de Morale Sociale* (1901).

44. "Programme," 1–2.

45. "Histoire d'un plébiscite," *Revue de Morale Sociale*, no. 5 (March 1900): 4–25, esp. 8–18.

46. "De toutes parts," *Revue de Morale Sociale*, no. 2 (April–June 1899): 197–208. The rather different translations of the question probably also contributed to the divergent responses. The English version, for example, does not mention feminism, though it contains a definition of it that is even more leading: "In what way will the participation of women in public life elevate the standard of social ethics?"

47. "De toutes parts," 201–2.

48. "De toutes parts," 201.

49. See *Pro Finlandia: les adresses internationales à S. M. L'Empereur-Grand-Duc Nicolas II* (Stockholm: H. W. Tullberg, 1899), 125. Not a single female signature appears on the French petition to the czar, confirming that national sovereignty was clearly a domain of "masculine" public authority.

50. On the use of such strategies by writers during the Dreyfus Affair, see Charle, *Naissance des "intellectuels,"* 204.

51. French historians of women and gender have begun to consider the problem of women's absence from the history of intellectuals, but curiously little attention has been paid to the emergence of the public intellectual. For exceptions with regard to women and the Dreyfus Affair, see n. 21. See also Nicole Racine, "Intellectuelles," on the recent state of the field, in *L'Histoire des intellectuels aujourd'hui*, ed. Michel Leymarie and Jean-François Sirinelli (Paris: PUF, 2003), 341–62. See also Nicole Racine and Michel Trebitsch, eds., *Intellectuelles: du genre en histoire des intellectuels* (Brussels: Éditions Complexe, 2004); "Intellectuelles," special issue of *Clio: Histoire, Femmes, et Sociétés*, no. 13 (2001): esp. Florence Rochefort's introduction, "À la découverte des intellectuelles," 1–14; and "Figures d'intellectuelles," special issue of *Mil Neuf Cent*, no. 16 (1998).

52. One of the best-known objections to intellectuals taking political stands was expressed by Julien Benda in *La Trahison des clercs* (Paris: Grasset, 1927). But intellectuals had already been quarreling about their proper role since the late nineteenth century. Most debated, particularly since World War II, have been the political role and moral responsibilities of the engaged intellectual.

53. William B. Cohen, "The Algerian War, the French State, and Official Memory,"

Historical Reflections 28, no. 2 (2002): 219–39. The controversy unleashed by the law of February 23, 2005, on France's colonial past, as well as subsequent polemics, indicate that this process is far from complete. Margaret H. Darrow has addressed the related problem of gender and the production of public memory of war in *French Women and the First World War: War Stories of the Home Front* (Oxford: Berg, 2000).

54. See, for example, Ben-Amos, *Funerals, Politics, and Memory*; Bonnet, *Naissance du Panthéon*; and Priscilla Parkhurst Clark, *Literary France: The Making of a Culture* (Berkeley: University of California Press, 1987).

55. Gender has not been the only grounds for exclusion from the French intellectual canon: the "right" kind of political engagement at the right time has always been required. Intellectual canonization, made real (though not necessarily permanent) through a process that may include a state funeral and the transfer of an individual's remains to the Pantheon in Paris, has always been a matter of politics. Because talent, genius, personal charisma, and notoriety are not sufficient to secure one's place as a French Intellectual, many public thinkers who were well-known in their own day may not be remembered as true French Intellectuals—or indeed remembered at all. On the politics of memory, see esp. Ben-Amos, *Funerals, Politics, and Memory*.

56. According to Christophe Charle, "The social genealogy of the 'intellectual' underlines to what degree this neologism is a product of its time, whereas subsequent efforts continue to make of it a transhistorical ideal." *Naissance des "intellectuels,"* 63–64. Julliard and Winock's introduction to the *Dictionnaire des intellectuels français* reflects the delicate politics of definition, inclusion, and exclusion.

57. Recent research supports the hypothesis that concerted efforts to link intellectuality and masculinity actually began during the Dreyfus Affair. Christopher Forth suggests, for example, that facing a gender identity crisis, the male intellectuals involved in the Dreyfus Affair consciously worked to construct Dreyfusism as a "masculinist discourse." If exceptional women such as Séverine appeared to "[carve] out a place for intellectual women" within this discourse, it was on terms set essentially between and for men. Forth, *Dreyfus Affair*, 142, also 137–42, 151–60.

58. On the gender politics of cultural canons, see, for example, Berenice A. Carroll, "The Politics of 'Originality': Women and the Class System of the Intellect," *Journal of Women's History* 2, no. 2 (Fall 1990): 136–63; and Linda Nochlin, "Why Have There Been No Great Women Artists?" in *Women, Art, and Power and Other Essays* (New York: Harper and Row, 1988), 145–78. On the particular case of Simone de Beauvoir and politics, see Toril Moi, *Simone de Beauvoir: The Making of an Intellectual Woman* (Oxford: Blackwell, 1994), 73–92.

59. At Bourdieu's passing the text of the official communiqué of the president of the Republic, dated January 24, 2002, could be viewed at www.elysee.fr.

60. The sales rankings of recent French and American studies of intellectuals on

Amazon.com's French and U.S. Web sites provide anecdotal information about the relative popularity of such works in France. In June 2007 Winock's *Le Siècle des intellectuels* (in pocket paperback, Seuil, Collection Points, 1999 ed.) ranked 6,642nd on the French site (www.amazon.fr). Two American studies of intellectuals and politics, one polemical (Mark Lilla's *The Reckless Mind*, paperback, New York Review Books, repr. ed., 2003) and the other historical (Thomas Bender's *Intellect and Public Life*, paperback, Johns Hopkins University Press, repr. ed., 1997) ranked 391,356th and 867,842nd, respectively, on Amazon's U.S. site (www. amazon.com). Lilla's book seems also to interest customers of the French Web site, where on June 20, 2007, the 2004 edition of his book ranked 83,484th in the category "Books in English." The globalization of the literary market, the constant fluctuation of these rankings, the varying amounts of time elapsed since the books came out, the relative size of the French-language and English-language markets, among other factors, naturally make this a very blunt instrument of comparison. But the significant difference in rankings—and the fact that books such as Winock's *Le Siècle des intellectuels* and Ory and Sirinelli's history of French intellectuals both exist as pocket paperbacks (the former now in a second pocket edition)— suggests that a more carefully controlled study might lead to similar conclusions.

61. On the international circulation of French "symbolic goods," such as ideas, see Niilo Kauppi, *The Making of an Avant-Garde: Tel Quel* (Berlin: Mouton de Gruyter, 1994), 362–73. On French literary culture, see also Clark, *Literary France*.

62. Indeed, Brigitte Bardot, now known for her animal-rights activism and controversial political views, offers an emblematic example.

63. On the intellectual as a symbolic construct with a political and cultural role, see Daniel Brewer, "The French Intellectual, History, and the Reproduction of Culture," *L'Esprit Créateur* 37, no. 2 (Summer 1997): esp. 18–19. On the continued unifying role of the "founding myth" of the intellectual's origins and the connection between past and present, see Eric Fassin, "Play It Again Sartre? New *Dreyfusards* in Search of a New Dreyfus," *French Politics and Society* 16, no. 1 (Winter 1998): 21–37.

64. "Table thématique: les personnes," in Julliard and Winock, *Dictionnaires des intellectuels français*, 1509–21. Interestingly, Simone de Beauvoir appears on the back of the paperback, Émile Zola and Albert Camus on the front.

65. Media commentary on the spring 2007 presidential debates between Ségolène Royal and Nicholas Sarkozy made this amply clear.

9

Family Dramas

Paternity, Divorce, and Adultery, 1917–1945

Rachel G. Fuchs examines the impact on family legal cases of the concept of core and periphery in France and its empire. These family histories detail how the intimacies of daily
life transpired between the center of Paris and the peripheries of Algeria and Indochina
under Vichy, depicting the material and emotional hardships of those years. In examining the relationships of the French in matters of paternity, divorce, and adultery, Fuchs
illustrates that the nineteenth-century bourgeois family unit of the nuclear family, which
had become France's social and cultural core family identity structure, was perforating in
the first half of the twentieth century. As a consequence, in part because of the changing
geography of core and periphery in France and its empire, the very identity of the French
family was changing. French society was becoming more accepting of peripheral family
formations such as single-parent households and unwed partners residing together raising a common child. These changes were evident in the verdicts of French family courts,
often rendering decisions against the interests of a patriarchal father and legitimizing
marginal family structures. Fuchs's research shows how the conjugal family was only
one possible family model, albeit at the core of the bourgeois family discourse, while
peripheral family formations existed, competed, and sometimes won.

⊕ ⊕

The private and most intimate lives of many Parisians involved communication and travel between the core capital city and regions on the periphery—
the rural areas within France and the more distant colonies.[1] Since early
modern times, men and women moved to and from Paris and the other
departments within France in carrying out their social, marital, and sexual
relationships. In the nineteenth and twentieth centuries people also went
to the colonies, specifically to Algeria and Indochina (present-day Vietnam,
Laos, and Cambodia). Communication between Paris and the periphery did

not stop during the Occupation and Vichy governments of the wartime period from 1940 to 1945. Although these five years brought untold deprivation of food and freedom, men and women tried to live their private lives much as they had always done. For Jews, however, this was impossible. Family formation and dissolution from the 1920s through the 1950s reveal how people moved about and conducted their most private affairs between the geographical core and the periphery.[2] They filed paternity suits, divorced, and sought child custody, all of which involved correspondence between Paris and the geographical periphery.

The study of family history inspires another way of thinking about core and periphery. The traditional heterosexual married family with children had long pervaded nineteenth-century thought on the family and constituted the social and cultural core of the nineteenth-century social order. This revered bourgeois vision of an ideal family included a paterfamilias who expected to receive obedience from his wife and children. Divorced and adulterous women and women with ex-nuptial children existed on the periphery of the ideal family. Increasingly in the late nineteenth and early twentieth centuries, traditional ideas began to lose their hold or became more modern and accepting of how people actually lived their lives. Families that had existed on the periphery of the family culture became part of that now highly perforated core. Society increasingly accepted divorced and single-parent families, including the mother-child dyad. Some women divorced and formed new, socially and culturally approved, families. Moreover, French society increasingly accepted men and women living together in nonmarital relationships that the French called "concubinage," a relationship that resembled marriage but without a legal ceremony. Thus, families that had been at the periphery of acceptance entered the core in terms of culture and the law.

Living in consensual unions had long been common among the urban poor throughout the nineteenth and twentieth centuries. For women it was a prelude to marriage, or often a marriage strategy that failed when the men did not marry them.[3] Toward the end of the nineteenth century, and even more during the 1920s and 1930s, men and women of all social classes increasingly entered these unions, either on a long- or short-term basis, for economic, cultural, or sexual reasons. Social and cultural mores among many strata of the population were shifting away from only accepting the core legally married conjugal family and acknowledging, although sometimes with reluctance and disapproval, alternative family forms that had been on the periphery. With a greater interest in protecting the children (in part resulting from fears of demographic depopulation), jurisprudence and law in the late nineteenth century came to reflect the private lives of many French citizens and recognized concubinage as a fact of life. In part this was to make single men responsible for their ex-nuptial children and assure those children a viable life. In the Third Republic the change from the patria potestas was gradual and also sporadic. The Vichy regime vehemently reinforced the core patriarchal family in the political discourse but only in the discourse.

This essay discusses several family histories discovered in the private papers of a Paris law firm from the 1920s through the 1950s. The family stories included here are those that best illustrate different concepts of core and periphery. In all other respects they bear amazing consistency with the many hundreds of family histories presented before the Civil Tribunals of Paris between 1900 and 1940, analyzed elsewhere.[4] Even the cases that came before the Paris courts between 1940 and 1945 corresponded with those of the earlier period, revealing that in family matters politics did not always have a major effect on people's private lives, unless an individual or family, by virtue of morality or religion, was on the periphery of accepted values.

The relationship of Lucienne Hilleret and Henri Parent remained on the periphery in terms of their family formation as well as in terms of geography. In the 1920s Indochina, far from the Parisian core, provided overseas jobs and opportunities for Frenchmen as the French government sought to colonize and develop that land. But the distance also presented difficulties of travel and delays of up to six weeks for letters to travel from Paris to Hanoi. The distance was also sufficient to prevent a man and woman from being together—perhaps because he was reluctant to return to Paris and she could not get the money to go to Hanoi. The story of Lucienne Hilleret and Henri Parent, partially revealed in the letters that Henri wrote to Lucienne from Indochina, indicate how a relationship floundered over time and distance.[5]

The story begins in October 1923, when Lucienne Hilleret married Gaston Girard. Their wedded bliss was short-lived, and they legally separated a year later, in September 1924, with a divorce awarded in Gaston's favor in 1925. This meant that Gaston did not have to provide her with alimony or monetary support. Lucienne appealed the decision. At some point during the divorce proceedings, and perhaps during her marriage with Gaston as well, Lucienne had a sexual relationship with Henri Parent. Shortly after Lucienne knew she was pregnant, Henri went to live and work in Hanoi as an employee of the French Railroad Company of Indochina and Yunnan. A pregnant Lucienne remained in Paris to attend to the final stages of her divorce. She lost her legal appeal, and the divorce became final on April 12, 1926. On June 30 she gave birth to a baby boy, Georges Hilleret, whom she immediately legally recognized. A mother could legally recognize her ex-nuptial baby, thereby assuming official responsibility for the child and also giving the baby her last name and a civil identity. A father could recognize his ex-nuptial child as long as he was not married to someone else and the child was not born of his adultery. Lucienne's legal recognition of the child was also essential to her later filing a paternity suit against Henri, although at the time of Georges's birth she may not have been contemplating a later paternity suit.

Henri Parent's letters to Lucienne during spring 1926 reveal much about his life in Indochina and his initial desire to make his peripheral relationship to Lucienne and baby Georges more like the cultural core. In one of the first letters he described his six-room, two-story house surrounded by a garden. Henri, eager to have Lucienne join him, told her she would have a "true little chateau," a "boy" to do the housework and laundry, and a chef to prepare the meals. He promised that their "great love would spare [her] any boredom." There is no indication whether this appealed to her because her letters to Henri, which he acknowledged that she wrote with great regularity, are not available. In his next letter, dated March 31, 1926, he regretted that he would not have her and "our child" near to him. He was sorry, however, that he was not able to send her money for her trip because his moving to Indochina and furnishing a house there entailed many debts. Two months in Hanoi had not been enough for him to save large sums, but he wrote that he was "making a household for her" and was also sending her five hundred francs each month. Her divorce appeal, lack of money for the trip, and perhaps the pregnancy were the ostensible reasons for her remaining in Paris and not joining Henri in Hanoi. In his letter of March 31 he asked her how long after the birth of the baby she needed to wait until she could make the trip and warned her that she might not want to travel in the summer because it was too hot there. In his letter two weeks later, written on April 14, he mentioned that he had just received her letters of March 1 and 7. It was quite likely that in each of her letters to him she had asked for money so she could make the trip to Indochina, because in each of his letters to her he reiterated that he lacked the money to pay for her trip. He repeated that he could not ask his parents for the money because Lucienne's divorce was not yet final.

Henri could only surmise what might have happened between her letters of the beginning of March and his reply to her in mid-April when he wrote, "Now that you are free I will write to my sister and my father [to ask them to give you money from the bank account in Paris]." He also discussed provisions for the child, saying that if she wanted to leave the "kid" (gosse) with a wet nurse, that was fine, but he wanted her to join him in the shortest amount of time, because at his age he could not be without a woman for long. He mentioned that "all the French here are married and their wives are here also, and very happy. For distraction, there is only family life, a little tennis, and walks on Sunday." In a letter two weeks later he echoed the same refrain that appeared in all his letters: he asked her to find the money and come to him as soon as possible. He instructed Lucienne to talk to his sister, make arrangements for the trip, and decide whether to leave the infant with a wet nurse or bring him to Indochina. He was still eager for her to come and said that he had investigated whether marriage by proxy was possible but expected not. On May 10 he mentioned that he had just received her letter of March 28 and guessed that she had now delivered the baby. Apparently, he did not have a good sense about the length of the pregnancy. He told her that he had asked his sister and his parents to accept their union and wanted his father, who had control of his money, to give Lucienne money for the trip. In this letter he provided for a transfer of five hundred francs per month from the Banque de l'Indochine in Hanoi to its branch bank in Paris. He wrote that as soon as she arrived in Indochina, they "would get married because in the colony it is impossible to live together otherwise, and it is necessary to legitimize our kid."

The tone of Henri's letters changed at the end of April. He told Lucienne that he could not send her any more money than he was already doing. Moreover, he said that he was beginning to tolerate their separation more easily because now he had made good friends. Moreover, his work never ended and could consume all his days. A month later, in his letter of May 24, he mentioned that he had just received her letters of April 10 and 13 and was very happy that her divorce was now over—despite the result. As he said, "You are finally free." He reiterated that he wanted her to come to him and that he had written to his sister and father and instructed Lucienne to get the money from his father. The last letter in the file is dated July 7. In this letter Henri begged Lucienne's forgiveness for not having written in a long time. He wrote all about how very ill he had been and still was. The doctor had feared it was cholera, which had afflicted much of the indigenous population, but it was only a very bad bout of dysentery. He mentioned that although the doctor wanted him to return to France, he chose to remain in Indochina until his health improved. He now asked her to be patient and mentioned that the temperature was a torrid thirty-five degrees Celsius in the shade. This is the last letter in the file. He transferred money to his bank in Paris for her, however, as late as August 1929—three years after this letter. The records do not indicate if or why he ever returned to Paris or why she never went to Indochina. He remained geographically on the periphery; their relationship and young Georges likewise remained on the periphery of the cultural ideal of a core family.

As soon as payments stopped, Lucienne initiated a paternity suit against Henri. By March 1932 the lawyer had collected his letters from Lucienne and had decided to file the suit based on Henri's implicit avowal of paternity. Lucienne never paid the five hundred–franc retainer fee that the lawyer demanded, however, and she then suddenly moved from Paris, leaving no forwarding address. The law firm had trouble locating her, and when someone found her living in a somewhat distant suburb, he advised the firm not to handle the case because she was "dangerous." There is no further explanation or evidence. Paternity suits had to be filed in the domicile of the putative father. Perhaps leaving the metropole for a distant periphery in Indochina saved Henri from a paternity suit.

The paternity suit that Jeanne Victoire and her son Henri Victoire, both living in rural France, brought against Henri Roget, who lived in Paris, illustrates how families relied on one another and how communication was possible between Paris and the provinces, even during World War II, the Occupation, and the Vichy government. It also demonstrates how an ex-nuptial child, on the periphery of core nuclear families, could eventually legally become part of that cultural core. This drama begins during World War I, in the winter of 1916–17, when Jeanne Victoire was working as a waitress in a hotel near her family home in the department of the Vosges in eastern France, not far, but a reasonably safe distance, from the trench warfare at the front during this time. Over that winter of 1916–17 she had a sexual relationship with a young soldier, Henri Roget, who was stationed there.[6] By April 1917, when he was deployed elsewhere, Jeanne realized that she was pregnant. He wrote fourteen letters to her between March 1917 and May 1918, all of which she saved and turned over to her lawyer when she began a paternity suit in 1939. In one of Roget's first letters, of March 1917, he wrote tenderly of the nights they had spent together "in your little room where we were so happy . . . Each day I loved you more." In April, after learning that she was pregnant, he was solicitous of her welfare: "You know well, my little Jeanette, that I will do all that is possible for you. I would really be a heartless lout, my little treasure, to let you suffer after all that you have done for me. I am astonished that no one . . . perceives anything. Can you hide . . . [the pregnancy] from them?" In July he wrote, "I made you suffer my little Jeannette, and you respond with kindness; what must you think of me, my little treasure, you know that there was never a question of a future between us and you know that we would never marry, but bear in mind that I'm not heartless and I will never forget my little Jeannette. I have not ceased to love you and you are always 'la petite amie.' When you . . . need something write to me." Calling her "la petite amie" suggests that he thought of her as a young lover or little mistress, the meaning of little here meant to indicate not her size but, rather, her importance to him more as a sexual playmate than a marital mate. He visited her on his military leave in October and again said he was sorry he had made her suffer. His letters did not change significantly after she had a nine-pound boy on November 4, 1918. Jeanne recognized her baby son and named him Henri, after his father. Until the end of May 1919 Roget continued to write to her, worried about her well-being. He promised to help her out materially if she asked, but there is no confirmation that he did. Jeanne paid her sister and brother-in-law a monthly stipend to raise young Henri until he was fourteen. For the first year after the boy was born, Jeanne went to the hospital for several surgical procedures, and the following year she was very weak. Therefore, she could not file a paternity suit within the two-year limit stipulated by the 1912 law that permitted paternity suits in France for the first time in over a century.

There is no indication of contact between Roget and either Jeanne or young Henri Victoire from 1919 until 1939, the year in which Henri reached his majority and his last chance to file a paternity suit, according to law. Although de jure young Henri filed the paternity suit, de facto he was not a legal presence. This paternity suit lasted from 1939 through January 1943, taking about a year longer than similar suits had lasted before the war. Jeanne and Henri Victoire lived in the department of the Vosges, but the paternity suit occurred in Paris because that is where Roget lived. Her lawyer in her rural hometown corresponded with the lawyer in Paris and traveled there, although she did not. Jeanne's lawyer based his argument on an implicit avowal of paternity contained in the letters, which acknowledged sexual relations during the possible time of conception. Although Roget did not explicitly acknowledge paternity, he expressed love and promised material support. In 1943 the judge ruled that implicit written indications of paternity were acceptable proof of paternity, but Roget appealed. According to the law, in his appeal Roget had to bring proof of Jeanne Victoire's immorality with testimonial evidence of her having had several lovers; she brought proof to the contrary. On March 3, 1944, the judge of the appeals court denied Roget's appeal, agreeing with the lower court judge, who had ruled that Henri Roget was the father of Henri Victoire. The decision meant that henceforth Henri Victoire was entitled to carry Roget's name, and he also had right to a portion of Roget's inheritance. Henri Victoire, who had lived as an ex-nuptial child, now legally was part of a core family with an acknowledged father, albeit one who had not wanted to recognize the existence of his son.

Immediately after this decision, on April 21, 1944, Jeanne Victoire sued for damages to cover the fifty thousand francs she had paid to her sister and brother-in-law for rearing her son. The legal grounds for this type of suit, unchanged since the early nineteenth century, were abuse of authority or fraudulent seduction based on false promises of marriage. The letters divulged, however, that he had never promised marriage and that she had engaged in sexual relations with Roget without coercion. Her lawyer therefore did not think she had a chance. After February 1945 the case was dropped.

By the terms of 1912 legislation permitting paternity suits, a mother (in the name of her child) could take the putative father to court for child support—provided he was not married to another woman at the legal time of conception. To win her suit a mother had to provide proof of paternity consisting of: (1) written letters in which the putative father indicated that the child was his; (2) witnesses who attested that the couple had lived together maritally during the probable time of conception; or (3) evidence that he had contributed materially to rearing the child, such as paying the wet nurse. If a mother did not file a suit for child support during the first two years of the child's life, an adult child could bring charges within two years of reaching legal adulthood.[7] A woman's morality was crucial. The putative father could bring countercharges against the mother, including witnesses who testified that she had sexual relations with others besides him, thus disputing his authorship of the pregnancy. If a woman did not have explicit written letters giving an unequivocal affirmation of paternity, proof that the man had contributed to the rearing of the child, or witnesses that she had cohabited with the man in a manner resembling marriage she usually lost her case.[8] The legal issue in the 1930s and 1940s was whether an implicit indication of paternity contained in the letters of Henri Roget and Henri Parent was sufficient. Implicit indications of paternity were not new in the 1940s because the lawyers brought an example of a court case of 1930 as a form of legal precedent allowing implicit indication of paternity. To avoid paying child support, men would bring witnesses attesting to the woman's immorality, thereby throwing doubt on his paternity.[9]

These two paternity suits, one that never went to court and one that was successful, were like many hundreds of such cases in the 1920s and 1930s.[10] Travel back and forth between the provinces and Paris marked many of them. The details of the paternity suit carried out during World War II indicate that in terms of jurisprudence and the conduct of paternity searches the government of Vichy and the Occupation was not an aberration but, rather, was on a continuum from the Third Republic. Lawyers in 1942 and 1943 even invoked jurisprudence of the 1920s and 1930s as a type of precedence. Furthermore, there was no mention on any piece of paper in these dossiers of the war, occupation, or government policy. The Victoires did not have to travel from the department of the Vosges to Paris during these years; lawyers made the connections, demonstrating the close connections between center and nearby periphery as long as both were in the Occupied

Zone and no one had to cross the demarcation line between the Occupied Zone and the so-called Free Zone, or Vichy, during the war. In keeping with Third Republic jurisprudence as well as Vichy policy, fathers could legally be forced to acknowledge their children. Neither the law nor jurisprudence before or after the 1940s condemned single motherhood, if the mother tried to support her child. In the case of Jeanne Victoire she relied on her sister and brother-in-law for survival strategies and social networks. But even in this respect her actions were emblematic of a culture of expediencies within a climate of calamities that had typified single women's lives since the early nineteenth century.[11] Reliance on her sister and her family made her part of a core traditional family, even though as a single mother she was outside that core.

During World War II the private lives of Parisians continued much as they had before, within the framework of great political restrictions and a constant need for food and fuel. If they were Jewish, however, their situation was fraught with the horrors of deportation and death. Most French, however, tried to live lives barely perturbed by the Occupation and Vichy regime; they continued to commit adultery, get divorced, and file paternity suits. They also continued to use the French civil courts, which operated under the Napoleonic Civil Code and Third Republic laws, to settle family matters. This essay details two further family dramas that went to court during the Occupation and Vichy years: one child custody case and one case of adultery, divorce, and disavowal of paternity. Aside from some comments about fuel shortages, difficulties in travel, or the dire situation of Jews during the war, there was little to distinguish these court cases from the many hundreds brought before the Civil Tribunal of Paris during the 1920s and 1930s.[12] Men and women dealt with their private lives and loves, despite the hardships and legal delays from 1940 to 1945.

One family drama involving child custody demonstrates an obvious impact of the Occupation and Vichy government because one person was Jewish; all the other parties were Catholic.[13] This story begins and ends in Paris, with intervening travel between the core of Paris, the zone of Vichy, and Algeria. In 1927 Léon Kahan, who was Jewish, married Arlette Ponelle, and they had two boys. Arlette's brother Jean-Pierre Ponelle married Renée Chavet in 1929, and a year later they had a daughter, Doris. Jean-Pierre was a *couturier* (dress designer), and Renée managed his *maison de couture* (designer shop). The Kahan and Ponelle households were closely tied in terms of marriage, friendship, and residential proximity, so closely tied that Renée Chavet Ponelle and Léon Kahan had intimate relations. The Kahan couple divorced in 1937, with Arlette Ponelle Kahan granted custody of their two boys and Léon Kahan paying a sizable sum in child support. Two years later Renée and Jean-Pierre Ponelle divorced. The judge left guardianship of Doris to Renée's mother, Mme LeBois, with both parents having visitation rights. One can only speculate that the judge made this decision because of Renée's relationship with Kahan and perhaps her desire not to retain guardianship. At the beginning of 1940 Renée Ponelle married her former brother-in-law Léon Kahan.

In September 1940 authorities in Occupied France ordered a census of all Jews, and the Vichy Statutes of October 1940 excluded Jews from positions of responsibility in government, teaching, and cultural life. From 1940 to the winter of 1942 Jews were able to pay for exit visas and passports, but it was expensive and difficult to do so. Léon Kahan, who had been one of the directors of a large petrol company, had the financial means to leave. Large numbers of Jews fled the Occupied areas for the south of France, and the privileged (or lucky) among them left the country, Kahan among them. By spring 1941 Kahan was in the southeast of France, and by summer he left for Algeria. Kahan was fortunate not to have been in Paris because in December 1941 one thousand Jewish notables there were arrested; given his position in industry, he would probably have been among them.

From letters addressed to Jean-Pierre Ponelle, which he retained and gave to his lawyer, it is evident that since the divorce in 1939 his daughter, Doris, lived in the sixteenth arrondissement with her grandmother, three blocks away from her mother and just across the Seine River from Ponelle. She walked back and forth between her mother's home and her grandmother's. Her father saw her on Sundays. In July 1940, just after the German invasion, Jean-Pierre Ponelle discovered that Doris and Mme LeBois (Doris's grand-mother) had fled Paris, as did so many thousands of Parisians at that time.[14] He apparently stayed. Her grandmother took Doris to a resort in Arcachon in the Gironde in western France. Jean-Pierre must have put out a search for them because he received a note from someone in Arcachon saying that they were there and were well. Then, a year later, in April 1941, Léon Kahan wrote to his ex-wife, Arlette Ponelle, asking for custody of his boys so he could take them to Algiers. This letter provided the motivation for the custody battle. Arlette refused Léon's offer and warned Jean-Pierre that his ex-wife would soon take his daughter to Algeria. Arlette alleged that they had already left for the Free Zone and were headed for Algeria and then the United States—with Doris. A few weeks later Jean-Pierre Ponelle brought his suit to obtain legal custody of his daughter, who was then twelve years old. He alleged that "because of certain questions of religion, Mr. Kahan left the Occupied Zone to go to the Free Zone with the goal of going to Africa if not America." By the end of 1941, however, when French Jews and Jewish refugees to France wanted to leave France in droves, the United States had closed its borders.

Renée Kahan (Doris's mother) did not want the custody case to go to court, so her lawyer proposed that guardianship rest with Doris's maternal grandmother, with child support from Jean-Pierre fixed at 1,500 francs per month until Doris was eighteen. Renée Kahan's lawyer further stipulated that in case Renée left for Algeria, Doris should remain in Paris with her father for six months of the year and in Algeria with her mother for the other six months.[15] Ponelle rejected this arrangement, and in August 1941 Renée Kahan brought a countersuit demanding guardianship and custody of Doris.

At the same time, in August 1941, Doris's grandmother, Mme LeBois, under the orders of the doctor in Paris, left for two months of vacation in Mégève, high in the French Alps, in the Free Zone, but near Switzerland. They managed to cross from the occupied to the nonoccupied zone, despite the severe restrictions on travel between the two that German authorities imposed during the first two years. Ponelle alleged that their departure was clandestine and sudden, and there was no actual medical need, but the only way they could get across the line of demarcation was with a doctor's certificate for a "serious illness." Even for a temporary permit to travel, like everyone else they had to wait in lines for innumerable hours to get the authorization to pass the demarcation line and head on to Mégève.[16] Jean-Pierre Ponelle complained that he could not get permission to go visit them. In a letter to Ponelle, in August 1941, Renée Kahan said, "Doris and maman under the orders of Dr. D. [the Paris doctor] left for the Mégève for two months and we no longer think they will arrive at the beginning of the week since they've lost a lot of time in passing [the boundary]. . . . They will send their address when they arrive and will return to Paris at the beginning of October, where I will wait for them, having renounced my trip to Algeria in order to pursue the legal proceedings you have begun." This is the only news we have of Renée. Doris's first postcard to her father from Mégève indicates that her doctor in Paris said that she was getting thinner and had a fever so he recommended mountain air for a cure. By September 1941 she was at a "Home for Children" in Mégève. Aside from a diagnosis of mild scoliosis, it is unclear what her ailment was. In October 1941 Doris and her grandmother returned to Paris. Although they had reason to go to Algeria, and probably the money to do so, they stayed in France.

None of the letters contain a word about the war or shortages or really express much difficulty in traveling from Paris to outlying regions. On the contrary, this upper-bourgeois family continued their lives as before—except for Léon Kahan. Part of the reason for the silence on wartime problems may have been because letters were subject to censorship. Most letters and postcards were from Doris discussing her health or her new dress or were requests from Mme LeBois for more money for the doctors' bills. Throughout the war Ponelle continued to contribute a minimum of one thousand francs per month to Mme LeBois for taking care of Doris. The family traveled, although their travel was limited to places within Occupied France, except for the one visit to Mégève. In June 1942 Mme LeBois and Doris went to a thermal spa in the department of Nièvre (near the demarcation line and close to the border with Vichy France) for a "cure"—Doris for scoliosis and Mme LeBois for rheumatism. Doris and her grandmother were among the few who had the money to take the cures during wartime. Wherever they went, Doris visited doctors for some ailment.

Ponelle did not win his case for custody, although he was Catholic and his ex-wife was now married to a Jew. Ponelle's lawyer based his case on the attributes of Ponelle as a good father (*bon père de famille*) and on Renée Kahan's alleged immorality as a mother. He argued that the welfare of young Doris would therefore be better with her father than with her mother or grandmother. Yet the judge ordered that custody remain with Doris's grandmother and that guardianship be shared between the two biological parents. Ponelle's lawyer further alleged that Kahan had "sacrificed" his two sons when he divorced, although he materially supported them in relative affluence until he left for Algiers in 1941. In a nonaccusatory statement, however, Jean-Pierre's lawyer acknowledged that Kahan and Renée Ponelle "sacrificed two homes, but it had a moral dénouement; they married." If there was anti-Semitism in the case, it was coded. Ponelle said that he had not contested the divorce because Kahan had "more money in this battle." According to his lawyer, "he was beaten by the money of his brother-in-law."

Ponelle's lawyer based his argument on the same criteria that lawyers had used in family cases before 1940. One indication of good fatherhood was that the father had participated "materially and emotionally" in rearing the child. Evidence shows that Ponelle not only paid a monthly pension for Doris's care, but he also paid for medicines and vacations, sent her presents that she could show off, and spent Sundays with her when they were both in Paris. So, why did he not get custody? It is possible that the time-honored custom of awarding custody of a young girl to a mother or grandmother prevailed in traditional Vichy France, despite the patriarchal nature of that society. Furthermore, the Kahan-LeBois countersuit focused on Ponelle's immorality and on Doris's best interests. In 1940 and 1941 Ponelle was living with a mistress who was one of his models. In response he married her in 1942, just before the case went to court and the judge issued his decision. The judge denied both the mother's and father's arguments for custody. Instead, he ruled that because Doris's grandmother had raised her for nine years, it was in Doris's best interest to remain with her. Questions of the child's best interest and that of morality trumped a Jewish connection. Moreover, the Jewish connection was slim, in part because there was no blood connection but mostly because Doris's grandmother was raising her Catholic, ensuring she had a Communion. Life for the haute bourgeoisie went on during the war, much as it had before—unless you were Jewish.

A final illustration of communication between the core of Paris and periphery involves the nearby periphery within the Occupied Zone during the war. It also involves adultery, divorce, and the denial of paternity. According to law, any child born into a marriage was legally the husband's; he was responsible for the child's education and for providing the child with a legal status and inheritance. Only if he could legally prove his wife's infidelity could he deny paternity. The story of the Duprès family shows the complications of adultery, divorce, and paternity during the war and reveals some of the problems of wartime shortages, because these letters did not go through the post but were, rather, hand-delivered and slipped under doors.[17] Pierre and

Suzanne Duprès married in 1934. He was a twenty-nine-year-old government employee working in the Paris region. A year after they married they had a son, Alain. In 1939 Pierre became the assistant head of a department in the Ministry of Finances but was relocated to Chinon in the Loire Valley, about a day away from Paris. On April 16, 1939, he was mobilized and spent the time at nearby Tours until June, when his unit left for the Charente in western France. He was demobilized at the end of July 1940. While he was away, Suzanne remained in their suburban Paris house, close to her parents.

On December 24, 1940, Suzanne had a son, Daniel, whose paternity became an issue. Between August 1940 and December 1941 Pierre Duprès took a separate residence. Louis LePont, Suzanne's lover, moved in with Suzanne. On January 1, 1942, Suzanne visited Pierre, and not finding him home, she slipped a note under the door. She was peeved because he had promised to give her something each month for the care of her son. She wrote, "I know that I have acted badly, but what you have done is not much better. . . . If you don't want to see me, or if you want nothing more to do with me, I prefer that you take revenge on me rather than make my little one suffer. . . . You are wicked to wish to humiliate me. I have given you pain and sorrow, it is not your fault. . . . I think of my little Alain. . . . Nevertheless, I embrace you affectionately." This closing to the note is formulaic among close friends. Almost three weeks later, on January 20, he wrote to her saying that he would not be responsible for paying for the electricity for everyone living in her house. But he added,

> Your place is next to me and you should take it for your sake and that of the little ones. Believe me, it's your duty and it's in their interest. . . . Don't continue in your error. You have had the time to think . . . and you must decide. I need to know what you intend to do. Think of your little Alain. If you return, Suzette, be assured that I will forget all. But you must break completely with the past. I want you to understand that it is your duty and also your happiness to return and take your place near me.

She replied the next day, saying that she was quite sick. In each letter she mentioned her need for coal to heat the house and to cook. "I thank you a thousand times for the coal. You do us a great service because we no longer have any fire in the house. . . . Would it be possible to have a little more?" She added that she was still in turmoil: "I do not want to be separated from my little Alain. I love him as much as Danny and I don't see life without either one. This is too serious a decision for me to make right away. I need more time." She ended by asking him not to judge her too badly: "I am not as guilty as you believe. It is only death that will separate me from either one of my children. I love you always with affection."

On January 26, 1943, she asked for more coal. The lack of fuel was a universal and serious problem under the Occupation; it was severely rationed, and supplies were inadequate. On January 30 Suzanne implored Pierre for more coal but was also tortured about her decision not to return to him:

> Sometimes I would like to go back to the past and erase all that has happened . . . My heart refuses that, however. Pierre, do not make me miserable. Do not take Alain, I beg you. I am so unhappy. Don't look at me with such hard eyes. I am not as sinful as you think. I cannot find my place next to you. I often miss your sweet words. You have asked me to return to you. Have you thought carefully of what would happen if I returned? Would you love me as before? I would like to make you happy, but for the moment it is not possible.

She wrote that she missed him but could not return to him: "Please have a little patience and if my health gets better I will tell you frankly what I will do. Pierrot, if I become even sicker, you will come to see me won't you? I would not like to die without having seen you." This was her last letter, but she did not die at that time.

In March 1942 Pierre Duprès began divorce proceedings, charging Suzanne and Louis LePont with adultery. Police came to her house, and LePont answered the door. They responded to police interrogation, acknowledging that they were living together as a married couple and had a child together, Daniel, born in December 1940. A judgment of nonconciliation issued in July 1942 was followed by the birth of a daughter to Suzanne, on January 11, 1943. Suzanne's father filed the birth certificate reporting Duprès as the father because she was still technically married to him. The divorce was final on July 7, 1943, in favor of Pierre. Then proceedings for disavowal of paternity began. During the legal process Suzanne's father was named as the legal guardian of the children. LePont said that the girl born in January 1943 was his, but his saying so was not enough. According to the law, because Suzanne and Pierre were legally separated at the time of conception, the child could legally be LePont's if Pierre filed a simple suit to disavow. The child born in 1940, however, was another story. Pierre had to bring witnesses attesting that he had been away from home during the legal period of conception (180 to 300 days before the child's birth) and that he never went home and that his wife never came to visit him. This he did. She did not contest the divorce or the disavowal of paternity. The disavowal was effective as of May 24, 1945, at which point Suzanne was no longer Suzanne Duprès but Suzanne LePont. Nothing distinguished these proceedings from similar ones carried out before the war. Even though the documents about the case were in the files of Pierre's lawyer, there is no rhetoric condemning Suzanne for immorality, for her lack of fulfilling her role as "good mother," or any rhetoric one might expect from Vichy policies. Suzanne had three children, stayed home to care for those living with her, married her lover, and thus helped to repopulate France—all part of the Vichy government's designs for reemphasizing traditional families.

Family formation and dissolution relied on ongoing connections between Paris and the nearby regions of France as well as between Paris and the colonies. Even during the years of World War II, family life under Vichy and the Occupation differed little from how it had been during the Third Republic; all evidence indicates that the years 1940 to 1945 perpetuated many of the policies of the Third Republic. Lucienne Hilleret and Henry Parent maintained a correspondence between Paris and Hanoi, although their relationship did not survive the great distance of the separation. Jeanne and Henri Victoire's paternity suit could have taken place at any time after 1912. Although historians report that people's daily concerns during the Occupation centered on food and heat—either standing in line or using the black market—in these letters used as evidence in court the problems of provisions were not crucial, in part perhaps because of censorship and in part because the correspondence only provides a snapshot of family life relevant to paternity, custody, adultery, and divorce. Only Suzanne Duprès, who hand-delivered her notes, wrote of the ever-present desperate need for coal. No one mentioned food packages. Suzanne Duprès may have grown some of what she needed in her garden; the Ponelles were well-to-do; and Jeanne Victoire lived in a relatively rural part of the Vosges. Instead, negotiating precarious marriages and paternity was crucial. For Léon Kahan, however, being Jewish gravely disrupted his life; he had to flee the country.

His two sons and his ex-wife no longer received their pension, and the legal proceedings for custody evolved only because Kahan was Jewish. His eventual fate is unknown.

Likewise, on a most basic level there is little to distinguish social networks or survival strategies during the war years from those during the Third Republic. Relations between core and periphery remained strong, but people had greater difficulty maintaining them. Family strategies are driven by an interaction of social forces as well as people's emotional bonds. Distance can be a problem, such as when a lover goes to Indochina or when a Jew flees to Algeria to save his life, which led to a custody suit back in Paris. Women relied on their families for help in rearing their children. Suzanne Duprès relied on her father, who lived upstairs in the same house. Furthermore, during the divorce, the court declared him the guardian of her children. Renée Ponelle Kahan relied on her mother to care for her daughter, and Jeanne Victoire paid her sister and brother-in-law to raise her son. In these families, as in the many other examples of family life during this era, relatives stepped in as part of survival strategies of the middle classes, just as they did among all classes during the nineteenth and early twentieth centuries. Yet it is also possible that Henri Parent's father and sister refused to step in and help him get his lover to Hanoi. During the war the extent to which Vichy policies influenced family strategies varied more by religion than by gender. Suzanne Duprès and Renée Ponelle were not rhetorically stoned for their adultery or Jeanne Victoire for having an ex-nuptial child. Surprisingly, Jean-Pierre Ponelle was denied custody even though he was a good father and a material provider.

Unsurprisingly, adultery and divorce continued under the patriarchal and pro-family Vichy government. Adultery, excessive cruelty, or failure to fulfill the duties and obligations of the marriage were the major grounds for divorce. Catching one of the parties in flagrante delicto was almost always required for disavowal of a child born within a marriage. Vichy ideology viewed adultery as a "social danger" as it sought to regulate women's sexual behavior.[18] Although Suzanne Duprès may have lost her older son in the divorce settlement, she remarried and remained in the house. She may have been one of many bourgeois women outside the metaphorical surveillance cameras that Vichy rhetoric established to control illicit female activity. According to rhetoric and policy, women were above all to be good mothers, to love their children and rear them well. As symbols of the National Revolution, they were also to be pious and maintain a good household. Yet there was a difference in the roles that Vichy assigned to women and how they lived their lives. Suzanne Duprès committed adultery, but in her correspondence she regularly expressed love for all her children and struggled to maintain a home for them. She refused, however, her legally married husband's enjoinders to fulfill her duty and return to take her place by his side. Only his letters contain the Vichy rhetoric. Moreover, she married her lover and the father of two of her children.

In her superb book historian Miranda Pollard wrote, "Appropriating and regulating sexuality was at the heart of Vichy's politics."[19] Reading the legal narratives, Pollard is surely correct, but there was a disjuncture between discourse and practice. During Vichy, and to some extent during the Third Republic, ideal families were strong, secure, and calm, glorifying both fatherhood and motherhood. Vichy's gender policies applied to people in Paris as well as in the rest of France, and the court cases differed little from those of the Third Republic. In these stories, despite adultery and divorce, the *femme au foyer* (housewife) existed—whether as a single mother or a woman who married her lover and raised her children. In the patriarchal National Revolution the role of the father increased in importance. In the cases examined here, however, none of the fathers are strong patriarchs, no matter how hard they tried. The courts ruled against two of them. All the men in these dramas were good fathers, materially providing for their children. Only Henri Roget was derelict, and for that the courts called him to account. Henri Parent paid child support but did not manage to marry his child's mother.

A father's performance of his duties remained a key aspect of paternity, as Ponelle's lawyer tried to prove and as Henri Roget's letters implicitly showed. The ideal family with the strong patriarchal *père de famille* was the ideological goal. Yet tensions and contradictions abounded between policy and people's lives. Even law contradicted policy and rhetoric. On September 3, 1941, Philippe Pétain's government decreed that a man could legitimate his children born of his adultery if he divorced his wife who was not the mother of those children. This so-called Gardener's Law originated with Pétain's wife, who wished to regularize the situation of their private gardener, who wanted to legitimate his children born of his adultery; all preceding laws on adultery and legitimation had denied him this right. All restrictions against paternity suits directed at married men and legitimation of children born of adultery during the Third Republic were ostensibly to keep the legally married family sacrosanct. The Gardener's Law demonstrated the loosely woven fabric of the family and an obliteration of the concept of a core nuclear family with nonmarital families on the periphery. This juridical reform was counter to prior law, jurisprudence, and the moral imperatives of Vichy—and of the Third Republic. There was much uproar in 1941 that this would mean the end of the family, just as there was uproar against paternity searches prior to 1912. This law, however, was justified on the grounds that it was pro-family, sanctioning legitimacy. Legitimacy was equated with moral order—in the Third Republic as in Vichy. Although the Gardener's Law did not outlast Vichy, in fact during wartime—both the Revolutionary and Napoleonic Wars and again in 1917—governments took action to legitimate children not born within legal wedlock.

Private lives and public policy ran along different roads, if not at cross-streets. Personal life continued, with all its ups and downs, despite the horrible stresses of the Occupation and Vichy. Wartime Occupation and Vichy governments had surprisingly little control in intimate family strategies— unless you were Jewish, mobilized by the war, or deported, which applied to all too many people. Vichy or the Occupation authorities were directly absent from people's personal lives, except as they forced the Jews out, made travel intensely more difficult, or created severe shortages of food and coal. Collaboration or resistance was not part of the vocabulary of the letter writers, in part perhaps because correspondence was censured but also because their personal lives were more important to them.

This essay has endeavored to show that in family life people moved between the geographical core of Paris and the periphery—whether within France or between France and the colonies. Moreover, when historians examine family life, a cultural core and periphery appears less clear than the geographical one. The nuclear heterosexual family of mother, father, and children has long constituted the social and cultural core. Divorce, adultery, ex-nuptial children, and single-mother families have always been on the periphery. The family dramas depicted in this essay—the letters from Hanoi, the Victoires' successful paternity suit, the divorce and custody battles, and finally adultery and disavowal of paternity—all demonstrate that in the twentieth century these peripheral families could become integrated into the cultural core.

Notes

1. For a general survey of European migration, see Leslie Page Moch, *Moving Europeans: Migration in Western Europe since 1650* (Bloomington: Indiana University Press, 1992).

2. The Parisian law firm of Leveillé-Nizerolles deposited its records from the 1920s through the early 1950s at the Archives de la Ville de Paris, where they form part of the fonds Mermet. Under the terms of the *dérogation* allowing me to consult these files, I have changed all the names and precise identifying information of the people involved. This essay is based on a few of the dossiers contained in the private papers of this law firm, which I chose because of their diversity and relevance for this collection.

3. Françoise Battagliola, "Marriage, concubinage et rélations entre les sexes, Paris 1880–1890," *Genèses* (January 1995): 68–96; Michel Frey, "Du mariage et du concubinage dans les classes populaires à Paris (1846–1847)," *Annales* (July–August 1978): 803–29.

4. I have analyzed over five hundred judicial decisions concerning divorce, *recherche de paternité*, and *désaveu de paternité* of the Tribunal Civil, 1880–1940. The discussion of these cases forms part of my book *Contested Paternity: Constructing Families in Modern France* (Baltimore: Johns Hopkins University Press, 2008). I initially focused on the cases brought to the courts with the aid of Assistance Judiciaire, hoping to get a composite picture of the less well-to-do segments of society, those who qualified for what we might call legal aid—e.g., seamstresses, servants, and clerks. By a random sample of every ten of the numerous volumes of judgments before the Tribunal Civil of Paris under Assistance Judiciaire, I discovered hundreds of instances in which a woman had brought suit against a putative father for child support under the law of 1912. I also examined the cases brought before the Tribunal Civil by members of the middle classes, who could afford to pay their own lawyers and did not have need of Assistance Judiciaire. Much fewer in number, these cases did not differ significantly from those brought with the aid of Assistance Judiciaire. All these judgments are in bound volumes in the Archives de la Ville de Paris in the Tribunal Civil, series D1U5. Just how many women sued for child support is impossible to determine because these suits are buried in the multitudinous civil judgments among the more extensive divorce cases and arranged by date and court.

5. 8.Mermet.89.1.23 folder 693 H . . ./P . . . 17965, Archives de la Ville de Paris (hereafter cited as AP). Unfortunately, there are only ten letters from Henri P in the file and none from Lucienne H. She saved the letters that Henri wrote and turned them over to her lawyer as evidence in her paternity suit.

6. D10 J34, folder 816, dossier 22510, AP. Only his letters and not hers were in the file.

7. Some authorities have argued that the demand for "written proof" undermined the law, resulting in very few cases of *recherche en paternité* brought before the courts.

8. See, for example, DIU5 Tribunal Civil, Assistance Judiciaire (287), January 1–8, 1920, decision of January 3, 1920, AP; R. Perruchot, *Résultats de la loi du 16 novembre 1912 sur la recherche de la paternité* (Paris: Sirey, 1931), 70.

9. See, for example, DIU5, Tribunal Civil, Assistance Judiaire (370), January 18–31, 1923, case no. 1940 of 1921, judgment of January 18, 1923, AP. See also DIU5, Assistance Judiciaire (530), July 1–10, 1930, case January 1928, judgment of July 1, 1930, AP; DIU>5, Assistance Judiciaire (550), May 1–14, 1931, case no. 5112 of 1928, judgment of May 12, 1931, AP; and DIU5, Assistance Judiciaire (710), March 9–17, 1937, case no. 2495 of 1934, decision of March 12, 1937, AP.

10. See, for example, DIU5, Tribunal Civil, Assistance Judiciaire (287), January 1–8, 1920, decision of January 3, 1920, AP; Assistance Judiciaire (370), January 18–31, 1923, case no. 1940 of 1921, judgment of January 18, 1923, AP>. See also DIU5, Assistance Judiciaire (530), July 1–10, 1930, case January 1928, judgment of July 1, 1930, AP; DIU5, Assistance Judiciaire (550), May 1–14, 1931, case no. 5112 of 1928, judgment of May 12, 1931, AP; and DIU5, Assistance Judiciaire (710), March 9–17, 1937, case no. 2495 of 1934, decision of March 12, 1937, AP.

11. See, for example, Rachel G. Fuchs, *Poor and Pregnant in Paris: Strategies for Survival in the Nineteenth Century* (New Brunswick NJ: Rutgers University Press, 1992); and Rachel G. Fuchs, *Gender and Poverty in Nineteenth-Century Europe* (Cambridge: Cambridge University Press, 2005).

12. See n. 4.

13. DIO J32, folder 783, dossier 22926, AP.

14. For the context of daily life in France during the war years, see Dominique Veillon, *Vivre et survivre en France, 1939–1947* (Paris: Payot, 1995).

15. Because the Germans occupied Paris at the time, this proposal indicates that the lawyer may have thought that the Occupation would soon end or else that it would not disrupt daily life.

16. Veillon, *Vivre et survivre*, 83–85.

17. DIO J32, folder 811, dossier 23514, AP.

18. Miranda Pollard, *Reign of Virtue: Mobilizing Gender in Vichy France* (Chicago: University of Chicago Press, 1998), 63–64.

19. Pollard, *Reign of Virtue*, 56.

The Writings of William B. Cohen

"Pity, Shame and Fear: American Opinion of Germany, 1932–1936." BA thesis,
Pomona College, 1962.

"Rulers of Empire: The French Colonial Service in Africa, 1880–1960." PhD diss.,
Stanford University, 1968.

"The Lure of Empire: Why Frenchmen Entered the Colonial Service." *Journal of
Contemporary History* 4, no. 1 (1969): 103–25.

"A Century of Modern Administration: From Faidherbe to Senghor." *Civilisations*
20, no. 1 (1970): 40–51.

"The Colonized as Child: British and French Colonial Rule." *African Historical
Studies* 3, no. 2 (1970): 427–31.

"The French Colonial Service in West Africa." In *Britain and France in Africa: Imperial
Rivalry and Colonial Rule,* edited by Prosser Gifford and William R. Louis. New
Haven CT: Yale University Press, 1971.

Rulers of Empire: The French Colonial Service in Africa. Stanford CA: Hoover Institution
Press, 1971.

"The Colonial Policy of the Popular Front." *French Historical Studies* 7, no. 3 (1972):
368–93.

*Empereurs sans sceptre: histoire des administrateurs de la France d'outre-mer et de l'École
coloniale.* Paris: Berger-Levrault, 1973. (French edition of *Rulers of Empire.*)

"Imperial Mirage: The Western Sudan in French Thought and Action." *Journal of
the Historical Society of Nigeria* 7, no. 3 (1974): 417–45.

"Literature and Race: Nineteenth-Century French Fiction, Blacks, and Africa
(1800–1880)." *Race and Class* 16 (1974): 181–205.

"Gambettists and Colonial Expansion before 1881: The *République française.*" *French
Colonial Studies* 1 (1977): 54–64.

"Henri Brunschwig." In *Proceedings of the Second Annual Meeting of the French Colonial
Historical Society.* Athens GA: French Colonial Historical Society, 1977.

Robert Delavignette on the French Empire: Selected Writings, editor. Chicago: University
of Chicago Press, 1977.

"The French Governors" and "Gentle Ruler: Robert Delavignette." In *African
Proconsuls,* edited by Peter Duignan and Lewis Gann. Glencoe IL: Free Press,
1978.

European Empire Building: Causes and Motives of Nineteenth-Century Imperialism, editor.
Problems in European Civilization. St. Louis: Forum Press, 1980.

"Français et africains: les noirs dans le regard des blancs, 1530–1880" (livre montage). Le Débat 4 (1980): 169–92.

The French Encounter with Africans: White Response to Blacks, 1530–1880. 1980. Reprint, Bloomington: Indiana University Press, 2003.

"Legacy of Empire: The Algerian Connection." Journal of Contemporary History 15, no. 1 (1980): 97–123. Reprinted in Colin Holmes, ed., Migration in European History (Cheltenham: E. Elgar, 1996).

Français et africains: les noirs dans le regard des blancs, 1530–1880. Paris: Gallimard, 1981. (French edition of The French Encounter with Africans.)

"Health and Colonialism." In Études africaines offertes à Henri Brunschwig, edited by Fernand Braudel. Paris: Editions de l'École des Hautes Études en Sciences Sociales, 1982.

"Malaria and French Imperialism." Journal of African History 24, no. 1 (1983): 23–36.

"The Roots of Popular Anti-Semitism in the Third Republic," with Irwin Wall. In The Jews in Modern France, edited by Frances Malino and Bernard Wasserstein. Hanover NH: University of New England Press for Brandeis University Press, 1985.

"French Racism and Its African Impact." In The Double Impact: France and Africa, edited by G. Wesley Johnson. Westport CT: Greenwood, 1986.

Six articles in Historical Dictionary of the French Third Republic, edited by Patrick H. Hutton. Westport CT: Greenwood, 1986.

"Symbols of Power: Statues in Nineteenth-Century Provincial France." Comparative Studies in Society and History 31, no. 3 (1989): 491–513.

"De Gaulle and Europe prior to 1958." French Politics and Society 8, no. 4 (1990): 1–12.

"De Gaulle et l'Europe avant 1958." In De Gaulle en son siècle. Vol. 5. Paris: Plon, 1992.

"Le città francesi—Aspetti politici et sociali." In I Regimi della città—Il governo municipale in Europa tra '800 e '900. Milan: Franco Angeli, 1992.

Western Civilization: The Continuing Experiment, with Thomas F. X. Noble, Barry Strauss, Duane J. Osheim, Kristin B. Neuschel, and David D. Roberts. 3rd ed. 1994. Reprint, Boston: Houghton Mifflin, 2001.

"European Nationalism." In Bonds of Affection: Americans Define Their Patriotism, edited by John Bodnar. Princeton NJ: Princeton University Press, 1995.

"Finland and the Holocaust," with Jorgen Svensson. Holocaust and Genocide Studies 9, no. 1 (1995): 70–93.

The Transformation of Modern France: Essays in Honor of Gordon Wright, editor. Boston:

Houghton Mifflin, 1997. Contribution: "The Development of an Urban Society."

"Les Fonctionnaires des municipalités." In L'Administration territoriale de la France, 1750–1940, edited by Michel Pertué. Orléans: Presses Universitaires d'Orléans, 1998.

Urban Government and the Rise of the French City: Five Municipalities in the Nineteenth Century. New York: St. Martin's, 1998.

"The Algerian War and French Memory." Contemporary European History 9, no. 3 (2000): 489–500.

"Finland," with Jörgen Svensson. In Encyclopedia of the Holocaust, edited by Walter Laqueur. New Haven CT: Yale University Press, 2001.

"French Empire" and "Theories of Empire." In Encyclopedia of Colonialism, edited by Melvin E. Page. New York: East River Books, 2001.

"The Sudden Memory of Torture, the Algerian War in French Discourse, 2000–2001." French Politics, Culture, and Society 19, no. 3 (2001): 82–94.

"The Algerian War, the French State and Official Memory." Historical Reflections 28, no. 2 (2002): 219–39. Coedited issue with James D. Le Sueur: "France and Algeria: From Colonial Conflicts to Postcolonial Memories."

"The European Background." In American Philanthropy, edited by Larry Friedman. New York: Cambridge University Press, 2002.

"The Algerian War and the Revision of France's Overseas Mission." French Colonial History 4 (2003): 227–39.

"Robert Delavignette et les responsabilites de l'administrateur colonial." In Robert Delavignette savant et politique (1897–1976), edited by Bernard Mouralis and Anne Piriou. Paris: Karthala, 2003.

"Becoming a French Colonial Historian." French Colonial History 5 (2004): 1–6.

"Language and Politics: A New Revisionism." In Algeria and France, 1800–2000: Identity, Memory, Nostalgia, edited by Patricia M. E. Lorcin. Syracuse NY: Syracuse University Press, 2006.

Contributors

KEVIN J. CALLAHAN is Associate Professor of History at Saint Joseph College, Connecticut. He has published articles in *International Review of Social History* and *Peace and Change* on international socialism and served as a member of the Peace History Society board from 2004 to 2007. His current research is a cultural history of European socialism.

SARAH A. CURTIS is Associate Professor of History at San Francisco State University. She is finishing a book on three French women missionaries in the early nineteenth century. She has published *Educating the Faithful: Religion, Schooling, and Society in Nineteenth-Century France* (2000; French ed., 2003) as well as articles on gender, charity, religion, and education.

ANNE R. EPSTEIN teaches at the Institut d'Études Politiques, Université de Strasbourg 3 (Robert Schuman). Her current research focuses on intellectuals, gender, and citizenship in historical and comparative perspective. She is completing a book manuscript provisionally entitled "Joining the Fray: Gender, Civic Engagement, and Interpretations of Citizenship in Fin-de-Siècle France."

RACHEL G. FUCHS is the Distinguished Foundation Professor of History at Arizona State University. She is the author of six books, including *Poor and Pregnant in Paris: Strategies for Survival in the Nineteenth Century* (1992), *Gender and Poverty in Nineteenth-Century Europe* (2005), and *Contested Paternity: Constructing Families in Modern France* (2008).

SAMUEL HUSTON GOODFELLOW is Professor of History and Director of Global Education at Westminster College in Fulton, Missouri. He has published *Between the Swastika and the Cross of Lorraine: Fascisms in Interwar Alsace* (1999), along with articles on fascism, Alsace, and the Holocaust.

STEPHEN L. HARP is Professor of History at the University of Akron. He is the author of *Learning to Be Loyal: Primary Schooling as Nation Building in Alsace and Lorraine* (1998) and *Marketing Michelin: Advertising and Cultural Identity in Twentieth-*

Century France (2001; French ed., 2008). He is currently at work on a book tentatively entitled "Au Naturel: Naturisme, Nudism, and Beachfront Tourism in Modern France."

SEAN M. QUINLAN is Associate Professor of History at the University of Idaho. His scholarly work has appeared in *Eighteenth-Century Studies, French History, History of European Ideas, History Workshop Journal, Social History,* and *Textual Practice.* His book *The Great Nation in Decline: Sex, Modernity, and Health Crises in Revolutionary France, c. 1750–1850* was published in 2007.

JEREMY RICH is Associate Professor of History at Middle Tennessee State University. He is a specialist of colonial Gabon, and his book *A Workman Is Worthy of His Meat: Food and Colonialism in the Gabon Estuary,* was published in 2007. He is currently working on a new project on canoe workers in early colonial Gabon.

LEE WHITFIELD is Associate Professor of History at Wheelock College. Her recent scholarship on colonialism and the postcolonial era includes "The Politics of Power and Ethnicity: The Maghreb at a Crossroads," in *North African Mosaic: A Cultural Reappraisal of Ethnic and Religious Minorities,* ed. Nabil Boudraa and Joseph Krause (2007); "Embattled Boundaries of the African Mind in the Colonial Era: Albert Memmi's *The Pillar of Salt,*" in *Revue des Lettres et Sciences Humaines des Universités de Republique Tunisienne;* and an article on French public opinion and the Algerian War in *Proceedings of the Western Society for French History.* She is finishing a book manuscript on the same subject.